SECRET SERVICE IN THE COLD WAR

'To a gallant British airborne "soldier", Colonel J.B. Sanderson.

With warm regards and appreciation.'

Joseph H. Harper, former commanding officer of the 401st Glider Infantry Regiment,

6 July 1977, Atlanta, USA

A tribute by Major General J. Harper, written inside the cover of Harper's association history Rendezvous with Destiny. A History of the 101st Airborne Division. *The book was presented to John Sanderson by Joseph Harper, a fellow airborne veteran, who in December 1944 had personally delivered General McAuliffe's famous 'Nuts!' reply to the German negotiators at Bastogne.*

SECRET SERVICE IN THE COLD WAR

AN SIS OFFICER FROM PHILBY TO THE CUBAN MISSILE CRISIS AND THE BALKANS

LIEUTENANT COLONEL
JOHN B. SANDERSON
AND MYLES SANDERSON

FRONTLINE
BOOKS

SECRET SERVICE IN THE COLD WAR
An SIS Officer from Philby to the Cuban Missile Crisis and the Balkans

First published in Great Britain in 2018 by Frontline Books,
an imprint of Pen & Sword Books Ltd, Yorkshire - Philadelphia

ISBN: 978-1-52674-090-8

Typeset in India by Vman Infotech Private Limited
Printed and bound by TJ International, Padstow, Cornwall

Pen & Sword Books Ltd incorporates the imprints of Pen & Sword Archaeology, Air World Books, Atlas, Aviation, Battleground, Discovery, Family History, History, Maritime, Military, Naval, Politics, Social History, Transport, True Crime, Claymore Press, Frontline Books, Praetorian Press, Seaforth Publishing and White Owl.

For a complete list of Pen & Sword titles please contact:

PEN & SWORD BOOKS LTD
47 Church Street, Barnsley, South Yorkshire, S70 2AS, UK.
E-mail: enquiries@pen-and-sword.co.uk
Website: www.pen-and-sword.co.uk

Or

PEN AND SWORD BOOKS,
1950 Lawrence Road, Havertown, PA 19083, USA
E-mail: Uspen-and-sword@casematepublishers.com
Website: www.penandswordbooks.com

Contents

Plates and Maps

Plates

Section 1

1. Marriage (a) 18 November 1919 of (c) Major Alexander Sanderson DSO MC bar to (b) Gladys Royle Burden; son John as (b) child and (d) Para officer.
2. JBS's childhood: (a, e) in India 1921–9; with Gladys and Richard (b, d); with brothers Peter, Richard and their ayah (c).
3. Sanderson family: (a) in peacetime, 1935; (b) brothers and sisters (Janet, 4 years) in wartime, 1940; (c) A/Major Sanderson 152nd Btn, 50th Para Bde, 1944.
4. A young teenage JBS (b, c); (a) Territorial Army enlistment form, with father's consent, for the Queen's Westminsters Regiment, March 1938.
5. JBS: (a, b) junior soldier: kit inspection at Bisley camp, 1938; (c) Dover, 1940.
6. Alex Sanderson (a) with Tony, Gladys, Janet, John; (b) Gladys' diary entry about Hitler for 27 January 1941; (c) Alex's secret 'tilt-engine' aircraft plans, 19 October 1942.
7. (a) John Aldwinckle, RAF officer; (b) Enigma machine; (c) John's wife Helene, an analyst in (d) Hut 6 at Bletchley Park; (e) Helene meeting HRH The Duchess of Cambridge in the Registration Room of Hut 6 at Bletchley Park, where Helene worked in 1942–6, on the occasion of the royal reopening of Hut 6 and Hut 8 on 18 June 2014, after a major restoration.
8. (a) Fort Lockhart, 1942: .303 rifles; (b) JBS flanked by Lieutenant Hari S. and *Subedar* Udhey Singh; (c) Captain Sanderson's 'A' Coy 6th Btn of 11th Sikh Regt (all Singhs).
9. (a) Sikhs relax; (c) JBS gives rifle instruction near (b) Fort Lockhart, 1942; (d) route march on North West Frontier; (e) briefing: map drawn on British officer's chest.

10. (a, b) Sikh Regt patrol in an Indian Pattern Armoured Carrier Mk 2; (1c) JBS with binoculars in tribal hills; (d) JBS sits at the front of a group of officers; (e) JBS with Jeep and trailer.
11. (a, e) Turbaned JBS (pistol case on chest) on patrol, Khyber Pass area, India, 1942; (b) Sikh Regt (Lieutenant) ID; (c) JBS portrait; (d) writing letter home.
12. Paratrooper's gear, note padded helmet and quick-release harness: (a, d) JBS; (b) RAF Meteor jet pilot: Ted Cooper, 1944; (c, e) Major John Sim MC.
13. Parachute training in Rawalpindi, 1944: (a) JBS during indoor attached harness jump; (b) sergeant waits his turn; (c) practising parachute 'rolls'.
14. (a) Douglas Dakota C-47, India, 1944; (b) Mohn Kahn and Jock Grimmond; (c) letter from home; (d) parachute balloon jumps, through hole, 1944.
15. (a) Indian Paras line up next to a Dakota C-47; (b) Paratrooper's chute deploys; (c) stick boarding a Whitley bomber at Chakala Airfield, 1944; (d) Paras in training wait to drop through hole in Whitley fuselage floor.
16. (a) JBS (centre) with 152nd Btn, 50th (Indian) Parachute Bde group, 1944; (b) JBS; (c) JBS and 152nd Btn; (d) Sangshak veteran Maurice Bell and Sylvia.

Section 2

17. (a, b) JBS on weekend leave with his then fiancée Marian Painter, her sister Doreen and Raymond Lloyd, Lake Gardens, Srinigar, Kashmir; (c) Marian in uniform in the Officers' Mess; (d) Jeep trip Bhurban, Murray Hills, 1944.
18. (a) RAF officer John Aldwinckle's 148 Squadron Halifax aircraft, bomb bays being loaded with containers; (b) John, aged 21, with his pilot 'Mac' McLean, 1944; (c) John's 'M' aircraft BB 338 being loaded for Yugoslav drop; (d) John, aged 19, on navigator training, Canada; (e) John, Brindisi airfield.
19. JBS's Demolition and Assault Pioneer Course in Roorkee, India, November 1944.
20. Victory: VE and VJ Days, 1945. (a) Sanderson family, Gladys, right of Macmillan in the car, and Janet, right with flag, cheer (b) Churchill; (c) statue of Churchill, Parliament Square; (d) Major General W.A. Crowther DSO, OC 17th Indian Div. takes sword and surrender of 33rd Japanese Army; (e) 'A' Bomb.
21. (a, b) Audrey Jones visits the Reichstag garden, by Hitler's bunker, January 1946; (c) plan of Hitler's bunker.
22. (a) York and Lancaster officers, Berlin, July 1947; (b, d) Captain John Sanderson and Audrey Jones' wedding, Luneburg church, February 1947; (c) Audrey Jones.

23. (a, d) 'RECOGNISING SERVICE AT HOME AND ABROAD: PROTECTING THE UNITED KINGDOM SINCE 1909. SIS–GCHQ–MI5–ER' Memorial, Westminster Abbey. SIS personnel: (b) JBS; (c) traitor 'Kim' Philby; (e) John Aldwinckle in Berlin with the burnt-out Reichstag building in the background, 1956.
24. Mission to Paris as AM: (a) Chateau des Ombrages; (24b) Bulgarian/Russian émigré/D.P. Batchinski's shack, Marly-Le-Roi; (c) Major Peter Greenhalgh DFC; (d) JBS; (e) JBS studying Bulgarian; (f) lottery ticket, '*Qui ose gagne*'; (g) JBS and James Wheen, MI4 officers, London, 1948.
25. (a) Denis Greenhill article; (b) JBS attends (c) Pastors' Sofia Show Trials as civilian press officer, 1949; (e, f) Sandersons' Bulgarian Diplomatic IDs, 1961–2; (d, g) the Sandersons with John and Jasmine Blakeway, Bulgaria, 1949.
26. (a) The author at a Sudan railway station, 1954; (d, e) the Sandersons' 1952 reconnaissance trip around west Turkey in (b, d, f) Philby's Jeep; (c) JBS – with Luger pistol in pocket – and a traveller with performing bear.
27. Sofia, 1961. Lieutenant Colonel Sanderson and MAs learn of (a) Yuri Gagarin's 12 April 1961 space flight: JBS and US Colonel Edward R. Cleary; (b) JBS and a Bulgarian major; (c) JBS and a Soviet lieutenant colonel (left) and Bulgarian colonel (facing); (d) JBS toasts Yuri Gagarin with a Bulgarian Lieutenant Colonel.
28. Sanderson (d) clandestinely photograped a (b) MiG-21F jet with (a) Minox camera, August 1962; (c) JBS jokes with other MAs; (e) JBS converses with Colonel Paul Murat, French MA, 1961; (f) a major instructs on Gagarin's flight.
29. JBS, Liaison Officer with French Army, Baden-Baden, 1970–1: (a) JBS takes parade by Royal Artillery on the Queen's birthday, June 1970; (b) JBS entertains; (c) a French general introduces JBS to Russian General Sawitzki, Chief of SOXMIS; (d) the Sandersons with a German NATO *colonel-oberst*, Second World War veteran, wearing Iron Cross 1st and 2nd class (de-Nazified version of Second World War medals), Winter War Medal (Russia, 1941–2) and Luftwaffe Ground Combat Medal (he was probably a Luftwaffe Feld Division soldier under General H-B. Ramcke, OC Paratroop forces: Crete, North Africa, Russia, France).
30. (a) JBS front row left of a group of 152 Btn Paras, one with a long machete, 1944; (b) 11 Platoon, 4 Coy, 10th Btn Para Regt of 5th Airborne Div. play Spetsnaz 'Orange' forces on Exercise Lionheart, 1984; (c) Paras prepare for heliborne assault on key bridge of the River Weser. Tank-busting role as part of the 16th Armoured Bde, indicated by 84mm Carl Gustav weapons; (d) Paras lift off in a USAF Chinook before (e) disembarking. No insignia worn.

31. (a) East Berlin Wall death strip near the Brandenburg Gate; (b) sign: 'WARNING you are now leaving West-Berlin'; (c) ground-to-air radar-guided 23mm anti-aircraft cannon on a T-72 tank chassis; (d) Scott Charman tests the effectiveness of a Russian SA13 missile by rotating a lit cigarette in front of the guidance system; (e, f) secret T-72 tank and WTO arms shipment ex-Szczecin to South Africa, 1989.
32. John Sanderson from young TA soldier aged 16 to old veteran, 1938–95: (b) medals, dogtags and regimental cap badges; (c) Loyal Queen's Westminsters Regt; (e) Sikh Regt; (f, g) York and Lancaster, Yorkshire, 50th Indian Parachute (wings), Yorkshire (horse), 2nd Wessex TA; (g) JBS wears a Dennison Paratrooper's smock with a York and Lancaster cap badge.

Acknowledgements

All photographs from the Sanderson Archives except the following, courtesy of: 7a–e, 18a–e, 23e: Richard Aldwinckle; 12b: Andrew Cooper; 12c, 12e: Sim family; 16d: Bell family; 20d: James Chalmers; 24c: Dr M. Verbrugge; 30b–e: Prosper Keating; 31a–f: Scott Charman; 7(d) Courtesy of GCHQ, 18(a) Imperial War Museum CNA 3231, 18(b) IWM CNA 3138, 24(c) Dr M. Verbrugge, Museum of Army Flying, 20e: free web use.

Maps

Abbreviations

'A' bomb	Atomic bomb
ABM	Anti-Ballistic Missile
AFCENT	Allied Forces Central Europe
AK	Armia Krajowa (Home Army, Poland)
AMA	Assistant Military Attaché
AOP	Air Observation Post
ARP	Air Raid Precautions (Warden)
ASA	Anti-Soviet agitation
AVO (AVH)	Predecessor of AVH (Hungarian intelligence and security agency)
BAOR	British Army of the Rhine
BG/FIEND	Top Secret US CIA/OPC plan of 1951 to infiltrate Albania; BG refers to comunication codes, FIEND refers to the operation
BND	West German foreign intelligence agency
BRIXMIS	British Commanders-in-Chief Mission; Military Liasion with GSFG
BRUSA	British and US (SIGINT sharing) Agreement
BSP	Bulgarian Socialist Party
Btn	Battalion
BUF	British Union of Fascists
'C'	Chief of SIS (Initial of Captain Sir Smith-Cumming, RN)
CCCP	Russian abbreviation for the Soviet Union
Cheka	Bolshevik Secret Police; predecessor of the KGB (1917–22)
CIA	Central Intelligence Agency (USA)
CIG	Current Intelligence Group
CIGS	British Chief of the Imperial General Staff
CO/OC	Commanding Officer/Officer Commanding
Comintern	Communist International organisation (1919–43); founded by Lenin, advocated world Communism

COY	Company
CPGB	Communist Party of Great Britain
CPSU	Communist Party of the Soviet Union
CSS	Chief of the Secret Intelligence Service
DEFCON	NATO's five alert stages (5–1) up to imminent war: Operational–Readiness No. 1
DFC	Distinguished Flying Cross
DG	Director General of MI5
DGSE	Direction générale de la sécurité extérieure; French foreign intelligence service
DIS	Defence Intelligence Staff (GB)
Div.	Division
DP	Displaced Person (i.e. at the end of the Second World War)
DS	Durzhavna Sigurnost; Bulgarian intelligence and security service
DSO	Distinguished Service Order
DST	Direction de la surveillance du territoire; French domestic intelligence agency which in 2008 merged into Direction centrale du renseignement intérieur
Enigma	German coding machine
EOKA	National Union of Cypriot Combatants; seeking union (enosis) with Greece
ERP	European Recovery Plan (Marshall Plan)
FBI	Federal Bureau of Investigation (USA)
FCO	Foreign and Commonwealth Office, created in 1968
FO	Foreign Office; formed in 1782, merged with CO to create the FCO
FOB	Forward Observation Officer
FRG	Federal Republic of Germany (West Germany)
GC & CS	Government Code & Cypher School (GB)
GCHQ	Government Communications Headquarters (SIGINT Agency)
GCMG	Knight of the Grand Cross, Order of St Michael and St George
GDR	German Democratic Republic (East Germany)
GRU	Glavnoye Razvedyvatelnoye Upravleniye (Soviet Military Intelligence)
GSFG	Group of Soviet Forces in Germany
GSO1/2	General Staff Officer Grades 1 and 2
'H' bomb	Hydrogen/ thermonuclear bomb

HBBASIS	Covert German site where OPC trained Bulgarian and Albanian agents for infiltration
H/SIS	Head of Station, i.e. H/Turkey
HMG	His/Her Majesty's Government
HMT	His/Her Majesty's Transport (Ship)
HUMINT	Intelligence gained from human sources (through espionage)
HVA	GDR foreign intelligence service (East Germany)
IC	Iron Curtain
ICBM	Intercontinental Ballistic Missile
INF	Intermediate-Range Nuclear Forces (Treaty)
IoH	Indicators of hostility (range 1–9)
IRBM	Intermediate-Range Ballistic Missile
JBS	Lieutenant Colonel John Burden Sanderson
JCS	Joint Chiefs of Staff (USA)
JIB	Joint Intelligence Bureau (GB)
JIC	Joint Intelligence Committee (GB)
KGB	Komitet Gosudarstvennoye Bezopastnosti (Soviet intelligence and security service (1954–91))
KI	Komitet Informatsii (Soviet foreign intelligence agency (1947–51)); formed from combining GRU and MGB
KPÖ	Austrian Communist Party
KRD	Counter-revolutionary activity (crime in USSR)
KYP	Greek intelligence service
LDV	Local Defence Volunteers
LMG	Light Machine Gun
MAD	Mutually Assured Destruction
MBE	Member of the British Empire
MC	Military Cross
MGB	Ministerstvo Gosudarstvennoye Bezopastnosti (Soviet Ministry of State Security (1946–54))
MI3	Operational side of intelligence gathering
MI4	SIS/FCO German and East European desk
MI5	British domestic security up to 3 miles offshore; responsible for protecting the UK against threats to national security from espionage, terrorism and sabotage on British territory
MI6	Inside the service known as SIS; British foreign intelligence service, works secretly abroad to develop foreign contacts and gather intelligence
MiG	Soviet jet fighter planes named after Mikoyan and Gurevich, Russian aircraft designers

MIR	Military Intelligence Research (GB)
MOD	Ministry of Defence; formerly the War Office until 1964
MP	Military Policeman
MPLA	People's Movement for the Liberation of Angola
MRBM	Medium-Range Ballistic Missile
NAAFI	Navy, Army and Air Force Institutes
NATO	North Atlantic Treaty Organisation
NCO	Non-commissioned officer
NKGB	Narodnyi Kommissariat Gosudarstvennoye Bezopastnost (Soviet intelligence and security service (1941–6), part of NKVD (1941–3))
NKVD	Narodnyi Kommissariat Vnutrennikh Del (People's Commissariat for Internal Affairs incorporating GUGB)
NSA	National Security Agency (SIGINT) (USA)
NSC	National Security Council (USA)
NSDD	National Security Decision Directive (USA)
NTS	People's Labour Alliance; Social democratic movement, used by Ukrainian émigrés, financed by the USA
OAS	Organisation Armée Secrète; clandestine French group aiming to keep Algeria as part of France
OB	Order of Battle
OC/CO	Officer Commanding/Commanding Officer
OCTU	Officer Cadet Training Unit
OEEC	Organisation for European Economic Cooperation
OPC	Office of Policy Coordination
OSS	Office of Strategic Services (USA)
PCF	Parti communiste français (French Communist Party)
PLAN	People's Liberation Army of Namibia
PNG	*Persona non grata*
POW	Prisoner of War
PUS	Permanent Under-Secretary
PUSD	Cover name for SIS
PX	Military Service Store (USA)
PSYOPS	Psychological Operations of a tactical nature
QKSTAIR	Operation launched by OPC against Bulgaria in 1950
QR	Quiet Room of Bletchley Park
RAF	Royal Air Force
Regt	Regiment
Rezident	KGB Head of Station (*Rezidentura*) in Russian embassy abroad

RPF	'Rassemblement du peuple français' ('rallying of the French people'), political party founded by General Charles de Gaulle
RR1	Registration Room 1 of Bletchley Park
RYAN	Raketno-Yadernoye Napadenie (nuclear missile attack); Soviet operation to detect an imagined Western First Nuclear Strike
SAAF	South African Air Force
SAC	Strategic Air Command (USA)
SACEUR	Supreme Allied Commander Europe
SADF	South African Defence Force
SALT	Strategic Arms Limitation (Treaty)
SAM	Surface-to-Air Missile
SAS	Special Air Service
SB	Służba Bezpieczeństwa (Polish Internal Security Service)
SBS	Special Boat Section; formed in 1940
SCI	Special Counter Intelligence (GB)
SDECE	Service de documentation extérieure et de contre-espionnage (French foreign intelligence service); replaced by the DGSE; 'Deck' in US slang
SDI	Strategic Defense Initiative ('Star Wars')
SHAPE	Supreme Headquarters Allied Powers Europe; NATO HQ
SIB	Special Investigations Branch (GB)
SIGINT	Signals intelligence gathered from intercepted communications between people (COMINT) or from electronic signals (ELINT)
SIS	Secret Intelligence Service (MI6); gathers secret intelligence and carries out counter intelligence abroad to protect the UK, its people and interests
SMA	Soviet Military Administration in the GDR
SMERSH	*Smert Shpionam*! ('Death to spies!'); Red Army counter intelligence unit replaced by Soviet Department 13 in 1946.
SMG	Submachine gun
SOE	Special Operations Executive (GB)
SOS	Socially dangerous element (criminal charge in USSR)
SOSUS	Sound Surveillance System
SOXMIS	Soviet equivalent of BRIXMIS
Spetsnaz	Soviet special forces
SQN	Squadron

SR	Service de renseignement ('Secret Service' in French)
SSBM	Surface-to-Surface Missile
START	Strategic Arms Reduction Treaty
STASI	GDR state intelligence and security service
SWAPO	South West African People's Organisation
TA	Territorial Army (British Reserve Army)
TNT	Trinitrotoluene explosive; used with a detonator
U2	Ultra-high altitude CIA spy plane used for reconnaissance over USSR
UDF	Union of Democratic Forces (Bulgaria)
UKUSA	1946 agreement of GCHQ and NSA to share all SIGINT; superseded 1943 BRUSA agreement between GC & CS and US War Department
ULTRA	Security classification for signals intelligence obtained from intercepted German wireless communications enciphered by the Enigma machine
UN/UNO	United Nations/Organisation
UNIPROFOR	UN Protection Force
UNITA	National Union for Total Independence of Angola
UNRRA	United Nations Relief and Rehabilitation Administration
UPA	Ukranian partisan group (post-war)
USAF	United States Air Force
V-1	Vergeltungswaffe 1 (reprisal weapon) V-1 flying bomb; in slang a 'buzz bomb' or 'doodlebug'
VAD	Admirer of US democracy (crime in USSR)
VCO	Viceroy commissioned officer
VCSS	Vice Chief of SIS
VE Day	Victory in Europe Day, 8 May 1945
VMN	'Executed', codeword under Stalin
WO	War Office (GB)
WTO	Warsaw Treaty Organisation; Warsaw Pact of Russia and Soviet Bloc
YMCA	Young Men's Christian Association

Acknowledgements

In preparing this book, I am indebted to my former tutor at college, the historian Dr Robert C. Mowat (1913–2006), for extracts from his fine book, *Ruin and Resurgence 1939–1965* (Blandford, 1966). The legendary slide-show which he presented in his home, 'the history of the world in sixty minutes', has led me to be ambitious in the content of this book.

I am very grateful to those who knew and worked with my father, for passing on their stories. Colonel Herbert Stobbe, of the NATO Deutsches Heer (ex-Wehrmacht), recalled his service in AFCENT HQ. Richard Aldwinckle kindly provided the comprehensive details of his father John Aldwinckle's career in the RAF and SIS, as well as the fascinating account of his talented mother Helene's work in Hut 6, Bletchley Park.

Another family friend, a York and Lancaster Regiment officer who served with my father, patiently recalled his memories of John's service in Suez and Bulgaria. Richard Sim so helpfully recalled our lives together as children in Sudan and Egypt. My eloquent paratrooper friend kindly recalled the story of how his squad nearly started world war three in West Germany. Mark Meaton, a flying museum archivist, spent hours researching the history of Major Peter Greenhalgh DFC (Distinguished Flying Cross), my father's SIS colleague in Paris and Turkey. Dr Marjolijn Verbrugge kindly located Greenhalgh's photograph in the museum archives. Many thanks are due also to my helpful bookseller friends, Kevin and Darryl, for keeping me supplied with useful Cold War reference books, and for their encouraging good humour.

I am especially grateful to Richard Crompton, a fellow 3rd Australian Tunnelling Company descendant, who casually mentioned that he would be happy to contribute a couple of maps for this book and then produced twelve meticulously detailed and beautiful maps.

I would like to thank the brilliant Emeritus Professor Archie Brown of St Antony's College, Oxford, an expert on Mikhail Gorbachev and the

Cold War. Although busy completing a new book, he kindly gave his time to share some of his perceptive articles on the end of the Cold War. His advice on Mikhail Gorbachev's significance as a possible General Secretary, given to Margaret Thatcher in Number 10, helped persuade the Prime Minister to invite the 'up and coming' leader to Britain.

I was very fortunate to have had the privilege of meeting Major Maurice Bell, aged 96 years, and his very welcoming, 'young at heart' wife Sylvia (she lived to five days short of her 99th birthday), who invited me to spend the day with them in 2015 to hear about Maurice's part in the Battle of Sangshak on the border of India and Burma in April 1944. To hear first-hand, over seventy years after the event, from a Signals officer fighting not 50yd from my father was extraordinary. The intrepid Maurice Bell died two months later but his account survives.

Introduction

by Myles Sanderson

Excepting my father's Sarajevo mission two decades ago, half a century has passed since the majority of the events described in this book took place. Techniques and methods of warfare, diplomacy and espionage have changed immeasurably over these fifty years. I feel sure, given the passage of time, that the contents, revelations and accounts detailed here will not prove damaging to British national security. My father, Lieutenant Colonel John B. Sanderson, knew from our close and long relationship that any of the few confidences he passed to me from an early age would be strictly between ourselves. From early childhood, the shared isolation of a diplomatic family living behind a hostile Iron Curtain, and previous residency in the then rather basic countries of Turkey, Sudan and Egypt, created a rather unique family situation, and explains the strong bond and mutual respect between father and son, forged in many countries and over fifty years. My father was an optimistic, happy and positive man – 'all his geese were swans'. My mother was a very active 'working' diplomatic partner and helpful 'counterbalance' for my father and obviously privy to his unique security situation. (She once described, in a light-hearted way, an obviously harrowing experience when leaving Bulgaria in a car protected by diplomatic status: in the boot were secreted weapons for repatriation from the British Legation.)

My childhood was wonderful, varied and exciting. At the age of 12, I was present when British security officers 'swept' our Sofia house for hidden microphones. Seated in the back of my parents' car, I listened as they discussed their friends Denis Greenhill and Bruce Lockhart or counted Bulgarian T-64 tanks as they drove along the road, followed by the 'Georges', as we called the Bulgarian secret police who always shadowed our car. I travelled with my sister across Europe in 1961 on the Simplon–Orient Express from Paris to Sofia, watched over by the armed Queen's

Messengers with their diplomatic bags, who rustled up bacon and eggs for us in the guards' compartment.

On leaving Paris in 1961 we saw OAS (Organisation Armée Secrète) slogans painted on walls, hinting at deep divisions within French society. We were told that this was a clandestine group aiming to keep Algeria French ('*L'Algérie est française et le restera*'). '*Vive l'Algérie française*!' de Gaulle had declared in 1958 after his election, but then pragmatically carried out a political volte-face to recognise an independent Algeria in 1962. The SDECE (Service de documentation extérieure et de contre-espionnage) was engaged in a 'dirty war' with the OAS: the bearded Barbouzes were secretly contracted to find, abduct and kill terrorists opposed to French policy.[1] We didn't guess that the following year we would be living near Paris when our father was based in the Intelligence Division of SHAPE (Supreme Headquarters Allied Powers Europe), the military HQ of NATO (North Atlantic Treaty Organisation) during the Cuban Missile Crisis. Nor imagine that this crisis, in which our father was directly concerned, would take the world to the brink of nuclear catastrophe, as this book will explain.

We didn't know in 1962 in Versailles that John Aldwinckle, RAF (Royal Air Force) father of our friends, was a member of SIS (Secret Intelligence Service) like our own father. Nor did the Aldwinckle children know that their vivacious and charming mother Helene had worked in Hut 6 at Bletchley Park during the war. She would keep this secret for many more years. Later I was permitted the unusual, unforgettable experience, for a young boy of 14 years, of joining my father's soldiers in firing a Sterling SMG (submachine gun) on his Yorkshire base range. I was in Italy in August 1968 with my father when he learned of the Russian invasion of Czechoslovakia, an event that demanded his immediate return to AFCENT (Allied Forces Central Europe), NATO's HQ in Holland. Similarly my sister and I would be present around the family table at social functions, when discussions took place with friends from varied diplomatic, political and military backgrounds. It was a privilege to meet Major General Harper of the 101st 'Screaming Eagles' Airborne Div., a veteran of the Battle of Bastogne during the 1944 Ardennes offensive. All these small, unusual childhood adventures have spurred me on to investigate and write about what these soldiers, spies and diplomats of the 'Hot' and 'Cold' wars experienced.

There was in the background, however, as the Cold War intensified, an awareness for both adults and children that 'a Damocles sword' (as Nikita Khrushchev aptly described it) of global nuclear annihilation was hanging over our heads.[2] It was a Cold War which very nearly became a

Hot War, with the Soviets' Operation RYAN, a paranoid fear of a Western 'first strike', at the time of the NATO exercises ABLE ARCHER in 1983 and LIONHEART in 1984. My father, I believe, carefully preserved and stored, in two well-travelled and battered metal trunks in his shed, the many photographs, letters and documents covering his military, personal and diplomatic life, so that one day a fuller history of events that he witnessed could be told. These 'time capsules' were only noticed and opened after his death. In the following account there are many gaps and silences, simply because the world of the SIS was by definition 'secret'. It was natural though that a father would let slip certain confidences to a son, confidences that were well-kept in his lifetime and for over a decade beyond. My father John left the door of secrecy a little ajar, so that we can peer inside this fascinating, complex world and get some idea of what it was like to have lived through these tumultuous times, when patriotism was the rudder and when individuals could make a difference. So I am grateful to my father and his family for realising it was important to put pen to paper and record their time in history. Their conscientiousness in communicating their thoughts so clearly in letters to each other throughout the Second World War and afterwards during the Cold War has left a clear picture of the eventful times they lived through. The correspondence between the Sanderson family in Beckenham, Kent and my father in India was sent via sheets called airgraphs. These letters were written on 21 x 28cm letter forms that were sent to special V-stations where they were photographed on 16mm film. This film was then flown to India to a photo V-station where the images were processed, enlarged and the half-size 10.5 x 13cm airgraph letters sent on by ordinary mail to the addressee. Service personnel could send their forms free and they were delivered free. A normal letter would have taken three to six months by sea to the Far East and been one-hundred times heavier. The beauty of this ingenious system was that all airgraph letters reached their destinations: each sheet was numbered and photographed. When the flying boat *Clare* was lost in September 1941, carrying mail home from India and Africa, duplicates of the lost film were received in London in October and all the letters processed for delivery. By October 1942, when John was in India, a million airgraphs were being sent in each direction every week.[3]

In the photographs of John Sanderson you will see that he was almost always smiling: he was determined to preserve his internal happiness and humanity throughout the conflicts. He was prepared to die in battle, exhorting his soldiers to 'Die like men' in the face of repeated Japanese attacks, yet he was determined to survive, as his father had the First World War. During the war in India he was planning his post-war army career. He was brought up by a young, optimistic and strong mother with great common sense, firm political views and a religious faith. A world in turmoil and conflict is recorded in her detailed wartime diary and letters to her son in Dover and India. John's childhood journeys to, within and from India made him at ease in the world and fluent in Urdu. His early responsiblities as the eldest of six children, four boys and two girls, taught him restraint and authority. The whole family survived the war. His brother Richard served in the RAF in Canada and Peter in the ARP (Air Raid Precautions). His little sister Janet spotted V-1s (flying bombs) coming from the rooftops. In 1940 John survived being blown off his feet near Dover by a German bomb, and his family in Beckenham were shaken by another large bomb dropped by the Luftwaffe. Luckily his Royal Australian Engineer father, a former Tunnelling officer, had reinforced their cellar with railway sleepers. His younger sisters were equally defiant. Let Hitler come to this island, they will deal with him.

In the Soviet Union another tyrant was terrorising an empire. Tens of millions died before the war through his paranoia, inhumanity and cruelty. Stalin was obsessed with his own survival and waged an internal Cold War against his fellow citizens. Posted after the war to Communist Bulgaria, John Sanderson would condemn the show trials he attended in Sofia. His reports to London described the cruelty of the Communist system which he witnessed first-hand.

This is the story of resistance to tyranny by free men and women. It involves a terrible weapon, the atomic bomb, that ended the war with Japan and provided an umbrella of protection to the West and kept the peace for almost half a century until the Soviet Union's Eastern European empire broke up, the Communist Party was dissolved and the Soviet Union fractured. The courage of one particularly courageous Russian politician, Mikhail Gorbachev, was central to this process.

The book also tells the human story of three families, the Sandersons, the Sims and the Aldwinkles, caught up in the tides of history. It describes the organisation to which the two Johns belonged, SIS (Secret Intelligence Service or MI6), which fought a clandestine war against the Soviet secret services, the KGB (Soviet intelligence and security service) and the GRU (Soviet Military Intelligence). 'Kim' Philby, the traitor, and John Sanderson have much in common. They had both spent their childhood in India, both were attractive and sociable individuals, fond of telling amusing anecdotes (as was the politician Ernest Bevin incidentally) with great charm and charisma, self-confidence and intelligence, as well as that vital espionage asset, an ability to be duplicitous. They had served together in London, followed the same fieldcraft courses and were posted to Istanbul on SIS operations in the same era. Philby became the MI6 liaison with the CIA

(Central Intelligence Agency) and FBI (Federal Bureau of Investigation) and John Sanderson was later offered this Washington liaison post but turned it down. Of the four main SIS officers described here: Kim Philby, George Blake, John Sanderson and the brave John Aldwinckle, two were traitors and two patriots. The treacherous Philby saw Britain as 'the enemy camp': 'all through my career, I have been a straight penetration agent working in the Soviet interest . . . dedicated to smashing every vestige of imperialism off the face of the earth'.[4] The traitor George Blake embraced Communism like a religious faith. For Lieutenant Colonel John Sanderson and Wing Commander John Aldwinckle patriotism was their rudder. Their loyalty was to their King, their Queen and their country.

> Within the house of espionage, with its myriad of reflective walls, truths are uncertain and elusive. Our former allies become our enemies, enemies become our friends and allies, the friends of our enemies become our enemies, the enemies of our enemies become our friends and sometimes those we trust the most reveal themselves as traitors.
>
> Myles Sanderson

Espionage in the Cold War

In both the Second World War and the Cold War that followed, a priority was to discover to what use the opposition planned to put the weapons they possessed, and to discover their strategic intentions and threats. HUMINT (Human Intelligence: spies and agents), BRIXMIS (British Commanders-in-Chief Mission), military attachés abroad, aerial photographic and satellite surveillance as well as SIGINT (Signals Intelligence) all played an important part in gathering intelligence.

1. A major objective was 'acquiring' the secrets of the rivals' technology. Weapons systems had to be developed or stolen through espionage, simply because their possession by their Cold War enemies created an unacceptable imbalance of power which left the weaker side vulnerable to a superior threat. The logic of deterrence and MAD (Mutually Assured Destruction) led to systems and equipment being designed and built mainly to prevent wars not fight them. Weapons like the 'A' and 'H' bombs posed, as today, such a threat to the environment and civilisation that neither side was willing to take the risk of using them in conflict (apart from those that ended the war with Japan). An accidental outbreak of nuclear war or a devastating, unexpected nuclear

first strike were the most feared scenario. Where the Soviet Union did not actually possess the weapons to match the Western arsenal, they created the illusion that they did: Khrushchev's missile posturing was an attempt to psychologically deceive the West (*maskarova* – deception).

2. HUMINT. The motivations of defectors or agents differed. In the inter-war years, and early 1940s, spies and moles in the West (the Cambridge Five) were generally spurred on by ideology. The poverty and seemingly dysfunctional inter-war capitalist system was compared to a perceived 'fairer' Communist system in the Soviet Union. As the truth was revealed about the harsh reality of life in Stalin's totalitarian state, spies were recruited into espionage against the Soviet Union mainly through financial inducements, sexual blackmail or dissatisfaction with the routine of their daily lives. Another effective way of spying was to 'embed' an agent in the rival's country, as an 'illegal' with a false identity. Sometimes the fruits of espionage were so rich, and the documents stolen so copious in quantity, that, in the case of the Cambridge Five, unjustified Soviet suspicions were aroused.
3. Ironically, ideological despair was the main motivation for the successful recruitment of Soviets as double agents by Western intelligence. The two greatest Russian spies recruited by the Western secret services were individuals disillusioned with the ideology of Communism and the reality of the brutal repression of Soviet satellite states: the GRU Colonel Pentovsky with the invasion of Hungary in 1956 and the KGB Colonel Gordievsky with the 1968 invasion of Czechoslovakia. The intelligence provided by the two Olegs, Penkovsky and Gordievsky, was invaluable in revealing the deliberations within the Kremlin walls.
4. SIGINT from either COMINT, human communication, or ELINT, electronic communication. The information provided by the advanced technology of overflying SIGINT bombers, U2 spy planes and satellites revealed to the West the Soviet deficiencies in bombers and in ICBMs. There was no 'missile gap' as the Americans had feared. Decrypting an enemy's communication traffic was the best way to reveal their intentions, military operations or plans, or to discover foreign agents, burrowing as moles within one's own organisations or abroad. In the 1980s the CIA could listen in to the conversations between Communist Party leaders driving around Moscow in their large Zil official cars.[5] 'Ferret flights' over the Soviet Union revealed gaps in Soviet radar that could be exploited by bombers in time of war. Defecting technical experts or spies working within the SIGINT field could reveal secrets of encryption, enabling other agents to be uncovered, i.e. the Venona (Soviet encrypted messages) traffic.

5. After the war the US OPC (Office of Policy Coordination)/CIA and British SIS sought to obtain intelligence, and to encourage resistance, within the occupied Soviet satellites by sending in undercover agents, usually émigrés. These risky and costly operations were betrayed by spies such as Blake and Philby within British intelligence, or by Soviet agents who had infiltrated the émigré organisations. The Soviets were skilled in 'turning' the infiltrating émigré agents to entice further compromised operations, a method employed to good effect by the British in the 'doublecross' spy ploys in the Second World War before D-Day.
6. The Soviet Union's KGB departments provided its satellite bloc allies with the technology and specially developed poisons, chemicals or radioactive substances to carry out 'revenge' assassinations to eliminate 'enemies' abroad. The Soviet Union and the USA (called Glavny Protivnik, the 'Main Adversary', by Moscow Centre) and their European allies differed in the way they handled spies discovered within their own countries. If not imprisoned (or shot, as in the Soviet-controlled states), the adversaries in the Cold War, on occasions, exchanged the illegals or 'double' agents found operating clandestinely within their country for their own agents detained abroad. The U2 pilot Gary Powers and a US student were exchanged in February 1962 at the Glienicke Bridge in Berlin for an 'illegal', the spy 'Rudolf Abel', alias KGB Colonel Vilyam Fisher. None of the Cambridge Five Soviet spies were ever prosecuted.[6]

Chapter 1

Indian Childhood

In 1909 the Secret Service Bureau was founded on the initiative of Herbert Asquith, the Prime Minister, in response to the threat posed to the British Empire by Germany's Imperial ambitions. The first Director of this Secret Service was Captain Smith-Cumming, a naval officer who signed his corespondence 'C' in green ink, a tradition that continues to this day.[1]

Ten years later, on a fine autumn day in 1919, five months after the signing of the peace treaty in Versailles, a New Zealand-born officer stood happily in the sunshine outside a church in Otford, Kent with his young bride, an 18-year-old 'English Rose', Gladys Royle, on his arm. Two decades later, as a mother of six children, she would write a perceptive and passionate wartime diary.

On his uniform, Major Alexander Sanderson wore the red and blue ribbon of a DSO (Distinguished Service Order), the rainbow ribbon of the Victory Medal with an oak leaf 'Mentioned in Dispatches' and a purple and white ribbon with an attached miniature silver metallic rose, signifying a bar to his MC (Military Cross), awarded following an evening raid into enemy trenches to destroy German mineshafts. The two wound stripes on his left sleeve witnessed the wounds received during each of the two actions that earned him an MC.

Alexander's fortunate survival in the killing fields of the Western Front was to convince his eldest son that he too would come through his own wartime service unharmed. John Sanderson's *'kriegsglück'* (fortunate survival in battle) would permit him post-war to pursue a long and eventful diplomatic and military career in Her Majesty's Secret Intelligence Services. John Burden Sanderson's account of his life begins here:

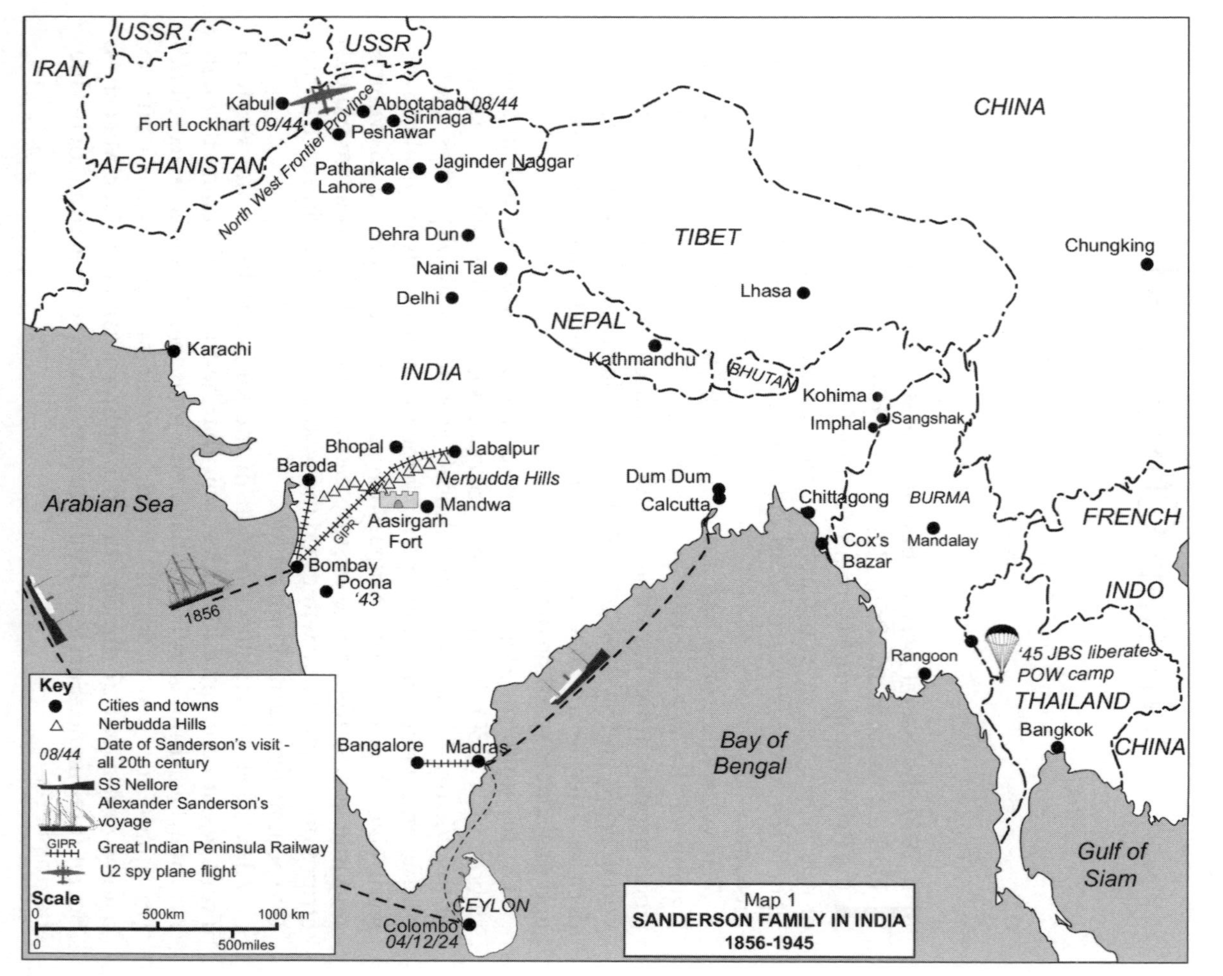

Map 1
SANDERSON FAMILY IN INDIA
1856-1945

My code of living by John Sanderson:
The following has been my philosophy throughout life:

- To earn a day's pay for a day's work
- To relax and enjoy life, both at work and at play
- To love and be loved
- To laugh and be friendly
- To be honest and not selfish
- To be generous and kind, where kindness is deserved
- To support our family and friends

And most important of all:

- To love our country, and to appreciate and be thankful, for being British.

Where Central India meets the sky,
When June and heat were in,
I met a tiger passing by,
A Burra Bagh, and there was I
All armed and most afraid to die –
And now I have the skin.

Anon.

I was born on 6 August 1921 in 'The Brambles', Otford, Kent. It was the home of my maternal grandparents, a large Victorian house with an extensive garden with a sizeable orchard. My mother Gladys Burden lived there with her parents, and two brothers.

Gladys's father 'Jack' Burden was a charming person, extremely handsome with fine hair which had turned completely white in his twenties. He was a managing director in London, and a member of the London Corn Exchange. He was head of the Special Constabulary for twenty years, vicar's warden and a local school manager. One might describe him as a member of the affluent middle class, with a lovely house, a housemaid and a chauffeur/gardener, horses and pigs. I thought he was wonderful, and was always very happy there. His wife Alice was equally charming. An extremely elegant lady who looked and behaved like Queen Mary! Needless to say, she managed the household like an efficient hotel, with excellent food, exquisite entertainment and with never a harsh word to anyone. I adored her.

At the outbreak of the First World War, aged 39 years, my grandfather had volunteered for army service. At the recruiting office, however, the duty sergeant had other ideas, shouting out at him: 'What are you doing here Grandpa, fall out!'

My mother married my father, Alexander Sanderson, in November 1919, almost exactly a year after the Armistice of the First World War. Alexander, an officer of 38 years, with a distinguished war record, had fought with the Australian Imperial Force, commanding a Tunnelling company for three years. He was due to return to Australia the month after his wedding. My mother fell in love and, although apprehensive about leaving her family, she decided to accompany Alexander aboard the SS *Runic*, of which he was OC (Officer Commanding) Ship, to his family home in Perth, Western Australia.

My father was released from the Australian Army in April 1920 and accepted an offer from the government of India of a three-year appointment with the Military Works Department. He was posted as Garrison Engineer with the rank of major to Allahabad in the central provinces. During this posting, my mother became pregnant. When my father was transferred to Calcutta a year later, she decided to travel home to her parents in Kent to have their baby, me.

My First Voyage to India

Four months after my birth in Kent, on 2 December 1921 we embarked aboard the SS *Peona* from Liverpool, arriving in Calcutta on New Year's Eve. We were met at the quayside by my father, just after the departure of the Prince of Wales. Edward VII's visit had been met with widespread rioting in Bombay, Allahabad and Calcutta, and as a consequence sixteen Gurkha troops were killed by anti-British rebels. Ghandi used this visit to draw attention to his campaign against the import of foreign cloth. I remember nothing, of course, of these events, but refer to them briefly because I was to experience similar rioting during the Second World War, some twenty-three years later.

Another significant event at this time was the British government's signing of the agreement granting independence to Southern Ireland on 6 December. Six of the counties of Ulster remained part of the United Kingdom. The ministers at the time believed that ultimately Ireland would be best served by having its own parliament in Dublin. Today Ulster's leaders still show no sign of bowing to Dublin rule.

My mother was pleased to return to India. However, she was soon pregnant again. Calcutta in the height of summer was no place to have a baby so in July 1922 my mother and I were back on board ship, on the SS *Malda*, for the six-week voyage back to England. We arrived in Kent in time for my 1st birthday and my mother soon gave birth to a second son, Richard. According to my mother, I had grown up a 'sturdy boy and, like all boys, full of mischief'. I was found in the garage one day pressing the self-starter button on the car, with the engine ticking away. It was from this happy household that we had to set off back to India in November 1924.

My mother recorded in her diary that: 'this time [over two years] spent at "The Brambles" [with her two sons] did the children so much good, instead of the heat of Calcutta. They were able to have plenty of milk and cream as father kept two Jersey cows.' It was with some apprehension and regret that my mother finally set off for the return journey to India aboard the SS *Mori*. However, the prospect of being with her husband again, and avoiding the English winter, cheered her up.

We stopped off at Malta, Port Said, Aden and Colombo. I vaguely remember playing on deck with Richard, and the heat on board ship in the Red Sea; we all caught colds from the fans, which were constantly revolving. I had been presented with a pedal car on leaving England, and this was a great joy to me on the boat deck, which was virtually a circular race track. When I drove off a gangway onto the deck below, I completely wrecked the car. Nobody knew why I was not killed in the accident! I suppose I was destined to survive a dangerous life.

We arrived in Colombo at about 6 a.m. on 4 December 1924, where we were met by my father – a great excitement! We then all sailed on together to Madras. From there we set off on an 8-hour train journey to Bangalore where my father had been commissioned to design a bridge. We enjoyed a pleasant week's break in the West End Hotel, after the long voyage, before returning to Madras and the final four days on board the *Nellore* to Calcutta.

In Calcutta, for virtually the whole time, my younger brother and I were looked after by our ayah and the Indian servants:

as a result I was fluent in Hindustani by the age of 4 years. We continued to use the language until our return to England when I was 8 years of age. I gradually forgot how to speak it, other than the odd sentence or two. When I returned to India thirteen years later, during the Second World War, and was given Urdu lessons on board the ship by a Colonel Hewett of 13th Frontier First Rifles, all the language came back to me. In fact, to the Colonel's surprise, I was more fluent with the language on arrival at Bombay than he was ever likely to be!

We used to play with the servants' children in the garden, with its lines of delphiniums, seemingly fashioned from silver. We fished in the local stream with a bamboo rod and a length of cotton. A bent pin served as a hook and a piece of bread as bait. We caught many fish in this way and carried them proudly up to the servants' quarters where our ayah used to cook them for us, served with chippatio flat bread.

There were memorable occasions during my childhood in India. One morning my brother and I awoke to a rustling noise beneath our beds. Peering down, we saw a large snake coiled up. Terrified, we realised that it was a King Cobra, a very poisonous snake that must have slid in through the plug-hole of the bath. Richard let out a piercing yell, 'Snake!', and father rushed in with a large alpenstock, before shifting the snake outside. My father gave us a model railway: a clockwork Hornby train with carriages and we built tunnels into the bank of the house and spent hours watching the trains pass through. My father explained that his grandfather, also named Alexander, a railway engineer, had been sent out by Robert Stephenson in 1856 to survey the Great Indian Peninsular Railway, but within weeks of the railway line reaching the Nerbudda jungle he had died of malarial 'fever jungle'. This was during the Indian Mutiny. After his grandfather's burial at Agra fort, his grandmother, Susannah, made her way back to Bombay, travelling by night and armed with a silver-handled pistol which she would not have hesitated to use. (This firearm remained in the family until 1940 when we had to hand it in to a police station for the Home Guard to use!) Susannah remarried a sergeant, a veteran of the Crimean War, and sailed to Otago, South Island, New Zealand where in 1881 her grandson, Alexander, my father, was born.

I cannot have been much older than 5 when my parents packed me off to St Joseph's Convent School, in the hills at Naini Tal. As the extreme heat of the Indian climate lasted most of the year, the terms at St Joseph's were nine months long: we had three months of holiday during the 'cool' season. During this long term time, we saw our parents only once at half term. The school was designed along the lines of an English public school, with dormitories holding about twenty-four boys, all of whom were much the same age as myself. We were taught and looked after by Catholic nuns, most of whom seemed to relish handing out corporal punishment. One of the items specified in the list of belongings, to be brought by each school attendee, was a hairbrush with a handle. These were rarely used to brush one's hair, but provided useful implements with which the nuns could beat us for every misdemeanour!

There were only two exciting episodes during my sojourn at the school. The first was a tiger shoot which I viewed from the windows of my dormitory, in the middle of the night. A rogue tiger – a mankiller, a *Burra Bagh* ('big tiger') – had been roaming the villages close to the school and attacked some of the villagers. A game hunter came and had a bait of a young calf tethered in the middle of the playing field, directly adjacent to our dormitory. On a well moonlit night, he took up his stand in one of our windows. I well remember the tiger appearing, and being shot dead. Great excitement for all of us! The other surprising occasion was when my parents appeared unexpectedly at the school to announce that we were going home to England.

It was whilst I was at St Joseph's that my parents moved to Dehra Dun, in the United Provinces, north of Delhi. They had rented a large furnished bungalow in the Rajpore Road, that goes on to the hill station of Mussoorie. We had a huge compound, and I enjoyed playing in the garden during my holidays. The only problem with Dehra Dun was the snakes – the grass grew very high during the monsoon, and the snakes were very difficult to spot. I remember walking with my father one day when he was struck on the leg by a snake. Fortunately, he was wearing riding boots, and the head of the snake became embedded in the leather boot. He simply drew out a knife, and cut the snake from his boot! He was used to dealing with the desert death adders in the Australian outback.

My brother and I had our own horses which were stabled in the compound at the rear of the bungalow. We rode regularly, a skill I found useful in the Indian Army. One day we decided to have a race home. Richard's horse bolted for the stables when we neared our house and I was afraid his head might be chopped off by the iron roofing covering the stables. Fortunately, he had the good sense to thrust both hands upwards towards the corrugated roofing, and the horse trotted into the stable door leaving my brother suspended in the air.

I keep asking myself why I remember so little about my father in those formative years of my life, and can only conclude that his workload was spread far and wide, and we saw so little of him. My father was always very conscientious and had to work extremely hard all his life. In 1923 he designed and constructed the first reinforced concrete bridge in India in Calcutta. He was away for long periods with his engineering works. However, when he was appointed Chief Engineer of a hydroelectric scheme at Joginder Nagar, in Mandi State, he came down to Dehra Dun to collect us. We travelled up by train to Pathankale, then along a narrow winding road, a journey of 100 miles in total, up into the Himalayan mountains. It was the first time the family had lived in the hills in India, with snow-topped mountains in the distance. Our home was a comfortable bungalow with a garden and enough land to keep two cows, horses and chickens.

The work on the hydroelectric scheme, at an elevation of 6,000ft above sea level, included the design and construction of a surge shaft 400ft deep and a 3-mile concrete-lined tunnel through a high mountain spur. It was a technically challenging project but my father was an expert in all aspects of tunnelling through rock, skills acquired in the goldmines of Australia. Enormous quantities of water, collected in the mountains, would flow through this tunnel and down to the turbines, located in the Indian foothills. In December 1929, with the project half completed, my father decided to resign. I suspect that by this time my mother had seen enough of India and, moreover, she was pregnant for the fifth time. Also the Indian people were becoming more antagonistic towards the British Raj.

The servants employed by my father, however, were sad to see us leave. They had grown fond of the children and told me: 'John Saab, Burro Saab, you will return here to be a Major when you grow up.' They would have been interested to know that, twelve years later, that is exactly what I would do.

Chapter 2

Return to Britain, 1929

JBS:

We sailed from Bombay to the south of France. The journey home was long and tedious. Richard and I got into mischief on the first-class deck promenade where a wealthy passenger's child had left his treasured pedal car. What fun and games we had pushing each other around the deck, until we had wrecked his car! We hurriedly disappeared back to the tourist-class deck. The early mornings were great fun, when the sailors cleaning the decks laughingly splashed us down with their hoses.

From Marseilles we travelled north across France by train, retracing the journey my father had taken with his Australian soldiers in May 1916. It was a harsh winter and the Channel crossing was on the roughest sea I have ever experienced. We were all thankful when we eventually arrived at the Port of London.

At Tilbury docks, on a cold, misty morning, we descended the gangway onto English soil to be met by our grandparents and their chauffeur Graves, dressed in uniform. We all packed into the large Alvis car and Graves drove us across London and into the beautiful Kent countryside, to arrive eventually at the house of my birth. Here we were allowed to pick the fruit, including the delicious apples, but grandad always insisted that we eat every part of the apple, core and all. Graves used to drive us to see the local fox hunting and, afterwards, we would wait for him outside the Royal George pub, where he gave us large glasses of ginger beer and big round arrowroot biscuits, whilst he went inside for a pint. One day I slipped away and went up to Petticoat Lane market in London where I bought a Rhode Island Red chicken. Much to my satisfaction, it laid an egg when I got home.

In India, the All-India National Congress passed a resolution demanding 'complete independence' from Britain. Perhaps it had been the right time for us to leave India. Job prospects at home, however, were far from favourable: some 2 million were unemployed. The world economy looked grim after the Wall Street Crash. Sterling had devalued by 30 per cent, the gold standard was abandoned to stop the run on the pound and servicemen found their pay cut by as much as 25 per cent.

During this time 'The Brambles' must have been bursting at the seams, which is no doubt why I was dispatched to boarding school. I attended the junior prep school for Sutton Valence Public School but was so far behind in my schooling that I never really caught up with the other boys. I spent a miserable two years there: my only pleasure being some success at sport. I participated in athletics events with Sydney Wooderson, the future 'Mighty Atom', the 4-minute miler of national repute. I never did graduate to the main school.

In March 1933 the US President Herbert C. Hoover left office: his economic policies were unpopular during the Great Depression, with US unemployment figures of 25 per cent. The stock market had crashed in 1929, on Black Tuesday, six months into his presidency. As a young man, in 1898 Hoover had been a mining manager working with my father at the Berwick Moering 'Sons of Gwalia Gold Mine' in Coolgardie, Western Australia.

In May 1933 my father set up a factory producing pipes, manholes, sleepers and reinforced concrete towers. He had previously run a company in Australia before the First World War in partnership with his friend John Monarsh (later appointed Commander-in-Chief of Australian forces in France, as General Sir John Monarsh GCMG (Knight of the Grand Cross, Order of St Michael and St George)). I well remember visiting my father's factory, and being impressed by the products. There undoubtedly seemed to be a need for steel-reinforced concrete items, and there was nothing of equal quality on the market at the time. Unfortunately, the largest pipe-producing company in the UK had just spent over £2 million developing their new factory. They made absolutely sure my father's firm was not going to take over their business and it never got off the ground. We were once again living on the breadline.

Iosif Vissarionovich Dzhugashvili chose to name himself Stalin, 'Man of Steel', in 1912, the year Lenin made him editor of *Pravda* (*Truth*) and a member of the Bolshevik Central Committee. Exiled to Siberia in 1913, Stalin had been judged unfit for the Czar's army in 1916. After Lenin's death, Stalin had proceeded to neutralise all opposition, starting with those on the left of the Communist Party, then those on the right who stood in his way to achieving absolute power.[1]

During the First World War, in 1917, the German decision to arrange for Lenin to travel back in a sealed train to Petrograd from Switzerland had set in motion an unforeseeable chain of events.[2]

Lenin, on his deathbed, had warned against the power Stalin had accumulated: 'I am not sure that he always knows how to use that power with sufficient caution . . . Stalin is too rough . . . becomes insupportable in the office of General Secretary . . . I propose to the comrades to find a way to remove Stalin . . . and appoint to it another man . . . more patient, more loyal, more polite, and more attentive to comrades, less capricious'.[3] It was not to be. The man responsible for the confrontation between West and East, the Cold War, had already become too powerful and feared. Khrushchev would recall Stalin's 'utter irresponsibility and complete lack of respect for anyone other than himself.'[4]

The Soviet flag, created in 1923, displayed the three symbols of the State: the red flag (dating from the French Commune of 1871) displayed a gold star above a hammer and sickle, representing the Communist Party leading the proletarian class, the industrial and agricultural workers, in building Communism. In the 1930s the Soviet Union was going through hardships, as was Britain, but many times worse. The Marxist economy had always been essentially 'the sickle': agricultural. Now, with a ruthless disregard for those who depended on their land for feeding themselves, Stalin was seizing their property for collective farms and exporting the bulk of the Soviet crops to finance his drive for the 'hammer': industrialisation. Those that resisted this policy were arrested by the secret police and either exiled to Siberia or liquidated. Millions starved.[5]

In 1937 Stalin, launched a campaign of 'social purification', not unlike Hitler's, when an initial quota of social 'criminals' was seized across the Soviet Union, region by region, and the people either executed (70,000) or sent to the Gulag (200,000). Thousands were used as slave labour in the early 1930s, when 1.5–2 million were prisoners. Nearly 800,000 citizens were executed. From 1929–53, it is estimated 29 million Soviet citizens had spent time in camps.[6] In Britain in this inter-war period, the poverty of many in the Depression, contrasted starkly with the evident wealth of a privileged minority. This inequality was to have a profound influence on many young students studying at Cambridge University, taught by lecturers with Socialist and Communist Marxist views and unsettled by the Cambridge hunger march. Philby was to be the most successful of these 'Cambridge Spies' (with Donald Maclean, Guy Burgess, Anthony Blunt and John Cairncross, the fifth).

Harold 'Kim' Philby, was a student at Trinity College, Cambridge, reading economics, a radical subject at the time. Philby was born in 1912 into a privileged family in Ambala, India: his father was the diplomat and soldier St John Philby. Sir Denis Greenhill, later a FO (Foreign Office) colleague of Sanderson, noted: 'The rise of the Nazis did not seem to agitate my friends at Oxford as much as our counterparts at Cambridge. Amongst us there were few fierce arguments about fascists.'[7]

Harold Philby was nicknamed 'Kim' after the eponymous protagonist in author Rudyard Kipling's book *Kim*. Kim is a young Irish-Indian boy who spies for the British in nineteenth-century India. The book, drawing on Kipling's own Indian childhood experiences, is set against the background of a covert war, the 'Great Game' between the two rivals Russia and Britain in central Asia. Kim is torn between his West–East background and must decide where his loyalties ultimately lie, whether he is a *chela* ('disciple') of an ancient Tibetan lama or a British spy. Kipling's Kim tells his guru: 'I am not a Sahib, I am thy chela, and my head is heavy on my shoulders.'[8]

Philby was recruited as a Russian agent after a meeting with Arnold ('Otto') Deutsch in Regent's Park. He was told: 'We needed people who could penetrate into the bourgeois institutions. Penetrate them for us.' Christopher Andrew and Vasili Mitrokhin noted that Philby was not told he was becoming a Soviet agent: he thought he was joining Comintern's (Communist International organisation) underground war against international facism. Philby was given the codenames 'Sohnchen' in German or 'Synok' in Russian, 'Sonny' in English.[9]

After time in Austria, where Philby established links with the KPÖ (Austrian Communist Party), he smuggled Communists out of Germany. On the orders of his KGB controllers, Philby was to distance himself from his Socialist society friends, joining the Anglo-German Fellowship and becoming an accredited reporter for *The Times* newspaper with Franco's forces in Spain.

John Sanderson was to be given the similar cover of an accredited Reuters agent by MI6 in 1949. Nigel West wrote that the Reuters News Agency had been purchased by SIS in 1916 through an intermediary. Funded secretly through a government budget, the many overseas branches were useful sources of intelligence for SIS. For example, an SIS officer named Frederick Heuvel was posted throughout the Second World War to the British Embassy in Berne, officially as the assistant press attaché, a cover that Sanderson would use in 1949 in Sofia.[10]

JBS had an early experience of Communist agitation:

> The Sanderson family moved to Beckenham, where I was able to live at home, and attend the local grammar school, at a cost of £12 a term. This was much more to my liking. I was able to play rugby, and even managed to reach the semi-finals of the schools' boxing championship at the Holborn Stadium, in London.
>
> Fortunately, the London Passenger Transport Board appointed my father as the Constructional Engineer in charge of the rebuilding of the King's Cross, Aldgate East and White City Underground stations. In 1936 he was building Aldgate East Underground station. The work often took place at weekends, when the electrical power system could be disconnected. When my father visited the construction site I liked to accompany him, mainly because, from the rooftops in the area, I had a perfect bird's-eye view of Oswald Mosley's BUF (British Union of Fascists) having 'ding-dong' battles with the extreme, pro-Communist Left. These Cable Street riots were described as Britain's worst for thirty years but, for a 15-year-old schoolboy, they were a sight to behold, so long as one was out of 'stone's throw' distance of the mob. I cannot remember if I was in sympathy with any particular side. After Aldgate East my father was posted as resident engineer at King's Cross Underground.
>
> In 1934, at the age of 13, I had joined the local Beckenham Troop of the Boy Scouts, and attended two of their summer camps; the last one as a section commander. Eventually, my uniform sleeves were covered in qualification badges and I was proud of the title 'King's Scout'. In 1937 I left school and found myself a job as a clerk in the Secretary's Office of the International Sportsman's Club, in the Grosvenor House Hotel, Park Lane, London. The club had a splendid swimming pool, gymnasium and squash courts; facilities I was permitted to use during my lunch breaks. I very much enjoyed the few months I spent there, but having decided that the prospects for advancement were limited, I found a job in the City with a small firm of importers of tools for manufacturing and repairing motor vehicles. There was a very happy atmosphere and I remained with them right up to outbreak of the Second World War, when I was mobilised with the TA (Territorial Army). In fact, the firm was generous enough to continue to pay my salary each month during the war, until a day in 1942 when a German bomb destroyed Finsbury Square, leaving no trace that the firm had ever existed.

Chapter 3

Army Enlistment, Cliffs of Dover and War, 1938–42

JBS:

This verse from William Shakespeare sums up succinctly my feelings about our situation in Dover in 1940:

This royal throne of kings, this sceptred isle,
This earth of majesty, this seat of Mars,
This other Eden, demi-paradise,
This fortress built by Nature for herself
Against infection and the hand of war,
This happy breed of men, this little world,
This precious stone set in the silver sea,
Which serves it in the office of a wall
Or as a moat defensive to a house,
Against the envy of less happier lands,
This blessed plot, this earth, this realm, this England.[1]

In March 1938, after leaving school and working in London, I decided to join the TA. Aged 16, I turned up one evening at the drill hall of the 1st Btn (Battalion), the London Scottish Regt (Regiment) in Buckingham Gate, Westminster, only to be told that I could not join before the age of 17 years. So I went next door to the drill hall of the Queen's Westminsters Regt and signed on under the false age of 17.

I was sworn in by the Orderley Room Quarter Sergeant as a rifleman, issued with a rifle, a full set of clothing and equipment, and posted to the signals platoon of Headquarters Coy (Company). Six or seven members of the platoon were present that evening in the Signals 'bunk', and I was introduced to the radio and line equipment available. On conclusion of training that evening, everyone adjourned to the bar. It was a custom that each attending member of the platoon buys a pint of beer for a new recruit! The outcome was devastating. I had the greatest difficulty making my way to Victoria station, and home to Beckenham, loaded down with a kit bag full of clothing and equipment. My mother opened the front door and cried out: 'My God! He has joined the army!'

The next day, my father was told the whole story, and seemed to have no objection to my joining the TA, other than to say that, should I ever want to apply for a commission, I might not be accepted having given a false age on enlistment. Consequently, I was forced to own up to the fact, and put up with the ignominy of being a 'boy' soldier for nine months. He was quite wrong about this since the London Rifle regiments have basically been officer-producing units in the event of an emergency: had I not owned up to giving a false age, I would have been commissioned at least nine months sooner than I was at the outbreak of the war. In any case, the army has a long tradition of young men joining under a false age, and I cannot imagine them being punished for doing so. I have never been asked for my birth certificate!

By the age of 17, I was very proficient in Morse code and had qualified as a driver of army vehicles and motor cycles, regularly driving my colleagues in a 15cwt truck to the Bisley ranges at weekends. The unit owned a bungalow there and we spent many happy hours shooting on the ranges. I became an expert shot with the rifle and the LMG.

In September 1938 Prime Minister Chamberlain returned from Munich having signed a 'Peace for our time' agreement with Hitler but we all knew it could only be a matter of time before war might be declared. In January 1939 the RAF was taking delivery of more than 400 aircraft a month, and in March it was decided to double the strength of the TA. The Queen's Westminsters were ordered to form a second battalion. Recruits started to pour in to the drill hall, including a number of well-known actors such as Frank Lawton.

When called up for active service with the TA in August 1939, I was by then a well-trained and useful member of the unit. On 14 August 1939, when I heard the message at work over the wireless that all members of the TA were to report to their drill halls, I knew exactly what to do.

> It was an exciting time for most of us, but, I daresay, a worrying time for our families. I was just 18 years old when the war commenced. For the next six years I was to lead a quite different lifestyle of active military service at home and abroad. It was the beginning of a full-time army career which would last thirty-five years.

A non-aggression pact signed with Hitler on 23 August 1939 demonstrated Stalin's brutal pragmatism. He intended that a future war should be fought, not on Soviet territory, but in the buffer zones of Eastern Europe. Ironically, Stalin's misplaced trust in Hitler's intentions, contrasted with the paranoia that had led him in the show trials of 1936–8 to eliminate the very Red Army commanders who would have stiffened Russia's resistance to the invasion by the Wehrmacht.[2] In one day in June 1937 Stalin had his best Red Army generals and three admirals arrested, tried and shot. In addition, 57 of the 85 corps commanders were removed and 50,000 military officers were put on trial.[3]

Long after the war, in 1969, with the Soviet Army now the threat, John Sanderson would be directly responsible as a lieutenant colonel GSO1 (General Staff Officer Grade 1) for a complete rewrite of the NATO plan for the defence of the whole of Central European Region against the Warsaw Pact threat. *JBS*:

> War was declared at 11 a.m. on 3 September 1939. By that time, volunteers had trickled in to the drill hall from far and wide, and both battalions of the Queen's Westminsters were well up to strength. The 1st Btn was in billets in the Praed Street area of Paddington, and at the time of the declaration of war was actually on a route march through the streets of London. Half an hour after the declaration, air raid sirens sounded. It was a false alarm but everyone ran for cover. Whether or not this persuaded the WO (War Office) to move the troops out of London, we soon found ourselves in billets in Folkestone, on the south coast. Headquarters Coy took over a girls' boarding school called Brampton Down. Unfortunately, the ladies had been evacuated! Quite a few of the men went off to OCTUs (Officer Cadet Training Units), and we received 200 recruits from the East End of London. I was promoted to lance corporal, and placed in charge of a section of ten of these new recruits, their morals and language being a complete shock and a revelation to me. I was considered too young to be sent off straight away to a OCTU, and had to wait nearly a year before going.

> This was a year of relative peace and quiet during the 'phoney' war. Not much happened until May 1940 when the Germans invaded Belgium and Holland, and the Allied forces were evacuated from Dunkirk. Now the British people awaited Hitler's next move.

The Soviet Union, Britain's future wartime ally, was at this time materially aiding the Nazi war machine. The historian C. Andrew and former KGB agent Oleg Gordievsky noted that KGB files would later reveal the extent to which Stalin was supplying Hitler's war machine with raw materials. General Heinz Guderian was the advocate of 'Blitzkrieg', the 'lightning war'. His Panzer tanks 'operated largely on Soviet petrol as they dashed for the sea at Abbeville. The bombs that levelled Rotterdam contained Soviet guncotton, and the bullets that strafed British Tommies wading to the boats at Dunkirk were sheathed in Soviet cupro nickel.'[4]

Stalin's misjudgement in trusting Hitler and ignoring warnings of invasion would prevent him from taking defensive measures when Hitler turned against Russia in 1941. Another individual who totally misjudged Hitler was even now starting up his aircraft on a runway in southern Germany. On 10 May the Deputy Führer Rudolph Hess, on his own initiative, flew alone in a Messerschmitt Bf 110 bomber from Augsburg to Scotland, where he abandoned his aircraft and parachuted out. His aim was to meet with the Duke of Hamilton and persuade Britain to negotiate a peace with Germany. Hess felt he was losing influence with his hero Hitler and thought this bold and brave flight, and a successful agreement with Britain, would win back the Führer's favour.[5] Hess evidently believed that he could interpret Hitler's will. In *Mein Kampf*, written when Hitler was in prison and published in 1925, he had noted:

> No sacrifice would have been too great to gain England's alliance. There was a moment when Great Britain would have let us speak to her, for she understood very well that, owing to her increased population, Germany would have to look for some solution and find it, whether in Europe with Great Britain's help, or elsewhere in the world without it. Yet no nation ever prepared better for economic conquest with the sword, or later maintained it more ruthlessly than the British.[6]

In the autumn of 1940 as Hitler prepared Operation SEALION to invade Britain, Hess and Hitler had talked about Churchill's refusal to sue for peace. Hitler had said to Hess: 'What more can I do? I can't fly over there and beg on bended knee.'[7] Hitler, however, was unimpressed with Hess's flight of fantasy and on 12 May declared that Hess had betrayed him. A month later Germany invaded Russia.

On 14 May 1940 a Soviet agent in London codenamed 'Sohnchen' ('little son'), or 'Zenkhen', under the control of the *rezident* (head of intelligence of the *rezidentura* in the Soviet Embassy), first reported to Moscow the arrival of Hess in Britain. This agent was Kim Philby, who in a 'speculative and malicious assessment' hinted that Hess could become 'the centre of an intrigue' in a 'peace party' between Hitler and Britain. The suspicious Stalin would later accuse Churchill of 'keeping Hess in reserve'.[8]

After a thorough interrogation by the former First Secretary in Berlin, then the Lord Chancellor and afterwards by Lord Beaverbrook, the Minister for Air production, Hess was imprisoned in Britain. Here he remained for five years until transferred post-war to Spandau Prison in Berlin, where JBS's battalion would mount guard.[9]

Churchill would write in his memoirs of this threat of a 1940 German invasion:

> Here perhaps was a chance of striking a blow at the mighty enemy which would resound throughout the world. One could not help being inwardly excited alike by the atmosphere and the evidence of Hitler's intention which streamed in upon us. I see only one way through now – to wit, that Hitler should attack this country, and in doing so break his air weapon . . . The heavy [German] cannon I preserved from the last war fired constantly from the heights of Dover in this war.[10]

JBS had a ringside view in Kent:

> In July 1940 we were deployed east of Dover to meet any invasion threat from across the Channel. We spent most of the time in slit trenches along the cliffs of Dover. During this period we were on constant guard, sleeping in our clothes. The Luftwaffe started attacking Allied shipping in the Channel, and a month later, they attacked our airfields along the south coast. Over 1,000 German planes were being sent over Britain daily. We then found ourselves filling in bomb craters during the day and 'standing to' in our slit trenches at night. Our Sergeant had a motto: 'Never put off until tomorrow what someone else can do today.' When not required for duty on the airfields, we simply rested on our backs, in glorious sunshine, watching the RAF fighters taking on the German aircraft.

'Luna Habitabilis', a prophecy translated by Thomas Grey (1716–71):

The time will come when thou shall lift thine eyes
To watch a long drawn battle in the skies
While aged peasants, too amazed for words
Stare at the flying fleets of wondrous birds,
England, so long mistress of the sea
Where winds and waves caress her sovereignty,
Her ancient triumphs yet on high shall bear
And reign the sovereign of the conquered air.

We saw some wonderful dogfights in the blue sky. My brother Peter was hop-picking in Kent and they also used to watch the fights in the air and see the Messerschmitts fall to earth.

Recently issued with a motorbike and tasked with getting to the location of any crashed or parachuted pilot with all haste, one day I arrived on the scene to find a farmer holding a pitchfork to the throat of an RAF pilot who had just drifted down in his parachute into a field. Having survived an air battle, this Polish pilot was extremely grateful to be rescued by a young soldier from the clutches of an irate Kent farmer who had mistaken him for a Luftwaffe crew member!

One RAF pilot, Flight Lieutenant B. Kingcome, had the same experience with patriotic English farmworkers, who had been warned to expect invading German parachutists:

There was a rattle of bullets . . . and one went through my leg. Three Spitfires drew alongside me and took one look and rolled away. I don't know whether they had shot me in error . . . or whether they had shot a German plane off my tail. I bailed out . . . I pulled my ripcord and sailed gently down and landed in a ploughed field . . . A number of farmers gathered with pitchforks. I was a bit nervous, because some Polish pilots who had been shot down had been set upon because of their accents, and I was wearing a German Mae West which I had taken off some German pilots. As it happened they were very friendly, because my Spitfire had landed before me.[11]

In the summer of 1940, during the Battle of Britain, *JBS* wrote home from Dover:

Dear Mother and all, Dover 1940

At the moment I am on another 24 hour guard. I do hope you are OK? I am naturally anxious when I hear of several of our lads having their homes bombed. I spent the afternoon in Dover on Sunday. What a mess they have made there. Five of us were walking along the road from the station when we heard a whistling bomb coming, it seemed, straight for us. Our noses were in the gutter in a flash and the bomb fell on a block of houses nearby. This was flattened by another bomb that fell dead on the station and smashed all the platforms except one. This is the only one in use now. We have just had lunch, which was bought up to us by the guard orderly stone cold. It probably was very nice hot but when we had it, it was awful. Some Canadians are on a charge near here. A short while ago a couple of Germans bailed out of their plane and were captured by the Canadians before the LDV [Local Defence Volunteers] got down there. When they did arrive the Germans were hanging dead – strung up by their own parachutes: 'We take no prisoners in this war!' said the Canadians.

I wonder what is holding up the invasion? Rough seas, I should think. I really believe he intended or intends to come over. He had better make his mind up soon or it will be too late. We are having a NAAFI cinema show in our mess hall this evening. I asked the officer commanding our company what was happening about my application for India yesterday. He said that they were doing nothing about this whilst the 'flap' is on, but I ought to hear soon, after it is over.

Your loving son, John

Audrey Jones, John's future wife, who lived near Kenley airfield, had made friends with a Polish soldier. *Plutonowy Podchorazy* (Officer Cadet) Koiluk Aleksander was based at RAF Kenley before being moved up to Fife in Scotland in late 1941 to train. He wrote many letters to her:

[11 Jan 1942] I see that I will soon have to leave England. So I went yesterday to English Taylors, who are making me a fur coat and a fur suit. I will go overseas, northwards. It's pretty cold over there now. I will keep warm this way. I have very little time as I have some matters to settle still. Cheerio. Koiluk

[28 July 1943] Glasgow I am wait for knowledge from you. Near one week I live in Glasgow. I am very glad from my new job. I study chemistry in Glasgow. It's necessary for my job.

> It's very interesting job. After the chemistry course, I must go for parachute course again. It's indispensable. Now I have a good rest in the school. I hope to see you again one day if I survive. Koiluk

Sadly, the brave Pole special forces officer did not survive. News of his death arrived in a letter from a Polish RAF pilot. He was probably killed fighting with the Polish Underground Home Army.[12]

Gladys Sanderson's diary:

> [6 August 1940] Today it is John's 19th birthday – he is a soldier following the tradition of his father in the last war. John writes how he would like to be with us to spend his birthday, but says his thoughts are so often with us at home. He is stationed near Dover with his regiment 1st Btn The Queen's Westminster 'C' Coy 15th Platoon. He has been recommended by his Brigadier for a commission and is now gaining further platoon experience, until he can be transferred to an OTC company. How sad it is to think that one country, Germany, should twice plunge the World into so much horror and sorrow through their greed. This time, please God, we will defeat them and see that they never have a chance again to rise and cause another war. My thoughts go back to my girlhood days in the last war. It hardly seems 26 years ago and now our son, like so many other mothers' sons, is doing his share in the defence of Liberty and Freedom and today, with the threat of Hitler's invasion of Britain hanging over our heads, the defence of our homeland.
>
> Today has been a perfect summer day with a beautiful sunset. We have had such a fine spring and summer this year, it seems to have made us realise what a lovely little country England is. If that were possible, we must show we love her and all she stands for.

Within a week, Churchill and Roosevelt would meet to discuss exactly this strategy of ensuring that Germany, following her defeat, would live within her boundaries. Churchill and Roosevelt's 'historic meeting', as they cruised in the *Prince of Wales* off the Newfoundland coast from 9–12 August, was to agree: 'Certain common principles . . . on which they based their hopes for a better future for the world'. The sixth clause of eight in the Atlantic Charter read: 'Safety within national boundaries, freedom from fear and want.'[13]

JBS:

In August 1940 my mother wrote that they were sitting in a hay field at the back of our house in Beckenham when suddenly she heard and saw dozens of planes coming out of the clouds in the distance – they were attacking Croydon aerodrome. My little sister Janet, who is 5 years old, was down at Otford in Kent with our grandparents when the Jerries dropped bombs about ¼ mile away in daylight. 'Pat and I were sitting in the billiard room when we heard the whine of a bomb coming down,' she said. 'We had no time to run down to the cellar, so Pat and I got under the billiard table.' One night, when mother heard the sound of a bomb falling she pushed Janet under the bed. She writes that these are anxious times, it is hard to be brave and yet brave we must be: perhaps in the future we may have heavy bombing and perhaps gas attacks.

In September 1940, the enemy blitz on London had got underway, and we were able to observe 300 or 400 bombers, escorted by double that number of fighter aircraft, crossing the coast, and heading for London.

In October 1940, as an expert on reinforced concrete, my father was brought in for secret engineering works on the Cabinet war rooms and the air raid shelters for the Prime Minister and ministers. On one occasion, when Churchill had offered him one of his Havana cigars, the two old soldiers had sat on Winston's bed, discussing their experiences during the Great War. Churchill's battalion, the 6th Btn, the Royal Scots Fusiliers, had fought and suffered greatly at the Battle of Loos in 1915. My father Alexander had arrived in Loos-en-Gohelle in November 1916 and commanded the 3rd Australian Tunnelling Coy, waging a secret war under no man's land. From January 1916 Churchill had spent five months on the front line in the Belgian village of Ploegsteert.

In the middle of all this air activity, I was posted to Barmouth in North Wales, for officer training. My number was 165827. Alan Whicker, later of broadcasting fame, was posted to the same unit. It was four months of extremely hard work and study, for six days every week. One would have expected the locals to offer some hospitality on the Sundays we were free from duty. However, not even the public houses, or hotels, would open their doors on a Sunday. It was with a feeling of relief that we got home for Christmas, and that our Commissions were promulgated on 28 December 1940. I was then a fresh-faced subaltern aged 19.

I was told I was the youngest serving subaltern in the British Army. Whether this was true or not, I certainly felt apprehensive when posted to the Loyal (North Lancashire) Regt Depot in Preston, Lancashire for six weeks. There was another newly commissioned officer reporting at the same time, clearly a mature and well-established business man from the City. We were about to report to the Depot Adjutant, an elderly pre-war regular who obviously believed that newly joining subalterns should be kept waiting outside his office for long periods in order to subdue any enthusiasm that might be lurking in our breasts! We sat there for nearly an hour, and no doubt I would have continued sitting there for hours. But not so my older colleague, who jumped up, banged open the adjutant's door and told him that he had never expected to be received so rudely, and that if this was typical of the manners in the regiment, he did not wish to be part of it. Whereupon he stormed out! I did learn later, however, that he ended up in another regiment, and had a distinguished wartime service. This incident made a strong impression upon me, and I have never subsequently taken for granted anyone – of whatever rank – posted to me for employment.

I was just 18 years of age when the war commenced, and for the next six years I was to lead a quite different lifestyle of active military service at home and abroad.

After the three-week officer training course, for which I was graded 'A', my next posting was to the 7th Btn, the Loyal Regt at Ravenscar in Yorkshire. Here my platoon distinguished themselves by breaking all the windows in a seafront hotel with machine-gun bullets!

I was then given command of a platoon and sent to a lovely little village called Staithes, where we had to build seafront concrete defences on Runswick Bay. It was one of the loveliest little places I had ever seen: we lived in holiday huts.

Our regiment was later engaged in large-scale manoeuvres with Northern Command, spending days continuously marching, sleeping under trees and mock fighting. At 5 a.m. one morning we waded through the Tweed, 80yd wide, holding our equipment over our heads.

During the London Blitz my father had been put in charge of bomb repairs to the London Underground. He always said it was more interesting than his experiences on the Western Front and that he unfailingly had the Underground line up and running again in 24 hours.

John's mother wrote to her son:

> [13 January 1941] We had a heavy air raid on London on Saturday. Your father was called to go into the office as one of the Tubes had been hit and many killed. He did not get home till 3.30 a.m. on Monday. Such a terrible bomb had fallen through to the Underground station. It made a huge crater outside the Bank of England. The crater is so big they will have to build a temporary bridge over it to allow traffic to proceed. Poor people were blown on to the electric line and killed. Hundreds of soldiers are working clearing the debris. At one time everything was stopped to see if they could hear any sounds of anyone trapped.
>
> Last night we had snow lying on the ground. We had two air raid warnings during the night, with heavy gunfire. It was so cold taking the children down to the cellars that we have decided to sleep there. For the first time one of our RAF boys have shot down two German night bombers over London – soon we shall deal with them – same as we have beaten them off during the last time.
>
> Then I remember seeing a Zeppelin shot down. The air raids were really bad at Leytonstone in that war – they used to bring our aircraft right down our road to try and shoot at the Zeppelins, and one night my father opened the doors of the sitting room and said, 'Come inside the Zeppelin is throwing out fire bombs!'
>
> But it was the Zeppelin that was on fire – standing upright and in flames underneath! One morning in the Great War I went into the garden and saw about twenty-five aeroplanes coming over – and they were the first German air raids in daylight on London – bombs fell in the Royal Mint. Your grandfather was walking over Tower Bridge when a policeman said to him: 'Run sir!'
>
> But he said: 'Run? Where can I run to?'
>
> From the top of Tower Bridge the guns were firing at the aeroplanes.

JBS:

> My father Alexander, who was very experienced in building underground shelters, had shored up the wall and ceiling of the cellars beneath our Beckenham home with heavy wooden railway sleepers and had fitted bunks for the family to sleep on during night air-raids. During one raid, when the family were in the

> cellars and Peter was passing the end of the street on ARP duty, a German plane dropped a single bomb 100m from our home. My brother raced home to find all the windows were shattered but the building still standing. On looking into the cellar, he found the family safe, but looking like ghosts. The bomb had caused the limewash on the walls and ceiling to fall and cover everybody.

John's brother Richard wrote to him: 'I've started general duties at various aerodromes in Surrey. At Redhill I was issued with a pronged hayfork and told to defend the edge of the aerodrome. How could I defend an aerodrome against a German paratrooper equipped with an automatic machine gun!'

John's mother Gladys wrote in a letter: '[27 January 1941] We have had no air raids for seven days and we are wondering what it means – is Hitler nursing all his planes for a mass attack on this country? Anyway we are ready for him!' Patricia, his 14-year-old sister, added the defiant words: 'Good, I hope they do invade us – they'll get what's coming to them.' In February, John received a letter from his youngest sister Janet which read: 'Dear John, It is quite hot for February. We had a bad raid – they dropt a lot of little bombs. We are very well. I am well too. Love Janet.'

His mother continued in her diary:

> Good news today. Revolution has broken out in Yugoslavia. The ministers who signed the treaty with Germany are now imprisoned and Prince Paul has fled. Now perhaps we shall have a chance to open up the war and force a way to attack Germany, if the Slavs will fight and we go to their aid.
>
> [10 May] A great raid by Germans on London, They say 400 planes took part. Westminster Abbey, the House of Commons and the Hall damaged. 33 German planes were bought down. Alex and Peter were fire-watching here all night until the 'all clear' at 5.50 a.m. Then London Transport phoned calling Alex to London where a tunnel in the Underground had been damaged.

In May 1941 Captain John Sim, a lifelong post-war friend of John Sanderson and the author, was posted to Iceland on an operation with the Hallamshire Regt. Leading a mountain patrol to locate a Fairey Battle of 98 Squadron RAF that had disappeared in bad weather, he located the aircraft after two days, crashed on a glacier near Akureyri, with the bodies of its two crewmen and two passengers inside. Sim descended the mountain and, after finding a padre to conduct a religious service, erected a small cross on the crash site, which was rapidly being covered by snow and ice. (The aircraft reappeared in 2000 when the glacier melted.) Sim was Mentioned in Dispatches but contracted pneumonia following his efforts in the atrocious weather.[14]

Gladys Sanderson's diary:

> [11 August 1941] What an anxious year it has been, one of great triumphs but also of trials. Today, we are in the same position as I wrote last year, any day we might expect the Germans to try to invade. But we are far stronger today and are getting more arms and equipment. With the wonderful help of America, we are in a better position every day. A year ago, the Battle of Britain started off on the south and south-east coast of England. It was to have been the prelude to an invasion, but the RAF Fighter Command and the anti-aircraft guns scored such a success that the Germans gave up daylight bombing and concentrated on indiscriminate night raids. Our wonderful RAF boys saved us, Hitler then boasted that he would be in London by 15 August 1940. That was before our boys destroyed his Luftwaffe. Dover has been named 'Hell Fire Corner'. It must be a wonderful sight to see the huge convoys passing through the Straits, protected by the Navy and the RAF. They are attacked by Nazi planes and shelled from the coast of France, and yet they calmly carry on, these wonderful merchant men, in the face of so much danger. Mr Churchill, our wonderful Prime Minister, has warned the nation to be especially alert for invasion from 1 September. There's one thing, we will all die on our feet if needs be. No German will ever set foot on this soil, if we can prevent it.

Gladys quoted in her diary from an article in *The Sunday Times*:

> [10 August 1941] Both Mr Attlee and Mr Eden in the recent debate on the course of the war, were at pains to strike a balance between harmful pessimism and harmful optimism. The country is still in a situation of unqualified danger, fighting for its life against a gigantic, a cruel, and an implacable opponent, in a struggle where ultimate failure would spell, not merely our defeat, but our end. On the other hand, if we compare the position today with that of a year ago, there is larger ground for gratitude and for seasoned hope. We shall appreciate this better when we know, just how

> near to destruction 1940 brought us. Mr Eden lifted a corner of the curtain when he said that he could remember a week whilst he was in the WO when our trained and equipped forces in this country did not number a division.
>
> Through these waiting months, a heavy burden is being borne by our people. As I go among them I marvel at their unshakable constancy. In many cities their homes are in ruins . . . Women and children have been killed, and even the sufferers in hospital have not been spared; yet hardship has only steeled our hearts and strengthened our resolution. Wherever I go I see bright eyes and smiling faces, for though our road is strong and hard, it is straight, and we know that we fight in a great cause.

A week later on she added:

> [19 August 1941] Now there has been this week a meeting in mid-Atlantic between Mr Roosevelt and Mr Churchill and the Heads of the Navy and Military and other important heads of departments. Surely an historic meeting that will lead to far reaching results and help to us? Mr Churchill was on the Battleship *Prince of Wales*, escorted by destroyers, and today he arrived home safely, surely a proof that Britannia rules the waves. Russia is fighting stubbornly against the German invaders, if she can only hold out until the winter comes – and with our help they may be able to stem the advance. We are doing all we can to help, with the RAF bombing towns in Germany by day and night. This week about 300 of our bombers and fighters attacked Cologne in daylight and the power plant and station at Knapsack. A marvellous raid – our boys flew so low they could see the towering chimneys of the power station above them. They say it is three times the size of our Battersea one.

1942 was not a good year for Britain. The threat of a German invasion had receded but the Luftwaffe were still bombing London. German submarines were threatening to sever the vital supply route to America. In North Africa the British Army were retreating, after initial successes. The situation in the Far East had deteriorated rapidly. The pride of the British navy, the battleship HMS *Prince of Wales* and the battlecruiser HMS *Repulse* were sunk off the east coast of Malaya. The loss of the Island fortress of Singapore dealt a catastrophic blow to the British Empire. The Japanese occupied Malaya and were now making advances through Burma that threatened the very 'Jewel in the Crown' – India.[15]

2nd Lieutenant John Sanderson volunteered for attachment to the Indian Army on 11 November 1941 and was later posted to the 6th Btn/11th Sikh Regt. The Sikh regiments were the elite of the Indian Army. His mother's entries in her diary read:

> [22 January 1942] It is freezing and so cold. John came home unexpectedly on a week's leave. I was asleep in bed: it was lovely to see him at 6.15 a.m.
>
> [19 January] The Japs have made several landings on the west coast of Malaya, behind our lines. This forced the Indian troops on that side of the peninsula to make further withdrawals. The Japs occupy Tavey, a port on the Indian Ocean.
>
> [21 January] It is terribly cold. The hot water pipe has frozen in the kitchen. Snow is thick on the ground with 8 degrees of frost. How awful the cold must be in Russia with 57 degrees of frost. Alex and I went to the Gaumont in Bromley to see the film *Ships with Wings*. It was marvellous, showing scenes of our wonderful Navy, taken on the *Ark Royal* aircraft carrier. One day we will give those Japs, Germans and Italians such a beating and teach them such a lesson. They are nothing but robbers and thieves. In parts, the Japs are 75 miles or less from Singapore. I do hope we will be able to hold Singapore. If only we had more aeroplanes. General Sir Claude Auchinleck, in a personal message to the General commanding the 8th Army in Libya has written: 'Well done and heartiest congratulations on the capture of 1,400 prisoners and much material at a cost of less than five hundred casualties. This represents a fine feat of arms.'
>
> [23 January] The Japs have made landings in New Guinea. The Australian government have ordered the mobilisation of all defence forces at full fighting strength. Mr Curtin, the Prime Minister, says his government are asking for a representation in an Imperial War Cabinet.
>
> [25 January] It is now revealed that Mr Churchill's voyage to America last month was in the *Duke of York*, one of our battleships. The first American troops have arrived in Northern Ireland.

> Canada's credit in London has been concreted into a loan for Britain interest-free. Moreover, supplies shipped to Britain, up to an amount of hundreds of millions of pounds, will be free of charge without obligation.
>
> [27 January] Mr Churchill made a speech in House of Commons: 'We in this Island for a long time were alone, holding aloft the torch. We are no longer alone now. We are now at the centre and among those at the summit of 26 United Nations, comprising more than three-quarters of the population of the globe.'

Churchill described in Parliament Britain's substantial material aid to Russia:

> Three or four months ago . . . the German invaders were advancing, blasting their way through Russia. The Russians were resisting with the utmost heroism. But no one could tell what would happen, whether Leningrad, Moscow or Rostov would fall . . . but now the boot is on the other leg. We all agree that we must aid the valiant Russian Armies to the utmost limit of our power . . . the best aid we could give to Russia was in supplies of many kinds of raw materials and of munitions, particularly tanks and aircraft. Our Forces at home and abroad had for long been waiting thirstily for these weapons. Nevertheless, we sent Premier Stalin exactly what he asked for. The whole quantity was promised and sent. This was a decision of major strategy and policy, and anyone can see that it was right to put it first when they watch . . . the wonderful achievements of the Russian Armies. Our munitions were, of course, only a contribution to the Russian victory, but they were an encouragement in Russia's darkest hour. Far from regretting what we did for Russia, I only wish it had been in our power, but it was not, to have done more.' (Hansard)

Gladys' diary notes:

> [29 January] A vote of confidence in the government for Mr Churchill was passed with only one against. For some days it has been evident that our troops in Malaya could not force the Japs to a stand in South Johore. Last night they were withdrawn into the island of Singapore. John was able to get home on a few hours' leave and Richard was at home on leave. It was so lovely to have all our children around the tea table, pray God that they are kept safe and in future years we will have many more such birthday parties.

'The Battle of Malaya has come to an end and the Battle of Singapore has started', said Lieutenant General Percival GOC [General Officer Commanding] Malaya. He declares that the island fortress will be held until help arrives, as assuredly it will. The causeway has been breached. In Libya, British Armed Forces are being concentrated against Rommel. The Russians are advancing well into the Ukraine.

[3 February] Alex was on duty tonight in London. John came home for a few hours. Snow began to thaw but it was bitterly cold. One of the coldest winters ever known. Singapore are standing too – being continually dive-bombed by the Japs. The garrison are told to hold fast, as help is on the way.

[4 February] I have been listening to the service: the Padre prayed for the people of Singapore and for the troops.

[25th February] The news looks grave. All civilians have evacuated from Rangoon and the Japs are only 40 miles from Rangoon.

[6th March] John left at 7.00 p.m. to catch the train at Euston for his assembly point.

[5th April] The Japs bombed Colombo for the first time but twenty-seven of them were brought down. Alex is working tonight. They say the Japs bombed Trincomalee harbour. I once stayed outside there for two days in a liner, before John was born. I hope our fleet is moving up to the Indian Ocean.

2nd Lieutenant John Sanderson sailed for India from Glasgow on 19 March 1942, in one of the largest convoys of the war. His mother wrote in her diary some weeks later:

[6 May] We were delighted to get a cable from John today, to say that he was so far safe and well and sent fondest love. We think he must have reached Cape Town. We have landed troops in Madagascar to take possession so that the Japs wouldn't land. A great naval and air battle is going on in the Coral Sea of Australia. Sixteen Jap ships sunk or damaged, Evidently they were trying to go and invade Australia.

[9 May] Our Hurricane tackled six Messerschmitts today single handed and shot down two of them and drove the other off – what bravery! We are turning the tables on the Germans – sometimes we now send 600 planes over France.

[10 May] Mr Churchill has just made a wonderful speech in which he reviews his two years in office and sends us words of good cheer. He warns the Germans that if they use poisonous gas on our allies, the Russians we will use the same on the German people.

Chapter 4

Hut 6 at Bletchley Park and ULTRA

RAF officer cadet John Aldwinckle (later in Special Operations, and NATO Intelligence with John Sanderson) was studying meteorology in 1941 when he met his future wife, Helene Taylor, a university student in her home town of Aberdeen. In 1942 she was recommended by the principal of the university as a candidate for important government work. In an interview in 2013 for the Bletchley Park Oral History Project, Helene explained her recruitment to Bletchley Park and her work there.[1]

> I was well known at Aberdeen University, through being on various committees and through acting, so I was one of a number of female graduates recommended for interview in London at the Foreign Office.
>
> I remember it being quite a big thing as I had only ever been as far south as the north of England to visit an uncle. After leaving Scotland at 3.45 a.m., I eventually arrived in London during the blackout. I was very hungry, as I hadn't eaten on the train. Off I headed in the dark to the Lyons Corner House down the road. They served egg on toast, which was a great thing to have! But then the air raid siren sounded and off we went downstairs. It was so bare and cold and we stood around for what seemed an age. When the 'all clear' was given, we returned upstairs. After finally getting my egg on toast, I returned to the lodging.
>
> After a poor night's sleep, I went on to my interview at Burlington House with the Civil Service Commission. I didn't know that I was being interviewed for something specific: I thought it was for general Civil Service work. I recall at least twenty male interviewers around a long table, asking various questions relating to mathematics, crosswords, interests, languages, etc. The interviewers knew all about Bletchley Park but no mention was made of the place. Afterwards, exhausted,

I walked back to King's Cross for the long journey back to Aberdeen. Some time afterwards, Burlington House wrote to the Principal to arrange further interviews for selected candidates, at the Caledonian Hotel in Aberdeen.

On this occasion we weren't interviewed as such: I do remember interviewers signalling to each other, which didn't mean anything to me! It was obvious that they'd already selected those they wanted from the London interviews, that these interviewers were from Bletchley Park and that they were making final checks that we were 'the right sort of people' for the job. One particular tall and lean gentleman commented that he was pleased that I'd come along and that we'd spoken at the previous interview. As we were leaving, he took me to one side to confirm that I would be offered government related work. I remembered wondering how he could be so sure I would be any good, to which he replied 'I can tell you'll be alright'.

I realised then that he must be someone eminent in the organisation. He did warn me that I would receive departure instructions very quickly and would need to leave straight away.

I was taken on as a permanent Foreign Office Civil Servant, and four of us girls were made Temporary Junior Assistant Principals, being paid between £3 and £5 per week, which was more than the other recruits and a lot of money at that time.

In the summer of 1942, a card was sent to me with instructions, and a letter sent to my parents, reassuring them that I would be looked after. I caught the early train again. I remember my mother being very nervous, asking an Army chap on the station platform to take good care of me: he certainly kept an eye on me until Perth, anyway! I arrived at Bletchley late at night and went to the telephone on the station forecourt, as instructed on the card.

I had been given the number for Bletchley Park, with instructions on what to say when picking up the telephone. I had to give my name and a description of myself and was told that someone with a limp would meet me. Sylvia, whose surname I never found out, appeared very quickly, with a driver and car, probably within about three minutes! It was all very dramatic. I was put in the back of the car and driven to Bletchley Park. The driver jumped out at the gatehouse to announce us and jumped back in.

We drove straight up to the main office, not to the big house, but to the outside part. We stopped at the last hut. I was welcomed warmly inside by a gentleman I had met at the interview in Aberdeen, and he asked if I was prepared to sign the Official Secrets Act. I remember very clearly that there was no pressure to do so, other than that he couldn't offer me the job if I didn't sign. But he did say: 'If you sign there, you're with us.'

I read it quickly. Once I had signed, he took me over to Hut 6 and introduced me to everyone, who were all very, very nice. One particular memory stands out: seeing rows of girls, all with similar hair styles. Then one of these girls, a Wren called Agnes Smith, recognised me from Aberdeen University, and said she'd voted for me for the Student Council! It was a lovely way to start.

Helene had been recruited to work as a codebreaker at the GC & CS (Government Code & Cypher School). Hut 6 was where German Army and Air Force Enigma machine cyphers were decrypted. The Registration Room arranged intercepts by call sign and frequency.

My work started straight away. I was based initially in Registration Room 1 [RR1]. We worked on encrypted signals, brought in by motorcycle from places like Beaumanor and Chicksands. I worked in both RR1 and RR2, for at least a year altogether. In RR1, I simply worked by myself at first. There was so much to learn as I'd never worked on codes before. I sorted the traffic, looked at the call signs to see if there were any repetitions or trends. I was doing a fair bit of analysis work and didn't have any managerial responsibility.

Helene was then put in charge of the training programme for Americans joining the staff, after the BRUSA agreement (British and US (SIGINT sharing) agreement) was signed in May 1943, in which GC & CS and the US War Department agreed to share signals intelligence. This was the forerunner of the UKUSA agreement in 1946 in which GC & CS's successor, GCHQ (Government Communications Headquarters), and its US equivalent, the NSA (National Security Agency), agreed to share all SIGINT. This is still at the core of today's 'Five Eyes' intelligence alliance.

After a while, I was invited to lead the training programme for American service personnel and, of course, I accepted! I remember the school building being high up some stairs. It may have been one of the brick-built blocks separate from Hut 6. These were used from early 1943 to make more space. Hut 6 moved into Block D at some point.

One of the senior people told me that it was a big job taking on these Americans, but that they were keen to learn. And indeed they were. They were full of banter and used to flirt at every opportunity, e.g. trying to accompany me to lunch. But it was always in good jest. They were enormous fun, a breath of fresh air in a rather stuffy environment. It was simply lovely to have them there. There were about seventeen personnel on the first course which lasted several weeks and I remember them being a particularly nice bunch. There were fourteen on the second course. In between the two courses, I also trained a few British personnel.

We would instruct them on what was going on at Bletchley, not just about my previous Registration work, but also wider information from higher up, for which we would have a lecturer. I was very much running the school, rather than doing all the teaching. I did the straightforward teaching (showing them call signs, etc.) and I called in other lecturers as needed, from anywhere in Bletchley Park. The exciting thing for us was that we'd just got the Colossus machine (the world's first electronic computer used to decrypt Geheimschreiber messages, radio signals) and we used to round off the whole programme on the last day by one of our personnel showing them the machine. They'd never seen anything like that before!

After the courses, I went to work in the Quiet Room [QR] in Hut 6, where more difficult, non-routine work was done.

In the 'Quiet Room' Helene worked on cracking codes that others hadn't managed to crack. German codes were sent using a machine called Enigma which, through a complicated plug board and set of rotors, made it very difficult to crack the codes, as it produced thousands of permutations and the codes were changed every day. However, because of the way Enigma was designed to code and decode, a letter once coded could not be the same as itself. This quirk helped Helene and her colleagues to try to guess words or phrases that might be contained in a code. These might be phrases such as 'weather forecast' or 'Heil Hitler' or 'nothing to report'. These were known as 'cribs'.

They were helped by a machine called 'the Bombe' which could be set to work to try to establish if the crib was correct and thereby break the code. This could take a while but, as the war progressed, the codebreakers got better and faster at cracking each day's code. Being able to break Luftwaffe and Wehrmacht codes gave the Allies an enormous advantage.

It is estimated that the work that was done at Bletchley Park by Helene and her colleagues saved thousands, if not millions, of lives and shortened the war by two years.

> We would often work on longer-term problems and look for unusual trends, standing back a bit from what was going on day to day. Because I had a wider knowledge from my involvement in the course, I was quite suited to the work. About ten to twelve people were working there. Jack Winton was in charge, with his own, separate office.
>
> I went back home to Aberdeen just once for a week, on the instructions of Jack Winton, who thought I was working too hard and needed a break. Other than that, all I could do was sit in digs, being quite bored as there was no real bus route to get out and about! I would have loved to have followed my interests such as acting.
>
> I travelled in on a special Bletchley Park bus each day. I mostly worked days in the Registration Room, with maybe one or two night shifts, while other people worked a three-shift system. In the School and QR I also worked days. Whilst I was at Bletchley Park, we had a P.O. Box for correspondence. I remember receiving correspondence from my fiancé [John Aldwinckle] that way, because he didn't have a specific address for me. It was difficult to stay in touch. No one had a straightforward life in those days!
>
> I came across some wonderful characters: British chess champion Hugh Alexander and the rather intense-looking, white-faced Dennis Babbage, who would walk past you, looking as though you might shoot him on the way! There was James Aitken, Scottish chess champion, who wore these great glasses and a hat pulled down very low. Aitken also walked past very quickly. Of the Americans, I remember Bill Bundy, who went on to become Foreign Affairs Adviser to Presidents John F. Kennedy and Lyndon B. Johnson, and Howard Porter who went on to become Professor of Classics at Columbia University. I also met some of the Americans subsequently, because my husband worked in Intelligence after the war, such as Arthur Levenson, who became very senior in NSA.
>
> We were all bound by the Official Secrets Act, of course, and didn't talk about our work with anyone, not even after the war.

Bletchley Park, and the breaking of the Enigma codes, was itself a secret until RAF Group Captain F.W. Winterbotham, who had worked at

Bletchley Park, had a book published.[2] Helene Aldwinckle disapproved of his book:

> When I first heard about the Winterbotham book (the first book to reveal the existence of Bletchley Park and the breaking of Enigma), I thought it was awful and shouldn't have been written, as it let down everyone who had stayed quiet. After 1974, when it was published, I felt a little more relaxed about talking generally about Bletchley Park, though I've never discussed detail. I think we were all very clear of our responsibilities under the Act and that's why we were shocked when the book was written.

At the end of the war, Helene was one of the authors of the official history of Hut 6, only published in 2014.[3]

Because Helene had signed the Official Secrets Act on her first day at Bletchley in 1942, she remained reluctant to talk about her work to anyone, and her parents died without ever knowing what she did in the war. Churchill, whose codename for Bletchley Park intelligence was ULTRA, described the Bletchley team as 'the geese that laid the golden eggs and never cackled'.

Chapter 5

Voyage Back to India, Khyber Pass and Sikhs

Lieutenant Sanderson was returning to India after thirteen years. To avoid submarines his convoy sailed almost to the coast of America and then turned east to Freetown, West Africa.

JBS:

Our ship left from Glasgow on 19 March 1942. After a safe voyage, avoiding any U-boats, our troopship docked in Cape Town, South Africa. We were given shore leave for five days. As we came down the gangplank, we saw lines of families in smart cars queuing to welcome us. I was met at the docks by the Warr family, with their daughter Joyce, who lived in a splendid house called 'Tara'. I had a wonderful time, treated to tours of the Cape and dances at the 'Rotunda' in Camps Bay. The memories of this happy time remained with me throughout the war and I vowed to return one day to thank my hosts. (I did exactly this fifty-four years later, flying to South Africa to meet up with Joyce Atwell of Fish Hoek, who remembered: 'It was a bad time for the world but we had some marvellous fun'.)

When I returned to the docks at the end of the leave, my convoy had already left, sailing early no doubt to stay one step ahead of the enemy. I had literally missed the boat. Quite a few of the soldiers who arrived in our convoy were not so keen to go to war and decided to stay put in South Africa. The pro-British Prime Minister Field Marshal Jan Smuts, whose country was short of manpower, turned a blind eye to these able-bodied men jumping ship and they were permitted to stay. A friend and I, however, soon made our way across to Durban. This was the largest port

> in South Africa and a holiday resort for South Africans. We were taken on as crew of an armed merchant ship, bound for Calcutta, and manned the ship's gun for the journey. In fact, when our convoy arrived in India, we were there to meet them! They had taken a zig-zag course to avoid submarines.

John arrived in India in the summer of 1942 at a critical time for the British Raj. Churchill knew, through intelligence intercepts, that a campaign of civil disobedience was imminent and had sent the Labour politician Stafford Cripps in March to negotiate an agreement with Jinnah and Gandhi. (Cripps had recently returned from Moscow where he had been British Ambassador since 1940, after Churchill had sent him to negotiate with Stalin.) Cripps would promise India self-government after the war, if the Congress Party would support the British war effort. To no avail. Cripps noted: 'Unrest is growing amongst the population. The food situation is causing disquiet. Outlook, so far as the internal situation goes, is exceedingly bad.'[1]

Letters came from John's mother:

> [5 June 1942] Yesterday we received your letter before reaching port. I read that the rains have started in Ceylon. Hope they have with you. Keep your boots up off the ground or white ants will eat them in the night. I enjoyed the pictures. Errol Flynn's *They died with their boots on*. Oh boy! What love scenes. Flynn's certainly good looking. It is good that we can get in touch with you now. Will be better still when we get replies to letters. What do you think of the general situation now? We are certainly on the upwards – one day the Japs will get the surprise the people of Essen and Cologne get. Those brave RAF boys. Every day I am more proud than ever to belong to the British Empire. Can you receive the BBC in India? Perhaps it is picked up and relayed. I always pray and think of you at 9 p.m. when Big Ben sounds. What time is that with you then?
>
> [23 June 1942] John, I am afraid you will be finding it very hot at Mhow, it's very near Ahmedabad and that's a very hot place. Mother
>
> [27 June 1942] Dear John, We are all well, but it has been such an anxious week. Whatever went wrong in Libya? I hope we'll hold Egypt. Perhaps things will look better when Churchill gets back. Our RAF are giving it to them. 1,000 planes again on Bremmen.

I suppose it is just a matter of time and holding out until we get new equipment. Don't touch a jackall, John, as they are full of rabies. Watch out for snakes at night time. Leggings would be good to wear. Have the rains started? Don't the frogs croak at night? Can you sleep? Ghandi seems to be saying plenty lately. Wasn't I right about them never agreeing? Mother

[7 July 1942] My Dear John, Congratulations on your reaching 21 years old on your birthday on 6 August. I do hope you have a happy day. Perhaps one of your fellow officers will give a party for you? Perhaps we'll have a small party and drink your health. You will have a small party and wedding combined when you come home. I wish I could have sent you a gold watch but these days it's as much as we can do to carry on. We love one another and that's all that matters. I'm very proud of my eldest son. I'm sure you'll always be a credit to us and our dear Country. Like Churchill's message to the Middle East RAF: 'We are sure you will be to our glorious army the friend that endureth to the end.' Wasn't it great! It looks as if we might defeat Rommel – what a wonderful stand the army have made – the New Zealand and Yorkshire regiments have fought so well. Poor men in tanks with 130 degrees inside. What an interesting experience you had on that troopship. Mother

[8 July 1942] John dear. Your cable came from Mhow! 15 days' training. You tell us not to worry so I musn't. Good luck Boy & God bless.

[16 July 1942] My dear John . . . The Russians seem to be having a hard fight. I wonder if we will open a second front. I have seen some American troops in London, Mother.

[22 July 1942; a part-censored letter from John's mother] I wonder where you are? I expect the monsoon is on. Have any scenes of your childhood returned to you? We are all well, carrying on, in these anxious days. We are certainly holding them in Egypt. The King's Royal Rifles and Green Howards have been fighting well. Wonder how many of your pals are there? The nation mourns F., he was a good sort and pilot. We saw a fine film: *Joan of France*. One of the airmen hiding in France dies and the priest reads the 23rd Psalm: The Lord is my Shepherd. If only we didn't have such a struggle to make ends meet these days. Never mind if one laughs. We are going to be rich when your father's ship

> – censored: ('his aircraft design') comes home. He is still working on the ideas he had when you were at home.
>
> [28 July 1942] My dear John, We are all well but tired this morning. We had an air raid alarm at 3.a.m. this morning: guns but not bad. They said on the wireless that we had brought eight aircraft down. Pray God he will help us in the next two months: they are evidently going to be the most critical. I wonder if we shall open up a 2nd front? The paper today says the Germans think we shall. It is hoped we don't until we have sufficient material. Churchill knows what he is doing. Mother
>
> [29 July 1942] Those poor Russians. The war has got to be won and will soon. Looks as if we have enough of a 2nd front now to cope with in Egypt. I think when the Americans get going with us, it will be the bombing of Germany that will do them in.
>
> [1 August 1942] John, If you weren't engaged I would say you were looking at the girls . . . I was pleased to see the government are going to be firm in India with Ghandi, if he continues to hinder the war effort.
>
> [6 August 1942] Today is your 21st birthday. We have been thinking of you all day and, when we had our early tea downstairs, we all kissed one another for John and said: 'Happy birthday and Good Luck.' Little Janet sang 'Happy Birthday'. No doubt they will toast you in the mess.

On 9 August, the morning after Gandhi had declared that the British should leave India and that it was time to: 'Do or die for nothing less than freedom', he was detained in the Aga Khan's Palace and Congress leaders arrested across India.[2]

> [11 August 1942] Dear John, How lovely to go to Darjeeling. I never went. Bound to be some trouble storming in India: it will be the police who will suffer. It is just like the time twelve years ago, when we were in India. I see the Sikhs are in Libya. I hope you won't go there. Mother

JBS later explained to the author:

> On 11 August 1942 I was appointed an acting captain. I was first sent to officer's training school in Mhow in June. In August

I received language training in Urdu and in September I returned for a camouflage course to Kirkee, reporting to the 6th Btn of the 11th Sikh Regt. We were then posted to a remote fort on the borders of India, near the Khyber Pass, supposedly to protect India against a possible German thrust on India.

On leave periods, we spent time in Simla, the summer residential station of the Raj, or at Srinagar ('Sri' – 'Hindu Goddess' or 'Sun', Nagar –'City') with my English fiancée Marian. She is one of two beautiful sisters I met. I hired a houseboat on Dal Lake in Kashmir. It is backed by snow-capped Himalayan mountains and fed by the Jhellum River, a tributary of the Indus. I happened to know Paul Scott, who was to write the *Raj Quartet* and the *Jewel in the Crown*. I suggested to Scott that these two beautiful army officer's daughters would make wonderful characters in a novel.

For the 'forgotten army' of India, letters from our family and friends were important for morale. One anecdote; in the local town, there was a popular Indian fortuneteller that our men visited. His personal predictions were uncannily accurate. His income took a steep dive, however, when it was discovered that his brother was working in the post-office and steaming open our soldiers' letters and reading all about their lives.

John's mother and father wrote to India expressing their concerns:

[13 August 1942] I hope you are well. Bengal is a beastly climate. I hope you won't get dengue fever and watch your milk and water. You need to get prickly heat powder in Calcutta. You will be seeing the country if you fly to Karachi.

[21 August 1942] These are momentous days – this week the raid on Dieppe. We are certainly on the upgrade to bring back all those men. 500 Spitfires over France escorting bombers and not one lost. How proud one feels of those men in the convoy to Malta. Mother

[25 August 1942] Dear John, If only this war would end. Sir E. Page thinks it will last 10 years. I don't think so. When the Yanks get going with their Flying Fortresses . . . they are already bombing the hun. Father

[28 August 1942] Dear John, I hope you look after yourself. I read in the paper today that the Japs had their 5th Div. massed on the Arakan Border. They will get a hiding. Mother.

The 6th/11th Sikhs were in the isolated Jhikergacha Ghat, 60 miles north east of Calcutta, where they had been completing training in an area of bad sanitation and excessive humidity. In 1942 the summer air was humid and steamy. The monsoon brought the discomfort of wet, warm clinging clothes and prickly heat. There was only one main road, with paddy fields on either side. However, when the rains stopped, the Bengal climate made life more pleasant.

The letters continued:

> [1 Sept 1942] My Dear John, How are you? I wonder if you are still in the same village? Soon it will be the end of the monsoon and you may be on the move to fight the Japs. Take care of yourself and look to your health and I pray you will keep safe. Things look a bit brighter. The Japs have had a hiding at Milne Bay but there have been articles lately telling us not to underestimate the Japs. I read they can march 40 miles a day and they are clever devils, fanatical. We want to send Flying Fortresses to bomb Tokyo. They are over France now and doing a lot of damage. We like the snaps of you in tropical kit. Watch those snakes after rains in the dark. Tell me if Alex's name is still on the bridge he built in Dum Dum? He also put in water pipes at Srinagar. I wonder if the Congress party are giving trouble in your area? Seems as if the government have the situation under control. In two days time it will be the Day of Prayer, going into the fourth year of the war. Oh, I hope it will be over in a year but I doubt it. It was a wonderful trip of Churchill's to Moscow. Very sad the Duke of Kent being killed – his little children – no daddy! I hope you boys will be spared to come back, be happily married and have children. When I see our family, I thank God for you all. I love my country and am proud I have sons to serve her. I know your father is too. Mother

> [5 Sept 1942] Dear John, Will the Japs attack? Will we make a 2nd front? If Stalingrad falls, it won't be good for us all. You must be homesick but you have a job to do for your Country, same as all of us, until we have beaten those devils. There are men gassing thousands of Jews now. What would they do to us? It is the sea that has saved us. Mother

> [9 Sept 1942] I do love this month in England. P. Strong wrote: 'Sunlight breaking through the birches turning gold.' In a world so beautiful, dear God, why should there be men with dark, evil

> hearts. War. Bloodshed. Misery. There is one thing, war has taught us to appreciate the simpler things of life. I am bottling plums. Peter has been digging the garden potatoes up. Mother

On this day, Lieutenant John Sanderson reported back to the 6/11th Sikhs at Jhikergacha after attending a camouflage course.

> [14 Sept 1942] There are anxious days ahead. Lord Milne [Field Marshal CIGS: Chief of the Imperial General Staff, 1926–33] was addressing ex-servicemen yesterday and he said we had a hard year in front of us. No matter if they all did not meet next year as long as England stands. I think we shall have big air raids this winter but I am sure they cannot do any worse than they did on that big blitz; we stood up to that and we are ready for them. Mother.

On 15 September, as the designated Intelligence Officer, Lieutenant Sanderson attended a 'Lecture on Security'.

> [16 Sept 1942] Looks as if we are about to attack to get Burma back. They are cunning devils those Japs. *The Times* had a long article about their tactics in New Guinea. Wait all day to stalk an Aussie. Hide in trees. They seem to be so well equipped in guns. Don't trust anything: they pretend to give up or lie down wounded but they have a grenade behind their back. You need to train your men to be as cunning as them. The next twenty days will be most critical in our history. Pray God we will have greater strength and help in the coming days. Take care of yourself. Mother.

A letter arrived in India from Sanderson's former employers dated 17 September 1942:

> Major Ingram and the staff read your letter with much interest. We are glad to see you are amongst brother officers and men who work together so happily. As regards news from the Home Front, we are all well. Although we get a little disturbance from above, nobody takes much notice of it. We wish you good fortune.

Soon after this letter was written, a Luftwaffe bomb completely destroyed their office building at 36–8 New Broad Street, London EC2.

The letters between *JBS* and his family continued:

> [23 Sept 1942] The Russians are still holding out in Stalingrad. Wonder if we will make a landing in France soon? Be some casualties when we do. Mother.
>
> [30 Sept 1942] My Dear Mother, Dad and all,
> I have just returned from a recce after being out all day: today has been one of the hottest for a long time. I have been driving one of those little 'jeeps', you may have seen about in London. They are grand little things and you can get through a foot of mud and over any type of country when on a road reconnaissance, as they have a four-wheel drive. I was looking for a place to billet a platoon that will be on a detachment near a river, and found it very difficult to get a place away from the jungle and away from a village, but near the river. We try not to get too near villages because of the malaria and disease. John
>
> [3 October 1942]: For a leader I do not think we could have a finer leader than Churchill. I think after him, General Smuts is a fine man. Wasn't it a marvellous feat the convoy getting through to Russia? Men are certainly as brave today as they ever were. I think some of your aerogrammes may have gone down in the flying boat? Mother
>
> [14 October 1942] Wonderful Malta – they have bought so many planes down this week. Churchill doesn't seem to think we'll have worse raids than we had before.

On 19 October 1942 Major Alex Sanderson completed his revolutionary 'TOP SECRET' drawings and designs for double-decked aircraft with tilt-wings for submission to the Air Ministry. The concept was for heavier bombing of Germany. Alexander wrote to his son:

> Many non-co-op's in India, it is to be hoped it won't turn to Civil War. Time the British Government put them down. I am all for Indian Home Rule when they can all agree. Good to know you have such a fine Colonel: I know you will do your best to be a credit to him. We read the Japs were 120 miles from the Tibet frontier. Looks as if they'll come that way – but we are ready for them, no doubt. Last night I have never heard such an armada overhead. When the Americans bomb, I pity the Huns. Father

Gladys wrote to John:

> [22 October 1942] Salaam Captain Sahib! Congratulations. We got your cable saying you were made Captain. We are all so pleased. Mother

On 24 October 1942 *JBS* sat down to compose a letter:

> My dear father, it is Sunday evening and I am sitting writing by the light of my flickering hurricane lamp with the usual insects dive-bombing the paper and lamp as I write. My best wishes and loving thoughts to you on your birthday, more especially than any other day. No doubt you are being kept quite busy these days building heaven knows what, but I was so glad that you were able to get way for a few days to Cornwall. I have just returned from Calcutta, where I spent three quiet days, quiet because the beer costs 2 *6d.* a bottle and drinks taste like medicine. I saw an excellent picture, which was easily as good as the book. You have probably read it. *Let the People Sing* by J.B. Priestley. It's an excellent tonic to have a good laugh. I went shopping in Calcutta. The dhobi knocks hell out of our clothes and we always have to buy new ones. No, women have not been evacuated from Calcutta but they are nearly one type, I don't have to tell you what they are. There are so many troops from different countries that the hotels are not very particular who they let in and you get a pretty rough crowd. I spend my time in the pictures, the 'Saturday Club' and the Swimming Club, both excellent places for good food, billiards, drinks and bathing. I spent an evening with Frank Ides, the Brigade Intelligence Officer. Poor Frank had his clothes ruined by the dhobi – you know, we have an anti-malarial unit who spray all buildings and water tanks with pools of water. Our wretched dhobi thought he would wash Frank's clothes in a tank, instead of the river, as it's nearer: all his clothes have grease stains! Cheerio for now, love to you all, and give a huge big kiss to my little sister Janet, Your son, J. B.
>
> [25 Oct 1942] My Dear father, I am looking forward to moving from our outpost to a little more hostile country. Of course one never knows, but the news that three large battleships and an aircraft carrier are in the Indian Ocean means quite a lot and shows signs of good things to come. I think you know when we

[the allies] do get started we will give the Axis such a boot up the b.s. that it will knock their spinal column 'out of joint'. Everyone knows that with the troops we have in England, India, America and the Dominions and together with the gallant resistance of the Russians, the end of the war is not so very far away – eighteen months perhaps. Who knows, if I am lucky, I will come out of this war a regular Captain and then the pay is not so bad for a married officer. I think after the war there will be a radical change in the government's attitude towards the army and the soldier will get enough to live on. What do you think? Cheerio for now Dad, your loving son, John.

JBS wrote a second letter home that day:

I walked for miles through the jungle and then gave it up and hired three coolies to paddle me upstream. As I write, I'm being pestered by dozens of those flying ants, moths, beetles etc. that keep landing on the paper, and I seem to be spending most of my time flicking them off. You get a little 'browned off' at times in this country and it's usually the small things that annoy you: I was in Calcutta last weekend and brought a new pair of shoes. I wore them out of the shop, and asked the wretched shopkeeper to send the other pair to the hotel. Of course he never did, and I lost a good pair of shoes.

I have just finished playing a hectic game of handball with the Havildars. They are terribly keen on the game and hockey in this unit. Now that the weather is a little warmer, I have started Physical Training in the company at 06.15, three times a week with bathing three times a week. They are learning to swim with the use of empty petrol cans used as lifebuoys.

Now being the Intelligence Officer as well, I have to see to the censorship of the battalion mail, look at the training and write out my company orders for the next day. Last night or evening, I had my usual Sunday evening ride. It was grand, as the evenings are getting cooler now and it was not too hot. I was actually able to wear my thick riding breeches I bought in England. We are getting six more horses in this battalion soon, and they will probably come with new saddles, so I am going to bag a good horse for myself and go down each day and see that they are looking after it. In a few weeks time, it will be cool enough to go every evening and then I expect some of the officers will come out with me.

> Cheerio for now all, I hope you had a happy Christmas. Your ever loving son, John

The correspondence continued:

> [28 October 1942] Dear John, Our RAF is going to help save us with the other services. The Huns are on the defensive in Libya in the air. The wonderful RAF daylight raids on Italy. I bet Hitler is beginning to think. Daylight raids into Germany too! Mother.
>
> [28 October 1942]: Dear Mother and all, I received an aerogramme from you today – the first in three weeks. It was posted five weeks ago. I am afraid I've not had time to write lately and when I do it is under quite difficult circumstances in the heat and in bad light. I get up so early, which necessitates turning in early. I am defending officer on a courts martial tomorrow. In a week, all the officers are going out on a scheme for three days. No doubt we shall get wet, hungry and tired, but it is good practice for things to come. Robby comes back today, having got over his fever. I enjoyed my month as adjutant, as one knows what is going on all the time. I am returning of course, to command HQ Coy and will have to learn 365 new names! John

With growing civil unrest and increasing violence on both sides, in November 1942 Churchill made his position quite clear in the House of Commons: ' I have not become the King's First Minister in order to preside over the liquidation of the British Empire.'[3]

Gladys wrote to John:

> [5 November 1942] My Dear Son John, I must write to you today – it is such wonderful news this morn. Rommel is in full retreat! At last the news that we have been waiting for. I bet you are as excited as we are! Perhaps the war will be over next year? Now we have them on the run in Libya. It looks as if the Americans are going to get cracking the other side in W. Africa. Once we have control of the Med, Italy will be finished. I read that things are moving on the Burmese Frontier. The Japs will get it soon too. Mother

The Second Battle of Alemein was fought from 23 October until 11 November 1942. General Auchinleck's view at the time was that: 'without Ultra Rommel would certainly have got through to Cairo'.

The former MI6 historian H. Trevor Roper noted the impatience expressed by the analysts of HUT 3 at Bletchley Park with General Montgomery's excessive caution after El Alemein. They knew that the Afrika Corps' supply ships had been sent to the bottom of the sea, thanks to the ULTRA decrypts, and that Rommel had only 11 Panzer tanks facing Montgomery's 270 tanks. They could not understand why Montgomery did not annihilate the Afrika Corps.[4]

The tone of Gladys's letters was upbeat:

> [11 Nov 1942]: John, It's Armistice day today so I knelt down by the kitchen table. Those men have not died in vain and we are doing so marvellously. It is certainly the turn of the tide. They couldn't stand up to our bombing, could they? They say our infantry advanced with their rifles, as if on a parade ground. What a marvellous leader and orator Winston Churchill is. At the London Mayor's banquet he said: 'The Germans have been outmatched and outfought with every kind of weapon and by every technical apparatus they hoped would give them domination of the World. This is not the end; it is not even the beginning of the end, but it is perhaps the end of the beginning.'
>
> Just now the news – things are moving – Hitler has moved into unoccupied France and parachuted troops in Tunisia. It will be a big flare up, won't it? Pray God that we are strong enough to beat them. I'm sure we are. Mother.

> [12 Nov 1942] Thursday. The news is so good and we are so excited – all the church bells are to ring on Sunday morning [15th] for victory in Egypt! You can imagine how our hearts will be uplifted. What do you think? How long will the war last? If we defeat Hitler in Tunisia, we'll soon get the Japs. Cheerio Darling.

> [18 Nov 1942] Wonderful news from Libya, isn't it? Good Old 60th Rifles. I wonder if Hitler will come through Spain or Turkey – he won't stand still but I reckon he's in a funk with so much territory to defend. What a feat of arms to send that armada to Egypt. Good old Churchill. It was lovely to hear the bells on Sunday.

> [25 Nov 1942] John Dear, I see we are heavily bombing Burma airfields – perhaps prelude to our attack? The wonderful news from Libya does your heart good, doesn't it? Today's paper uplifts one. Did you read of the 19-year-old girl Jennie who for

nearly three weeks shared the tortures and perils of an open boat with injured and dying men night and day: they tended the sick and eleven men died. The girl's clothing was torn and battered by wind, salt water. They were covered with boils. I am glad she has been awarded the BEM.

[4 Dec 1942] The war news is splendid, isn't it? And Churchill's wonderful speech again. Mussolini didn't like being called a hyena. It seems hard fighting in Tunisia, doesn't it? But it's just a question of getting enough supplies there. Just reading Churchill's message to India.

[16 Dec 1942] How are you Son? And what do you think of the war news? Good! We have Rommel on the run again. A Great British regiment has been fighting so magnificently near Tunis. The Surrey Regt? They had only landed a week and we read about the bravery of the young company commanders. I hope they soon have all the support they need.

Chapter 6

The Arakan Battle, December 1942–May 1943

The March on Delhi has begun.
Tanahashi, victor of Arakan, will be in Chittagong within a week.
New British Fourteenth Army destroyed.
Why not go home? It's all over in Burma.

Tokyo Rose broadcast on Japanese radio in English (Tokyo Rose was Iva Toguri D'Aquino, an American Japanese). Major General William Slim wrote later: 'Actually, it was just starting.'[1] General Archibald Wavell had made a rather more downbeat comment on the dangers ahead, in a play on Kipling's poem 'On Mandalay':

The anopheles is buzzing, and his bite is swift and keen,
The rain falls down in torrents, and the jungle's thick and green:
And the way back into Burma is a long and weary way
And there ain't no buses running from Assam to Mandalay.
On the road to Mandalay
Where the flying Zeros play
And the Jap comes up through the jungle like a tiger after prey.[2]

JBS would witness a Japanese Zero 'play', and in late 1942 he described an extraordinary event.

> One morning when riding my horse across a wide paddy field, I heard the engine of an aeroplane and looked up. A Japanese Zero had spotted me and was descending rapidly like a hawk diving on its prey. As it turned and flew low, directly up the field towards me, I was a defenceless target in the middle of the field and I waited for the impact of the bullets. Inexplicably, they never came.

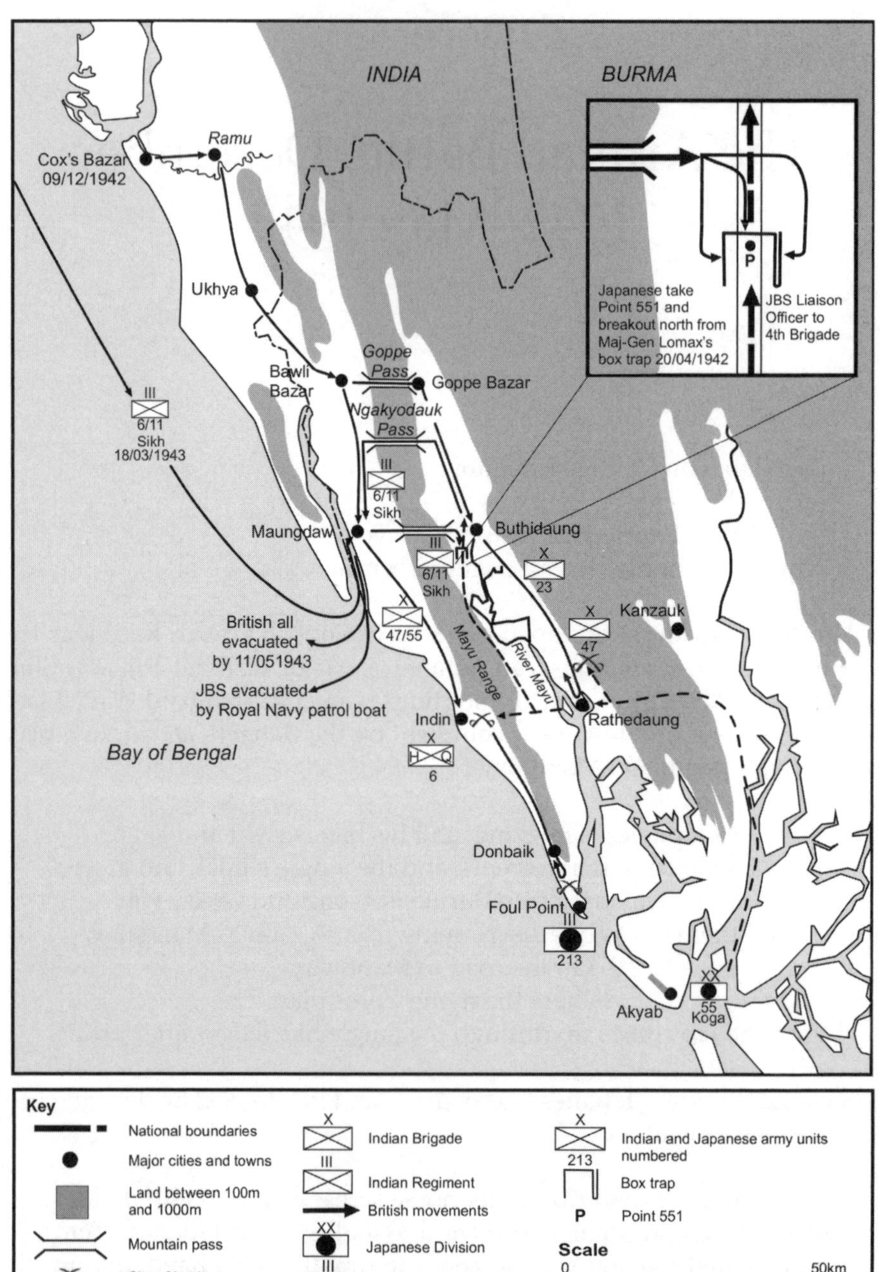

Map 2 **FIRST ARAKAN CAMPAIGN AND RETREAT DECEMBER 1942-MAY1943**

> I rode on unharmed. The Mitsubishi fighter banked and flew off low above the jungle until it was just a dot in the sky. Perhaps the pilot had run out of ammunition? Who knows? Perhaps, in an ugly war, seeing a beautiful horse galloping through shallow water, the pilot had decided to spare it out of Samurai chivalry.

An account by Flying Officer Cecil Braithwaite of 60 Squadron RAF in Burma may explain why the Zero was flying so low:

> The Japanese aircraft were not armoured and could not take damage. If attacked, one solution was to fly low as close to the ground as possible. Some Japanese fighters had telescopic sites, which required the pilot to put his eye to it to aim, unlike the gunsight in most fighters which allowed the pilot to fly with his head up. With his eye to the side, the pilot could not fly low and fast without risking piling into the ground'.[3]

Slim described the Japanese air raids on Calcutta in December 1942 and January 1943. Although the damage from the raids was negligible, the civilian population were scared and 'hundreds of thousands of all class of citizens surged out of Calcutta by rail and road'.[4]

The Japanese plan for operations in Burma in the winter of 1942–3 was to advance into India and seize northern Assam. Captured Japanese documents later revealed that these plans were frustrated by the Allied offensive in the Arakan and Wingate's 77th (Chindit) Brigade's penetration of northern Burma. Wavell's operations, in which Sanderson's Sikhs took part, achieved their objective of diverting and engaging Japanese forces through bold, disruptive action and so stalling a Japanese attack on an unprepared India. An earlier Arakan offensive was not a good precedent: an expedition in the First Burmese War, one-hundred years previously, had resulted in the British force being almost entirely wiped out by disease.[5]

General Wavell originally planned an amphibious operation along the Arakan coast as far as Akyab Island. A lack of landing craft, however, meant a land-based attack was the only alternative, a 'hard slog' down the Arakan peninsula. Preparation involved building an all-weather road from Chittagong as far as Cox's Bazar.[6]

In September 1942 Major General Lloyd's inexperienced and jittery 14th Indian Div. advanced slowly southwards. In December Lloyd sent a probing force down the Mayu range. The ambitious objective, intended primarily as a psychological offensive to raise British fighting morale, was to expel the Japanese and to seize Akyab Island, which had an airfield suitable for long-range RAF bombing purposes and which lay at the mouth of the two main Arakan rivers. The geography of the Arakan was not welcoming. The central, 20-mile-wide Mayu range, with a precipitous and dense jungle-covered spine of hills up to 1,500ft high, ran 90 miles down the middle of the Arakan peninsula.[7] On one side was a flat strip of land with swamps and tidal creeks, difficult to cross. On the other side, beyond the foothills, lay the Mayu range valley, leading to the Mayu River which was infested with leeches up to 9in long, which could slip through the lace holes of boots. It was here that Sanderson was sent, as Liaison Officer with the 4th Brigade. It was inevitable that Sanderson would go down with malaria: the Arakan was highly malarial and the most virulent type of mosquito bred there. The wonder drug mepacrine and mosquito repellents would only be made available later in the year.[8]

The port of Maungdaw on the estuary was connected to Buthidaung by a road that ran through two old railway tunnels. There was also a narrow packhorse track crossing the range. Lloyd's mistaken judgement that the Mayu range jungle was impassable to troops was not shared by the Japanese Commander General Koga, with tragic results.

Lloyds' forces advanced west of the ranges until they stopped, 10 miles from Foul Point on the end of the peninsula. On the Mayu estuary, patrols of the 14th Div. entered the outskirts of Rathedaung and waited whilst supplies were brought up by boat.[9] This delay was a crucial tactical error. Until the end of January, when the 112th Regt of the 55th Div. reached Akyab, there were only two battalions of the Japanese 33rd Div. facing the 14th Indian Div.[10] Until the 14th Div. renewed their advance on 6 January, the Japanese 33rd Div. made good use of their time by strengthening their defences in both Donbaik and Rathedaung, installing solid bunkers constructed from thick tree trunks covered with earth, light artillery machine guns, grenade launchers with barbed wire and bamboo sticks, sharpened in fires, protecting their approach.[11]

The 14th Div. attacks were repeatedly repelled. Reinforcements sent from India now brought the divisional strength up to nine brigades, with eight Valentine tanks, though too few to be effective. Slim had advised against bringing in armour in such small numbers in so constricted an area but his advice was not taken.[12] The Royal Armoured Corps tanks was soon destroyed. Lloyd used the 6th Brigade in a frontal attack on Dombaik, an assault that harked back to the First World War for its futility and heavy casualties. Fusilier W.C. Smith reported that: 'It was like a scene from Dante's Inferno – as screams and yells from the wounded and dying filled the air, even above the bombardment, and all the casualties seemed to be our own.'[13] Sergeant Jones of the Royal Welch Fusiliers described one attack:

> At 0500 the attack on Donbaik began. All hell was let loose. Three quarters of 'A' Company got on the bunker but couldn't hold it. I lost half my men trying to attack similar bunkers . . . The Jap is very astute and shouted out in English: 'British soldier, why are you here? Your wives are waiting for you.' The CO shouted in Welsh through a loudspeaker to 'D' Company to hold on. That flummoxed the Japs.[14]

Slim, who had been summoned by Irwin to report on the situation, condemned the repeated frontal attacks and said it would be a disaster to continue. Irwin ignored him.[15] Slim recommended positioning a brigade up on the Mayu range but Lloyd made a major tactical error in ignoring Slim's advice. The Japanese now counter-attacked aggressively. On 25 March a strong enemy column of the Japanese's 112th Regt, having arrived from central Burma under Colonel Tanahashi Seizo, now crossed into the Mayu valley opposite Rathedaung and attacked the British 55th Brigade, which made a fighting retreat up the Mayu River. When Lloyd attempted another attack, Major General Irwin replaced him with Major General Lomax, who arrived with part of the 26th Div., including the 4th Indian Brigade.

Captain Sanderson and his Sikhs had left Jhikergacha for the Arakan on 18 March, the day the final attack on Donbaik took place: 'The former relaxed, idyllic and diverse life that we young officers led was soon replaced by tough weeks fighting the Japanese in the jungle across the border in the Arakan in Burma.'[16] The Sikh Regt had been trained for mechanised warfare but their role was now changed: in place of the motor transport, twenty-eight saddleless mules were issued to the battalion. The 6th/11th Sikh Btn was part of the 4th Indian Brigade of Lomax's 26th Div., with whom Sanderson had been appointed a Liaison Officer on 4 January 1943.[17]

Just as the recently arrived Lomax was studying his maps and dispositions, a small force of Lieutenant General Koga Takeshi's 55th Japanese Div. (of which there were only six battalions in the Arakan) audaciously crossed the Mayu River on the night of 24 March.[18] It attacked the left flank of the British 47th Brigade, deployed along the Eastern side of the Mayu range. The Japanese almost annihilated the 47th, whose shaken survivors left all their equipment and withdrew in small groups through the hills.[19]

Sanderson's 6/11th Sikhs had received their movement orders on 11 March. They had left Jhikergacha on 15 March for Calcutta docks, where they embarked on board the SS *Ellenga*, sailing on 16 March as part of the

4th Infantry Brigade. They disembarked at Chittagong on the 19th and transferred to paddle steamers for the 20-hour journey by sea to Maugdaw in Burma. Captain Sanderson's Sikhs moved inland by night to Buthidaung, where they deployed under previously unmet conditions, against a well-prepared and jungle-hardy enemy. Two companies proceeded on patrol down the Mayu River. On 27 March the battalion reached Hpaybyn village, where they set up a defensive perimeter. When they approached Theindaungpara village, the enemy opened fire. Sanderson's battalion, meeting heavy resistance from machine guns and small arms fire, was pinned down and suffered four killed and fourteen wounded. They dug in on a piquet hill. When intelligence reports identified two companies of enemy nearby, a flanking movement was made on Prainagdaung. The Sikhs fought at night, unaware of the locations or exact movements of their own forces or of the enemy. On 30 March Sanderson and his Sikhs advanced down the west bank of the Mayu River as a reinforcement for troops hard-pressed by the Japanese.[20] On 2 April there were skirmishes with the enemy. The Japanese begin to shell the battalion positions every half an hour.

There was 'great RAF activity over the area'. Sanderson later recalled the brave pilots who flew over the jungle in support: 'The pilots in Burma took great risks: the jungle downdrafts and mountainous terrain made flying extremely hazardous. I saw one Spitfire pilot on close support clip a wing on the trees and crash. We tried to reach him to pull him out of his cockpit but unfortunately the flames made it impossible to get near the plane.'

The 26th Div. attempted to hold a defensive zone south of Buthidaung, and even tried to surround the Japanese as they pressed their advantage.

JBS:

> I was leading a patrol in the jungle. Hearing the sounds of an enemy camp ahead, we crept carefully forward and rushed out to confront the surprised Japanese infantry sitting in a group. The Japanese patrols often had a complement of between 30 and 50 men. Pressing the trigger of my submachine gun, I found that it had jammed. Turning around for support, I observed the rest of my patrol beating a hasty retreat into the thick jungle. Reluctantly, I too decided, on this occasion, that 'discretion was the better part of valour'.
>
> My men had to clear vines with machetes for a crossing. Some had been bitten by water snakes. I made sure I was in the water alongside them. Leadership is about sharing in their hardships.

When making camp in the jungle after patrols, our patrol used lighted cigarettes to burn off the leeches that had attached themselves to our skin and were taking our blood. When defending a position, and lacking barbed wire, we took the time to place in front of our lines primitive obstacles of bamboos, called *panjis*, that we had sharpened at night on our camp fires. These faced forward to pierce the thin sandals of the Japanese when they charged. They were a very effective defence and went through both their sandals and their feet.

One of the Sikh soldiers in my company, when we were in India, had arrived back once late from leave. He explained that his return had been delayed by the slow Indian trains. In the Arakan, when one of the Japanese called out from the jungle 'We'll be in Calcutta in a week', the same Sikh shouted back, 'Not on our trains you won't!' As a reward, I promptly awarded him extra days of leave when we went back to India!

Further south, having dispersed the 47th Brigade, the Japanese commander Colonel Tanahashi took his men across the steep slopes of the Mayu range, marching along small, narrow tracks, or cutting his way through the jungle that Lloyd had considered impassable. On the night of 5 April the Japanese had streamed out on to the coastal western strip from the west of the Mayu range and fell upon the rear of the 6th Brigade.[21] They overran the 6th Brigade HQ, bayonetting the wounded and shooting the doctors. Brigadier Cavendish was killed. (A Japanese soldier later killed in an ambush was found to be wearing Cavendish's socks.[22]) Slim withdrew the remaining exhausted and demoralised forces from a chaotic battlefield. He had taken over command on 14 April and knew he was up against a tough, resilient enemy. He had earlier written to Irwin: 'We are fighting an enemy army in which the best men go into the infantry.'[23]

The 6/11 Sikh war diaries report that on 10 April there was heavy rain for an hour. Japanese were reported near the battalion position at Hparongyaung. Patrols were fired on from the snipers in trees. 'At 08.30 on 13th April the Battalion Commander and LO [Liaison Officer] Captain Sanderson check the camp perimeter.' At 17.00 a Japanese aircraft overflew their position from east to west. A patrol laid an ambush that killed three of the enemy and two marked maps were subsequently discovered on the bodies. A returning patrol was ambushed by the enemy who threw grenades and fired bursts from LMGs (light machine guns), killing one and wounding six. On 18 April 'B' Coy reported an enemy column of 250 Japanese with mules heading north and fired on them, sending them scattering into the jungle. The Japanese returned mortar fire from the jungle. From 7 a.m. the next day the enemy shelled for an hour. The Japanese then engaged the right flank of the battalion but were driven off.[24]

Slim, aware that Koga had bold ambitions and would be heading for the Maungdaw–Buthidaung road and the railway tunnels, decided to set a classic trap to encircle and defeat the Japanese. M. Hickey described Slim and Lomax's plan to trap Koga's forces in a tactic from a Japanese textbook.[25] Slim ordered a brigade to set up a defensive box below the road, with the high Point 551 in the middle. The Japanese would enter the box and the lid would then swing shut from the east, where the 4th Brigade, including Captain Sanderson's Sikhs waited.

On the 20th 'C' Coy's telephone was cut. Sanderson's Company was attacked from all sides by an enemy strength of 150. At 8 p.m. Brigade orders were received to move back 3 miles to the old Brigade HQ's camp. Slim's box trap was being set. All rations were destroyed, except for heavy amounts of ammunition.

Positioned east of the Mayu range, Captain Sanderson and the 4th Indian Infantry Brigade now had its left flank on the range. The Japanese were skillfully infiltrating, working their way through the jungle on top of the ranges and foothills, threatening the flanks and rear of the retreating 4th Brigade.[26]

JBS later told his family:

> When retreating northwards in the Arakan, I was given the responsibility for destroying many crates of whisky, to prevent the Japanese drinking it. We could not bear to smash up such fine alcohol and buried the lot under a tree, with booby-traps hidden in elephant droppings, thinking perhaps to return again on some advance. We never did return, of course and the crates must still be there.

Some abandoned British alcohol was not wasted. A Japanese officer, 2nd Lieutenant Satoru Nazawa of the 112th Regt 55th Japanese Div., later described the scene:

> At Maungdaw we captured a British field storage. We drunk a bottle of water which we found was Gin. Some were gulping down the gin, happier than ever. We had this kind of excitement, or more like comedy. We thought: 'These people are fighting in such a luxurious condition. If they took our camp, they would find just a bit of dried fish and a bit of rice, nothing else.'[27]

The 6/11th Sikhs were now part of a force defending the southern approaches to Buthidaung with 2/1 Punjab on the left and 1/15 Punjab on the right. On the 23rd a small party of Japanese approached. The battalion fired as sixty Japanese advanced north west from Gudabynin. Throughout the day the enemy shelled the battalion position. *JBS* later described such Japanese shelling to the author:

> Once in India one day, after we had downed a few whiskies together, I had said jokingly to a fellow officer: 'I am going to shoot your girlfriend' and had fired a bullet from my revolver, across the room, and into the framed picture of his beloved. This officer possessed a wind-up gramaphone with two records which he often set up and played when out in the field. I suppose to calm his nerves. One day, however, a Japanese shell flew over and blew the officer and his gramaphone to kingdom come.

At 5 p.m. on the 23rd April there was a heavy enemy attack on the 2/1 Punjab position and they withdrew. Heavy LMG and mortar fire fell on the area. On the 27th twenty-five enemy were reported at Point 510 in the centre of the box. The British artillery fired on the approaching Japanese. During the night of the 27/28th 'D' Coy fired on an enemy party who scattered. 1/15 Punjab repelled an enemy attack on the right flank.

At dawn the enemy shelled Sanderson's position at Kanthe. 'D' Coy ambushed and fired on twenty Japanese who were trying to work their way around the right flank of the Brigade, on the high ground between 55 and 4 Brigade. The RAF bombed areas on 'D' Coy's right flank where the enemy were known to be situated. The 6 /11th Sikh war diaries report that on 28th April: '2nd Lieut Rajkhewa takes over as Liaison Officer as Captain Sanderson in being sick.' Sanderson was now beginning to suffer from malaria, with symptoms of aching bones, shivering and a high temperature.

Two battalions were positioned on each side of the box. The Japanese attacked as planned, flowing into the box. When Lomax was about to order the closure of the box, however, the two weary battalions at the top of the box, and south of the road, gave way in the face of ferocious Japanese assaults.[28] The Japanese seized Point 551, holding this strategic position and the vital road. The troops around Buthidaung were cut off. They were ordered to destroy all vehicles and to withdraw over the Mayu range.

Ordered to retreat, Sanderson's made his way over the Mayu hills in a malarial condition to the coast, holding a last grenade to kill himself to avoid capture by the Japanese. By serendipity, he spotted an inshore Royal

Naval Patrol Boat of HQ Coastal Force (nicknamed 'Wavell's Navy' and based in Chittagong) and was evacuated.[29] As Sanderson left the shore, he threw his grenade into the water. It was a dud and failed to explode. On 5 May Captain Sanderson was admitted to Chittagong Hospital, one of the 7,500 cases of malaria from the disasterous Arakan campaign.[30]

After Sanderson's evacuation, the battalion fought on. On 5 May they spotted the Japanese on high ground in the box area. A hundred Japanese with mules advanced along their right flank. 'D' Coy observed the Japanese climbing the hills to the west of their position, where a group of twenty-five were seen digging in. An ambush party was attacked by the enemy with grenades and forced to retire.

On 6 May the battalion withdrew through the positions of 36 Brigade, which was defending the Maungdaw–Buthdaung Road. During the night of 7/8 May the Sikhs next passed through 55 Brigade's positions and retired east of the Mayu Ridge. On 8 May they made their way through the Ngakyedauk Pass, over the high Mayu range of mountains, which was very slippery and difficult for the mules. West of the Mayu ridge, they found motor transport and were taken north of Maungdaw. The town had been abandoned and the RAF bombed it on 13 May. The battalion was then moved south 2 miles, astride the Maungdaw–Buthidaung Road, to permit 4 and 6 Brigade in turn to pass through their positions. On 14 May they reached Bawli Bazar. Heavy monsoon rains were now falling, and there were many cases of dysentry. On 28 May they reached Zebin on the coast and a waiting steamer, which evacuated the battalion to Cox's Bazar in pouring rain. In early July the battalion were back in Chittagong, from where they were evacuated by train.

Six weeks later Captain Sanderson was granted a month's sick leave and on 20 July he rejoined the reminder of his battalion who had returned from Cox's Bazar to Jhikergacha, where they would remain until Christmas Eve.[31] Slim had withdrawn all forces from Maungdaw by 11 May, returning to the rice field area of Cox's Bazar until the monsoon ended. A force was left at Bawli Bazar to observe the Japanese. Three days later Slim wrote: 'Here we are back where we started, a sad ending to our first and much heralded offensive.'[32] Corporal Fred Cottier (a Section Commander in the 2nd Btn, Durham Light Infantry) had a more positive view of the campaign, later commenting: 'The Arakan campaign was the best training we ever had for fighting in Burma.'[33]

The 14th Div. was finished psychologically and never returned to active service. The Command Psychiatrist reported that 'no useful purpose would be served by counting psychiatric cases, for the whole of 14th Indian Div. was for practical purposes a psychiatric casualty'.[34] John Sanderson, however, was regaining his strength slowly after the recurring bouts of malaria and had volunteered for a transfer to a parachute regiment to take the fight to the enemy. He later told the author the story of Gurkhas sent back to Nepal to recruit fellow countrymen for the Parachute Brigade: 'Some Gurkhas were "roughed" up because the Nepalese thought they were lying to them. It was not possible to jump out of an aircraft at 600 feet and survive . . . at 300ft perhaps. This was before it was explained that they would be wearing parachutes when they jumped.'

Major Maurice Bell, who had sailed to India on the aptly named *Empress of Japan* troopship described how he came to join the Parachute Brigade on its formation in September 1941:

> The Assistant Adjutant drew me into a remote corner of the mess where we were beginning to assemble for lunch. He whispered that the Indian Army had decided to form a parachute brigade. Applicants would have to possess specified qualifications – fit, single, first class tradesman, over six feet in height. The Adjutant and CO had been through the records of all British ranks and only two qualified; Sgt Latham and myself. The CO was happy to recommend both of us and Sgt Latham had already volunteered. Two days later we learned that, of all the people in the unit we had left, we were two who were totally unacceptable. We were both over six feet and should never have been put forward because the landing casualty rates climbed steeply for parachutists exceeding six feet in height. Fate sometimes deals strange hands but I never, even for a moment, regretted joining 50 Para.

In October 1943 Churchill, who tended to think ahead strategically, surprised the Chiefs of Staff with his prescient view that: 'We mustn't weaken the Germans too much . . . after all, we may need them to fight the Russians'. This was dubbed Operation UNTHINKABLE.[35]

On 19 January 1944 the Second Battle of the Arakan began when 'the British XVth Corps began their advance down the Arakan coast. At the same time the Allied air forces redoubled their efforts, and, with the aid of newly arrived Spitfires, gained a degree of air superiority which was shortly to prove invaluable.'[36]

JBS recalled the difficulties of transporting mules in aircraft:

> The majority of the mules we used came from Argentina. They were very hardy animals, very useful in carrying equipment like ammunition and heavy radios on steep jungle trails and taking

casualties out but very stubborn on river crossings. The handlers became very attached to their animals: I saw one man in tears when his mule had to be destroyed, as was the fate of thousands at the end of the war. Many were airlifted for Wingate's forces in gliders towed by Dakatos: half crashed. Then someone had the bright idea of making mules honorary paratroopers. An accompanying soldier had strict instructions to shoot the animal if it got out of control. Of course, the mule panicked in the plane and it was shot by its handler. Unfortunately, the same bullet continued inside the plane and killed the pilot. They afterwards tried tipping the mules out on rolled trolleys with three chutes but the idea was eventually abandoned.

Gladys Sanderson's wrote in her diary:

[21 January 1944] This evening the Germans tried their biggest raid for two years on London. About 90 aeroplanes crossed the coast but only about 30 reached the London area – they were met by our guns with a terrific barrage – never heard such heavy gunfire before. Several bombs dropped on our neighbourhood. Five fell in Downsbridge Road – which did not explode – one wonders if the underground movement are sabotaging the bombs? We brought down ten Hun planes. In comparison 1,000 RAF aircraft bombed Magdeburg, 200 tons were dropped. It was the second great raid on Germany in 24 hours and followed Thursday night's onslaught on Berlin. At 5 a.m. we had another German raid in London, very heavy barrage met them.

[2 February 1944] General Montgomery the C-in-C of the British Invasion forces addressed thousands of troops, assembled in a SE town, so that they could get to know him:

I want you men to know that I never put an army into battle until I am certain it is going to be a good show. Never we will have any question of failure . . . This war began a long time ago, I am getting fed up with the thing, I think it is nearly time we finished it. We could not see at the beginning how it would end. That is not so today, definitely not. The only thing we cannot see is when. But we must make a great effort to finish it off this year. We can do so and we will. You and I will see this thing through together.

Describing the German soldier, General Montgomery said that, though he was a good fighter, there had never yet been a case which the British soldier could not see him off.

> [16 February 1944] We made the biggest raid over Berlin last night – 1,000 planes took part on the sorties, we lost 45 RAF crew. Our poor boys, God rest their souls.

Churchill described the situation now threatening India:

> In February 1944 there were sure signs that the enemy were preparing an attack on the central front against Imphal . . . Wingate's Long-Range Penetration Force, the Chindits operation, was a part of our offensive plan. Although it was clear that the Japanese would get their blow in first . . . Wingate's brigades would principally cut the enemy's communication . . . thereby dislocating their supply system. The enemy would be forced to detach troops to deal with the menace behind his fighting front.[37]

The Chindits 16th British marched across 450 miles of mountains and jungle and were supplied solely from the air. On 5 March, sustained by 250 US 'Air Commando' aircraft, their fly in began of two of Wingate's brigades, 260 miles from transport base. The landing strips were 100 miles inside enemy territory. The first landings were of troops in gliders, whose job was to prepare the strips for the transport aircraft. Between 6 and 11 March 7,500 men were successfully landed, although some gliders were lost. The operation appeared to be a complete surprise for the Japanese. On 24 March Wingate was killed when his aircraft crashed into a hillside. The pilot probably lost his way in poor weather.[38] John Sanderson remembers seeing Wingate: 'I once saw [Major General] Orde Wingate of the Chindit fame, on an airfield, heading for another of his guerilla operations behind the Japanese lines. He was very brave but a complete madman. Wingate was later killed in a plane crash.'

On 8 March the Japanese division began their expected attack on the central front, repeating the tactics they had used in the Arakan. The Japanese divisions were advancing, however, with greater speed than predicted and in an area where they were not expected in such force.

Major General 'Uncle Bill' Slim, was working on his detailed plans to fight the Japanese on his own terms. He would draw them to his defended positions, which had close air support and shorter lines of supply and communication and then destroy them. The Japanese had planned to capture the stores they needed. This he would deny them. Slim had an astute understanding of the Japanese psychology of war and valuable experience of their tactics in the jungle. He was confident of success.

The historian Frank McLynn noted it was always a matter of regret for General Slim that he had not predicted a Japanese attack through Ukhrul, Litan and Sangshak. The Japanese 15th Div. made an unopposed crossing of the Chindwin River at Thaungdut on the night of 15–16 March and advanced rapidly through the jungle-covered hills towards Sangshak and Litan. By the evening of 18 March they had advanced as far as Ukhrul, only 50 miles as the bird flies from Imphal. Eight columns of the Japanese 31st Div., meanwhile, had crossed the Chindwin near Homalin and then separated, one force hastening to support the 15th at Ukhrul, the other heading for Kohima.[39]

Lieutenant General G. Scoones of 33rd Corps had little understanding of the predicament of his brigade. As the historian J. Thompson described it: 'His brigade was cut off, out on a limb, with minimal support . . . The conduct of the 50th Indian Parachute Brigade penned into a perimeter 400 by 500 yards was heroic: their eventual breakout equally so.'[40] On 14 March 1944 John Sanderson had been appointed as an acting major with 152 Indian Btn of 50th Indian Parachute Brigade. Days afterwards, they were out on a forward training exercise in the jungle, under-equipped and under-manned. The Brigade soldiers would soon be fighting for their lives, surrounded by elite spearhead troops of the Japanese 15th and 31st Divs, in an epic battle akin to the stand at Arnhem, on an isolated, exposed hilltop village, with no hope of reinforcements.

For the moment in mid-March 1944 the hilltop at 6,000ft presented a delightful aspect, with cool, clean air and magnificent views in all directions, with alpine flowers growing in profusion and orchids entwined in the trees. This was soon to change.[41]

Chapter 7

The Battle of Sangshak, March 1944

Parachute Regiment motto: *Utrinque paratus* – 'Ready for anything'.

> 'When you go home, tell them of us and say for your tomorrow, we gave our today.'[1]

On 14 March 1944 John was appointed an acting major with 152nd Indian Parachute Btn of 50th Indian Para Brigade. The Japanese had launched a final full-scale offensive on India. The enemy had unexpectedly crossed the River Chindwin on their planned Operation U-GO advance towards Delhi and the Indian plains. The Japanese 31st Div. moved forward on a wide front, heading for Kohima to cut the main supply road to Imphal. They divided into Right, Centre and Left assault groups. The Left force of the 58th Infantry Regt was under the command of Colonel Utata Fukunaga but accompanied by Major General Shigesaboro Miyazaki, the 31st Div.'s Infantry Commander.[2]

Brigadier Maxwell Hope-Thomson had difficulty obtaining transport to take his Parachute battalion from Kohima to Imphal, where they were unexpected and given no food, information or ammunition. After a long wait a few old lorries transported half the battalion to Sangshak.

50th Indian Para Brigade were volunteers drawn from every regiment of the British and Indian armies: 4/5th Mahratta Light Infantry, 152nd (Indian) and part of 153rd (Gurkha) Paratroop Btns, as well as Medical, Engineer and Signals units, all keen to get to grips with the enemy.

Hope-Thomson's Brigade was on a 'jungle warfare training exercise in a threatened area' to the east of Kohima and Imphal, on the border of India and Burma. Raj Singh described the harsh terrain they faced. Their orders were to patrol on foot with mules, as far as the Chindwin River, and to intercept any Japanese patrols within a vast area of mountainous jungle measuring 50 by 80 miles. The ridges rose to 4,000ft. It was considered highly unlikely that a large Japanese force could penetrate this thick jungle

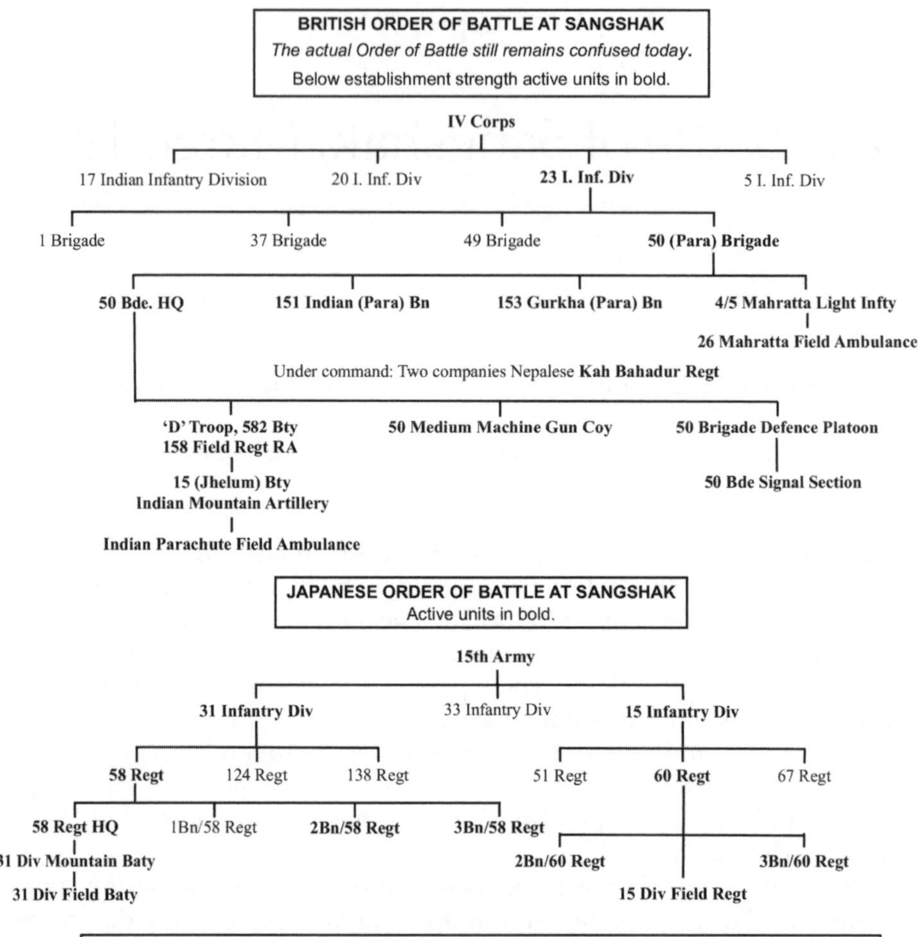

Adapted and corrected from *The Battle at Sangshak.* With permission of the estate of Harry Seaman

area of narrow tracks and footpaths, in places vertical and edged with steep 1,000ft drops. It was thought that the main Japanese attack would come from the south. The enemy, however, were closing fast.

On 18 March, the Japanese 58th Regt was approaching Ukhrul, 25 miles north east of Imphal and 8 miles north of Sangshak. Local Nagas had reported small Japanese patrols in Pushing, moving steathily forward.

Lieutenant Colonel Hopkinson, commander of 152nd (Indian) Btn sent 'B' and 'C' Coys to positions dominating the only two east–west Jeep-tracks over the hills. 'B' Coy were at Point 7386 and 7000. Near the Chindwin

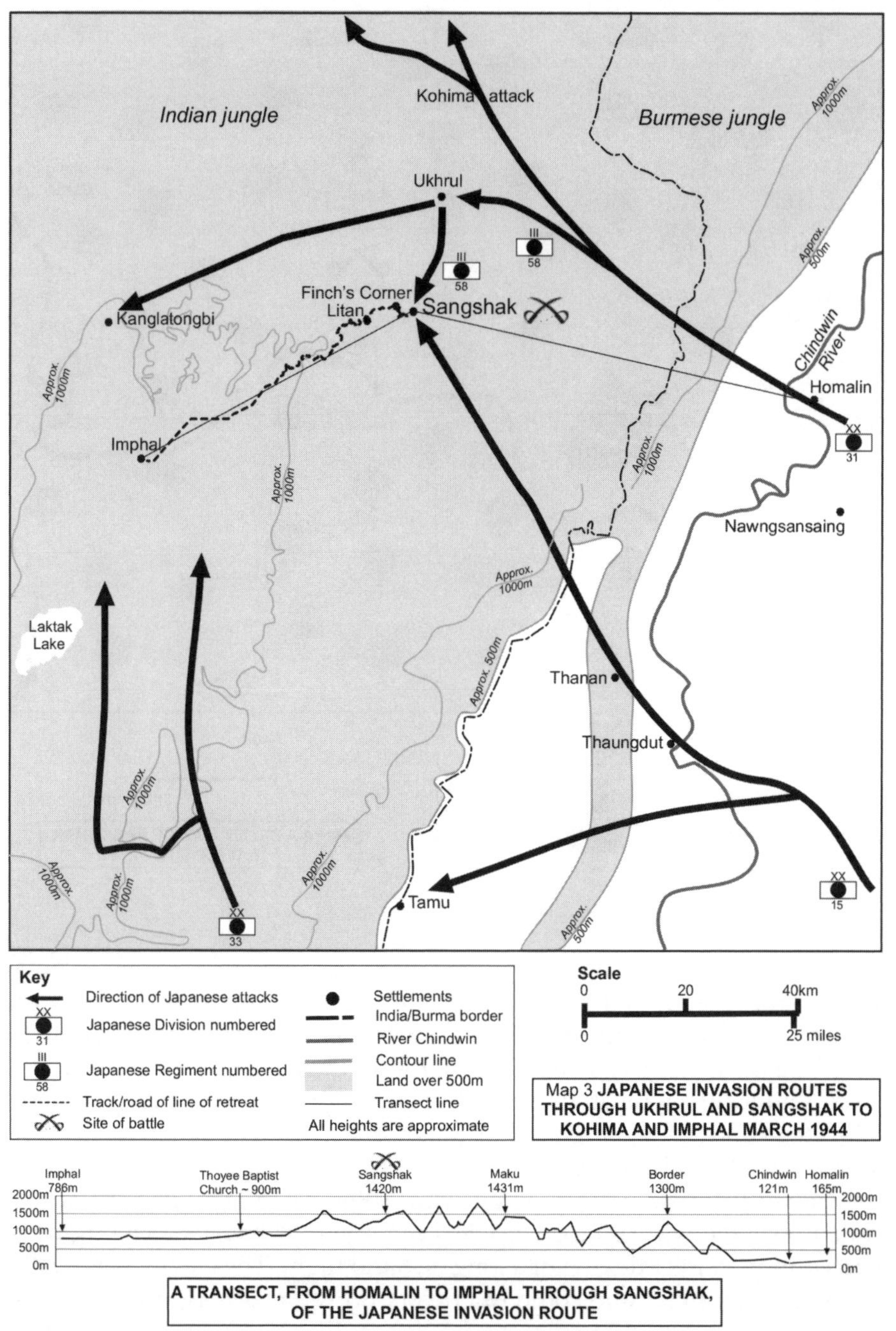

Map 3 **JAPANESE INVASION ROUTES THROUGH UKHRUL AND SANGSHAK TO KOHIMA AND IMPHAL MARCH 1944**

A TRANSECT, FROM HOMALIN TO IMPHAL THROUGH SANGSHAK, OF THE JAPANESE INVASION ROUTE

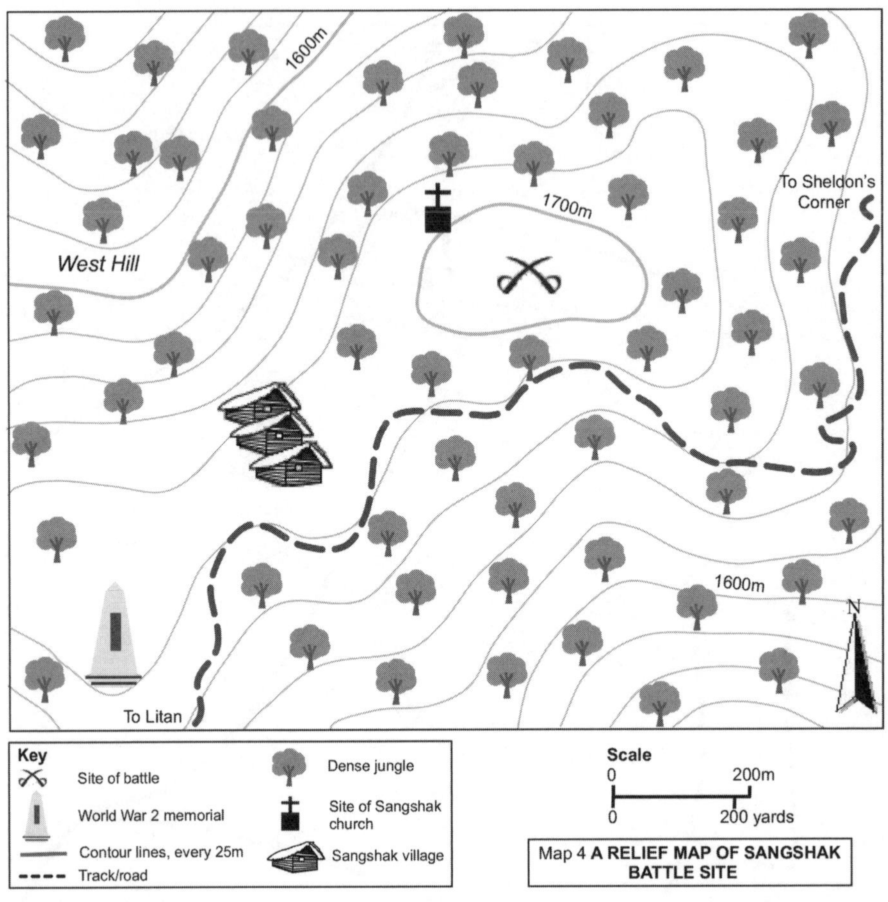

Map 4 **A RELIEF MAP OF SANGSHAK BATTLE SITE**

River, 3 miles from Point 7378, Major Fuller's 'C' company's dawn patrol spotted 200 Japanese approaching, the lead elements of a whole battalion. By 9.30 a.m. 152nd's isolated 'C' Coy found themselves on a hill at Point 7378, under ferocious attack from two enemy battalions of the Japanese 58th Regt under the command of Major Shimano. The other 152nd Coy attempted to send reinforcements to 'C' Coy but these were blocked by the enemy. Just before dawn on the 20th Fuller put in a counter-attack and called over the wireless for help. His men were exhausted. The fighting had continued relentlessly for a long day and night. The enemy was vastly superior in numbers and could use fresh troops for each assault. By 6 a.m. Fuller and his second-in-command, Captain Roseby had been wounded.

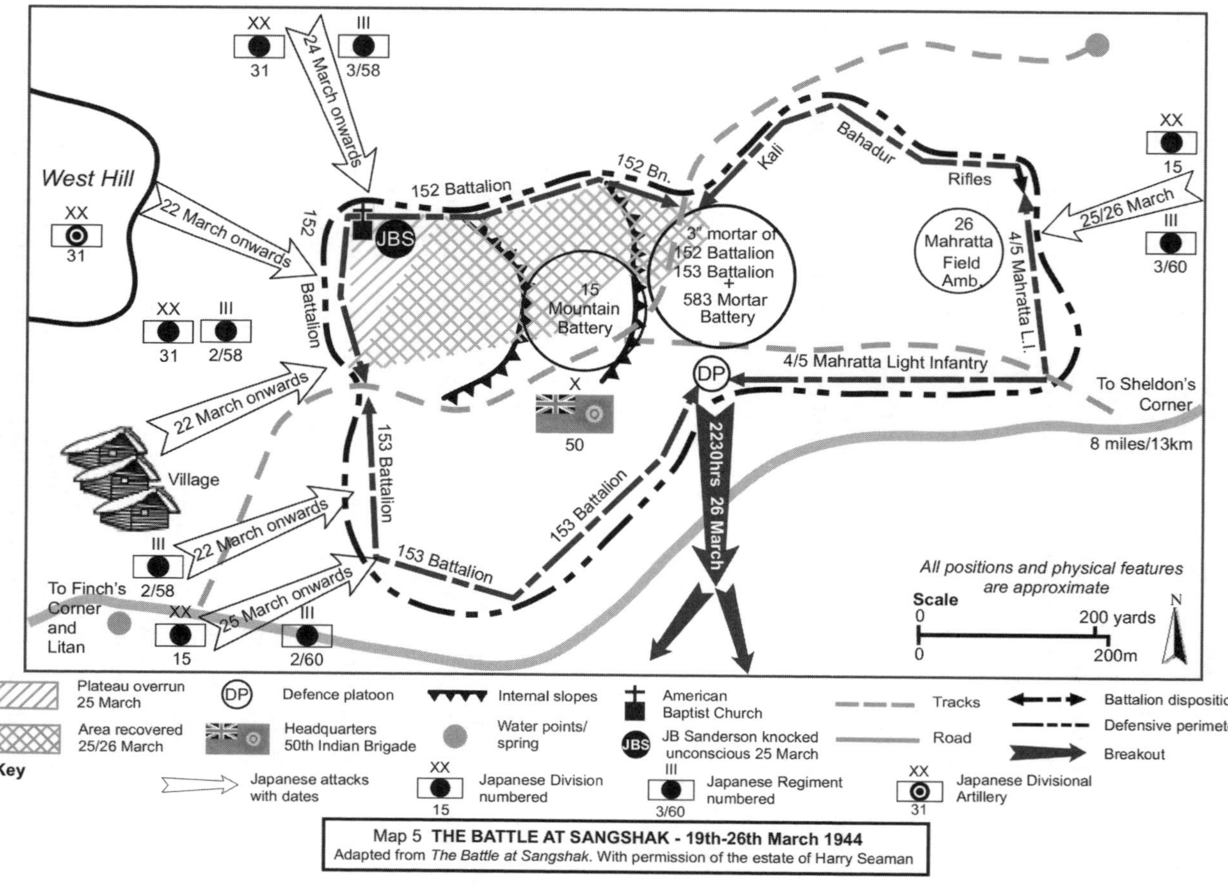

Map 5 **THE BATTLE AT SANGSHAK - 19th-26th March 1944**
Adapted from *The Battle at Sangshak*. With permission of the estate of Harry Seaman

An hour later they had died of their wounds. Easton was now in command. At 10 a.m. he reported that the company was being overwhelmed, with most of his men killed or wounded. Twenty of the British and Indian paratroopers had made a desperate charge downhill, firing and shouting as they came. Their way was blocked by a wide ravine into which some fell, whilst others escaped and twelve were captured.[3]

Colonel Fukunaga, commanding the Japanese 58th Infantry Regt, later recorded in his diary: 'At the very top of the position an officer appeared in sight, put a pistol to his head and shot himself in full view of everyone below. Our men fell silent, deeply impressed by such a brave act.'[4] Only Easton himself and a small party of wounded escaped through the jungle. The Japanese suffered 450 killed, including 7 officers.

On 19 March Lieutenant Colonel Hopkinson was informed that a strong Japanese force was now only 2 miles away and was closing rapidly. His war diaries recorded that he thought everyone had been deluded into thinking that the country was far too challenging for the Japanese to be able to move large forces across the mountain ranges and through the very dense jungles. After initially concentrating his forces at Sheldon's Corner, he pulled them back, first to 'Kidney Camp', 4 miles to the west, and then to Sangshak.

The three 152nd companies, including John Sanderson, withdrew under fire along the 10 miles of mountainous tracks back to the high ground of Sangshak, a small Naga village on the Jeep track between Imphal and Ukhrul. Here the 2,000 men of 50th Brigade were preparing, as best they could, to block the Japanese advance on IV Corps at Imphal.

The 50th Brigade were only lightly equipped, with very little barbed wire or sandbags, and only a few picks or shovels to dig weapon slits for protection in the rocky ground. The outcome of the battle would have been very different if rolls of barbed wire had been available. The 'strong box' defensive position, 600yd yards wide and 200–300yd deep was well-sited tactically but defended by only one battery of 3.7in Howitzers, 2 and 3in mortars and its Indian troop of field artillery. Only the Paratroop Brigade stood between the Japanese and the almost undefended Imphal HQ of airfields and huge storage dumps.

The Brigade arrived in the area at virtually the same time as the Japanese. When the force from Sheldon's Corner arrived at the Sangshak position late on the afternoon of 22 March, the Japanese were already at Finch's Corner. Their patrols were in range of the perimeter; the 15th Battery of the 9th Mountain Regt TA, which had joined the Brigade, was in action and shelling enemy columns coming down the track from Ukhrul. The company of the Mahrattas (Light Infantry), which had not been with the remainder of the battalion at Sheldon's Corner, was in action covering the concentration of the Brigade from a ridge about 500yd west of the perimeter.

Brigadier Hope-Thompson's 50th Brigade was ordered to hold the Japanese onslaught at all costs and fight to the last man with their remaining grenades and bullets of their Sten guns and Mark III rifles. Optimism was raised by Corps HQ's assurances that reinforcements would eventually reach their isolated garrison and that the holding of Sangshak was crucial for the overall battle plan. The 153rd Gurkha Btn and the Medium Machine Gun Coy were digging in as fast as possible. Part of 153rd Btn and two Nepalese companies arrived in haste from Kohima late on the 21st.[5]

On the night of 22 March Captain Nagara's infantry, without artillery support, charged in courageous suicidal waves up the three slopes, the fourth side being close jungle. Within 15 minutes 90 infantry soldiers of 2nd Btn Japanese 58th Regt were killed, including the commander; twenty Japanese dead were found around the football field.

As soon as it was really dark the Japanese started to attack. They continued to attack throughout the night, regardless of casualties. They made no attempt at surprise, using lights to aid direction and shouting to each other whilst they set fire to the Naga village, the flames from the burning buildings lighting up the battlefield. As daylight came, the Japanese withdrew into the jungle and firing ceased temporarily.[6]

On 23 March Dakotas attempted to drop supplies but most floated down to the Japanese positions. The 152nd's Btn's Gurkhas attacked in an attempt to recover the parachuted supplies, supported by British fighter planes that had escorted the transport planes. Although they were driven back empty-handed, they had inflicted heavy casualties on the enemy.[7]

On the 23rd there were few enemy attacks during daylight, although any movement in the open attracted fire from snipers, who were mainly concealed in trees in the surrounding jungle, and from medium and light machine guns, sited to sweep the plateau with fire. The defenders lost a number of officers, VCOs (Viceroy Commissioned Officer) and NCOs (Non Commissioned Officers) from this deadly fire whilst visiting the platoon and section posts. This lack of cover within the perimeter also made the distribution of ammunition, rations etc. very difficult in daylight.

The 153nd and 152nd Btns were in the most exposed part of the perimeter: the volcanic rock near the surface making it impossible to dig down for adequate cover. The Brigade Medium Machine Gun Coy suffered especially heavily through this inability to take the gun pits deep enough. The Number Ones firing the machine guns were very exposed and many were killed including Major Ball, the company commander, and Captain

Caydon, shot through the head whilst keeping the guns firing after the original Number One had been killed.

During the morning patrols reported large Japanese columns with motor transport and elephants moving up towards Sangshak from the east. At about midday the Japanese started shelling the position, having brought up artillery. They attacked in considerable strength. Fierce hand-to-hand fighting took place before they were repulsed. A call was made for air support and a number of Spitfires came over and attacked the enemy. The jungle target, however, was very difficult to locate and some of the British positions were shot up as well.

The shortage of water began to be felt. Fortunately, there was heavy rain in the evening and the defenders managed to collect some in mess tins. There was insufficient water for the mules. Once the mules had gone the Mountain and the Mortar batteries were immobile. They now found it very difficult to bury the dead, owing to the hard ground and the heavy shelling that was disinterring those already buried. There were piles of Japanese dead lying in front of weapon pits and slit trenches.[8]

On 24 March the surrounded Brigade was fighting off a force four times its own number: six battalions each with two Japanese infantry battalions and their reinforcements. General Miyazaki was directing fire from four field guns from Lungshang, about a mile north east of Sangshak.[9]

A lucky discovery was the complete enemy plan of attack for the Imphal offensive on the body of a dead Japanese captain, pulled in using a rope and an improvised hook. However, despite the Brigade Intelligence Officer risking his life carrying a copy of the map back to HQ and then returning to the battlefield, due to confusion at HQ, the valuable information about the 15th and 31st Japanese Divs was not used. The maps had shown that the Japanese had to take Sangshak for their plan to proceed: this knowledge made the defenders even more determined to resist.[10]

The British officers were dressed in green jungle trousers and shirts (without their usual Dennison smocks, paratroop wings or regimental badges) and were equipped with a water bottle, compass, binoculars and holster. Gripping their .455 revolvers tightly in their grasp, they ordered their men to 'open fire'.[11] John Sanderson recalled the resolve of the defenders, faced with repeated ferocious onslaughts.

JBS:

> I told my soldiers we had to 'die like men'. The enemy kept attacking in waves, time after time, and were shot down. At one stage in the fighting, a very brave Japanese officer charged

> straight towards me with his samurai sword raised above his head, only to be shot dead and fall directly in front of me.

On the night of the 24th, there were almost continuous attacks, each of which was driven off. Everyone was now beginning to feel the effects of lack of sleep. Ammunition and water were running low. Casualties were mounting, and the field ambulance was crowded with wounded and dying. The doctors and the surgical team were having to work without sleep or a break to cope with the numbers. During the morning the defenders were heartened by the sound of transport aircraft and a supply drop took place.

Everything now depended on successful air supplies of ammunition, water, rations, and medical supplies but the supply drops proved a failure.[12] John Sanderson described to the author his feelings when the airlifted supplies, which they desperately needed to survive, missed their target.

JBS:

> Supply drops were called for and Dakotas flew over with parachuted supplies of ammunition, water, food and equipment. We were frustrated to see almost all these containers floating down into the Japanese-held positions. The mountainous region and low clouds made the pilots' task difficult but only one pilot regularly flew low enough, on a steady course at great personal risk, to ensure supplies landed in our position.

The aircraft came in high to avoid the enemy's fire from the ground and slung their loads out in one run over the position. The defenders watched their urgently needed supplies drift away over the jungle to be collected by the Japanese. One aircraft, however, came over very low and made a number of runs over the hilltop, dropping only two parachute loads each run so that they were able to collect the entire aircraft load. The brave pilot made every flypast so low that the beseiged soldiers could see him waving. They could clearly make out the dispatchers in the doorway, as they watched and shouted encouragement. The Japanese directed intense small arms fire from the jungle as the single Dakota flew over their heads. All subsequent supply drops followed the same pattern. Of every flight on subsequent days they could only rely on being able to collect this one precious load. The pilot and crew of this aircraft had taken part in the Brigade air training. On hearing that 50th Bde (Brigade) was cut off, and having to rely entirely on supply from the air, they were determined that whatever happened, and regardless of the risk to themselves, the Brigade should at least get their entire aircraft load.

This failure to keep Sangshak adequately supplied by air meant that the stock of essential supplies dwindled very fast and the defenders ran very short of ammunition, including shells for the guns and mortar bombs. In 152 Btn their supply of hand grenades was now completely exhausted, a dispiriting situation as throwing grenades amongst the attackers was the most effective way of disrupting night attacks at close quarters. Rations were reduced to a bare minimum. What little water there remained had to go to the field ambulance for the wounded. Every man had only one small mug of tea each day.

They defenders now realised that the failure of the air supply, and the large number of wounded, meant the only course open to them was to fight it out where they stood, inflicting the maximum casualties possible on the enemy. The longer they resisted, the longer the Japanese planned offensive would be delayed. This would be of very great advantage to their comrades busily preparing their defences at Imphal, Kohima and Dimapur.

The forward positions had to be kept fully manned for without any barbed wire, and with the jungle coming up to the edge of the perimeter, they were very vulnerable to sudden attack. The area of the high ground by the church was subjected to almost continuous attack. The fiercest fighting of the battle took place where John Sanderson and Maurice Bell were positioned. It was the key to the whole position and the Japanese seemed to be only too aware of this. From here they would have be able to sweep the whole plateau with fire and quickly destroy the Mortar and Mountain batteries' positions. Several times the enemy got up to the church but were each time forced out.[13]

The shelling and frontal attacks continued for five days, as the Japanese repeatedly attempted to break through, despite their many casualties scattered on the slopes around the besieged box. Lieutenant Kameyama Shosaku recalled: 'We attacked every night from the 22nd to the 25th and every night many soldiers were killed. Despite that, we went forward.'

The Indian gunners were firing their guns at point-blank range into the attackers. Soon the bodies of defenders and mules lay everywhere. The field ambulance area, exposed to small-arms fire, was full of dead, wounded and dying men. Snipers in trees were picking off individual soldiers: two of the 152nd officers were killed within minutes.[14]

After five days of continuous fighting by day and night, conditions were appalling. Sangshak was isolated. The Japanese had cut off the only supply road from Kohima. The airdrop on 23 March was a failure.

Ammunition, water and food were running out: even mule meat went into the cooking pots. Men were weakened, some delirious from dystentery and lack of sleep. They were pleading for more ammunition and grenades. On the evening of the 24th there was very heavy shelling and mortar fire, followed by a very savage attack on the 152 Btn's sector of the perimeter near the church. The enemy managed to gain a footing in some of the forward positions but was eventually driven out with heavy casualties. By 25 March everyone was physically exhausted by the continuous fighting on this sector and no one expected to survive. None complained.

At 4 a.m. on the 25th the Japanese made a further large-scale attack against the church position, preceded by very heavy artillery, mortar and small arms fire. They broke into the position but were driven out several times during the next few hours. Lieutenant Nakamura was killed. Still they came on. Fighting took place inside the church itself and after the garrison had all been killed or wounded, the defenders were unable to retake it. The enemy attacked in overwhelming numbers and used fresh troops for each attack. They were now well into this corner of the perimeter and into the gun and mortar battery positions, setting up their machine guns in the 152nd and 153rd trenches, despite a courageous resistance put up by the Gunners. In 152 Btn all the company commanders had been killed or badly wounded. The remaining men were withdrawn to new positions behind the church.

JBS:

> My men and I were fighting for our lives, hand to hand, when a grenade exploded and knocked me out. A fellow soldier's body fell on top of me. The Japanese came through bayonetting our men but they must have thought I was dead. A counter-attack finally drove the Japanese back again. When I regained consciousness, I found I was the only one left alive.

Most of the junior officers and many of the VCOs and NCOs were casualties. In Battalion HQ both the Signal and Intelligence Officers had been killed. The weapon pits were a shambles of dead and dying, both our own and Japanese. It was impossible to be certain who was still alive. Major Smith and Major Lock commanding the Mortar and Gun batteries were both killed fighting gallantly in counter-attacks to save their battery positions. The Bde Commander tried to restore the situation by using his own reserve, the Bde HQ Defence Platoon. This platoon has been originally from Mahrattas of 153 Btn and was commanded by Lieutenant de la Haye.[15]

Lieutenant Robert de la Haye of the 152nd, nicknamed 'The Red Shadow', was seen checking his equipment and calmly combing his hair. Ordered by Thompson to retake the church area, he was heard to say: 'Oh, I do believe it's another counter attack', before leading his men forward. As they tried to fight their way up to the church, they were shot down in minutes by withering fire from Japanese LMGs and mortars from the edge of the surrounding jungle. Repeated counter-attacks with bayonet and kukri were repelled by the Japanese.[16]

Colonel Hopkinson decided to attempt once more to restore the position. Having gathered every man he could find from amongst the personnel, runners, signallers and orderlies, he led a counter-attack in a vain attempt to regain the church position. It was very much a forlorn hope. They made it into some of their positions, but because of a lack of grenades could not hold against a counter-attack. Hopkinson was badly wounded by a grenade, with shrapnel from the exploding device injuring his leg and foot. The men next to him were killed or seriously wounded.

The HQ then took the risk of leaving part of the 153 Btn's perimeter very lightly held and 'A' Coy 153 Btn, under the command of Major Roberts' 153rd Btn, fired their howitzers over open sights before making a valiant attack which stabilised the position temporarily. The church position was still firmly in Japanese hands. The remaining guns, mortars and the field ambulance were now exposed to fire from the church position and had to be moved back towards the centre of the perimeter where there was little cover. After this there was a lull in the fighting, whilst the enemy reorganised and prepared for fresh attacks.[17]

Manning the radio as second in command of the Brigade Signals Section was Major Maurice Bell:

> Because the Japs had effectively surrounded us, our only link with 23 Div. was by wireless and this was, to say the least, tenuous. The set itself was not powerful enough for the distance involved – about thirty miles 'as the crow flies' – and we were using 'sky wave', bouncing our transmission signals off an ionized layer which reflected them back to earth, hopefully around Imphal. The altitude of the Heaviside layer varied through the 24 hours and this required us, and 23 Div., to change frequency from time to time. This was a tricky operation. One lost contact and one just hoped fervently that the theory would work and contact would be restored on the new frequency. Because of the low power of the set, we were also using a directional aerial which had to be tied

> to a tree in the right position. Periodically, the tree or aerial were broken by mortar fire or shells and the aerial had to be repaired and retied. At about 5pm on the 26th March we lost contact and it was not until about 5.30 that we managed to restore service on the new frequency. Conditions were not good enough for speech but our two experienced British operators were able to read the morse signals pretty well, in spite of the 'static' interference so common in mountainous areas. I stayed on to make sure that all was O.K. and to give a hand on the manually operated 'coffee grinder' that generated electricity for the set. This machine was effective and reliable but tiring on the arms.[18]

At 17.45 on the evening of 26 March, the signaller noted down a message received over the crackling radio from Major General Roberts:

> FIGHT YOUR WAY OUT, GO SOUTH THEN WEST. AIR AND TRANSPORT ON LOOKOUT. GOOD LUCK OUR THOUGHTS ARE WITH YOU.
>
> Then the message came. I could barely believe my ears (or the accuracy of my morse reading!) but the operator was writing what I thought I was hearing. A moment of bliss as there dawned the possibility – however slim – of a future life. Then came the doubts. Firstly, was this a genuine message or something sent by the enemy? Secondly, had the Japs intercepted the message? We had destroyed our code books early in the battle to prevent them falling into Japanese hands and had been communicating 'in clear' ever since. On the first issue, we asked for information on personnel in Brigade Signals. This was personal stuff unlikely to be known by Japanese intelligence and included such details as the nicknames of various signalers, including that of the C.O. All the questions were answered promptly and correctly and we were reassured that the message was genuine.
>
> On the second issue we could do nothing. I told the two operators to keep the news to themselves and took the message to Brigade H.Q., wondering on the way how we would cope with the many wounded in the field hospital. There were no helicopters to evacuate the wounded and even those severely wounded could be given only limited treatment. I explained to Colonel Abbott, the Brigade second in command, the possibility that the message may have been intercepted by the enemy. What an opportunity

> for a major ambush! Action was speedy and troops began to leave the site as soon as darkness fell. The suggestion of fighting our way out was discarded because we had very little to fight with and would, anyway, have been vastly outnumbered. Instead we were told to move quietly in small groups, avoiding roads and main tracks which would very probably be controlled by the Japanese. Just in case the enemy were monitoring our radio link and would be alerted if it suddenly fell silent we kept it busy with 'dummy' traffic as long as we possibly could. Then we destroyed the set, picked up our sten guns and joined the last stragglers leaving the site.[19]

On 26 March, with the 5th Indian Div.'s arrival in Imphal, the Brigade's delaying mission was fulfilled and they were ordered to break out and withdraw.

With the sound of the approaching Dakotas' engines, the Japanese were lighting fires, anticipating more parachuted supplies landing in their lines. Hope-Thomson decided the withdrawal would begin after 10.30 p.m. that night. In 152nd Btn 350 of the men were now dead, including 18 of the 25 officers. Only two officers were unwounded, including Sanderson. Given the Japanese mistreatment of prisoners, the Brigade intended to take with them as many of the wounded as possible, either as walking wounded or stretchered.

After firing off all their remaining mortars, and belts of machine-gun bullets, which fortuitously disrupted a planned midnight attack by the Japanese, all guns, mortars and stores etc. which could not be carried were destroyed.

Certain men were given the responsibility for those individual wounded whom it was considered had a chance of surviving the long walk to Imphal. Parties were also detailed to look after and carry any stretcher cases who might survive. Many of the wounded who had received treatment, however, were scattered around in any slit trenches available to give them some protection against the constant shelling. It was difficult at night to locate them and judge which were too badly wounded to have a chance of surviving the journey. Many had been given morphine and could do little to help themselves or even realise what was happening.[20]

It was difficult to ensure that, when the time came for the break-out, everyone received the order to go. There were cases where the order never reached individuals of the Battalion who were holding the northern face of the perimeter, the opposite side to which the break-out was made.

Some were too worn-out to realise that the time had come. The exhausted survivors of 152nd Btn were channelled through a gap in the rear of the defensive box through the 4th/5th Maratha positions. Only 300 men of the 500 left in the perimeter, out of the original 2,000 contingent, slipped away with the wounded. Several were afterwards captured by a battalion of the Japanese 60th Regt (Uchibori Btn) which had cut the track from Sangshak to Litan.[21]

On the first morning of the Sangshak battle, Lieutenant Basil Seaton had sustained a severe facial wound when a bullet shot away all his teeth and most of his jaw. On the Brigade's evacuation, he was left behind under heavy sedation. Kicked awake on the morning of 27 March by a Japanese soldier, Seaton was as surprised as the Japanese. Without hesitation, he hit the soldier below the belt, scuttled off into the jungle and dived into heavy undergrowth. When darkness fell, he crept down the track to the Sangshak village clearing and headed for Imphal. Seeing an enemy soldier coming along the track, Seaton lay motionless. When the soldier put his hand on Seaton's head, after a brief struggle, Seaton swung up his Paratrooper's fighting knife into the man's stomach and neck. Pausing only to collect two grenades from the body (for catching fish), and without food, water, map or compass, Seaton moved west towards the three ranges of hills, rejoining a colleague of his battalion on the way. Maurice Bell, who lived to 96 years old, noted that Seaton's trek back lasted three weeks.[22] *JBS* recalls the arduous journey back to Imphal:

> We were paired up with walking wounded. I treked through the jungle with two others, at one point hiding motionless amongst bamboos when a Japanese patrol passed by. One of the wounded was a very tough fellow officer of 152nd Btn who had much of his jaw blown away. (He later had his jaw wired up.) Left wounded at Sangshak, he had pulled a Japanese soldier down and killed him with his knife before escaping. We had been told to climb over the ranges, running north to south and then turn west, which involved many steep climbs over the ranges. We had to take long detours, often cutting through thick growth with Gurkha knives, to avoid the many Japanese troops, moving in great numbers up the tracks in the direction of Imphal. The Japanese had occupied the Naga villages and the villagers were hiding in the jungle. I was determined not to be captured by the Japanese – we all knew about their treatment of Allied prisoners. The journey back took us three weeks, although other parties did make it back to Imphal in a few days.

Maurice Bell described his way home:

> I began badly by tripping and falling from the path we were on, to one about 40 feet below, where I bumped in to another group, comprising a British sergeant from the Mountain Battery, three or four Gurkhas and a similar number of Indians, all strangers to each other. We were all exhausted from lack of sleep and hungry from lack of food. I had a compass but none of us had a map. I agreed with the sergeant that we would take turns in leading with the other one bringing up the rear. We set off in single file through the mountains that surround the Imphal Plain keeping to rough tracks in the higher altitudes. It took us five days but we all made it and rejoined our respective units now forming part of the defence ring being hastily formed around Imphal. We now had food but catching up on sleep would have to wait.[23]

The 50th Bde war diaries show that survivors from Sangshak gradually struggled back to Imphal, where the Brigade was immediately allotted a portion of the perimeter to defend. The wounded Lieutenant Colonel Hopkinson, Basil Seaton and two other officers were immediately evacuated by air. On 2 April Major General Roberts of 23rd Div. addressed the Battalion officers and NCO, thanking them for their efforts at Sheldons Corner and Sangshak. Survivors were reporting in between 3 and 24 April, after the arduous walk back through the jungle and along Naga tracks from Sangshak: 10 men arrived on 3 April, 10 on 7th, 7 men on the 9th and 2 men on the 20th April; 25 Indian troops arrived on 21 April, having escaped from Japanese captivity. On 24 April the last survivor reported in, some twenty-nine days after the break-out. Major John Sanderson was probably one of the two men who walked into Imphal on 20 April, twenty-five days after the break-out. Sanderson would have been held up, supporting his wounded comrade.[24]

The Brigade had resisted the ferocious Japanese assault on Sangshak for six days in appalling conditions, refusing to surrender and inflicting heavy casualties on the attackers, in spite of their own very heavy losses, 40 officers and 585 men. Through their sacrifice, the 14th Army was prepared and equipped to fight the Japanese to a standstill at Kohima and Imphal, at the gateway to India.

The 50th Indian Parachute Bde's achievement was recognised in a Special Order of the Day issued by General William Slim on 31 August, acknowledging their role in delaying the Japanese advance on Kohima for a valuable week and giving the 14th Army the breathing space it needed to move up men and supplies to reinforce Kohima.

Gladys Sanderson, John's mother, wrote: 'John's commanding officer later called on Alex and I in Beckenham to tell us that our son deserved a Military Cross for bravery. However, delay, and the state of the war in India, blocked such recommendations.'

Hope-Thomson's request for a decoration for the Intelligence Officer, who had carried the captured Japanese battle plans back to Imphal from Shangshak, was not actioned. After his march back to Imphal, he was evacuated back to England with concussion, before he could write a full report on the Sangshak battle. In spite of 50th Parachute Bde's stoic achievement in delaying the Japanese advance on Kohima, their efforts were not officially recognised for a considerable time. They were for many years a forgotten brigade, in a forgotten army.

Churchill made no mention of the stubborn March defence at Sangshak in his detailed account of this critical time in the Burma campaign which focused on the heroic Kohima and Imphal resistance:

> By the end of March the Japanese had cut the road to Dimapur and were pressing hard on the fringes of the Imphal plain from three sides. The 5th Indian Division was flown into Imphal from the Arakan front . . . and the 7th Indian Division was flown into Dimapur. At Kohima, a roadside town that commanded the pass to the Assam Valley, the Japanese northern attack was held. Here the garrison . . . was attacked on April 4th by the Japanese 31st Division, slowly forced back into a diminishing area, and finally on to a single hill. They had no supplies except what was dropped on them by parachutes. Attacked on every side, they held on steadfastly, supported by bombing and cannon-fire from the air, until they were relieved on April 20th by the 161st Indian Brigade. 4,000 Japanese were killed. The valiant defence of Kohima against enormous odds was a fine episode.[25]

The historian Julian Thompson noted that the delay involved in fighting at Sangshak completely wrecked the Japanese 31st Div.'s timetable for the march on Kohima, which allowed time for the 161st Indian Infantry Bde to arrive from the Arakan. The 'totally unjustified' dismissal of 50th Indian Parachute Bde's Brigadier Hope-Thomson, the leader of this heroic stand at Sangshak, followed 'recriminations that made him a scapegoat for the events that followed at Kohima and Imphal'.[26]

Lieutenant General Kotoku Sato remained for many years bitter about the lives lost and the time delay caused by Major General Miyazaki Shigesaburo's attack on Sangshak, which inflicted 16 per cent casualties on the Japanese and which 'undoubtedly had an adverse effect on the final operation at Kohima'. Sangshak was not in Mizazaki's operational zone and Japanese historians still question why he attacked there.

Maurice Bell was proud of his brigade's stubborn resistance at Sangshak:

> My memories fade but recollections of the battle at Sangshak remain as vivid as ever and will doubtless remain so until I die. In ferocity and casualties, Sangshak far exceeded anything in my experience of the war. Our orders were to fight to the last man in order to delay as long as possible the advance of the Japanese in their drive towards Imphal and Kohima. Every day counted and there was no hope of reinforcements.
>
> On Sangshak Day and the British Day of Remembrance in November especially, I recall Sangshak and mourn the deaths of so many brave men, including several of my close friends. Desperate situations produce acts of great bravery and I was proud to be a member of the Indian Army. Blessed are the peace makers.[27]

> They shall grow not old, as we that are left grow old:
> Age shall not weary them, nor the years condemn.
> At the going down of the sun and in the morning,
> We will remember them.[28]

Chapter 8

D-Day, 1944

They went with songs to the battle, they were young.
Straight of limb, true of eye, steady and aglow.
They were staunch to the end against odds uncounted,
They fell with their faces to the foe.[1]

A D-Day parachutist, a future York and Lancaster regimental colleague and a close friend of John Sanderson, and the author, was Captain John Sim MC of the 12th Parachute Btn, 6th Airborne Div. Sim landed on French soil in the early hours of 6 June 1944.

> Finally the evening came – the evening of 5th June, when we got into our lorries and we were transported to the airfield. We collected the chutes and the lorries took us around the perimeter, miles away into the countryside where our aircraft had been dispersed. It was a peaceful June evening – lovely and calm.
>
> We just sat and talked for a while amongst ourselves, and then the padre came whipping up in his Jeep and we had a little prayer. He wished us well before he dashed off again to another aircraft. Then came the Jeep of the RAF crew roaring up, and they got out and said, 'All right, you chaps. Don't worry! Piece of cake! We'll get you there!' It was a tremendous, exciting, light hearted atmosphere.

Approaching the French coast, Sim described the view from the Short Sterling's open door:

> With about five minutes to go, we all moved up closer. I was astride the door, looking down at the sea. I hoped to see some of the task force – some of the Armada – but I didn't see any ships at all, just the speckly wave tops of the sea below me. Suddenly

> I saw the parallel lines of waves coming ashore on the dark yellow beach, then a cliff, woods, copses, hedgerows – this was all about 800 feet below me. It was a moonlit night so I could see the ground quite easily. Then – red light on, green light and I jumped. The noise of the engine, the clean, crisp rush of air behind the ears and around one's body and then quietness. After the swelling of the chute above, as it developed, sensations quickly followed one another, and I found myself floating lazily down and, it seemed alone. I landed without any harm in a field, just to the side of a grazing horse and I had others landing around me.[2]

Warrant Officer Ted Cooper, also a post-war friend of Sanderson, had a memorable experience later that day, with a bird's eye view of D-Day from the air. Judged an 'exceptional' Spitfire pilot in his logbook, Cooper had recently returned from instructing Commonwealth trainee pilots in Canada and was himself on a normal training flight over the Channel in a Gloster Meteor jet. Flying out of the clouds with his flying instructor, Cooper was astonished to find himself over an 'Armada' of Allied aircraft heading south, and stretching as far as the eye could see. The Meteor pilots knew nothing of D-Day: it was all classified 'Top Secret'. When the Normandy bound flights' escorting Spitfires and Hurricanes turned without hesitation towards the intruding Meteor, Ted Cooper and his flight instructor scuttled off back into cloud cover.[3]

On the ground shortly before 1 a.m. on D-Day on his designated drop zone east of the River Orne, Captain Sim was amongst the first British soldiers in France. Major John Howard and his troops had landed in Horsa gliders at 12.16 a.m. to seize the Bénouville (later 'Pegasus') Bridge, over the Caen Canal and the Ranville Bidge (later 'Horsa') over the River Orne. It was imperative to hold these two bridges: the Orne River was a natural barrier to any German counter-attack on the Allied invasion flank. Furthermore, the bridges had to be held undamaged to enable the Allies to advance from the beaches. The 6th Airborne was protecting the east flank of the Allies' invasion and needed a bridge to bring its supplies up from Sword Beach.[4] Thus 12th Btn's task was to prevent the enemy using the two bridges to disrupt the Allied beach landings to the west. By 4 a.m. the battalion was digging defensive positions around the hamlet of Le Bas de Ranville. Sim was commanding an outpost line of only a dozen men with two machine guns, a 6-pounder anti-tank gun and a FOB (Forward Observation Officer) with a radio link to the twelve 6in guns of the cruiser HMS *Mauritius*. Positioned 300yd east of the rest of their battalion, they were amongst the most advanced British troops in Normandy, deep in German-held territory.

> My particular task was to command a forward screen in a hedgerow. By first light my party was dug in and well camouflaged. The FOB was engaged in ranging the cruiser's guns on likely targets, while one of my snipers scored a hit on a man 400 yards away. At about 10 a.m. we spotted some men positioning a gun on a hill towards Caen. My FOB directed fire on them and they vanished. Then came a long wait.
>
> At about 11 a.m. we were surprised to see a company of about fifty men straggling across our front from the left. They were wearing parachute-type steel helmets and camouflaged smocks. They were about 300 yards away across a large open field. (Then) they changed direction and advanced in line towards us. I asked the FOB to direct the cruiser's guns on them but . . . they were firing on a priority target. Meanwhile the enemy continued to advance, knee deep in long grass. . . . our plan was not to open fire until the enemy had come within 50 yards of us where there was a barbed wire cattle fence. We watched and waited as the enemy came closer and closer. When they reached the fence, I fired a Verey light straight at them and my men opened fire. The enemy went to ground in the long grass. Simultaneously, two self-propelled 88 guns lumbered up from behind a ridge to our front and opened fire while on the move. They stopped 70 yards from us, a sitting target for our 6-pounder anti-tank gun, but no gun opened fire. Shortly after a soldier crawled up to me on hands and knees and saluted! He was very sorry but the 6-pounder could not fire . . . and must have been damaged in the glider landing.
>
> We were now suffering casualties rather quickly. The man on my right was dead. Another of my men, while crawling up to me moaning and groaning, slumped over before he could reach me and lay still . . . The FOB had been badly wounded. Meanwhile the enemy, under the covering fire of the self-propelled guns, were crawling around to my right flank.
>
> As so often happens in action, all fire suddenly ceased and silence reigned for a while . . . Peeping through the thick hedge, I saw a German soldier standing up in another hedge running at right angles to our own. I ordered my batman to have a shot at him. The self-propelled guns had quietened down – one of them was

> only firing spasmodically into our position. To my amazement, I saw a hatch of one open and a German officer, splendidly arrayed in polished jackboots, stiff cap and Sam Browne, leisurely climb down and light a cigarette. He was allowed two puffs only.
>
> Again we were subjected to fire but this time from mortars, the bombs airbursting in the hedgerow trees. Most uncomfortable – and we could do little but keep our heads down and hope for the best while the hell lasted. Again that sudden silence. One of my sergeants . . . informed me that that there were only four of us left alive and asked what we were to do. . . . The four of us – my sergeant, my batman, a sniper and myself – made use of a shallow ditch, covering each other, leapfrog fashion, running a few yards, crawling, firing and so back to our position: the Germans firing wildly at us most of the time. Soon after we had evacuated the forward position, it was subjected to 3 inch mortar fire and re-occupied, the Germans having had enough and withdrawn. The FOB, badly wounded in the thigh, and two other badly wounded men were taken away by stretcher bearers, the remainder lay dead at their posts. The two self-propelled German guns were later destroyed by six-pounder anti-tank guns.[5]

Captain Sim was awarded the Military Cross for his action in defence of this vital outpost. 'He so fought his little force that the fifty German infantry were held and the three self-propelled guns were forced into point blank range . . . By his personal example of conspicuous gallantry he held together his force and warded off the attack for 2 vital hours. This enabled a redistribution of troops to meet the armoured threat, thereby ensuring the safety of the vital ridge held by airborne troops.'[6] In the early afternoon men of Lord Lovat's commando brigade linked up with them and Ranville became the first village in France to be liberated by the Allies.

Four days after getting his MC, Sim received a small, deep 'blighty' wound during the battalion's attack on the village of Bréville, which stood on high ground overlooking the bridges. He recovered and, in December 1944, fought in the Battle of the Bulge, supporting the overstretched US forces. Later, on 24 March 1945 Sim took part in Operation VARSITY, his second airborne operation, the attack on the east bank of the Rhine to prevent German counter-attacks on the Allied armour, as they crossed the river. Involving two airborne divisions with 15,000 men, it was the largest daytime airborne drop in history, achieving all its objectives within the one day. In 2006 Major Sim described to the author, his panoramic 'front row' position, standing in the open door of his plane within the impressive vista of a sky full of British planes, heading over the Rhine. As soon as his feet hit the ground and he was rolling up his chute, he saw a German officer running towards him with his hands outstretched in the air.

Sim was next flown to the Far East to prepare, like his Pegasus colleague John Sanderson, for Operation ZIPPER on Malaya which happily was aborted. When Sim did land in Singapore, he was appointed commandant of the notorious Changi jail, many of whose Japanese inmates were later tried and executed for war crimes.[7]

JBS recalled his family's stories of wartime Britain:

> In Beckenham, from June 1944, my father posted my little sister Janet, nearly eight years of age, to keep watch on the balcony of our house for the pilotless V-1 flying bombs. At night the V-1's exhausts could be seen from far away. When she spotted a noisy 'doodlebug' coming – one could hear them from 10 miles away – she would blew hard on her policeman's whistle and the family would all head down to my father's air raid shelter. His cellar bunker was solidly constructed with reinforced concrete and thick wooden railway sleepers, as you would expect from a Great War Tunneller.

Above little Janet's head, nearer the coast in Kent, RAF pilots were learning to bring down the pulse jet-powered V-1s with specially tuned Spitfires and fast jets: Hawker Tempests and Meteors. To shoot at V-1s with their cannon risked detonating the bomb's 3,000lb of explosive. By 28 July, thirty-two pilots of 616 Squadron had been converted in great secrecy to Meteors, flying seven jets out of RAF Manston. Frank Whittle's turbojet engines enabled the Meteors to intercept these V-1 flying bombs. Pilots developed the technique of flying their all-metal Meteor alongside the V-1, positioning their wingtip under the V-1's wing, then flipping it over to confuse its gyro and send it crashing to the ground. The Meteors' final tally was fourteen V-1 'kills'. By August 1944 80 per cent of V-1s were being destroyed, 1,000 by aircraft.[8]

In June 1944, Major Alexander Sanderson wrote to his son in the Far East, about an army career when the war was won:

> My dear John,
>
> We were so pleased to get your long letter telling us all about you joining the Parachute Regiment. What you wanted to do that for I don't know and yet I suppose I would have done the same myself under the circumstances, so I must say no more

about that. It must be a very thrilling experience. If I were not so old, I would like to go through it myself. No doubt many Parachute Regiments will be formed in future. It will become one of our main fighting features. I can imagine the Gurkhas taking to it like ducks to water. The principal training will not be the actual jumping but the methods to be adapted for quick cooperation on landing in enemy territory. Plenty of speed and pluck provide the best means of dealing with the Japanese and, if applied in force, you will find they will run like hell. There will be plenty of good interesting jobs in the Army of Occupation in Germany if you are accepted into the Regular Army. I have been very busy filling out estimates for about a million pounds war damage repairs still to be done to the London Underground, that is if the Government will allow us to make a start.

Your loving father

Gladys noted in her diary:

[12 June 1944] An article in the *Evening News* by L. Artic sums up our feeling on the invasion of Europe:

What is the most remarkable thing about the way the nation heard last week's momentous news? It is that people heard it with complete steadiness. There was no exultant hanging out of flags. There were no excited parades. No bands played. No crowds gathered elatedly. People's hearts quickened when they heard that the long suspense had ended. They felt the thrill of battle, but they did not need any orators to tell them their kinsmen and friends across the water were only at the start of a deadly and hazardous adventure.

Gladys described the V-1 attacks that began on 13 June:

[18 June 1944] German jet propelled planes were passing over last night. They fell in Beckenham. A piece of one fell in Mr Cox's garden at the end of our road. Several more came over during the day – but I think we are mastering them. It's certainly a devilish clever invention. I wouldn't be surprised if one day, when Mr Hitler knows he's beat, he'll send gas over by these pilotless planes. We've beaten his U-boats and in a few hours mastered his magnetic mine – soon we'll discover how to stop

> these. They are shooting them down fast at the coast. Yesterday we saw two Spitfires chasing one – must be dangerous for our boys to fly near.

General Montgomery said in a broadcast on the BBC from his HQ in France: 'All soldiers serving under me send their best wishes to their wives and families, wherever they may be. We in France are in very good heart and we hope that all is well with you at home.'

> [19 June 1944] We slept in the cellar last night. We have been a bit anxious to what extent Hitler can launch these pilotless planes against you. For four days he has been shooting them over here – they are something like a Spitfire to look at, can go at over 300 miles an hour – jet propelled we think – they make a noise like a motorbike engine. Suddenly they stop and drop within 5 seconds to the ground. One yesterday fell on a country church – 150 worshippers inside – many hurt and killed. It kind of fascinates you to watch them and how fast they are flying through the sky. We will certainly find a way to stop them – they say we are shooting them down in hundreds on the coast – there are certainly less today. There were two when Janet and I were coming back from shopping – we did not have time to get home after the warning. Just shows you what inhuman brutes the Germans are to send things like that to drop on civilians. Tony says they only make a small crater – but the blast is terrific. Brings houses down. The schools are closed today. Tony has been helping nail paper on windows damaged in a house in our avenue. I mated the Dutch rabbit today.

In Berlin also citizens were breeding rabbits to provide extra food. They called them 'balcony pigs'.[9]

Chapter 9

SOE – RAF Operations from Italy, 1944

A future SIS close colleague of John Sanderson was Major Peter Greenhalgh DFC TD of the Royal Artillery. John and Peter would be posted to Paris together in the autumn of 1948, attached to the British Embassy. In 1951 Sanderson would take over from Greenhalgh as head of the SIS listening station in Edirne, Turkey.

Major Greenhalgh, although an artillery man, had seen repeated service aboard RAF aircraft.

> On the night of 12/13th February 1944, Major Greenhalgh was flying in an aircraft which was severely damaged by anti-aircraft fire, while engaged in marking the target from a height of 200 feet. Casualties were suffered by the crew and Major Greenhalgh himself was slightly wounded. A crash landing was eventually made in Sardinia. While in Sardinia he seized the opportunity to carry out two sorties at Anzio in a Marauder aircraft of the 42nd U.S. Bombardment Division. The sound knowledge of the enemy's defensive system gained from extensive operational experience has been of great assistance to the Group and Major Greenhalgh's keenness and enthusiasm in his work and his gallantry in the face of the enemy has been an example to all.

The citation for his DFC (Distinguished Flying Cross) as RAF 'Flack' Liaison Officer in 1945 would continue:

> Major Greenhalgh has been Anti-Aircraft Air Liaison Officer at HQ No. 5 Group, Bomber Command, for the past eighteen months. During this period, to enable him to assess the enemy's flak potential, he has flown on 22 operational sorties as an Air

Map 6 **1944 FLIGHT LIEUTENANT JOHN ALDWINCKLE'S 148 (SPECIAL DUTIES) SQUADRON RAF - SOE HALIFAX PARACHUTE DROPS TO PARTISANS**

> Gunner or Observer, covering every type of operation undertaken by this Group. He has made a point of flying on operations only against targets where heavy opposition was to be expected.[1]

John Aldwinckle's Work with SOE and the Warsaw Flights, August 1944

Squadron Leader John Aldwinckle would work closely with his friend Lieutenant Colonel Sanderson, both later SIS officers, in the Intelligence Division of SHAPE, NATO's military HQ, near Paris in 1962. This and his previous MI6 work in Berlin during the Cold War (see Chapter 16) was not Aldwinckle's first involvement with the Secret Intelligence Services. In the summer of 1944, he was posted as a navigator with the rank of Flying Officer to 148 Squadron, one of only four RAF 'Special Duties' squadrons. These supplied the SOE (Special Operations Executive) and their various resistance movements with arms and equipment, as well as delivering and retrieving agents from under the noses of the enemy.

Based at Brindisi on the heel of Italy, Aldwinckle flew dozens of missions with 148 Sqn (Squadron) in Halifax aircraft, dropping agents and supplies to the partisans in Yugoslavia, Albania, Northern Italy, Greece and Czechoslovakia. These were very challenging flights across difficult terrain, requiring 'navigation of a very high order . . . that necessitated pin-point accuracy on a small, often ill-defined target after hours of flying across enemy territory'.[2]

In August 1944 Aldwinckle took part in a particularly dangerous mission that has been described as 'in the same category as the raids on the Mohne and Eder dams';[3] 'one of the great unsung sagas of the second world war';[4] and 'a story of the utmost gallantry and self-sacrifice on the part of our aircrew'.[5] Unlike the Dambusters' single sortie, what became known as 'the Warsaw Flights' was a succession of operations carried out in August and September 1944, to supply munitions to the Polish Resistance 'Home Army' during the Warsaw Uprising against their Nazi occupiers.

At the end of July that year, the Soviet Army had made rapid progress in pushing the German Army westwards across Poland to the Vistula River until they were, in the words of Churchill, 'standing before the gates of Warsaw'. Stalin had set up a Polish National Committee of Liberation in Lublin on 23 July and viewed both the Polish national government in exile in London and the Home Guard in Warsaw as undesirable challenges to his plans for a Moscow-controlled Polish government. The Soviets broadcast to the people of Warsaw as they approached the city: 'People of the Capital! To arms! Assist the Red Army in their crossing of the Vistula. Strike at the Germans! Drive out the German invaders and win freedom.'[6] The German garrison, threatened from both the south and east, were preparing to withdraw. On 1 August, Armia Krajowa (AK, the Polish Home Army), anticipating the Soviet Army's crossing of the Vistula, rose up to attack the Germans, to support the Soviet advance and to hasten the liberation of the city.

Although the Home Army was initially successful, the Soviet Army failed to cross the river. The Germans, instead of retreating, retaliated with merciless barbarity, killing thousands of men, women and children in the streets and torching the city. The Polish government in exile appealed to Churchill for help, requesting a large quantity of equipment to be dropped to the Home Army, who were holed up in and around the Old City. The nearest British squadrons to Warsaw at that time were based in southern Italy, a distance of over 800 miles. Dropping anti-tank guns and ammunition into specific streets in central Warsaw, whilst there was fighting on the streets and buildings were ablaze, was described by the British officer commanding the SOE section at Latiano near Brindisi, as something that 'might be done in a taxi but not a Halifax'. Air Marshal Slessor, Commander-in-Chief, RAF Mediterranean and Middle East, advised the Chiefs of Staff in London that he looked upon their request to send aircraft from Italy 'unfavourably'.[7]

Churchill, however, felt that the British could not desert the Poles in their hour of need. So on 4 August, the day Aldwinckle and his fellow crew members arrived at 148 Sqn's Campo Casale airbase, seven Halifax four-engined aircraft from his new squadron and seven from 1586 (Polish) Flight, also based at Brindisi, took off to supply the Polish Home Army with arms and equipment. Their mission was to drop supplies in the Kampinos and Kabaty forests to the north and south of Warsaw, although, contrary to orders, two of the Polish crews made drops on the city of Warsaw itself.

One of the Polish RAF pilots was Tadeusz Roman, a 25-year-old who had spent time in a Soviet prison when fleeing eastern Poland. A keen flyer, after the 1941 armistice he made his way to Britain, where he joined Bomber Comand. Roman was pleased to be able to fly to help Warsaw: 'They were my friends. My brother was there (in Poland) in the underground army – he could have been in Warsaw. Nobody refused (to help), not a single person. It was a long trip and the Germans knew we were coming.'[8]

Of the seven 148 Sqn Halifaxes that took off that day, one burst into flames on the runway, another successfully dropped supplies over the target, a third failed to do so and the remaining four did not return, shot down by night fighter aircraft over Poland.[9] It was not the most auspicious start to the new crews' arrival and must have made them fearful of what was to come. For the time being, Slessor instructed 148 Sqn not to fly any further missions to Poland.

On the ground in Warsaw, the situation was bleak. The Germans continued to massacre the civilian population and the Russians still refused to cross the Vistula. On 12 August, Churchill realised that the Soviets were not going to aid the Poles and that 'the airlift was of little military use'. However, despite the high casualty rate, not assisting the Poles was politically difficult. Churchill 'came to a painful decision. Help must be sent, he declared, even at the risk of heavy losses'.[10] The following day seven 148 Sqn crew, including Flying Officer Aldwinckle and his new Canadian pilot, Pilot Officer 'Mac' Maclean, were ordered to fly to Warsaw. For the first time, 148 Sqn and 1586 Flight were joined in Brindisi by two Liberator squadrons, 178 (RAF) and 31 (SAAF (South African Air Force)).

When all twenty-seven crews were assembled in the briefing room, the operations officer began by saying: 'Gentlemen, your target for tonight is Warsaw'. The Liberator squadrons greeted this announcement with nervous laughter, but he repeated: 'This is no joke. Your target is Warsaw'. For a moment there was silence, followed by a solitary 'Good God!' from the back of the room.[11] Warsaw lay 1,311km (815 miles) from Brindisi. The chosen route to Poland took the form of an elongated lozenge, with Brindisi at the southern end and Warsaw at the northern tip, a round trip of over 1,750 miles, more than twice the Halifax's maximum still-air range with a heavy load.[12]

The aircraft took off in the evening over the Adriatic, crossed the Croatian coast in the last rays of the setting sun, overflew the Danube in Hungary in darkness, and climbed north east over the Carpathians, before approaching Warsaw from the east, over Soviet-held territory. The return journey over Poland, Czechoslovakia, Hungary and Yugoslavia brought the fliers back to Brindisi the following morning after over 11 hours in the air.

The airmen faced many dangers. They had no fighter escort, relying only on their own guns to ward off German fighter planes, they were fully visible crossing the Adriatic coast in both directions, and they passed close to a German night-fighter training centre, several night-fighter zones, patrolled by Luftwaffe squadrons on the hunt for Allied planes, and numerous anti-aircraft batteries.[13] As the aircraft had no navigational aids, such as Gee, which were denied to Mediterranean based Special Duties squadrons, navigators had to rely on map-reading and dead-reckoning, forcing pilots to fly at low altitude for much of the journey, so that sites on the ground could be visually identified.[14]

This made them easy targets for anti-aircraft batteries and enemy fighter aircraft. And, as the crews were to discover, they were fired at, not only by the enemy, but also by their Russian allies when they flew over Soviet-held airspace. Furthermore, electrical storms were a common hazard in summer over the Carpathians, and pilots frequently reported instances of St Elmo's fire, when blue flames trailed from wingtips and propeller blades.[15]

Handley-Page Halifax heavy bombers were notoriously difficult to fly and were often referred to by their crews as 'flying coffins'. Each was filled with 2,300 gallons of fuel for the Warsaw flights, instead of a more normal load of 1,800 gallons. This extra fuel, along with their heavy cargo, made them even more difficult to get airborne and harder to handle in flight. For accuracy, a low-level drop was essential: height 150ft and speed 125mph. Target maps and photographs were provided by the briefing officer and three aligning points were given: Mokotov in the south, the Old City in the centre and the Citadel in the north. The mission target was to drop supply canisters attached to parachutes, containing anti-tank weapons, grenades, ammunition and medical supplies, to the Home Army in Krasinski Square. There, the crews were told, young women would shine torches into the sky to guide them to the drop zone. The crews were told to fly up the Vistula until they reached the third bridge, the Kierbedz Bridge between the Old Town and the suburb of Praga, and then to turn sharply to port. (They later learned that the women holding the torches were easy targets for German snipers and that whenever one fell, another quickly recovered the torch and took her place.)

As a result of the Soviets refusing the RAF permission to overfly their territory, each crew member was issued with 'blood chits' in case they had to ditch on Soviet-occupied territory. These were silk, with a Union Jack on one side and wording such as 'this chap is a British officer. If you return him in good shape and working order, you will be rewarded'. On the reverse side, the same message in Russian. Crews for the Warsaw operations were briefed to say nothing other than their rank, name and number if they fell into Russian hands, as with the Germans.[16] Three of the seven 148 Sqn aircraft became unserviceable before take-off. Aldwinckle's crew in Halifax JP 263 got airborne at 8.35 p.m. Flying singly, not in formation, at a low altitude and, in broad daylight, he plotted a route north over the Adriatic, crossing the Dalmatian coast near Dubrovnik. As the Carpathians loomed, Aldwinckle was alarmed by the rising crescendo from the aircraft's loud Merlin engines as 'Mac' pulled back on the control column to climb rapidly, straining to lift the aircraft over the mountains, which rise to over 8,500ft. One of the four remaining squadron aircraft could not gain sufficient height to cross the mountains and was forced to return to base, as did four of the Liberators, caught in a thunderstorm. Once over the Carpathians, as they descended into the plain of Poland, east of Kraców, Mac called Aldwinckle up to the cockpit. From there, they could see the red glow of the sky above Warsaw, over 150 miles to the north. As they got closer, it was as if:

> the city was covered by an inverted fish bowl, inside which the night was a dull red. Individual fires and gun flashes showed up as bright sparks; flak streamed across the area or burst above the dome amidst the coning searchlight. Inside the red dome, aircraft were seen in silhouette against the fiery city as they made their low-level dropping run.[17]

All three remaining 148 Sqn aircraft made it to Warsaw. The aircraft dropped to around 700ft, as they approached the city and the very dense barrage over the Vistula. From inside the aircraft, John could see only a red glow through the Perspex glass of the front gunner's turret and the bomb aimer's window. A vivid description of what happened is provided by one of the other pilots:

> Fires were burning in every district of Warsaw. The dark spots were places occupied by the Jerries. Everything was smothered in smoke through which ruddy orange flames flickered. It was terrible and must have been hell for everyone down there. The German flak was the hottest I have ever been through, so we got down to just 70 or 100 feet . . . The flicks [searchlights] in the Praga and Mokotov suburbs kept us constantly lit up – there was nothing we could do about it. We nearly hit the Poniatovski Bridge as we cracked along the Vistula: the pilot hopped over it by the skin of his teeth.
>
> Our reception point was Krashinski Square. So, when we passed the [Kierbedz] iron-girder bridge, we turned sharp to port and made ready for the run-in. The whole southern side of the square was blazing and wind was blowing the smoke south . . . We dropped the containers . . . It was time to clear out. The pilot came down still lower, keeping an eye for steeples and high buildings. The cabin was full of smoke, which got into our eyes and made them smart. We could feel the heat . . . We ripped along the railway line leading west [to Prushkov and Skiernievitse]. Some flak from an anti-aircraft train tried to hit us, so we let go

> some bursts. We had a breathing space until flicks near Bohnia picked us up again.[18]

On the way back, as Aldwinckle's aircraft reached the Adriatic coast, the fuel tanks were registering empty. All the crew strapped on their parachutes, expecting to be told by Mac at any moment to bail out, or for the aircraft to ditch in the sea. Somehow, there was just enough fuel to get them back to Brindisi, but when they landed and the ground crew looked inside the fuel tanks, they were completely dry. Aldwinckle's log book records arriving back at base at 7.40 a.m., a total flying time of 11 hours and 5 minutes.

The US Ambassador Averell Harriman met Soviet Foreign Ministry officials on the night of 15 August and afterwards sent a telegram to Washington: 'The Soviet Government's refusal [to help Warsaw] is not based on operational difficulties, nor on a denial of the conflict, but on ruthless political calculations.' A week later Stalin described the Polish Home Army as a 'gang of criminals', refusing to help the Allies with the air supply.[19]

Aldwinckle returned to Poland on 18/19 August, dropping arms and ammunition to the Polish underground near Łódź, 80 miles west of Warsaw. For the rest of August and most of September, his squadron and the three other squadrons continued to fly missions to Poland, some to Warsaw but mostly to the Kampinos forest or central Poland.[20]

Tadeusz's aircraft flew back to Warsaw on 28 August. At 2,000ft, just after unloading his supplies over Warsaw, one of his engines was struck by anti-aircraft fire. Over Kraków the aircraft received another hit. In spite of the damage, he coaxed the aircraft back to crash on the perimeter of the Brindisi airbase, with only 5 minutes' worth of fuel in his tanks. Tadeusz, later awarded the DFC for this mission, fell on his knees and kissed the ground. His was the only aircraft of the flight of four in his mission that returned safely.[21]

The Soviets did themselves finally drop – literally – 50 tons of supplies on Warsaw between 14 and 28 September. Cynically, the supplies were unloaded from aircraft without parachutes and most were destroyed on impact. A young Halina Szopińska who witnessed the drops called them a sham: 'They had small planes and would throw dry bread without a parachute and when it fell it would just break into powder . . . They would drop guns without a parachute as well. There was no way we could repair it. So they pretended they were helping.'[22]

The Soviets not only failed to cross the Vistula but on 22 August the Soviet Interior Ministry, the NKVD (People's Commissariat for Internal

Affairs), ordered that all Polish insurgents who fell into Soviet hands were to be arrested and disarmed. For sixty-three days, until they surrendered to the Germans on 2 October, the Home Army battled the SS and the Wehrmacht in the city's cellars and sewers. Defenceless civilians had been slaughtered in their tens of thousands every week. Before they withdrew, the Germans took their revenge by razing almost the entire city to the ground. A ¼ million Poles were killed in the 2 months of resistance and Warsaw lay in ruins as Soviet troops continued to watch from across the river.[23] Many historians trace the beginning of the Cold War to this moment.

SOE's 'History of Special Operations (Air) in the Mediterranean Theatre' records that 'from the air point of view, these flights to Warsaw probably rank amongst the most difficult operations, of any description, undertaken by Air Force units during the European war'.[24] The RAF and SAAF lost one aircraft for every ton of supplies delivered. Of 186 sorties attempted from Italy between 8 August and 22 September 1944, less than half were successful, with 31 aircraft lost and 155 aircrew killed, including 76 Polish airmen, 37 from the SAAF and 39 from the RAF. A further 49 aircrew were captured and interned or imprisoned in POW (prisoner of war) camps. The level of casualties, an appalling 16.8 per cent, was amongst the highest of the war for any RAF mission.[25] Aldwinckle was very lucky to survive, although no doubt good piloting and accurate navigation played their part. In Warsaw, following its liberation in January 1945 by the Red Army, came squads of NKVD to seize the surviving members of the Home Army and install their own Communist stooges. They were commanded by General Ivan Serov, who would later head the KGB and the GRU and play a crucial part in the suppression of the Hungarian Revolution in 1956.[26] One Nikita Khrushchev, who had been present in 1939 during the Russian invasion of East Poland, would arrive in Warsaw in 1945 to coordinate the reconstruction of the city's electricity, water and sewerage systems (Khrushchev also later oversaw the construction of the Moscow underground).[27]

While John Aldwinckle was flying missions with 148 Sqn, unbeknown to him, his fiancée, Helene Taylor, was working as a codebreaker in Hut 6 at GC & CS at Bletchley Park in England. Recruited in 1942 straight from university, she deciphered German Abwehr and Luftwaffe Enigma codes using traffic analysis techniques. In 1943 Helene was chosen by Hut 6 chief Gordon Welchman to instruct arriving Americans on the secret workings of Bletchley Park, including Colossus, the world's first programmable computer. In an interview she gave in 2013 to the Bletchley Park Oral History Project, she explained how, after she became Mrs Aldwinckle, she celebrated VE Day with her husband:[28]

> I was married in February 1945. VE Day [Victory in Europe Day] was an adventure for me in itself! I am not in the well-known photograph of Hut 3 and Hut 6 people on VE-Day, seen in some the Bletchley Park books. I had gone down to London to celebrate with my husband. John had been with an RAF special duties squadron, dropping SOE agents, and had arrived back in England only two days prior to VE Day, en route for London. I had no idea how to find out where he was and he didn't know where I was. Jack Winton, who was in charge of the business side of things at Bletchley (recruitment and administration, etc.), was so good to me: against the rules, he told me that my husband was staying overnight in Harrogate. My problem though was how to phone Harrogate: there was no telephone in my digs. The only place I could try was the Galleon pub, which involved crossing a dark field during the blackout! Then, out of the blue, a chap who I knew at Bletchley Park got on my bus. I told him my story and he offered to walk me across the field. As we walked in, everyone started clapping. He was the musician Daniel Jones (whose 4th Symphony was written in memory of his close friend Dylan Thomas) and they were pleased to see him because they knew his arrival meant that he was going to play the piano for them! He helped me ring Harrogate and I was able to arrange to meet my husband and celebrate VE Day with him in London. I stayed on after VE day and worked on the history of Hut 6. I knew I wasn't going to stay on with GCHQ. In those days, you had to leave if you were a woman and got married. We were all bound by the Official Secrets Act, of course, and didn't talk about our work with anyone, not even after the war.

The historian Hugh Trevor-Roper described how: 'No doubt this long preserved silence was partly psychological. Those engaged in this delicate work were so conscious of its importance, so careful of its security, and so bound together in loyalty that secrecy became second nature to them and its maintenance a point of honour.'[29]

The ULTRA (security classification for signals intelligence obtained from intercepted German wireless communications enciphered by the Enigma machine) secret was revealed to only six ministers, although, according to the historians C. Andrew and V. Mitrokhin, Stalin knew about it, as he did about the MANHATTAN project to construct the atomic bomb.[30] Nigel West noted that: 'there never was an Ultra secret as such . . . nor an overwhelming mastery of the Enigma's traffic . . . Hence the need to make use of every crib, error, slip and plain language indiscretion that was spotted.'[31]

The existence of Bletchley Park and the breaking of Enigma was not publicly revealed until 1974, when Group Captain F.W. Winterbotham, who was in charge of security at Bletchley Park during the war, published *The Ultra Secret*.[32] Trevor-Roper, a former fellow member of MI6 himself, wrote that he found Group Captain Winterbotham's 'pioneering breach' of the rule of absolute secrecy 'paradoxical' since Winterbotham's official function during the war had been to enforce the secrecy rule and, moreover, he had once told Trevor-Roper that he threatened any officer who broke it with instant execution.[33]

The secret that Gordon Welchman exposed in his book on Hut 6 in 1982, and that really upset the government and GCHQ, was that Bletchley Park would never have been able to crack the Enigma codes if the German operators had followed proper procedures.[34] The defences of the Enigma keys could only be breached when their operators failed to follow their security operating instructions. As Helene Taylor's Hut 6 colleague Sir Stuart Milner-Barry remarked: 'Fortunately the [German] operators continued to make sufficient procedural mistakes to keep us in business.'

As Nigel West pointed out, the true secret of ULTRA was revealed by Welchman's explanation: 'At any time during the war, enforcement of a few minor security measures could have defeated us completely.' Welchman elaborated on Bletchley Park's constant daily struggle with Enigma traffic decryption:

> That we managed to stay in the game until the end of the war was made possible only by a comedy of errors committed by the Germans . . . Looking back it is amazing that so much could hang on such slender threads. . . . Our Bombes . . . would have been useless without cribs, and we would never have found our cribs if the Germans had not made a number of errors in procedure.[35]

But luckily the Germans did. As Helene Aldwinckle, whose secret work must have saved scores, if not hundreds of lives, later modestly remarked: 'Today everyone seems to know about it. It's interesting that people regard Bletchley Park as something very special.'

Chapter 10

Elephant Point and POW Liberation, 1945

The Battle for Berlin

In November 1944 there had been a contingency plan, Operation ECLIPSE, to drop the 82nd and 101st Airborne divs on Berlin, but only if Germany suddenly collapsed. Churchill telephoned Eisenhower to urge him to let Montgomery's Army Group continue the northern offensive towards Berlin. But 'Ike' (Eisenhower) decided that 'Berlin itself is no longer a particularly important objective.'[1]

On 2 February 1945, before flying to Yalta, Roosevelt and Churchill met in Malta, where their planners got together to discuss military strategy. The British proposed a rapid thrust on Berlin to seize the German capital before the Red Army arrived, with a southern breakout from Italy to take Vienna and Prague before the Soviets. The priority for the Americans, however, in contrast to the British longer term political objectives, was a quick victory in Europe with the minimum number of casualties, before moving on to defeat Japan. Faced with a US threat to recommend General Eisenhower resign, the British commanders gave way. The Americans had estimated that an Allied assault on Berlin would have resulted in at least 100,000 killed. The Red Army figures for the Battle of Berlin were 361,000 casualties, including 81,000 dead. German losses were almost ½ million killed, with the same number captured.[2] Two months later 'Ike' cabled Monty: 'Berlin . . . has political and psychological significance but of far greater importance will be the remaining German forces'.[3]

At Yalta the three Allied leaders – minus the French – had agreed zones of occupation postwar, with reciprocal agreements for travel within each others' zones. This would be the basis for the future British Mission in East Germany (abbreviated to BRIXMIS) and the Soviet equivalent (SOXMIS). The aims of these post-war missions would be to prevent

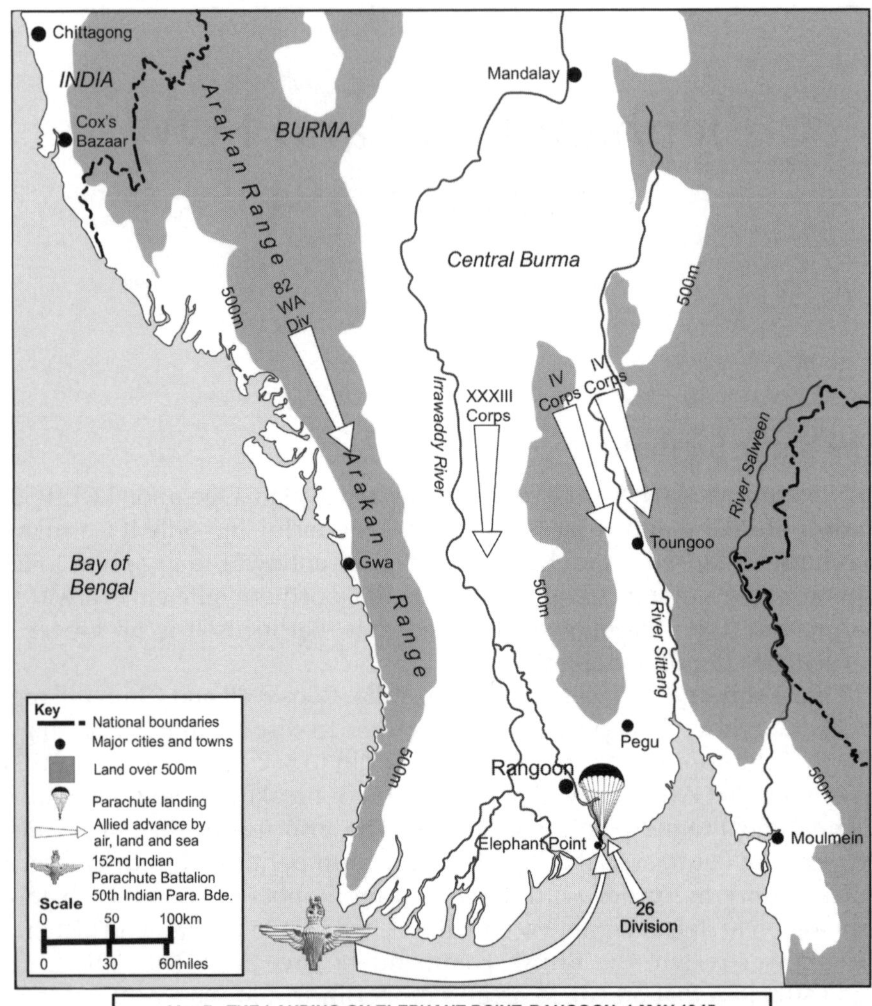

Map 7 - **THE LANDING ON ELEPHANT POINT, RANGOON, 1 MAY 1945**
Source: Based on Churchill, Winston, *The Second World War 'Triumph and Tragedy*, Cassell, 1954

misunderstanding between the occupying powers, to assess the military strength of the other powers and prevent any hostilities through accidents. BRIXMIS scouting operations would be a source of military intelligence, with objectives similar to those of military attachés. BRIXMIS would work closely with military attachés, with agents on the ground, with helicopters to extract defectors and RAF Chipmunks for photographic air surveillance flights providing integrated intelligence analyses.

Officially they would be meeting and liaising with their officer opposite numbers, operating under a Four Power 1946 Liaison agreement, but in practice the agreement was used to obtain intelligence assessments on Soviet readiness for conflict – IoH (indicators of hostility on a scale of 1–9), and their capabilities and equipment. The BRIXMIS team would consist of a major general and thirty-seven other military staff, including officer linguists, to cover East Germany and Berlin. SOXMIS, in practice, would concentrate their efforts on agent-running and espionage in West Germany. These arrangements would continue until 1990.[4]

Elephant Point, Burma

In Burma there was doubt that the 14th Army would take Rangoon before the monsoon season arrived. Two newly arrived Japanese divisions opposed it. Mountbatten decided to make an amphibious landing on the city. From the north IV Corps would chase the enemy south down the road and railway, whilst XXXIII Corps would attack on the west down the Irrawaddy to trap the Japanese.

The IV Corps pushed successfully, reaching the airfields at Toungoo. By the time the armoured brigades' troops reached Pegu, outside Rangoon, on 29 April the torrential monsoon rain had started. The Japanese blocked the bridges into Rangoon. Allied heavy bombers had been attacking Elephant Point, at the entrance to the Rangoon River, for two days when, on 1 May, Major John Sanderson's 152nd Parachute Btn dropped onto the defenders at Elephant Point. The river channel was then opened up for British minesweepers.

On 2 May IV Corps broke through and advanced on Rangoon. The very same day the amphibious assault began, as the 26th Div. ships reached the mouth of the Rangoon River. When a Mosquito crew landed on an airfield near Rangoon and walked into the city, they were greeted by British POWs, the Japanese occupants having left to fight at Pegu. That afternoon the heavy rains of the monsoon fell in earnest. Rangoon had been taken just in time. Many thousands of Japanese were taken prisoner or died attempting to flee eastwards.[5]

Fifty years after VE Day *JBS* was interviewed by Robert Kilroy-Silk on the ITV programme *Kilroy*:

> *JBS*: We landed on Elephant Point, elements of my unit: a naval task force was going in there to capture Rangoon. So there was a

war going in Burma while all the VE celebrations were going on over in Europe. This is why we talk about the 14th Army being a 'Forgotten Army', you see. When we landed at Elephant Point, the Burmese came out and, before we'd even got our parachute off, they were cutting the harness and taking the parachutes off, because they hadn't had any clothes for four or five years.

So there was really quite a lot going on. And then we were waiting to go on this 'Operation Zipper' on Malaya. So we had quite a lot to think about and, although we knew and were happy about what had happened in Europe, our minds were really over there.

Kilroy: When did you know about what had happened in Europe? When did you know that victory in Europe had actually been achieved?

JBS: Well, we knew the Russians were moving in January into Berlin and we were on the outskirts of Mandalay in Burma, so we knew the war was going the right way and we were just waiting for it to finish here. Even in January [1945] all the stuff was coming pouring over to the Far East – I mean Bombay harbour was full of all the equipment you could get out and we needed and everything else. So we had a good feeling that the war would soon be over.[6]

On 25 April 1945 at Torgau the US Army and the Red Army met on the banks of the River Elbe. On 8 May 1945, 'Victory in Europe' Day, the war with Germany and her allies was finally over. The Allies had prevailed.[7] Winston Churchill recalled:

> Thus ended the long struggle in Burma. On May 9th 1945, I telegraphed Admiral Mountbatten:
>
> I send you my most heartfelt congratulations upon the culminating victory at Rangoon of your Burma campaign. The hard fighting at Imphal and Kohima prepared the way for the brilliant operations conducted over a vast range of territory . . . In honour of these great deeds . . . His Majesty the King has commanded that a special decoration, the 'Burma Star' should be struck.[8]

Churchill made no mention of the 50th Indian Parachute Bde's defence of Sangshak, a stubborn delaying sacrifice that gave the command at Imphal and Kohima the vital time they needed to prepare for the Japanese onslaught. The Burma Star was the Forgotten Army's 'Medal of Honour', acknowledging its perseverance in the face of appalling hardships. It would be worn with pride by all Burma veterans.

Churchill sent a crucial telegram to President Truman on 12 May, outlining 'the grave challenge a disarming western Europe now faced with a powerful, totalitarian Russian army on its very doorstep'. Churchill was concerned that so many US aircraft and divisions were moving to the Pacific. The French army was weak and their politicians difficult. 'Soon our armed power on the continent will have vanished, except for moderate forces to hold down Germany.'

Churchill outlined his 'deep anxiety' regarding Russia, whose friendship he had tried to foster: their misinterpretation of the Yalta decisions, their attitude towards Poland, their overwhelming influence in the Balkans (except for Greece), the difficulties in Vienna and the power which Communist Russia exercised on the territories under their control. Russia could permanently maintain very large armies in the field. He worried that if British and US forces departed in a year or two, then a diminished Western military force of a 'handful of divisions', mainly French, would be inadequate to face Russia's 200 to 300 divisions.

Churchill described an Iron Curtain that was:

> drawn down upon their front. We do not know what is going on behind the scenes . . . the whole of the regions east of the line Lubeck–Trieste–Corfu will be completely in their hands. Soon there would be an 'immense flight of the German population westward' with 'this enormous Muscovite advance into the centre of Europe . . . and then the curtain will descend again.' Poland would be isolated behind . . . hundreds of miles of Russian-occupied territory.

Churchill invoked the image of a rapid Soviet military thrust across Europe to the North Sea and the Atlantic. 'A settlement with Russia before our strength has gone seems . . . to dwarf all others'.[9]

Chapter 11

The Atomic and Plutonium Bombs

> I am become death, the destroyer of worlds
>
> *Bhagavad Gita*

The thoughts of Robert Oppenheimer, the Scientific Director of the Manhattan Project, when witnessing the test detonation of the atomic bomb in New Mexico on 16 July 1945. His brother remembers his two words: 'It worked.'[1]

> Atomic bombs are meant to frighten those with weak nerves.
>
> Joseph Stalin.[2]

Simon Montefiore described how in Moscow Stalin asked for a map, which he spread out on his dinner table. Pointing with his pipe, he summarised the extent of his Soviet Empire:

> 'Let's see what we've got then: in the north, everything's all right, Finland wronged us, so we've moved the frontier further from Leningrad. The Baltic States, which were Russian territory from ancient times, are ours again, all the Belarussians are ours now, Ukrainians too, and the Moldavians are back with us. So to the west everything's okay. . . . China, Mongolia, all as it should be . . . Now this frontier I don't like at all. The Dardanelles . . . We should have claims to Turkish territory.'[3]

After VE Day the continent of Europe was now under the control of two opposing superpowers, Russia and the USA. Stalin was determined that Germany would never again attack Russia and was creating a buffer of satellite states occupied by the Red Army.[4] The Red Army on the borders threatened Turkey from Bulgaria and Azerbaijan. In May 1945 Stalin demanded a military base on the Bosphorus and the Dardanelles, against Molotov's strong advice: he knew the Americans would not accept such an arrangement. Turkey appealed to President Truman who noted: 'There isn't any doubt in my mind that Russia intends an invasion of Turkey and the seizure of the Black Sea Straits to the Mediterranean . . . Unless Russia is faced with an iron fist and strong language, another war is in the making. Only one language do they understand. How many divisions have you?' He would refuse to recognise Bulgaria and Romania until they complied.[5] In Berlin the bombing by the USAF (United States Air Force) by day and the RAF by night, followed by the intensive Russian shelling, had laid waste to the city. As much as 70 per cent of Berlin was reduced to rubble. The sacrifice in lives on these raids by RAF bomber command was staggering: on the 1,000 bomber raids one-sixth of crews did not return. Until late 1944, the chances of an RAF aircrew member surviving a 'tour' of thirty missions was just one in four. In total 55,000 of the 125,000 RAF bomber aircrew were killed in action.[6]

D. Middleton vividly described the utter devastation caused:

> In 1945 Germany viewed from the air was a country dying, or nearly dead. Berlin, Hamburg, the Ruhr cities showed mile upon mile of burnt, roofless houses and gaping tenements. Vast mounds of rubble and craters formed a landscape of the moon. Bombed and abandoned trains, like giant caterpillars, lay twisted or on their sides along the tracks. In the shells of factories where Krupps and other firms had poured out the steel, the tanks and the planes, acres of machinery lay silent and rusting, without protection from the elements. The only sign of life was the march of armies, the driblets of Germans walking back towards their homes, and the vast, pathetic movement of millions of . . . displaced persons.[7]

In Berlin most lacked a roof over their heads. Half a million appartments had been destroyed, and of the remaining only 30 per cent were undamaged, whilst 50,000 dwellings comprised cellars, ruins or garden huts.[8]

Churchill described Berlin on 16 July 1945:

> The city was nothing but a chaos of ruins . . . In the square in front of the Chancellery there was a considerable crowd. When I got out of the car and walked about among them, they all began to cheer. My hate had died with their surrender . . . Then we entered

> the Chancellery, and for quite a long time walked through its shattered galleries and halls. Our Russian guide then took us to Hitler's air-raid shelter . . . I went down to the bottom and saw the room in which he and his mistress had committed suicide.[9]

John Sanderson's future wife Audrey made the same tour in 1946, walking in the Reich Chancellery garden to the very spot where Hitler's body was burned (see 21a in the plates). Standing pensively in the former lair of the hateful Führer, she thought back to wartime Britain, two years previously, when she was the Welfare Officer in an English factory, a target for Hitler's Luftwaffe. On 1 August 1944 she had drawn up an instruction for her workforce:

> Warning System for Approaching Aircraft
>
> To bring our warning system in line with the Government system, as announced by the BBC, the following rings on the bells and klaxon will be given:
>
> * On the approach of Enemy Aircraft THREE RINGS will be given which is the warning to proceed to shelters.
>
> * When immediate danger is over ONE LONG RING will be given.
>
> The 'duck' signal [the 'duck' signal was the warning for bombs actually falling] for those remaining at work will be a series of short rings.
>
> Signed: Audrey M. Jones[10]

Churchill commented with satisfaction: 'The course Hitler had taken was much more convenient for us than the one I had feared. I have no doubt he would have shared the fate of the Nuremberg criminals.'[11]

On 5 July the Labour party led by Attlee were swept to victory in the general election. Churchill had anticipated a possible defeat as: 'on another occasion I inspected . . . many British troops and tanks. I opened a soldiers' club for the 7th Armoured Division. They all sang "For he's a jolly good fellow" . . . I thought I detected a certain air of sheepishness, which might be due to most of them having voted adversely.'[12]

On 17 July Churchill, no longer Prime Minister, was informed of the successful explosion of the first atomic bomb in the Mexican desert. He was handed a sheet of paper on which was written: 'Babies satisfactorily born'. Churchill now saw a way to end the war rapidly. He estimated that to invade Japan and fight it out yard by yard could cost the lives of 1 million American and ½ million British servicemen. 'Now all this nightmare vision had vanished. In its place was the vision . . . of the end of the war in one or two violent shocks.' He hoped that the Japanese would see this 'almost supernatural weapon' as an excuse to retain their honour and prevent a war of attrition to the last soldier. Such a solution would end the war in the Far East without Russia's aid. 'We might not merely destroy cities but save the lives of friend and foe alike.'[13]

When Churchill dined with Stalin on 18 July, the Russian leader spun a web of lies, promising that that Soviet policy was to see 'strong, independent sovereign states' in all the countries the Red Army 'liberated'. Stalin promised not to 'sovietise' these countries and to allow free elections. Stalin declared himself offended by American demands for a change in government in Romania and Bulgaria, explaining that, where there had been an 'émigré government', he had been obliged to help create a 'home government'. Stalin said that in Romania and Bulgaria, 'where everything was peaceful', this did not apply.[14]

Churchill replied that Western representatives in Romania and Bulgaria were prevented from assessing the true situation because 'an iron fence has come down around them'. The mission in Bucharest 'had been penned up with a closeness that approached internment'. To Stalin's response that this was 'all fairy tales', Churchill said he had complete confidence in his representatives in these countries.[15]

Churchill then said how anxious people were about Russia's intentions. He drew a line from the North Cape to Albania, and named the capitals east of that line which were in Russian hands. Churchill said that it seemed the Russians were 'rolling westwards'. Stalin denied this, pointing out that Soviet losses during the war were 5 million dead and missing. While the Germans had mobilised 18 million men, Russia had 12 million under arms. He apologised to Churchill for his failure to publicly thank Great Britain for the supplies she had sent to Russia during the war.[16]

Roosevelt had the foresight to sanction the MANHATTAN project whilst the USA was still officially neutral. He understood that if the Germans acquired the weapon first, it would be war-winning asset for them. Dwight Eisenhower was opposed to the atomic bombing: he said the Japanese were ready to surrender and that he hated to see the USA being the first country to use 'that awful thing'. But other military leaders considered the war could last well into 1946, with a loss of 250,000 US lives. General MacArthur predicted that an invasion of Japan would cost a million killed or wounded.[17]

In September 1949, after the Russians successfully exploded their first atomic bomb on 29 August, Stalin would voice similar fears of the destructiveness of atomic bombs: 'If war broke out, the use of A-bombs would depend on Trumans and Hitlers being in power . . . Atomic weapons can hardly be used without spelling the end of the world.'[18]

President Truman, who approved the atomic bombing, later commented that the atom bomb was 'no great decision . . . it was merely another powerful weapon in the arsenal of righteousness. The dropping of the bombs stopped the war, saved millions of lives. It was a purely military decision.'[19] On 26 July the USA's ultimatum was published, calling for an immediate unconditional surrender of the armed forces of Japan. When this was rejected, on 27 July, eleven Japanese cities were warned by leaflet that they would be intensively bombed. Six were attacked on the 28th, twelve more on the 31st and four on 5 August. Superfortress planes dropped over 1 million leaflets every day and 3 million copies of the ultimatum.[20]

At 2.45 a.m. a B-29 named *Enola Gay* took off from the long airstrip of Tinian Island and the 9,000lb 'Little Boy' uranium atomic bomb was armed in flight. At 8.15 a.m. on 6 August it was dropped from 31,000ft and exploded at 2,000ft over Hiroshima.[21]

As *JBS* recollected forty years later:

> The atomic bomb went off on my birthday, on the 6th August. I was 24 years old and I'd had six years in the war then and I was grateful, at that time, because we were apprehensive, as I said, you know, the attack on Malaya, I don't think we'd have come through. From my point of view I'd say it was worthwhile.[22]

On 9 August 1945, the day the Nagasaki plutonium bomb was exploded and the Russian Army invaded Manchuria, Truman made a radio broadcast:

> I realise the tragic significance of the atomic bomb . . . We have used it against those who attacked us without warning at Pearl Harbor, against those who have starved and beaten and executed American prisoners of war, against those who have abandoned all pretense of obeying international laws of warfare. We have used it to shorten the agony of war . . . to save the lives of thousands and thousands of young Americans . . . Only a Japanese surrender will stop us.[23]

On 10 August the Japanese government agreed to accept the ultimatum 'provided this did not prejudice the prerogative of the Emperor as a sovereign ruler'. The Emperor Hirohito authorised the signature of surrender and the Japanese surrendered unconditionally. The conventional bombing of Japan by B-29s was equally deadly. Incendiary bombs dropped on Tokyo on the night of 9/10 March 1945 killed 124,711 with 286,358 buildings destroyed, more than at Hiroshima or Nagasaki.[24]

JBS described his personal reaction to the atomic bombing:

> The war virtually came to an abrupt end on my 24th birthday, 6 August 1945 when the 'A' bomb (atomic bomb) was dropped on Hiroshima. At the time we were all geared up for the land, sea and air assault of the Malay Peninsula; I was in 152nd Indian Parachute Regiment, which formed part of 50th Indian Airborne Brigade, and I don't think we'd have come through had the 'A' bomb not been dropped on the Japanese mainland. Intelligence reports had greatly underestimated the enemy forces facing us.
>
> When the Japanese subsequently surrendered, I was then given the job of parachuting into a Japanese POW Camp in Thailand to free the Allied POWs. What we found there was horrific. One of the servicemen we tended had been confined to a small hole in the ground; this was a punishment for having constructed a small radio, to listen to the progress of the Allies, with parts smuggled in by a Korean guard. Sadly this brave British POW died soon afterwards; for him help had come just too late. Years later by chance I would meet one of these liberated POWs. He had never forgotten me landing in his camp.

Maurice Bell, who had fought at Sangshak was, like John Sanderson, scheduled to take part in Operation ZIPPER. This officer also went to Thailand after the surrender. At 20 years of age, as a young 2nd lieutenant, he was dispatched alone to a camp of about a thousand Japanese soldiers to verify their numbers: he counted them all on parade, whilst slowly driving along the rows on his motorbike.

James Wheen was another officer who had been due to take part in the cancelled Operation ZIPPER. Wheen had attended OCTU at Deolali near Bombay and was commissioned in July 1945 into the Indian Mountain Regiment. After the Japanese surrender, Wheen was sent to Thailand. Wheen and Sanderson (see 24a in the plates) were later both SIS officers and in 1948 would share a desk in MI4 (German and Eastern Europe desk) at the WO, where one day Sanderson would be surprised when picking up his telephone to hear a voice speaking in Russian! Wheen went on to study at the School of Oriental and African Studies, whilst Sanderson went to the School of Slavonic Studies to learn Bulgarian and Russian. He then departed for nine months' language training in situ to a Middle East country where he took private lessons. The traitor George Blake would attend a similar Arabic course in the Lebanon.

JBS recollected at the end of the war:

> I was astonished to witness the American sailors aboard supply ships push brand-new trucks and other equipment off the decks into the sea off Calcutta harbour and then promptly sail away. With the war in Burma and India successfully brought to a conclusion, it was decided that all this equipment was surplus to requirements.
>
> As a result of my experiences in the Far East during the war, I firmly believe that nothing matters much; most things don't matter at all. Add life to your day, rather than days to your life!

The cartoonist Ronald Searle was a young prisoner of the Japanese for four years on the infamous Burma railway. Searle somehow survived and after the war he directed his great art upwards, towards the light of humour. His thoughts were that those who returned from Burma had one advantage over everyone else: 'We now had in our grasp a thorny, but true, measuring stick against which to place the things that did or did not matter in life.'[25]

Denis Greenhill described how: 'After the Japanese surrender, there was a shortage of . . . ships to bring home as rapidly as they hoped both the P.O.W.s, recently released from their appalling conditions in Japanese camps, and the British troops in Indian camps who were rightly impatient to return to their families in Britain'.[26]

Back in Europe in August 1945 Kim Philby had had a close shave when a KGB agent, Konstantin Volkov, attempted to defect in Instanbul. Volkov had offered to hand over a list of the 314 NKGB (Soviet intelligence and security service (1941–6)), agents in Turkey as well as 'a list of the 250 known N.K.G.B. agents of the military and civil Intelligence in Great Britain'. Amongst other papers he offered to sell for £50,000 were the copies of material handed over 'by up to nine Soviet agents in the British Intelligence Service and the Ministry of Foreign Affairs in Great Britain', one of whom was 'fulfilling the functions of the head a Section of the British Counter Espionage Service in London'. This intelligence could have unmasked Philby. But he kept his calm and dealt with the situation adeptly. Delays by the British Ambassador in Istanbul, who insisted London dealt with the matter, gave Philby the vital breathing space he needed to warn his Soviet masters. He persuaded Menzies that he himself should fly to Turkey to investigate the defector's claims. By the time Philby finally reached Istanbul at the end of September, Volkov had been removed to Moscow and executed.[27]

Volkov had offered to sell his country's secrets for money. Philby, by contrast, received no money for his treachery. He betrayed his country for misplaced ideals.[28] Later Philby was to admit: 'All through my career, I have been a straight penetration agent working in the Soviet interest.'[29] Philby concealed his treachery for so long through operating a cunning 'double-bluff' method of never minimising the Soviet threat. In March 1946 he wrote:

> Our estimate of Russian sources in this country is that they are sufficiently numerous and well-placed to be dangerous . . . we cannot advance definite proof. Igor Gousenko in Ottawa has recently informed us that the G.R.U. was running an extremely well-placed agent in the London Intelligence world . . . but the details were too vague to enable us to identify the agent.[30]

Chapter 12

The Iron Curtain, Berlin and Hess

We all believed – or at least hoped – that the postwar world would be decent and human.

Andrei Sakharov[1]

This war is not in the past. Whoever occupies a territory also imposes his own social system . . . It cannot be otherwise.

Stalin, 1945[2]

The Second World War was over. Across Europe vast populations were on the move. In the 6th arrondissement of Paris, the Hotel Lutetia, formerly occupied by Nazi counter intelligence, was opened up on de Gaulle's instructions as a refuge for survivors of German concentration camps.

Nigel West noted that on 25 August 1944 Allied SCI (Special Counter Intelligence) units had entered Paris and headed straight for the Hotel Lutetia. Although many of the German files had been removed or destroyed, an Abwehr NCO, later the subject of a German assassination attempt, had cooperated in identifying many of the Abwehr stay-behind networks, handing over missing Lutetia files and accompanying SCI officers to hidden arms stores. Hotel Lutetia was afterwards offered as a refuge for returning French concentration camp victims, and POWs.[3]

The oppressive occupation of Eastern Europe by the Russians, former allies, was sending a further wave of DPs (displaced persons) towards France and into Paris. Many dreamed of obtaining visas for the USA or returning to their countries in Eastern Europe when the Communists left. In September 1945, a significant intelligence coup occurred. The secret revelations of a defecting Russian cypher clerk at the Ottawa Embassy, Igor Gouzenko, shocked the Canadian and US governments. The files he handed over from his *rezidentura* (NKGB Intelligence Department of the

Soviet Embassy) revealed an extensive Russian espionage ring in Canada run by the Russian Military Attaché Colonel Nikolai Zabotin, a GRU intelligence officer handling nuclear secrets and Uranium-235 samples obtained from Dr Alan May, codenamed ALEK, a British scientist. The case became known as 'Corby' after the whisky drunk by the Canadian intelligence investigating officers.[4]

Only five months after the US and Russian armies had met at the River Elbe in Germany, when US infantrymen had celebrated with vodka and danced with Russian female snipers and officers, the FBI learned that the USA had also been penetrated by a Russian spy network. Gouzenko revealed to Roger Hollis of MI5 the worrying news that 'the Soviet Union was preparing for war with the Western democracies' and that a 'large proportion of diplomatic representatives of Russian states' were 'Moscow agents'.[5]

Professor Jeffery described how Philby, as head of Section IX of British counter intelligence, attempted for obvious reasons to downplay the Gouzenko affair and to keep the Corby intelligence material within SIS. Ernest Bevin and the FO PUS (Permanent Under-Secretary) Sir Alexander Cadogen, however, considered the Gouzenko revelations to be of highly significant political importance. They were prepared to risk a public humiliation of the Soviet Union by making the affair known and by subjecting the suspected Soviet agents to arrest and a formal trial. The Canadians and Americans were not keen to make the Soviet espionage public for their own political reasons. President Truman was informed of the extensive Soviet spy ring in the USA but he was unwilling to rock the boat in Berlin.[6]

Military attachés often had a challenging relationship with their ambassador or minister in a legation. Duff Cooper in the Paris Embassy had the usual ambassadorial attitude to the activities of SIS. He wrote to Cadogen at the FO that he was 'averse to having as a member of my staff, working in the embassy, someone of whose movements I know nothing and over whose movements I have no control'. He desired 'to draw a very rigid line between the activities of the diplomatic service and those of the secret service'. He believed that 'a diplomatist has as much right to consider himself insulted if he is called "a spy" as a soldier if he is called "a murderer"'. Duff Cooper knew, of course, that the secret service existed but thought it 'would be impossible for a member of it to adopt the cover of a secretary or attaché at the embassy'. His comments must have fallen on deaf ears at the FO with the repercussions of the Gouzenko affair. When John Sanderson's colleague John Bruce Lockhart became Head of Station in Paris (1945–7), however, the situation had been eased and the ban on SIS reporting on France loosened. Bruce Lockhart was officially an AMA, attached to the embassy, as would be his colleague John Sanderson in 1948. The role of an AMA was a standard cover for MI6 officers.[7]

When the Gouzenko affair became public knowledge in 1946, with the arrest of Nunn May, the Chairman of the Joint Intelligence sub-Committee asked 'C' whether SIS could be embarrassed by reciprocal accusations of espionage from the USSR. Menzies replied that 'no widespread British organisation has yet been set up' but 'C' did have 'of course, individual agents who might conceivably be arrested'. Menzies stressed he would be 'failing in his duty' if he 'did not encourage the rapid building up of organisations within the satellite countries and, where opportunities presented themselves, for using these to obtain information from Russia'. He noted there was an old French adage, '*On ne peut pas faire le S.R. [Service de Renseignement] avec le curé*' ('One can't use a priest to run a Secret Service'). Looking forward, he promised to exercise caution but he planned within a year 'to have a far wider network than exists at present'.[8]

September 1945 saw the disembarkation in the UK of the 24-year-old battle-hardened Intelligence Officer Captain Sanderson, returning from the successful but harrowing liberation of British prisoners in a Japanese POW camp in Thailand. Five months later, on 9 February 1946, Stalin gave a speech declaring the inevitability of war between the Soviet Union and the West, due to the contradictions of Communism and Capitalism, a prediction that Khrushchev would disavow at the 20th Party Congress in February 1956.

In the famous 5,000-word 'Long Telegram' of 22 February, which followed Stalin's speech, the US Ambassador to Moscow, George Kennan, transmitted his recommendations for a policy of 'containment' of the Soviet spheres of influence. Kennan's analysis described the Communist leader Stalin as an insecure, paranoid dictator, motivated by self-preservation and using Marxist-Leninist theories as tools to justify Soviet external expansionism and internal repression. Stalin, he said, needed a hostile non-Communist enemy, and class enemies within, to legitimise his hold on domestic power and to reinforce his cult of the personality. 'We have here a political force commited fanatically to the belief that with the U.S. there can be no permanent modus vivendi.'[9] Kennan accurately and perceptively predicted that long-term containment, although very costly, would in the end lead to 'either the breakup or the gradual mellowing of Soviet power.' Kennan intended this 'containment' policy to be economic, rather than military, but it formed the basis for Truman's Cold War economic, diplomatic and military strategies.[10]

The Cold War, according to Robert Rossow, the Vice-Consul in Tabriz in Iran, began on 4 March 1946 when fifteen Soviet armoured brigades crossed into the Iranian province of Azerbaijan and deployed along the Iraqi and Turkish borders. Another large Soviet army moved south across Bulgaria to deploy along its frontier with Turkey.[11]

The day after the Russian invasion of Iran, at Fulton Missouri, Winston Churchill delivered his defining speech, awakening the US public to the reality of a looming Cold War.

> From Stettin in the Baltic to Trieste in the Adriatic, an iron curtain has descended across the Continent. Behind that line lie all the capitals of the ancient states of Central and Eastern Europe. Warsaw, Berlin, Prague, Vienna, Budapest, Belgrade, Bucharest and Sofia, all these famous cities and the populations around them, lie in what I must call the Soviet sphere . . . I am sure that our fortunes are still in our hands and that we hold the power to save the future. I do not believe that Soviet Russia desires war. What they desire is the fruits of war and the indefinite expansion of their power and influence.[12]

In Moscow, whilst Churchill was speaking at Fulton, the British Chargé d'affaires was recommending to London the same policy of resisting Soviet expansionism as Kennan's 'containment'.[13] In April the US battleship *Missouri* was sent to anchor off Piraeus, the port of Athens, sending a clear signal to Stalin of US intent in the region.[14]

Later the Soviet troops withdrew from Azerbaijan, having been granted an oil concession, and under pressure from the UN, Britain and the USA. Soviet influence would lessen, whilst Iran signed a military deal with the USA.[15]

Stalin had acknowledged Churchill's rough percentage plan for Greece, agreeing not to interfere. A challenge over Berlin was his main priority. In Yugoslavia the populace had not forgotten the 'liberating' Red Army of late 1944 passing through the north of the country, raping their local women. In response to these accusations, Stalin retorted that the Yugoslavs had showed insufficient respect for Soviet military sacrifices in failing to sympathise when a soldier 'who has crossed thousands of kilometers through blood and fire has fun with women'.

Stalin was worried that Tito might provoke the West and cautiously instructed Tito to slow down his plans to take over Albania and to cease aiding the Greek guerillas.[16] Tito, however, defied Stalin by arming the Greek Communists: he planned a Balkan Federation with the Bulgarians under Georgi Dimitrov. Khrushchev remarked later that Stalin had one demand always and that was 'absolute subordination'. The author Simon Montefiore describes a furious Stalin telling Khrushchev angrily: 'I'll shake my finger and there'll be no more Tito!' A long letter was sent to Tito with the menacing remark: 'We think Trotsky's political career is sufficiently instructive.' Stalin was totally ruthless: 'If you have a man who is a problem, kill the man. There; no problem.'[17]

In spite of Stalin's threats, Tito was to remain President of Yugoslavia for a further thirty-two years, surviving without a Soviet assassin's icepick embedded in his head, the fate of Trotsky in Mexico in 1940. Tito understood the threat of Soviet imperialism and was fortunate that he had no common border with the Soviet Union that the Red Army could cross. In the summer of 1948 50,000 loyal Greek troops were battling the Communist rebels. When they pleaded allegiance to Stalin, Tito cut off of the Communists' aid and effectively brought the Greek civil war to an end.[18]

In the middle of 1946, across West Germany and in Berlin, SIS had begun to establish undercover agents and contacts. The British SCI was interrogating and then employing suitable captured agents of GIS (Nazi German intelligence service), the documentation on whom was held on numerous file cards as there were many tens of thousands of suspects and Nazis. 'British interrogators began to look systematically for . . . German intelligence officers who had served on the Russian front or in the eastern sections of the GIS'.[19]

Stephen Dorril described the CIA flooding Germany with money. Intelligence officers of the OSS (Office of Strategic Services, the wartime agency later replaced by the CIA) took over the German General Gehlen's Fremde Heere Ost Eastern organisation with its detailed files from the British. MI6 could not afford to run it.[20]

> The Americans later in 1949 . . . persuaded Gehlen to run agent networks in eastern Europe. This proved a major mistake . . . the German Old-boy Nazi network . . . proved to be riddled with Soviet agents. The American agencies treated Gehlen's reports with (too much) respect, with the result that Gehlen's slanted intelligence was to have a distorting effect on the course of the Cold War.[21]

Dorril wrote that MI6 had committed some of its most experienced counter espionage officers to Germany. These intelligence officers were regarded as being particularly skillful in obtaining information from interrogated

Nazis. The skills and knowledge of ex-SS officers, recruited as informants, were employed to infiltrate the numerous Nazi organisations aiding war criminals to escape justice, as well as the various neo-Nazi groups which were rearing their ugly heads. To achieve this the savage wartime careers of these Nazi recruits often had to be overlooked.[22]

When OSS was disbanded in September 1945, it was a blow to the Soviets: they had penetrated the HQ staff of the organisation with seven NKVD agents. Soviet infiltration of the CIA would not match this success until 1985. The penetration of OSS was later revealed by a Soviet agent, Elizabeth Bentley, who regretted her espionage activities. The Soviets also lost two agents of influence in the British SOE, when its staff were dispersed.[23]

Due to the pressing Cold War Russian threat to Western Europe British Intelligence's priority was not to investigate war crimes, but rather to locate and recruit agents to deploy against the Soviet threat. War criminals such as Walter Schellenberg and Klaus Barbie, the former Gestapo Chief of Lyon, were used to identify German intelligence officers in hiding as recruits for a British backed anti-Communist counter-intelligence group. The CIA later helped Barbie down an escape route from Germany to conceal his CIA and MI6 involvement from French war crimes investigators. This exercise in pragmatism showed that for the Allied intelligence services national and military priorities overrode moral questions of accountability for wartime misdeeds.[24]

In October 1946 *JBS* was posted to Berlin. He wrote home:

> The York and Lancaster Regiment are tasked with guarding the Nazis Rudolf Hess and Albert Speer in Spandau Prison. I am looking forward to driving into Berlin. A fellow officer has described the roads and buildings to me. Apparently the roads are wonderful, and so wide that Pall Mall looks like a cart-track in comparison. Bob made me laugh today. He was telling me how he turned a corner last night in Berlin and thought he was driving down the road, only to discover it was the pavement. Even that was as wide as an English road.

In 1945 Hess had been put on trial in Nuremberg with other Nazi leaders and in 1946 was convicted of committing crimes against peace and the planning, preparation, initiation and waging of an aggressive war. Hess would remain the only prisoner in Spandau prison for forty-one years until his suicide in 1987, aged 93 years. The prison was demolished after his death. Baldur von Schirach, the Gauleiter of Vienna, and Albert Speer, the architect of Hitler's unachieved capital city Germania and Minister of Armaments and War Production, were released in 1966, having served their twenty-year terms.[25] Speer would say that he was decently treated in prison:

> During the next twenty years of my life I was guarded in Spandau prison, by nationals of the Four Powers. . . . Along with my six fellow prisoners, they were the only people I had close contact with. . . . Yet not one of them bore a grudge towards me for my personal share in the tragedy: never once did I hear words of recrimination. At the lowest ebb of my existence, in contact with these ordinary people, I encountered uncorrupted feelings of sympathy, helpfulness, human understanding.[26]

Meanwhile, John met his future wife in Luneburg where she was a volunteer with the YMCA (Young Men's Christian Association). He saw her at a dance and said to a fellow officer, before he introduced himself to her: 'That's the woman I'm going to marry.' It was the classic *coup de foudre* and they hit it off straight away, as Miss Audrey Jones explained in a letter home to her parents on 19 January 1947:

> There is something very special to tell you but I just don't know where to begin – it all seems unreal that I hardly believe it is true . . . I have met 'the' John and he is so wonderful and exceptionally kind and thoughtful, not only to me, but to everyone. I know you will like him. How shall I describe him – he is very tall and fair and good looking – just the sort of person you love. Everyone likes him – he is a regular soldier now – he went through the Burma Campaign with the Airborne Division (but didn't tell his people at home in case it worried them). It is amazing he came through, as he did 41 'jumps' by parachute. He is a Captain in the York & Lancaster Regiment – Company Commander and Welfare Officer – there are lots of things to tell you about him. He was A.D.C. to a General in Southern Command – but he is so modest about it all – his family live in Beckenham – his father is Australian – he is the eldest of six – and they seem a lovely family. We went to the club last night and somehow it leaked out – and we were wafted off to the Colonel's table and toasted in champagne – all of it seemed a dream to me.

They were married on 18 February 1947 in Luneburg church, with a guard of honour of fellow officers. They would be happily married for forty-five years. The Sandersons were fortunate to be offered a subsidised honeymoon, during the coldest winter in living memory. Their journey to Denmark was onboard an icebreaker ship.

JBS:

> To kill two birds with one stone, we were sent to collect supplies for the York & Lancs regimental stores. I was sent with a Jeep and trailer to Copenhagen. The Colonel had kindly permitted my wife and I to have a subsidised honeymoon. The winter of 1946/1947 was one of the coldest in Germany and Europe for many years. An icebreaker had to force our passage across to Denmark. We were looking forward to a hot bath on arrival at the 'Hotel Angleterre' but were informed politely by the reception, in perfect English: 'It is only two years since the end of your war. No coal from Britain. Hot water is rationed in Copenhagen.'
>
> Although installed in a comfortable suite, we were obliged to boil a kettle repeatedly and pour the heated water into a large metal tub, placed in front of the empty fireplace. This was all part of the adventure, however, and the bacon and eggs for breakfast were excellent.

Whilst Captain Sanderson was honeymooning in Denmark (the country where Barbie was planning to flee) on the night of 22/23 February 1947 scores of British and US security officers swooped on an underground meeting of the group Deutsche Revolution, arresting almost a hundred neo-Nazis. Their Head of Intelligence, Klaus Barbie, was permitted to escape. The CIA later helped him down an evasion route from Germany to conceal his CIA and MI6 involvement from French war crimes investigators.[27]

A copy of the *Daily Telegraph*, delivered to the Sandersons in February 1947, carried a report that the British Army had suffered the tragic loss of eight soldiers burned to death, alongside eighty others, in a fire at a 'Cafe and Dance' ball in Spandau. Also reported was the end of an unofficial truce on immigration by Zionists, following the interception of a ship from Naples bound for Palestine with 650 immigrants. The ship was boarded by ratings. Three destroyers escorted the ship into the port which was lit up by batteries of searchlights and cordoned off by tanks and armoured cars. The ship anchored with the immigrants singing Jewish songs. Brigadier Faithfull requested them to leave quietly, stating that he had a large force which he did not wish to use. These were the 1,500 Sixth Airborne Div.

paratroopers, some of whom boarded the ship. Most immigrants left quietly but some fanatical youths, discovered in the hold, fought, kicked and punched until they were dragged off the ship.

The British government suddenly announced the end of its mandate in Palestine. There were 6 million unemployed in Britain, the gold reserves were falling due to a run on the pound and the occupation of Germany was costing £1 million a day. Coal reserves were low. Bread rationing was introduced: grain was being shipped to feed the hungry in Germany. The USA was told that Britain could no longer afford economic aid to Turkey and Greece, where British troops were still fighting. Truman sought $400 million for Greece and Turkey. Dean Acheson, the US Secretary of State, declared that if Greece and Turkey fell to the Communists, 'like apples in a barrel infected by one rotten one', then Western Europe, North Africa, Iran and the Middle East would be threatened.

On 12 March 1947, the President outlined in a speech what became known as the 'Truman Doctrine':

> The seeds of totalitarian regimes are nurtured by misery and want. They spread and grow in the evil soil of poverty and strife. They reach their full growth when the hope of a people for a better life has died. We must keep that hope alive. We believe it must be the policy of the United States to support free peoples who are resisting attempted subjugation by armed minorities or by outside pressures.[28]

JBS wrote home on 6 May 1947:

> [British troops Berlin] We are having a very busy time at the moment – the emphasis seems to be on sport, and every available opportunity is being spent on training the men in some form of sport, and I am firmly convinced that if we teach the men nothing else but that, then we shall have achieved something for them during their short training. I am swimming for my company in the gala event being held in the Olympic stadium pool.

The Olympic stadium was close to the Berlin SIS station which was staffed (in the 1950s) with over 100 officers and personnel, organised into 4 operational sections dealing with political intelligence and Soviet penetration, the Soviet and German armed forces, scientific intelligence and a technical section.[29] The Olympic stadium also housed BRIXMIS' main office, which also had a mission building in Potsdam, across the Glienicke Bridge in the Soviet zone. The planning in 1953 for the Berlin tunnel STOPWATCH (GOLD: USA codeword), described later (see p. 232–8), was kept deliberately separate from the SIS station, as well as from the CIA base.[30]

On 12 July 1947 Audrey Sanderson wrote home:

> HQ BRITISH TROOPS BERLIN BAOR [British Army of the Rhine], 1st Battalion York & Lancaster Regiment
>
> Dear Mother and Father,
>
> Just a note to say that I am going over to Luneburg next week for three days. I have booked a telephone call to you for Thursday. I expect John has told you that the Russian course is to be held in Cambridge, nine months of it, and he has applied for a vacancy. We played tennis on Thursday and this afternoon we are going to see one of Tchaikovsky's operas in the Russian sector, with a Dutch Naval Commander. We have to be out of the Russian sector before dark though, love Audrey

Responsibility for organising the Berlin Tattoo, held in the German Olympic stadium, fell to Captain Sanderson. The British soldiers' natural good nature served to lift the spirits of the German children of Berlin in the Olympic stadium.

JBS:

> [10 August 1947] We held the full dress rehearsals of the tattoo yesterday, which I was directed to organise. They were a great success. The children of Berlin (12,000 of them) came to the afternoon performance, and thoroughly enjoyed themselves. Every child was handed a bag of sweets on arrival, and we nearly had a major tragedy – thousands of them surged forward at the gates, and in spite of firm barriers, almost swept away the gate control personnel! But the British soldiers, always wonderful on these occasions, managed to cope with the rush, and I think every child received his ration. Some of them had more and, to make things worse, the children who had passed through the barriers, had the bright idea to hide the bag of sweets in their shirts, and to return to the gates in the pretence of not having received any, owing to the rush. Absolute chaos reigned for a couple of minutes while the gate control was besieged by thousands of eager children!! However, there were no accidents, and all were eventually seated to see what must have been to them one of

> the most colourful spectacles of their tender years. The evening performance brought 23,000 inmates of charitable organisations, hospitals, displaced persons' camps etc., and I mingled with the crowds on the way out to learn what they thought of the show, and the word 'Prima!' heard everywhere, assured me of full houses next week. John.

In may 2018 the author interviewed a German named Gerhard whose father was a German fighter pilot. Shot down in 1943, Gerhard had climbed over the fence of an American airbase during the Berlin airlift of 1948 as a boy and been given a box of bottles of Coca-Cola by airmen. A friend of his had been been a recipient of one of John Sanderson's bags of sweets at the stadium in Berlin.

Five days later, on 15 August 1947, the long rule of the British Raj in India ended on the second anniversary of the conclusion of the Second World War. The date that Lord Mountbatten had chosen for the handover of power in India had, however, been considered by Hindu astrologers to be 'so horrendously inauspicious' that a compromise had to be found. It was decided, to avoid offence, that India would gain independence at midnight exactly, between the 15 and 16 August.[31]

Meanwhile, in Berlin, Sanderson and a fellow officer had a close call when they were misdirected by a German, perhaps deliberately.

JBS:

> My best man and I were directed by a German policeman to the Luneburg road with the instructions to bear right and then follow the tram lines. We spotted the tram lines and turned our jeep as instructed. After one minute, we suddenly realised that what we took to be a tram line, was in fact the main Hamburg railway!

The living conditions for Berliners was dire: the population were undernourished and hungry. As *JBS* explained:

> In July 1947, when our dog Ripper was lost, we scoured Berlin for him. All the Germans we asked said it was most likely that the dachshund had been eaten as 'The Berliners are so hungry'. Luckily, however, a woman had found our dog and placed an advertisement in the newspaper. We were happily reunited with Ripper and the woman was grateful for her reward of food.

Chapter 13

Intelligence Corps Depot, MI4, London

By the time John had returned to the Intelligence Corps Depot in London in September 1947, the SIS had thirty-eight officers and fifty-three administrative staff working in West Berlin. Sanderson's colleague John Bruce Lockhart took over as Head of the Berlin Station in February 1948, having relinquished Head of the Paris Station in January 1946. Lockhart reported directly to 'C', Stewart Menzies, the SIS Chief since 1939. There were now 120 case officers in West Germany, many interrogating, and then employing, former German Intelligence Service agents with valuable knowledge and experience of running espionage networks in the Russian zones. Lockhart considered Germany to be the 'nursery of S.I.S.'.

In Paris at the Quai d'Orsay on 27 June 1947 a conference was held between Bevin, Molotov and Bidault to discuss the Marshall Plan. It was here four months before that the five peace treaties had been signed on 10 February with Italy, Romania, Hungary, Bulgaria and Finland in the Salon de l'Horloge. The historians A. Beevor and A. Cooper described the scene: 'The air was oppressive from the heatwave which reduced Paris to torpor, and the atmosphere was further weighed down by Molotov's suspicions. He was certain that a trap had been laid for him by Bidault and Bevin at their private meeting ten days before. Bevin was in excellent spirits. Molotov used blocking tactics from the start.'[1]

The mercurial Stalin was initially keen to benefit from US material aid and reconstruction funds. The next day, however, Molotov read from a statement he had just received from Moscow, demanding that the USA must say in advance how much it was prepared to give. The Americans made it clear that if the Communists returned to government, they would hold back all Marshall Plan money from France. The British Prime Minister realised that to involve the Soviets in the negotiations was out of the question: 'Bevin's mind was made up. Bidault's attempts to bridge the chasm between them and the Soviet Union was a waste of time.'

Stalin ordered his delegates to leave. The only decision which Stalin permitted his satellite states was their method of refusal, although the Poles and Czechs were reluctant to depart and still keen to take part. The Poles withdrew their interest under duress. The Czech Foreign Minister, who had hoped his country would benefit from the Marshall Plan, was summoned to Moscow to be rebuked. He later commented: 'I went to Moscow as the foreign Minister of an independent sovereign state, I returned as a lackey of the Soviet government.' Stalin's promises to Churchill had been hollow words.[2]

Whilst all discussions were off with Russia, invitations were issued to all the nations of Europe for a European conference. Molotov departed from the Quai d'Orsay as their summit broke up. Sixteen countries, out of the twenty-two invited, attended the Marshall Plan Conference which started on 11 July. Without Molotov there to throw a spanner in the works, by 15 July agreement was reached on almost all aspects.

The devil takes care of his own. Molotov, the great survivor of the purges and an unashamed Stalinist, who had authorised the liquidation of nearly a quarter of a million individuals whose names were on NKVD lists, was to survive until 96 years of age. As the Soviet Foreign Minister after the war, he saw the world as divided into opposing and hostile ideological blocs and earned the sobriquet 'stone-bottom' for his intransigent attitude to the West.[3]

The Second World War had cost the lives of approximately 50 million people: roughly 20 million Soviets, 5 million Germans, 1.6 million Japanese, 397,000 British and 300,000 Americans. Homeless refugees, without adequate food or employment, surged across Europe, their lives overturned by war. The Allies' strategic bombing of Germany by the RAF at night and by the USAF by day had left millions homeless in Germany. Europe required an organised and well-funded plan to rebuild these people's lives and to support them financially within stable economies.[4] The US Secretary of State George Marshall was keen to get things moving: 'The recovery of Europe has been so far slower than expected. The patient is sinking while the doctors deliberate.'[5]

The historian Alan Axelrod described the intense efforts of the USA, sponsored UNRRA (United Nations Relief and Rehabilitation Administration), to reunite families. The Soviet Union barely cooperated with UNRRA, placing refugees in grim camps in their eastern zones, often using them as forced labour. General Lucius Clay, the military governor of the Western zone, organised the feeding of those in his sector. They received a minimum of 1,500 calories per day, mostly through bread and potatoes, but it was enough to survive until more food arrived. Only the Allies could restore Europe's economies and organise the new infrastructure which was urgently needed to transport coal from the mines and farmers' food to those living in the bombed-out cities.[6] In Europe the Marshall Plan would soon restore hope and prosperity to lands ravaged by war. But in Russia, where the paranoiac dictator Stalin was tightening his murderous grip on his own oppressed nation, such generous gestures were sadly lacking.

Iosif Vissarionovich Dzhugashvili named himself Stalin, 'Man of Steel', in 1912, the year Lenin made him editor of *Pravda* and a member of the Bolshevik Central Committee. Exiled to Siberia in 1913, Stalin had been judged unfit for the Czar's army in 1916. After Lenin's death, he began to methodically eliminate all opposition, starting with those on the left of the Communist Party, then targetting those on the right who stood in his way to absolute power.[7]

Lenin, on his deathbed, had warned against the power Stalin had accumulated: 'I am not sure that he always knows how to use that power with sufficient caution . . . Stalin is too rough . . . becomes insupportable in the office of General Secretary . . . I propose to the comrades to find a way to remove Stalin . . . and appoint to it another man . . . more patient, more loyal, more polite, and more attentive to comrades, less capricious'.[8] It was not to be. The man responsible for unleashing the confrontation between West and East, the Cold War, had already become too powerful and feared. Khrushchev would later recall Stalin's 'utter irresponsibility and complete lack of respect for anyone other than himself'.[9]

Ignoring their past suffering or their patriotic bravery in battle, 4 million of the civilians and soldiers who returned home to the Soviet Union were treated as traitors. It was of no concern to Stalin if they had been forced combattants in the German Army, or Red Army POWs or civilians who had been pressed into labour. Having been in the West, they were suspects and security risks.

The writer John Keep explained how the NKVD, NKGB and SMERSH (Red Army counter intelligence unit) interrogated these hapless Soviet citizens and 'filtered them out' (*fil'tratsiia*). Over half were permitted to return home, only to meet further discrimination. Roughly 20 per cent returned to the army. Of the rest, 608,000 were sent to labour battalions and a staggering total of 273,000 Soviet officers, many of whom were ex-POWs in Germany, were dispatched under NKVD control to the islands of the 'Gulag Archipelago'. Stalin's political system was based on the repression of a vast section of the population. As members of the 'slave class' they were treated as nonentities and exploited. Victims of this forced labour system made a significant contribution to the Soviet economy and the projects associated with the atomic bomb production.[10]

The novelist Aleksandr Solzhenitsyn, awarded the Nobel Prize for Literature in 1970, would describe the horror of the workings of this oppressive prison system of arbitrary arrest and subsequent brief 'trial' in a quasi-judicial 'troika', often on the false evidence of a fellow citizen's denunciation. If you were not executed (the code VMN), the normal sentence was 25 years: 'for nothing you get ten years'. Escape was impossible. The food, clothing and accommodation provided were totally inadequate for the extreme climates. Ordinary citizens could be accused of a number of offences denoted by code-words: ASA for 'anti-Soviet agitation', KRD for 'counter-revolutionary activity', SOS or 'socially dangerous element' or (after the war) VAD (admirer of US democracy).[11]

Prime Minister Clement Attlee was initially willing to give Stalin and the Russians a chance to prove their peaceful intentions through the UN (United Nations) but the scales had finally fallen from his eyes, as the Soviet Union tightened its political and military grip on Eastern Europe and the Balkans. Attlee's Foreign Minister Ernest Bevin, with experience of Marxist agitation in the trade unions, was never under any illusions about Communism. His view was justified in July 1949 when a 'State of Emergency' was declared and the government sent in 13,000 army troops to suppress a Communist-led dock strike.

Keith Jeffery noted that in January 1947, with the international situation worsening, a secret meeting of the Cabinet was held and the decision reached to push ahead with a British independent nuclear deterrent (though this was not divulged to Parliament until May 1948). The Prime Minister would now pursue a strong anti-Soviet line, recognising that Britain's former wartime ally Stalin was a dangerous adversary, posing an imminent threat to Europe and Britain's security. Human intelligence on the Soviet Union and its allies was now vital. Targets for the SIS would be 'the scientific development by any country of new weapons or methods of war' and 'the intention and capability of any foreign country to wage war, together with its economic potential'.[12]

The role of a British military attaché abroad, John Sanderson's future remit, was discovering precisely this information. Major General J.F.C. Fuller summarised the precarious military situation facing the Western Allies in December 1947:

> The forward positions of the Red Army are less than 700 kilometres from the French border. This army consists of 4,500,000 men and 14,000 aeroplanes, reinforced by 1,121,000 satellite troops.

> 56 Russian divisions are stationed in Belorussia and the Baltic States, 43 in East Germany and Poland, 24 in Ukraine, 22 in the Moscow region and 30 in Siberia: in all 175 divisions. The Western allies' force numbers only 2,787,000 men. The British army will soon be reduced to 900,000 men. The American army has only 96,000 men in Germany: the rest are dispersed across the world. As for the French army, which numbered some 100 divisions in 1939, they are now scarcely 5 divisions. 150 divisions would be needed to defend Europe. Neither Europe nor America has such a force.
>
> To the military superiority of the Soviets must be added the communist cells that would disrupt our defence through espionage, sabotage and guerilla activities.[13]

The defence of the British realm depended on the British and US intelligence services above all, both at home and abroad, cooperating to confront and overcome precisely these challenging threats which the Soviet Union posed.

Within the British Army, Sanderson was considering his future career. A York and Lancaster regimental colleague recalled in 2018:

> At the end of the war, John wanted to become a Regular, having served in the Territorial Army before war. In spite of his frontline war service, because he had not been to Sandhurst, he was unlikely to stand a chance of going to Staff College, a theoretical pre-requisite to obtaining an appointment to command. John therefore decided that he wanted to learn Russian. An appointment as a Military Attaché in Moscow would result in him being 'Staff Qualified'. However, John was told that everyone wanted to learn Russian and that he would have to learn Bulgarian as his main language, with Russian the secondary language.

From July 1947 until July 1948 John Sanderson was posted to the Intelligence Corps Depot UK. *JBS*: 'Then to gain a grounding in the Bulgarian Language, I undertook a preliminary course in Bulgarian at the School of Slavonic Studies in London. In April 1948 I successfully passed the Preliminary Examination at interpreter level with 124 marks out of 200. The pass mark was 120 and Peter Greenhalgh just scraped through with 121 marks.'

Chapter 14

Start of the Cold War, Berlin Airlift, 1948

A country that does not respect the rights of its own citizens will not respect the rights of its own neighbours.

Andrei Sakharov

Sakharov was a Soviet nuclear scientist, who became a dissident activist for nuclear disarmament and was awarded the Nobel Peace Prize in 1975.[1] Stalin's oppression of Soviet citizens, as Sakharov points out, was matched by the harsh repression of his satellite neighbours. 1948 was a significant year for Europe. In February the Prague coup had established a Communist dictatorship in Czechoslovakia that would last until 1989. The former First Minister Jan Masaryk was found dead in front of his ministry, no doubt a case of defenestration, a term in use in Prague since 1618, for an individual forcibly ejected from a window. After the imposition of Communism in Poland, Hungary and Romania, the repression of Czech social democrats revealed the true intentions of Stalin in crushing any political opposition to Soviet rule.

Alan Axelrod described how the Americans responded to the worsening situation in Europe, by 3 April approving the $5.3 million Marshall Plan (ERP (European Recovery Plan)), creating an economic zone under US influence to 'act as a buttress against Communism'. Marshall had understood from Kennan's discerning analysis that economic means, rather than military action, would be the most effective tool for containing Soviet influence in Western Europe. Sixteen nations from Iceland, Norway and Sweden in the North, across Western Europe (excepting Spain) to Italy, Greece and Turkey on the Mediterranean signed up for the ERP. Stalin responded by creating the 'Molotov' Plan, economic subsidies to his East European satellites. In the UN, Andrei Vyshinsky stridently declared the Marshall Plan to be a blatant violation of UN principles.[2]

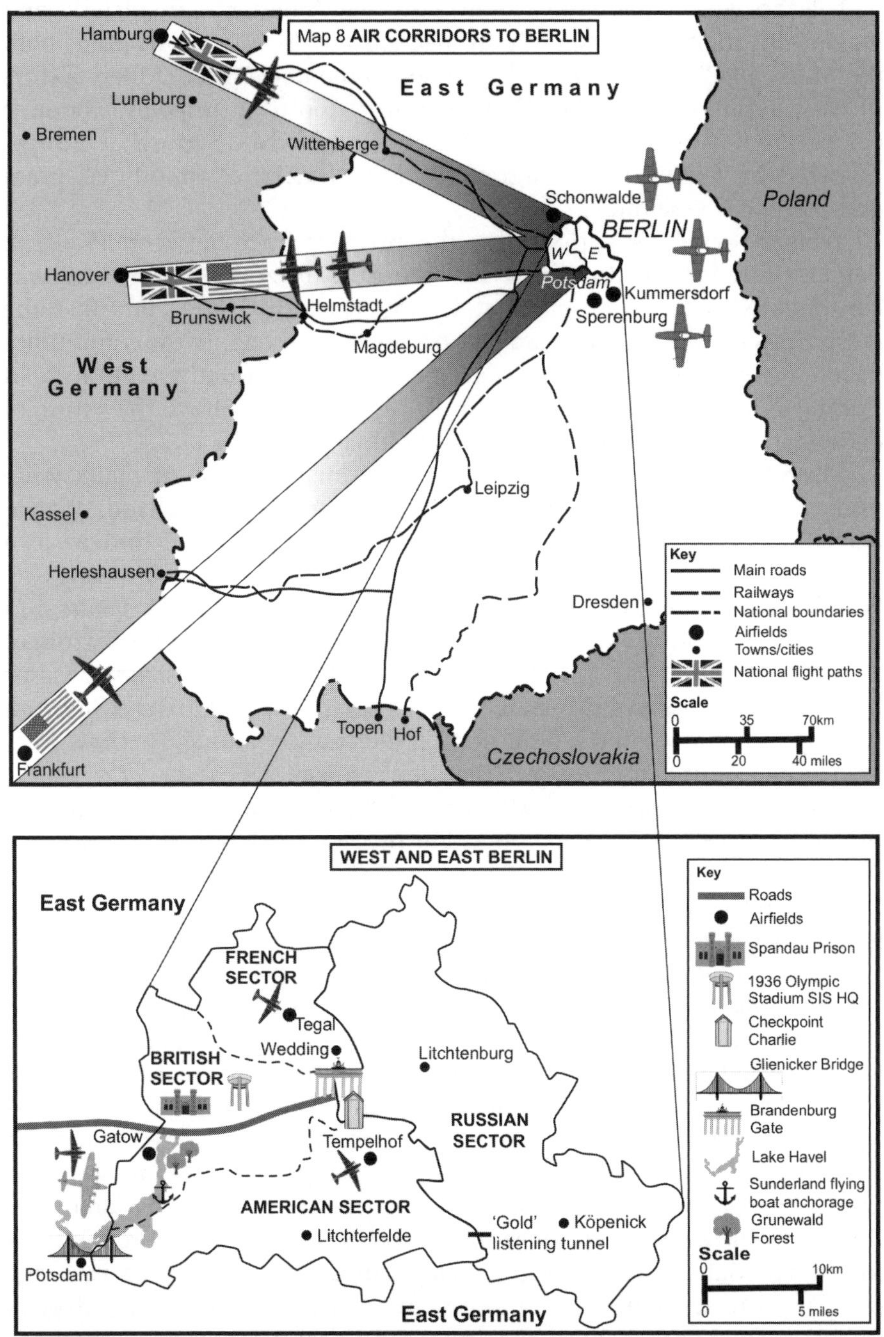
Map 8 AIR CORRIDORS TO BERLIN
East Germany
Hamburg
Luneburg
Bremen
Wittenberge
Schonwalde
BERLIN
W
E
Poland
Hanover
Brunswick
Helmstadt
Potsdam
Kummersdorf
Sperenburg
Magdeburg
West Germany
Leipzig
Kassel
Herleshausen
Dresden
Topen
Hof
Frankfurt
Czechoslovakia
Key
Main roads
Railways
National boundaries
Airfields
Towns/cities
National flight paths
Scale
0
35
70km
0
20
40 miles
WEST AND EAST BERLIN
East Germany
FRENCH SECTOR
Tegal
Wedding
BRITISH SECTOR
Litchtenburg
RUSSIAN SECTOR
Gatow
Tempelhof
AMERICAN SECTOR
Litchterfelde
'Gold' listening tunnel
Köpenick
Potsdam
East Germany
Key
Roads
Airfields
Spandau Prison
1936 Olympic Stadium SIS HQ
Checkpoint Charlie
Glienicker Bridge
Brandenburg Gate
Lake Havel
Sunderland flying boat anchorage
Grunewald Forest
Scale
0
10km
0
5 miles

J. Isaacs and T. Downing show how the Americans financially and logistically mobilised their vitally needed aid to Europe through both the Marshall Plan and airlifted supplies to the beleagured Allied sectors of West Berlin. In April the OEEC (Organisation for European Economic Cooperation) was created. Weeks later the first food aid arrived in Europe, followed by fertilisers and agricultural machinery, commodities, grain and industrial machinery.[3]

Truman gave his support for the Brussels Pact between Holland, Belgium, France and Britain. When the Russian zone of Germany was consolidated into a one-party state, the Western Allies identified the western sector of Germany as 'a democracy welcomed into the community of free peoples'. General Clay declared: 'If we mean that we are to hold Europe against Communism, we must not budge. I believe the future of democracy requires us to stay here until forced out.'[4]

Meanwhile, plans to 'rollback' Communism in the Balkans were underway. In 1946 MI6 had first turned its attentions unofficially to Albania, a small Communist country with a population of around 1 million, as a possible target for detaching from the Balkan Communist states. King Zog had fled into exile in 1939 with all the gold from the national treasury and Enver Hoxha now controlled the country from Tirana, after his seizure of power in the civil war of 1944. In wartime 1945 several resistance teams had been parachuted in by SOE but had disappeared. Hoxha's Sigurimi secret police maintained a tight grip on the country and show trials were held as an example for any with dissident aspirations.[5]

In early 1948 cooperative Allied planning for Albanian incursions was underway. The historian Stephen Dorril described how Frankfurt SIS liaised with DAD (secret US Department of Army Detachment), whose Washington Liaison Officer was Frank Wisner. In 1947 Wisner had been given an official Secretary of State responsibility for Occupied Territories.[6]

Dorril noted that Operation VALUABLE (infiltrating agents into Albania) was undertaken as an SOE–MIR (Military Intelligence Research) operation, with the involvement of MI6's Section D's irregular warfare specialists led by Colin Gubbins, who enlisted Julian Amery to gain senior Conservatives' support and financial backing. Amery was the imperialist right-wing MP who made the revealing comment one day over lunch that 'English foreign policy is founded on two principles: that God is an Englishman, and that the road to India must be kept open.'[7] In March 1949 Amery would argue that it was time to reply 'to Communist revolutions in China, Malaya and Greece by launching insurrection or sabotage campaigns in the Balkans . . . The vital need is to build up a powerful Resistance network behind the Iron Curtain and in threatened areas.'

Kim Philby commented drily on these plans that: 'given the drawbacks, I thought it surprising that the operation ever got off the ground'.[8]

Monty Woodhouse, a former SOE operative who had organised guerilla resistance in Greece during the war and was now Head of the Mission in Greece, was doubtful of the success of such operations. He believed that Ernest Bevin, who was still aggrieved by the aggressive mining of British destroyers in the Corfu Straits by the Communists in 1946, had been misled into giving implied approval for these operations by inaccurate reports of likely Albanian resistance to Communism. Woodhouse's judgement was correct, as would be his positive views on involving MI6 in a successful operation in 1951 in Iran.[9]

The plans for Albania went ahead, as Stephen Dorril further explained, with Malta chosen as the forward operations base. In June 1948 the US NSC (National Security Council) gave Wisner's OPC the go-ahead to oppose 'the vicious and covert activities of the USSR, its satellite countries and communist groups', as they thought fit. A recent agreement between Moscow and Tirana for a Russian naval base at Valona (thought to be for Soviet submarines) in exchange for aid to Albania, as well as the Albanian support for the Greek Communist rebels, swung the argument in Washington towards US support for military incursions into Albania. MI6 in Broadway was informed by Wisner that the US was now backing them in the operation they named BG/FIEND (Top Secret US CIA/OPC plan of 1951 to infiltrate Albania).[10]

On 20 March 1948 Marshal Sokolovsky, the Military Governor of Berlin, who had been Marshal Zhukhov's chief of staff during the Soviet advance on Berlin, walked out of the Berlin Control Council.[11] In Berlin a full-scale Cold War, within a hairtrigger of actual war, was now under way between Russia and the West. On 31 March the Russians began harrassing Allied transport on the rail and road routes into Berlin, by demanding special permits and travel IDs. When General Clay sent a troop train through to test access by rail, the Russians directed it into a siding. When they blocked the Helmstedt crossing with a barrier, General Clay considered its removal by force. In response to the halting of Allied trains, Clay ordered a small-scale airlift of thirty-five days' supplies. On 5 April came the first deaths, after a BEA (British European Airways) Viking plane was buzzed by a Soviet Yak-3 fighter. They collided and crashed, killing those on board both aircraft.

On 18 June the new Deutschmark, secretly printed in the USA, was introduced overnight replacing the old worthless Reichsmark, with the additional insurance policy of 20 million cigarettes, a 'de facto' curency available for barter purposes. Amongst the impoverished Germans, only those possessing valuables such as jewellery or antiques could obtain coffee, clothes or food from the black market or the US PX store (US Military Service Store).

On 24 June the Russians retaliated by introducing the Ostmark in their zone and imposing a total land blockade of Berlin, severing all canal, rail and land access from the West across Eastern Germany to Berlin and preventing the movement of personnel as well as vital supplies of food and coal. Power was cut off from West Berlin, supposedly due to 'coal shortages'. Soviet troops surrounding Berlin vastly outnumbered the diminished Western military presence in Berlin: Stalin was gambling that the Allies would not resort to the use of force and that all of Berlin would fall under Soviet control.

General Clay and the British were prepared to make a show of force to gain access. However, President Truman, faced with the coming US elections, considered the USA unprepared for a possible war with Russia: it would require a year-and-a-half to re-mobilise troops and prepare US forces for a possible conflict. There were grave doubts that this city of over 2 million people could be safely and logistically supplied through an airlift. Clay's conviction, backed up by Truman's resolve to stand firm, won over the Allies. They would not evacuate Berlin. (The French would have no part in the airlift.)[12]

The resulting 'Berlin Airlift' (Luftbrucke: Air bridge, named Operation VITTLES by the US and PLANEFARE by the British) was a symbol of collective Allied intent. Written agreements with the Soviets in 1945 had guaranteed the unrestricted use of air corridors from West Germany to Berlin. The Berlin airlift which began on 26 June proved to be an extraordinarily efficient logistical operation, advised by the USAF General Curtis LeMay, involving 'round the clock' transport plane flights (two-thirds US and one-third British), landing on the Templehof and Gatow runways. A third airport, completed at Tegel by 20,000 German men and women, working 3 shifts a day, enabled 60 more C-54s to land. Sutherland flying boats from Hamburg put down on Lake Havel. The Russians did occasionally buzz Allied aircraft in the three air corridors but the Russian air controllers in the four-power centre continued to participate in operational safety. At the height of the airlift, aircraft were arriving and departing every 45 seconds. It appeared that Berlin could be supplied from the air indefinitely.[13]

The Berlin blockade was finally lifted on 12 May 1949, by which time the Western Allies had formed the strong defensive alliance NATO, which was signed by the foreign ministers of the twelve founding nations on 4 April.[14]

1a

1b

1c

1d

2a

2b

2c

2d

2e

3a

3b

3c

Army Form E 507.

TERRITORIAL ARMY

Form of Parents' Consent to the enlistment of Youths under 18 years of age.

I consent to the enlistment, into His Majesty's Territorial Army,

of my Son, John Burden SANDERSON

who was born on 6th. August 1921.

Alex. Sanderson, (Father)
Major.

(Mother)

(or Guardian)

Signature of Parents or Guardian

R.A. RECORD & PAY OFFICE 17 MAR 1938 WINCHESTER

DATED Fifteenth day of March, 1938

Address 24 Kingshall Road.

Beckenham, Kent.

4a

4b

4c

5a

5b

5c

6a

JANUARY, 1941 27 MONDAY
New Moon 11.3 a.m.

We have had no air raid for 7 days & we are wondering what it means – is Hitler massing all his planes for a mass attack on this country – anyway we are ready for him – & as my Daughter Pat says – Good I hope they do invade us – they'll get whats coming to them. Had a letter from Dick he has passed his pt. & rifle drill. & expects to go on a morse course soon –

6b

SECRET. (Alex Sanderson 19.10.42.)

Backward tilt of Aircrew Units when landing

Tilt of Aircrew Units at take-off.

Alternative Profile

Alternative Profile

Alternative Profile

Alternative Profile with longer fuselage.

"SANDERSON I-S.2."

6c

7a

7b

7c

7d

7e

8a

8b

8c

9a

9b

9c

9d

9e

10a

10b

10c

10d

10e

11a

11d

11b

11c

11e

12b

12c

12a

12d

12e

"HOW DO YOU FIT THIS THING ON?!!"

13a

13b

13c

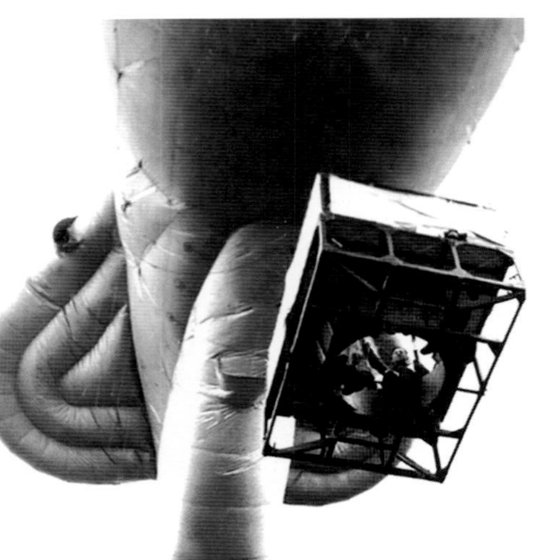

14a

14b

14c

14d

15a

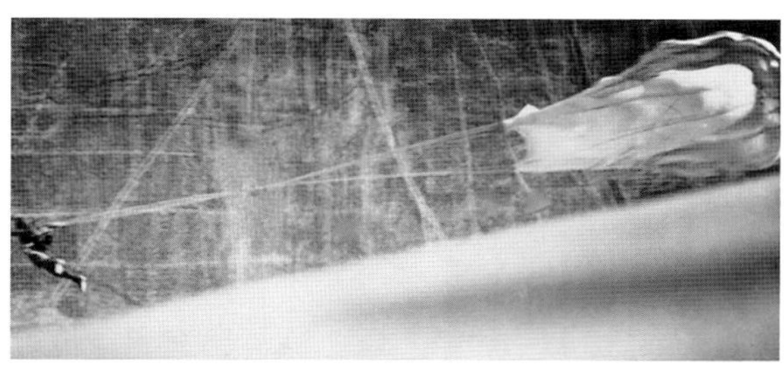
15b

15c

15d

16a

16b

16c

16d

In 1996 Lord Denis Greenhill, Chairman of the JIC (Joint Intelligence Committee) explained that the post-war threat from the Russians was 'absolutely clear'. Only with American military help could Western Europe be secure. 'Their support was absolutely essential': it was imperative that the US retained sufficient troops to defend Europe.

'France', Greenhill wrote, 'was a Communist country very largely' with a very strong Communist Party. British relations with the French were not good. 'There was the Communist element and . . . the Gaullist element', so the British could not rely upon French assistance. Relations with the Americans was naturally better.[15]

In August 1948 Captain Sanderson was 'posted to the Military Attaché in Paris for Bulgarian language duty overseas'. John Sanderson's activities would include attending the UN sessions in the place du Trocadero, on the right bank of the Seine over the bridge from the Eiffel Tower. The UN had its first General Assembly in October 1948 in the Palais de Chaillot, next to the Musée de la Marine and the Musée de L'Homme. Ironically, it was here that Hitler had been photographed eight years previously, in June 1940, with the Eiffel Tower behind him. His next stop was to visit Les Invalides, where Napoleon's tomb was placed. Both leaders had failed to invade England and invaded Russia.[16]

Chapter 15

Paris Mission and UNO, 1948

On 3 August 1948 Captain John Sanderson arrived in Paris for language studies, officially as an AMA (Assistant Military Attaché) at the British Embassy in Rue du Faubourg Saint-Honoré, near the Elysée Palace. John was accompanied by a fellow officer and 'student', Captain Peter Greenhalgh DFC (born 26 July 1919) of the Royal Artillery, who also had successfully passed the preliminary exam in Bulgarian in London in February. Greenhalgh had been commissioned as a 2nd lieutenant in August 1939, having served in the TA for a year. After flying in 'Special Operations' in the war, in 1947 Greenhalgh had applied to be an AOP (Air Observation Post) pilot and had started the course, only to be suspended. In November 1951 John would take over from Peter at the Edirne Intelligence Station on the Turkish European side of the Bosphorus, on the northern Turkish border with Bulgaria. From August 1957 for two years, until his retirement aged 40, Major Greenhalgh would be AMA in Warsaw, as a GSO2.

In Paris the Soviet intelligence services had a long history of hunting down opposition figures. The NKVD had abducted and killed several Soviet émigrés, including the Ukrainian General Petlura, murdered in 1926, a White Russian general, kidnapped in the street in 1930, and General Yevgeni Miller, who was abducted in 1937. According to the French Sûreté, General Miller, who was a former White Guard, was dragged off the street and driven to the Soviet Embassy where he was drugged, and dumped in a trunk. Taken aboard a Soviet freighter in Le Havre, he was returned to Moscow where he was interrogated and subsequently shot.[1]

More recently, General Ivan Ivanovich Agayants, a tall Armenian adopting the alias of 'Avalov' and the *Rezident* (Embassy KGB Head of Station) of the MGB (Soviet Ministry of State Security), would have been closely monitoring and organising the penetration of émigré groups from Soviet Bloc countries such as Bulgaria. Agayants, ensconced in the Soviet Embassy in Paris from 1946 to 1948, would later be appointed the head of the West European Department of the KGB. Until his death in 1968, he would be head of Service Department 'D' (later 'A'), the disinformation section of the First Chief Directorate, founded in 1959.[2]

Agayants liked to brag how he had penetrated the SDECE. In 1952 he contemptuously described to his colleagues, in a lecture at the Moscow Centre, how French intelligence was 'a prostitute I put in my pocket'.[3] After Agayants had left Paris, fewer reports were filed in 1949 to the Moscow Centre. Files on Agayants' activities surfaced forty-four years later when a retired KGB activist, Vasili Mitrokhin, codenamed JESSANT, who had begun his career as a Soviet intelligence officer in 1948 (when MGB and GRU military intelligence were combined), defected to the British in 1992 and was exfiltrated from Riga, Latvia. Christopher Andrew later co-wrote a book with him, *The Mitrokhin Archive*, on his extraordinary story. Mitrokhin was adamant that his files must be published, as a record of the harm the Soviet system had caused.

Mitrokhin was an extraordinarily determined individual. With admirable sangfroid, the KGB archivist, who from 1980 was responsible for the relocation of KGB archives from the overcrowded Lubyanka to the new HQ in Yasenova, had for twelve years secretly copied everything he could lay his hands on and smuggled it out to his dacha, where the 25,000 handwritten files lay buried in his garden until the end of the Soviet Union. His meticulous cache of files contained details dating back to 1918 of thousands of Soviet agents, including illegal agents, operating across the world.

Mitrokhin's handwritten notes revealed that fewer reports were filed from Paris to Moscow after Agayant's departure in 1948 because of a 'deterioration in the operational situation': the French DST (French domestic intelligence agency) and the Sûreté were heightening their surveillance. As a result the Paris *Rezidentura* was advised to avoid meeting agents on the streets, in cafes or in restaurants but rather to use dead letter boxes, notes in invisible ink or to communicate by radio.[4] (Of course, the reduction of expenses claims for French alcohol and meals could have been a factor.) In London at this time SIS had serious concerns about the possibility of a military conflict with Russia. In April 1948 Jack Easton, the VCSS (Vice Chief of SIS) had visited Washington to discuss a range of topics with the newly formed CIA: 'the handling of defectors, potential deception operations, signals intelligence, special operations and black propaganda operations'. Easton explained that the SIS had assimilated a 'small part of the old S.O.E. and was an integrated organisation for intelligence and special operations'.[5] (Christopher Andrew noted that Philby had been recruited into Section D of SIS in

1940 by Guy Burgess, before it was merged into SOE. Philby's role was a political officer preparing sabotage agents, before they flew off, in Churchill's words, 'to set Europe ablaze'.[6])

Six months later, in October 1948, SIS and the CIA held a series of meetings known as 'The London Conference on War Planning'. These were attended by senior CIA officials. Professor Jeffery's examination of official SIS files, for his officially sanctioned history of MI6, has revealed that much of the London discussions covered detailed practical matters, such as the joint arrangements for handling tactical intelligence at theatre HQ level, stay-behind projects, special operations planning, common training and how to deal 'with the French in peace and war.' The conference laid the foundations for a successful long-term relationship between the CIA and SIS. This led to the formation of the Clandestine Committee of NATO, which oversaw the co-ordination of stay-behind agents, secret intelligence collection and special operations in the event of a future war in Europe.[7]

In Italy CIA operations were successful in preventing the election of a Communist government, through the distribution of financial aid and contributions to politicians of moderate political parties. [8] In France the PCF (French Communist Party) was very strong, having played a leading role in the Resistance during the German occupation. In the 1945 elections, they had won a quarter of the votes cast, the largest support in Western Europe. In May 1947, however, when the Communists had voted a 'no confidence' motion in Paul Ramadier's government, the French leader expelled them from his cabinet.[9]

The historians Isaacs and Downing described the French Communist Party's determined efforts to undermine the 4th Republic. A strike at the Paris Renault factory led to industrial chaos. The Communist-led CGT Union (French transport union) staged strikes over rising prices. In the autumn of 1947, there were frequent disputes which shut down the coal mines, the electricity supply and the railways. Rubbish piled up in the streets of Paris. By December 3 million workers were on strike. Then the situation deteriorated and workers began sabotaging the mines. On the night of 4 December, when the express train from Lille to Paris was deliberately derailed, twenty passengers were killed. This tragedy finally swung public opinion and the French government offered a national wage increase and the strike action died down.[10]

In a nation riven by political and social unrest, Captain John Sanderson arrived in Paris to take up his SIS and military post as an AMA, attached to the British Embassy. *JBS*:

THE CASTLE OF SHADOWS – Le Chateau des Ombrages

[8August 1948] Number 1, Chemin de L'Aubergerie, Marly-Le-Roi, Seine-et-Oise,

Dear Audrey, I went down to Marly today with Mr Batchinski and we called in at the 'Chateau des Ombrages': it is the hotel owned by the cousin of the Batchinskis. She is an extremely pleasant woman, who speaks very good English and I am invited to tea there this afternoon. Marly is a very small place and has not more than a dozen shops in a tiny cobbled street. La Grande Rue! Not so 'Grande', but are quite amusing. Unfortunately, going to ruin for want of repair. In this street, there are a dozen or so shops and an equal number of cafés. Two-hundred years ago it must have flourished as a seat of the aristocracy of France, for one of the palaces of the King of France was here in 'Les Ombrages' but very little now remains. Surrounding it is the forest, which is on a little hill, overlooking the river valley. There are beautiful relics of lovely old houses in complete dilapidation. Nothing is being done to preserve them, and before many years, they will be in complete ruins. I have never seen such lovely scroll gates and iron railings, and they alone show evidence of the bygone splendour of this small town.

We walked from the shack, through the woods, to the town – a very lovely walk which I understand from Mr Batchinski is crowded with Parisians on Sundays. If you were to walk along one of the paths through even thicker trees and scrub than this you would come across a wooden shack in which are housed two Russians and one Englishman! But I warn you, unless you know the way, there is no knowing where you might end up! One thing is certain, you would enjoy the company. On my stroll around Marly yesterday, I came across this pond on the main road from Paris to St Germain. Children were having a glorious time bathing in the water, and on the side of the pond stood numerous caravans, either the advance guard or rear guard of a fun-fair that has or will entertain the locals. In the background is part of the grounds of a palace that is now destroyed.

Practically the main topic of conversation in France, as in England, is food. Bread does not seem scarce, but it is a dirty brown colour, and I believe flour is difficult to come by. Of course, everything is expensive, and if one had the money, even the food I mentioned as being impossible to obtain, can be purchased on a semi-legal black-market! This place where I am staying to learn Bulgarian is only a wooden shack and it will be impossible to live here in the winter. I am very fond of my hosts the Batchinskis (they are Russian DPs, displaced persons) and especially of Mr B. with whom I have long conversations on all manner of topics in Bulgarian. He is one of the most intelligent and well-informed old persons I have met for a long term. The photograph of the old couple is perfect – you can see pathos written all over their faces, and even their attitude is one of past sufferings and hardship. I feel sorry for them, and quite honestly, if it had not been for that, I would have left here the very day I arrived! As it is, I am staying here until the end of the month, and will then move somewhere temporarily and have the old chap coming to me once or twice a week to give me lessons – not that I really want him, but the money will help them out. My room is the open window behind the old couple, and the big window is the sitting-dining-kitchen.

[11 August 1948] The General at the British Embassy gave us a typical 'pet-talk' today, and we left his office to return to our various homes. Peter Greenalgh and I arranged to lunch together.

I was to spend two hours talking Bulgarian to Peter's landlord Sileyanov, for which the War Office will pay him 300 francs an hour (7/-). I am to choose someone to teach me for two hours each day for five days a week. We have been made temporary members of the Embassy club and we had lunch there today. It's far cheaper than anywhere outside. Peter and I strolled down the main boulevard, before going for my lesson. Sileyanov himself is one of those suave gentlemen who wear pin-striped suits, suede shoes and sleek black hair – you know the type! God only knows what he does for a living, for he never seems to go out to work. His girlfriend I saw for a fleeting second, a heavily made-up Mayfair face, tall and slender figure, beautifully dressed. From this brief description of them both, you can imagine they are quite congenial company to live with. He, incidentally, is awaiting his divorce before getting married again!! I liked him as far as conversation went – he speaks beautiful Bulgarian and he is very easy to understand. I may take him on for three days a week at a couple of hours a day. I gather from Peter he could do with the extra cash! After the lesson, I was walking back towards the station, and in my frantic questioning of the way from passers-by, I met a young Frenchman, who told me that he hopes to visit England next year, and wants to learn English. He has a wife and four children!! We got on quite well, he speaks enough English to make himself understood, and before we parted, we exchanged addresses: he wants me to go to dinner with him soon. I shall look forward to that, as it is always useful to hear what's going on amongst the French middle and working classes – politics, I mean!!

[12 August 1948] Whilst I was in Paris yesterday I thought I would buy a lottery ticket for fun – they cost 50 francs each and if one wins, one gets 1/10 of the total. I imagine one could buy the whole ticket for 500 francs, but I don't propose to keep the French government going as well as the British government! The results are announced in the daily papers. I enclose a cutting so you will see I haven't won anything!! I think we ought to have a national lottery in England. Look what a lot of money it would raise for the treasury. On Saturday Peter, his family, yours truly and my family are trotting off to Versailles for the day! What a jolly outing that ought to be – Mr and Mrs Batchinski and I chatting in Bulgarian, Peter talking to his hostess in Polish, the two families conversing in Russian, and Peter and I talking to Peter's host in English because he doesn't speak Bulgarian or Polish. This is his second wife: she learned to speak Polish before she met this husband! Koussef, the 'stick-in-the mud', has trotted off to Belgium but he has left me the addresses of several places in Paris where I might contact Bulgarians, mostly students. Apparently there is a Professor of Bulgarian at the Paris School of Slavonic studies, but believe it or not, he does not speak much Bulgarian! But Koussef suggests he might have several useful books in the language.

[13th August 1948] I went to Versailles today, and I was very impressed with the town and Palace. How wonderful it must have been in the 17th Century when the Court of France was the diplomatic centre of the world, and everything centred around the court at Versailles.

[14 August 1948] Chateau des Ombrages.

Dear Audrey, When I left the University I called on Peter Greenhalgh. I found him in his flat, dressed in a very smart dressing gown, complaining because he was having to clean his own shoes – and in the kitchen too! So I sat with him whilst he did them, which I might say was a little time, for he uses a toothbrush, and cleans them as minutely as he does his teeth!! However, the result was as shining a pair of shoes as I have ever seen, and whether it was to display their splendour, or to be sociable, but I don't know which, we then proceeded to walk down the Champs Elysées. What a wonderful avenue it is, much wider than the Kaiser Dam in Berlin, and at night time it's a real picture with all the neon lights lit up, the cafés full of people sitting on the pavements under bright-coloured awnings, drinking various assortments of wine at ridiculously cheap prices, young beauties trotting up and down showing off their latest creations from top fashion houses, huge American cars moving about like great black beetles, and the occasional street vendor lurking around trying to sell a complete set of dirty postcards – not I imagine without success!

Yes, that side of Paris is very fine, and I think the average visitor from abroad, with sufficient money to have a good time, only sees that side of France, and goes home thinking how wonderful France is, and what a b. awful country their own is! They don't see the way the present Frenchman despises the English (and more so the Americans), how they find it difficult to live at all on the present inflationary prices, how difficult some food is to obtain, and how uncertain the Frenchman is of his political future! Theirs is not a happy life at the moment, and indeed it's a mere existence for most of them, and although the shops are full of the most lovely things, one does not see much buying going on. One can get anything one wants, without any sort of coupon – if you can pay for it. Nylons at a pound each, shoes of any description, silks to equal the finest ever produced in Japan, and food of any description. That's France today.

[14 August 1948] I went to look up the places that Kusseff had given me in his letter. First of all, I went to the café where the Bulgarians in Paris have this club, but like everything else, it was closed until the end of August. I then went down to the 'University City' (opposite Le Parc Montsouris) – and true to its name, it very nearly is a city on its own: the most beautiful buildings covering square miles of grounds, and each country has its own 'house', except of course the Bulgarians! I went into the 'Maison Franco-Britannique' which was full of young English men and women, and enquired whether there were any Bulgarians in the University – nobody knew, in spite of there being 3,000 Bulgarian students in Paris!

In his dealings with the students whom he contacted John assumed the alias of 'John Wilkinson'. At the Embassy he reverted to his official role as an AMA.

[16 August 1948] I spent the afternoon reading the 'History of Bulgaria', but so far I have only managed to reach 5,000 years before Christ! However, I am plodding through it and hope eventually to reach Bulgarian history! The evening was perfect so Mrs Batchinski suggested we go into the woods to pick mushrooms. What a lot has happened in 18 months, hasn't it Audrey? We certainly have not been having a dull and drab existence, and now, when I look back over these months, I marvel that we have done so much in such a short space of time.

This is the Chateau des Ombrages where all your letters arrive. It is run by the cousin of Mrs Batchinski, and they are the kindest of people. I have already been to tea with them and this afternoon I go there for a bath! The place is full of émigré white Russians, Romanians, Slavs etc. who like to go there to be amongst friends. I have not met one of them I do not like. What a difference between these people and the snobs of Hampstead!

The Russians had no doubt penetrated these émigré groups.

[16 August 1948] Dear Audrey, I am going up to Paris today looking for a house. Everywhere I go they say: 'C'est très difficile, Monsieur', and open the palms of their hands and, with their head on the side, purse their lips at you! Today I worked for four hours without a break on Bulgarian and then when Mr Batchinski and I got together talking about the Army, we did not stop from 6pm until 11pm. It went on all through dinner as well, with old Mrs Batchinski joining in the odd argument.

Today after lunch, my hosts and I were chatting, as is our wont, when suddenly there was a knock on the door and a strange face appeared. He turned out to be the Bulgarian that Peter and I had tried to look up in Paris yesterday but who was out. I had left my name and address so he decided to come down here to see me – in spite of the fact that he is leaving for Austria tonight. I'm only sorry I didn't get in touch with him before, for a more charming chap, I have not met for a long time. He is studying to be a doctor in Austria, and is very well educated, and has a natural smile and manner – nothing affected about him. He stayed four hours talking to us, until he had to leave to catch his train. The Batchinskis were very impressed with him, especially as he knows many of their friends, and has been in Bulgaria until last year. He has promised to send me some Bulgarian books and he has told me to write to him whenever I wish, for anything I want.

Yesterday I got the 'gen' on having a car out here: I have seen one and the thought occurred to me of driving to Germany, having the car re-cellulosed in a Kraut workshop for cigarettes and bringing it out again, perhaps with a new hood on it!

[24 August 1948] Dear Audrey, It has been raining continually for the past 48 hours. I shall not be surprised if the ark comes sailing around the corner at any moment! I have been completely unsuccessful in finding a suitable house in Paris or the countryside around. I keep worrying about not being with you on the one hand, and my duty to the Army on the other – I must pass my interpreter's exam for my whole career depends on it. If I don't pass it after the army has spent so much on training me for it, then they will never give me another chance again i.e. for staff college etc. I must pass it for the sake of my family too. At the tennis club today I had a very pleasant afternoon – I listened to French, Bulgarian, Russian and English in quick succession, and answered half in English and half in Bulgarian. The War Office is right, when one is learning the language as well as we have to know our language on this course, the only way is to sink oneself into a Bulgarian family and begin to think like them, in their own language, and this can only be done if one lives with them 24 hours a day. I have found a Bulgarian family in Paris who will be suitable for this type of instruction, and I will have to go to the French School of Slavonic studies every day as well. The Batchinskis speak the most awful Bulgarian, which for the moment it's doing me no harm, but later on, when I progress more, their Russian dialect may make a lot of difference. Next week I am back on leave by train to England. I'll soon be there and finally take the trip across the Channel and see the white cliffs of Dover again. With my feet firmly on English soil again (and Kentish soil at that!)

After John's return from England and a briefing from the FO, in which he explained the importance of a more appropriate 'host' family, the British Authorities made relevant enquiries and arranged for him to move to the wealthy residential area of Neuilly, not far from the Arc de Triomphe, to live with a pre-Communist Bulgarian Foreign Minister Kiroff, his wife Lena and their daughter Ninka, a student. Kiroff, an anglophile, had held an important post in the wartime Sofia government, albeit briefly. US diplomatic conference papers from 1943 reveal that the Bulgarian government, of which he was a cabinet member, had refused to stop sending Bulgarian troops abroad, in particular into Albania.

Bozhiloff and . . . Kiroff, declared that they considered Bulgaria's war against England and the United States as purely symbolical . . .

> there has occurred sharp difference of opinion on the question of the recognition of Mussolini. Kiroff, who was formerly Minister of Foreign Affairs for a short period, opposed this recognition, but the other members of the Cabinet obviously under German pressure took a contrary decision, as a result of which Kiroff resigned.[11]

In Paris Kiroff was considered a European 'Leader in Opposition' and would be in a position to instruct John comprehensively on both Bulgarian society and its politics, before the Communists took over. In addition, Kiroff would had have many contacts within the Bulgarian Community in Paris (which had undoubtedly been infiltrated by Russian intelligence). Kiroff, given his opposition to Communism, would have been in danger from a unit of Department 13, the successor to SMERSH (Smert Shpionam! death to spies) after its disbandment in 1946. From October 1947 to November 1952 Soviet Foreign Intelligence had been transferred from the MGB to KI and they would have been aware of Kiroff's existence and been watching him. Philby would certainly have been aware of Kiroff's role in Paris. In Turkey since 1947, Harold Adrian Russell 'Kim' Philby at this time was head of the SIS station. The MI6 HQ in Istanbul, as he was to explain in his autobiography, 'was then the main southern base for intelligence work directed against the Soviet Union and the Socialist countries of the Balkans and Central Europe'.[12]

For MI6 it was becoming evident that the hostile and oppressive hold the Eastern bloc regimes were tightening on their satellite states made penetrating these countries increasingly difficult. SOE and SIS had successfully coordinated wartime resistance behind the German lines, and it was decided that this experience could be put to good use organising and infiltrating émigré groups back behind the Iron Curtain to obtain information and to attempt insurrection in their country of origin.

A great many of SIS operations were to be compromised both by Philby, who had been recruited by the Russians after a meeting in Regent's Park with a Soviet controller, and his Communist colleague George Blake, who probably betrayed the greater number of Western agents to the Russians. When SIS head of counter intelligence Philby had recommended:

> To establish penetration in depth, it was useless to look for agent-material locally . . . we would clearly have to concentrate on émigré communities to find agents of sufficient ability to be trained to our requirements. My first recommendation to HQ was that our stations in Paris, Beirut, Washington and other centres, where refugees tended to congregate, be instructed to institute a search.[13]

John Sanderson was well placed to identify possible recruits for this cause but would later remark to the author that Kim Philby had betrayed all the agents he sent behind the Iron Curtain. John Sanderson's attempts to recruit émigrés in Paris would have had a little chance of coming to fruition. As Dick White, the head of MI5 (British domestic security up to 3 miles offshore) counter espionage, later commented: 'No doubt Philby betrayed the Albanian operation, but overshadowing this is the fact that all émigré organisations are hopelessly infiltrated from the outset.' James Jesus Angleton of the CIA was also convinced that Russian Intelligence had penetrated all émigré groups. US FIEND intelligence officers, talking of Albania, commented: 'The recruitment of . . . émigrés was too hurried and insecure, with the result that word of the operation quickly spread throughout the émigré community and as quickly reached Russian agents.' Dorril notes that the Russians penetrated the Albanian VALUABLE operation with an agent who verified Philby's general reports and provided details of the time and place of landings.[14]

JBS:

> [17 September 1948] 126 Rue Perronet, Neuilly, Paris.
>
> Dear Audrey, we had another pleasant 'house party' at the Kiroffs yesterday – a big French tobacco producer brought along his Bulgarian wife and French sister. They had lived in Bulgaria for years before the war and spoke Bulgarian so I enjoyed talking to them. Fortunately her sister spoke English so occasionally I broke off and chatted to her. It was kind of the Kiroffs to chat in Bulgarian as their usual language is French to their friends. Later I gave the Kiroffs lessons in making tea, and before too long hope to have them trained!!

On the same day of 17 September de Gaulle placed a wreath on a memorial in Grenoble. From 19 July to 11 September France had been without a stable government. In response to the Communist threat, General de Gaulle was touring south-eastern France to promote his political 'Rassemblement' which he believed was the only group able to prevent the Communists seizing power. The following day, when de Gaulle was left with little police protection, his car was attacked by Communist demonstrators who attempted to smash his window. That evening there was a death and many wounded in shooting incidents between de Gaulle's party and the Communists.[15] The RPF ('Le Rassemblement du Peuple Français' – 'The unity of the French people') was a political party founded by de Gaulle in April 1947 to encourage French society to rise above its left–right divisions. The clever use of the word *une rassemblement* appealed to the disaffected military, as it also means a 'military parade'. The word is used in the French expression: '*Ceux qui se ressemblent s'assemblent*' ('Birds of a feather flock together').[16].

JBS:

> [20 September 1948] *Moya mela bulka* (My darling wife!), I shall spend most of my day at my Bulgarian, or with my Bulgarians! From 9.30 this morning until lunch time, Kiroff and I were at it solidly, and since after lunch I have been sitting in my room translating. My window looks out on to the quadrangle of the flats. At times I find it quite amusing looking out of this window, especially first thing in the morning when all the wives don their dressing gowns and old bedroom slippers before trotting round the corner to the local baker's shop to buy the bread for their husband's breakfast.
>
> Old Batchinski came this morning to give me a lesson, and I managed to sit through 2 hours of rather doubtful instruction! However, he knows quite a lot of other things that are very useful – at least they are when I have translated them into English. The Kiroffs had guests to dinner: between you and I only, a very pleasant youngish Bulgarian and rather attractive young wife who have just escaped from Bulgaria. He was one of the biggest businessmen in Sofia, and as you can imagine, he had a fairly good connection with nearly all that went on in the capital. He and his wife kept us amused with stories of the present regime. From all accounts, conditions in Bulgaria are so controlled by the Communists (dominated by so-called Russian administrators) that the people dare not speak a word against the regime for fear of being executed, and generally, I feel, the country would come over on to our side the very moment we walk into the country.

This was the prevailing attitude of the SIS and the CIA at this time; they optimistically thought that by inserting special forces or émigré resistance fighters behind the Iron Curtain they could successfully light the fire of revolution. Their betrayal by Philby, gossip amongst the émigré communities and the tight hold the Communists held over their satellites made these incursions doomed to failure.

At this very moment in Budapest, a former MI (R) officer and British wartime Military Attaché in Sofia, an explosives expert called Kavan

Elliott, was being interrogated by the Hungarian AVO (predecessor of AVH: Hungarian intelligence and security agency). During the war Major Elliott had made friends with the left-wing leader of the Bulgarian Agrarian Party, Georgi Dimitrov, who was funded with SOE gold to build a resistance network. Dimitrov later worked for an SOE radio station, Free Independent Bulgaria. Elliot was captured by the Germans in the war and imprisoned in Colditz. Elliott had continued to work post-war as an SIS 'unofficial asset' in Hungary, running a network of agents. His son later said his father was collaborating on a Vatican anti-Communist project, Intermarium, with connections to Cardinal Mindszenty, head of the Hungarian Catholic Church.

The Catholic resistance movement had ties with MI6 in Vienna. Their leader was Bela Bajomi, who owned a textile factory in Budapest. MI6 requested Bajomi to organise a resistance group for intelligence gathering and sabotage. A young student, Paul Gorka, noted types and registration plates of Russian vehicles, armour and tanks, as well as details of the Russian airport construction. Yugoslav intelligence officers were cooperating with MI6 to help send couriers and agents into Hungary. The unfortunate Bajomi was kidnapped in Vienna and executed in April 1951.

Gorka, who was arrested, imprisoned for life and later escaped during the 1956 Hungarian uprising, considered that MI6 had so many failures because 'the spymasters were more agents provocateurs than Secret intelligence agents'.[17] However, many workable operations and networks would have been betrayed by Kim Philby. He had knowledge of the recruitment of Hungarian exiles into organisations like Intermarium. Stephen Dorril pointed out that the security lapses of these badly organised anti-Communist groups, many of which were false police groups established by Soviet agents, were more likely to have been a result of Soviet-organised infiltration than betrayal in London.[18] As Head of Section IX, Philby had more than a counter-intelligence role, being in charge of Britain's anti-Soviet operations. He was effectively running British intelligence operations against the Soviet bloc. It is no wonder that John Sanderson said Philby betrayed all his agents.[19]

JBS:

> [20 September 1948] The Kiroffs were excited last night – I taught them how to play 'Liar dice'! Ever since then, after every meal, out come the dice for a few minutes, so before long, I know we are going to have to invite some more guests here in order to play this new wonderful game. Needless to say, I haven't lost a game yet!

The Swedish Count Folke Bernadette, the Swedish UN envoy to Palestine, was assassinated in September by the Stern group, led by Yitshak Shamir. Also assassinated was Colonel André Sérot the Chief UN Observer.

JBS:

> News is not very refreshing though, is it? Poor Count Bernadette. He was a good man, it does not seem right that he should have 'brought it'; one feels that there is no good left in the world these days, when chaps like him have to be killed, and a person like the Communist leader in Italy, who was wounded recently, be saved? Predictably Nina, when she heard the news, had to take to her bed with nervous convulsions!! She was convinced that Count Bernadette's death meant that the Russians were approaching Marly-Le-Roi!! However, by way of compensation, the news came from England of greater output all round and a halving of our adverse trade balance. Heartening news indeed, which no doubt my family put down to anyone but the Labour government! – we would have to find a very good Conservative government to do any better. The question is, could we?
>
> [25 September 1948] What will happen when the inevitable long strikes take place in France? It's certainly an unpleasant thought that before long the whole machinery of the country may be at a standstill. Unless de Gaulle comes to power, I can see no other hope for France – they need someone to give them orders, not necessarily de Gaulle (who is not a politician). But there is, I'm afraid, nobody else who can do it. It's perfectly obvious to everyone that the members of the present government, and of recent governments, are incapable of carrying out their job, because the average Frenchman will not accept a 'more utility' life, and these politicians know, that if de Gaulle comes to power, they will lose their present jobs – which are of doubtful value. At the same time France is swamped with underpaid so-called 'white collar' bureaucrats who have to live on the efforts of the productive population. Of course, if the machines used by the population were modernised (as in America) to produce more, then the standard of living would rise, and Communism in France would be negligible. This is the aim of Marshall Aid – to improve machines and methods of production, and only time will tell whether it will succeed in France. From our point of view (anti-Communist) it has got to succeed. Prices have been going steadily up – the Metro now costs 10 francs a ride, newspapers up

> to 7 from 5, petrol much more, food up by 20 francs etc I should not be surprised if we few officers in France decide in the end that it's impossible to live out here, and ask to be sent home!
>
> [28 September 1948] Dear Audrey, Darling do not worry too much about the news in the papers. I agree with you that things are not as good as they might be, and there is every chance, to my mind, of America getting fed-up with Russia, and having a stab at her with an Atomic bomb, but I am convinced that such action would put a finish to all this trouble and a war would not last very long. Not long enough to involve the army in the fighting that is, but there's no saying whether Russia would not, by way of revenge, drop a few bombs on London, so if anything does start, I want you to promise me to take our daughter down to Surrey the very moment there is the slightest sign of any trouble. Please don't be mistaken by my meaning in this letter – I know no more than the average man in the street, but I always believe in being on the safe side, and I would feel much happier if I knew that you were out of London. So please promise me this. But let's not think of war and pray that there will not be another in our lifetime.

The authors A. Beevor and A. Cooper confirm that Sanderson is not far wrong in reading the US mind – or had John received a briefing from the FO? In October 1947 Cold War fever had affected both side of the Atlantic:

> 'It was depressing,' Duff Cooper wrote to the British Foreign Secretary, 'but not surprising, that even Bidault should be catching it, when supposedly responsible people, such as the American Senator Bridges, shout down the dinner table at the American Embassy: "Say, Monsier Bidault, we want to know what you're going to do when we drop our first atomic egg on Moscow."'[20]

Bridges's joking bluster was a foretaste of Khrushchev's boasts over his huge, initially imagined, nuclear arsenal. Bidault had been the French Foreign Minister from 1944 until mid-1948 and had supported the Prime Minister Paul Ramadier when he expelled Communists from his government in 1947. Bidault had visited Stalin in Moscow and, witnessing his intransigence, realised that an accommodation with the Soviet dictator was impossible.[21]

US support for Western Europe was gathering pace. The US NSC, as part of the build-up associated with the Berlin blockade, had dispatched (as yet unarmed) B29 'nuclear capable' Superfortress bombers to bases in

Britain, under the command of the first US SAC (Strategic Air Command) base in East Anglia. These aircraft had the range to reach the Russian capital. In the autumn of 1948, on the occasion of the visit of the US Defence Secretary to Britain, the Chief of the Air Staff Air Marshal Arthur Tedder admitted that the guidelines for the use of the atomic bomb in case of war were unclear to the RAF Command.[22]

The AMAs' espionage activities were not at all popular at No. 38 rue du Faubourg Saint-Honoré. Duff Cooper's successor as British Ambassador to France was Oliver Harvey, who shared Cooper's negative views on SIS's role in his embassy. In September 1948 Harvey protested to the FO, quoting a reported incident of SIS operating in France. To placate Harvey, Sir William Hayter, Head of the FO Services Liaison Department, wrote to Menzies ('C') requesting 'a brief account of your present activities in France'. Hayter pointed out that Ambassador Harvey's negative views were not shared by the FO's Western Department or even Ernest Bevin, for that matter.[23]

JBS:

> [1 October 1948] Dear A., Yesterday Mr Kiroff and I went to the Champs Elysées and saw 'Fort Apaché . Quite a well produced, but typically American story about the American Army's fight against the hostile Red Indian tribes of the last century. On our way out of the cinema we bumped into Peter G., all dressed up in his nutting suit, new hat and gloves, on his way to La Rue to see if any of the chaps were there. So we dragged him in for a beer and heard of his latest trip. John

A. Beevor and A. Cooper noted the growing pervasiveness of US culture in Paris: 'Many disliked the way the French youth appeared infatuated with all things American – detective stories, films, clothes, jazz, behop, Glenn Miller. This . . . represented both a yearning to escape from the poverty and dilapidation around them and a preference for American informality after the stuffiness of Vichy.'[24]

The working life of the French was still being disrupted. Strikes by the CGT were forcing the French to find other ways of getting to work. The Communists and the CGT aimed to bring the economy to its knees before the Marshall Plan could begin to have an effect.[25]

JBS:

> [2 October 1948] Today I went down to the public baths where, as usual, I had a beautiful hot bath. In the middle of it, I discovered

why, for the second time in succession, the female attendant started screaming at me a torrent of abuse. I was whistling in the bath, an act strictly forbidden by the Mayor and the Corporation! Unfortunately I again caused her annoyance on leaving my cubicle, for I accidentally shut the door – a terrible thing to do, I gathered from her flow of talk. However, a few francs subdued her!

Turp made us laugh yesterday, whilst telling us about the worried manner in which David N. came into his office not long ago. You remember the female he was billetted with? Well, David came in to complain to Turp that perhaps his wife would not approve of him living there, and as she was coming out on a short visit, he was getting quite worried! He must have looked worried too, for at that moment the General walked in and seeing David there, asked him what was the matter! David told him, to which the General replied that he ought to think himself damned lucky! When David left, the General came in to see Turp and said: 'I don't know what's come over the younger generation of today, why when I was his age, my colleagues would have jumped at the idea of living with that young girl in Paris!!' Which only goes to prove that the youth of Britain is improving! Incidentally, the General did not know that she had once been a nun!

[3 October 1948] Dear A., America has refused the Bulgarians admission to the Senate Assembly of UNO on the grounds that they were not suitable to sit in a civilised assembly because of the present shocking state of government prevailing in Bulgaria. Well, believe it or not, nothing daunted, the delegation has turned up here in Paris, and are 'peeping' over the fence at the 'cricket match' like 'a lot of naughty schoolboys'. Not only that, they arrived here in an 'Air France' aeroplane, according to reports. They dare not bring their own aircraft in case the pilot refused to return – like so many others from Czechoslovakia!! What a farce politics are these days, and what an even bigger farce this UNO has turned out to be. There is only one way to World peace, and I have always maintained this, and that is to have the strongest arm, and then nobody else will try to cause trouble. The only reason we were not involved in a major war before the First World War was because of our Navy, and now the Air Force has taken its place as a deciding and preventative factor in war, and the sooner we, and America, realise that for all time, the better. We passed the UNO building last night. It's a splendid building, beautifully lit up and visible for miles around at night.

The Kiroffs and I set off with the Shishmanoffs for drinks at the flat of the Belhoffs: he is a young Bulgarian dentist with a French wife. As is inevitable in France, whenever there's a gathering of men, the talk always comes around to politics and, in this 'set' of people in particular (so-called diplomats!), it is even more certain to occupy half the evening! They have built a most splendid new restaurant in the grounds of their Chateau at Passy which can seat six-hundred people. From there we went to a night club to meet the Tyznkiwitz party, including Mr Zalecki (looking as glum as ever). It was a very small, well laid out and beautifully lit place but the gramophone pick up and records were of the 1890 vintage and poured out the most frightful music imaginable! I found a 'bumps a daisy' record and gave a demonstration to all present on how it should be done – my partner was the ample Ninka Kiroff, so you can imagine the 'bumps' were very effective! The Polish girl we met last time, wearing a very low-cut dress, was there with the same dress, and out of the corner of my eye, I expected at any moment to see anything happen, but through some unseen device, her honour was maintained. A very peculiar party. As Ninka was about to pass out, we had to go early! David and I literally had to carry the overweight girl home.

[5 October 1948] The hot sunny days have suddenly changed to bleak autumn weather and the 350,000 coal miners in France have chosen this day to go on strike. Let's hope that, with the lack of coal in this country, they will also freeze!

When I was in the Embassy this morning, the wretched welfare officer (Miss Price) got hold of all of us and persuaded us to attend a big Embassy dance tonight because there are going to be many more females there than males. Half of us had not the slightest desire to go because everyone will be wearing dinner jackets which we haven't got, and at the same time we have not seen anybody inside the Embassy worth dancing with!! So I shall pop along in my lounge suit about nine, have a few drinks with the chaps at the bar, keep well out of the eagle eyesight of Miss Price, and return home at a reasonable hour. If I am to follow a diplomatic career, as opposed to soldiering, I suppose I must get used to the idea of Embassy functions. Talking of diplomats, we had a charming Frenchman to dinner last night, and fortunately he spoke excellent English, having been the French leader in Geneva of the original League of Nations – no small fish! He told me at one stage in the evening that he reckoned Kiroff would one day be Prime Minister of Bulgaria, which I can quite believe, as he is the recognised leader of 'the opposition' here in Paris, and there is nobody in England to compare with him, which only leaves a few odd persons in America who might be given the job. With old Kiroff as PM in Bulgaria, we would never want for anything if we were there also!

[6 October 1948] It was a glorious afternoon so I decided to go to Paris to visit the French School of Slavonic Studies, near Pont Royal. It was closed until November, so I crossed the bridge, through the Tuileries, past Joan of Arc's golden statue and down Avenue Richelieu to the 'Bibliothèque Nationale', where I wanted to meet the professor in the Bulgarian section. But he was out! However, I spent a pleasant time scouting out the Bulgarian books, of which there are hundreds . . . They have nearly every book one could wish for.

[7 October 1948] The French friend of the Kiroffs came to dinner. He had just returned from a short visit to Hungary, where to my utter surprise, he said the conditions were better than in France! Apparently, unlike Bulgaria and, until recently Yugoslavia, the Russians have very little to do with Hungary, and although Communists control the country, conditions there are not bad at all – provided one does what one is told! He said there was plenty of food in the shops, absolutely no talk of war (which is forbidden in the newspapers) and people go about their business much as before – dances, restaurants, cinemas etc. I was very surprised to hear this, as it's not what one is led to believe from our daily newspapers. Also remember this man, being a friend of Kiroff's, is very anti-Communist, and is not likely to say that of Hungary if it were not true. He also said that he heard from Hungarians, that conditions in Bulgaria were terrible.

Today I received a long letter from Kalcheff in Austria, and yesterday a beautiful book of poems and writings by one of Bulgaria's famous author – Yavorov. He was an unfortunate customer, for he shot his wife and then tried to blind himself! In that condition, he lived the remainder of his life in abject misery, but not, as one might expect, in jail! Kalcheff also arranged for a friend of his in the British zone of Austria to send me a whole pile of 'Fatherland Fronts' which are most useful as they are fairly recent newspapers: from them one can see the political trend in Bulgaria at the moment – every word is downright foolish propaganda.

John Bruce Lockhart, the head of the SIS station, in a report to London in 1946, had 'discussed domestic French politics with details of French Communist Party finances and reflections on Communist penetration of the French army and air force'.[26] Another note from an SIS case handler in London noted that SIS was 'always interested in reports based on "off the record" remarks made by individuals who are known to . . . speak with inside knowledge and authority on the subject under discussion and who do not know that their remarks will get back to this country'.[27]

Sanderson and other members of SIS were regularly in touch with Paris contacts who were travelling behind the Iron Curtain. Keith Jeffery wrote:

> In the spring of 1948, the Paris station took up the baton and began a series of meetings with (a) target 'on a purely social basis'. Paris reported that the individual had now got a job with an international humanitarian organisation, which would involve him travelling frequently in the 'Russian satellites' in Eastern Europe, and added their impression that he would 'be prepared to carry out an observation mission for us' during his visits to Eastern Europe, and would accept payment.[28]

JBS:

> [9 October 1948] Wonderful news! The Foreign Office have approached the War Office and asked them to send me to Sofia for translation duties! I was sent for this morning and was informed by the MA that I am to consider it a warning order, and that attempts are being made to obtain the necessary visa. The letter pointed out that it would be to my greatest advantage to accept this offer, and the benefit of having served at a Legation will be great for my future career. The Military Attaché said that it was an honour to be accepted for this most responsible job, and that once having got there, it would be easy for me to get known by all the Legation and Military Attaché staff, and that a job as Assistant Military Attaché was almost certain, with the chance of eventually becoming M.A. later in my career. The present idea is that I will go there definitely for a year, and will take the interpretership exam in October 1949 instead of February. I'm hoping that within this year I can get sufficiently 'dug in' there to be given the AMA job.
>
> Poor old Peter is fed-up he won't be going to Sofia but he says he does not really mind as he has this Bulgarian girlfriend he is

thinking of asking to marry him! I only hope he gets what he wants, for, on top of this career blow, he would be thoroughly miserable if she refuses! Everyone says she is charming. She will have to be very charming to console his very critical Lancashire father and mother.

On the way to the Embassy we passed a big car exhibition at the bottom of the Champs Elysées. Outside there were so many cars burning up dollars in the form of petrol, whilst the people in England are doing so much towards recovery living on a basic ration. But what can you do with such a government? I was told that the American administrator of ERP in Europe informed the French government that America was not satisfied with the steps being taken by France for recovery, and if they did not improve, ERP funds would not be forthcoming for France. [Author note: The European Recovery Program of the Marshall Plan had been passed by the US Foreign Assistance Act of April 1948: it would last three years.]

There was even talk of an American Administration in France! This caused a great outcry in French circles, but the government realise that the recovery of France is imperative for America for obvious political reasons, and however much the Americans 'wag their finger', they can do nothing about it – except pay out dollars. French politicians are quite content to sit back and allow America to pay. I'm certain in the end de Gaulle will come to power, but how he will do it legally nobody seems to know, for the President is unable to dissolve parliament and call fresh elections until this has been passed three times in one year by the present assembly – who, of course, are reluctant to pass anything!! Daily the strikes are getting worse, and something is bound to blow up eventually.

Today I was most fortunate to witness an everyday, but to my mind, peculiar French custom. Out of the Madeleine Church suddenly appeared hundreds of people who lined the pavement to watch the exit of, not one, but a dozen newly wedded couples. They had all taken the plunge at the same time and, as the couples came out, they posed in turn for their photograph, with the next couple lining up to be snapped!

[13 October 1948] This evening Peter has invited us to a cocktail party at his place and I have just learned that it will be a large gathering, for our General here in Paris is attending as well! I can't think what it's in aid of, and what Peter expects to get out of the General here? Do you think it might be to impress his 'lady love'

> whom I understand will also be there! Poor old Peter, he does go to a great deal of trouble to further his matrimonial prospects, doesn't he?! Mind you, for a man to have so many friends around him, not to mention the odd General and Colonel, does help to further one's chances with a Bulgarian girl!

In June 1945 fifty nations had signed the Charter of the United Nations. The UN itself was created on 24 October 1945. Almost exactly three years later, in October 1948 in Paris, steps were taken by the FO to provide John Sanderson with open access to UNO debates, firstly to increase his awareness of current international politics, in advance of his planned posting behind the Iron Curtain, and secondly to familiarise him with the future role of a Press Attaché. He was as yet unaware that this would be his mission.

JBS:

> [14 October 1948] Dear Audrey, I have just returned from spending the afternoon sitting in a United Nations session. It was extremely interesting as I sat just behind Vyshinsky and had a perfect view of all that went on – they were discussing the disarmament proposals, and the Canadian delegate made by far the most impressive speech of the afternoon. (Incidentally, I thought that Vyshinsky looked like an old grandfather I know and not in the least like a Russian.) I was quite amused to watch Vyshinsky's face throughout this most strongly worded denunciation of Soviet aggressive aims – quite impressive, in spite of the fact that the Russian translator put, what I thought, even more expression into the speech than the Canadian delegate himself!
>
> They have a wonderful system of translation there – each seat has a set of earphones and a switch, and one can switch over and listen to the speech being being put over in English, French, Russian, Spanish, Chinese or Italian and I was quite interested to switch over occasionally to Russian, which I found not too difficult to understand. It's wonderful how the interpreters can speak in our own language and listen to the speech at the same time – I couldn't help wondering if I shall be able to do that!!

Stalin had Molotov, 'his faithful acolyte at the Foreign ministry', replaced by the infamous Vyshinsky who would be the prosecutor at show trials under Nikita Khrushchev: 'The principle of criminal analogy was much valued by the infamous Vyshinsky, and the punishment of an accused's kinsmen on the specious grounds that they must have known of his offence.'[29] Before the war Klaus Fuchs, the GRU agent who would betray details of the Allied 'A' bomb research, used to take part in dramatised readings of Soviet show trial transcripts. Fuchs read the part of the prosecutor Vyshinsky 'accusing the defendants with a cold venom that [one] would never have suspected from so quiet and retiring young man'.[30]

James Reeve described his own experiences of the UN in Paris in 1951 when the Palais de Chaillot 'reverberated for hour after hour with the Cold War invective of Andrei Vyshinsky', the Soviet delegate in the UN disarmament debates. Reeve observed that Vyshinsky, a cruel public prosecutor in Stalinist trials and responsible for the imposition of countless death sentences, generally ignored the contents of the resolution under debate. Instead, he resorted to telling sardonic anecdotes, ridiculing Western imperialism. Selwyn-Lloyd, however, turned the tables on him one day. Referring to Vyshinski's long-winded speeches, he quoted the Russian proverb: 'The cow that makes the most noise gives the least milk.' When Vyshinski protested, Lloyd repeated the proverb in Polish, much to the amusement of the Polish delegation and to the annoyance of Vyshinsky, who was of Polish origins.[31]

At the conference of Foreign Ministers in Palais Rose, Avenue Foch on 14 May 1949 the aide of Dean Acheson, the US Foreign Minister, described Vyshinsky as 'sinister, tight, gaunt, with the beadiest eyes I have ever seen'.[32] Dean Acheson and Anthony Eden, during the October 1951 UN General Assembly meeting in Paris, would be introduced to Teodoro Castro, the Costa Rican chargé d'affaires in Rome. They would have been shocked to learn that this diplomat was a Soviet 'illegal', a saboteur and an assassin, named Iosif Grigulevich, who had played a major part in the murder of Trotsky in Mexico.

Christopher Andrew noted that Vyshinsky's oratorical style was usually tedious and long-winded. Vyshinsky arrived with a caged dove to represent the innocent victim of Western imperialist aggression and then, referring to a speech by President Truman on arms limitation, demonstrated his facetious attitude to this serious topic by informing the UN Assembly: 'I could hardly sleep all night having read that speech. I could not sleep because I kept laughing.'[33]

JBS described meeting an important FO official:

> On Saturday evening I met quite an influential Englishman who has obtained a permanent card for me for all the sessions of both the United Nations, and the Security Council, so I expect I shall be going again in the future. I want to hear the debate on Berlin

later in the week, when I hope Bevin and Marshall will be there. I saw Sir Alexander Cadogan [PUS for Foreign Affairs 1938–46, Diplomatic Service 1908–50] walking away from the building afterwards – and the poor chap looked as though he had the world on his shoulders – and he probably has! France made what I thought was rather a wet speech and that of Greece was not much better. However, eventually Poland proposed a motion to adjourn as they had many things to answer, and wanted time to think about them, so we all packed up and went home. It really is a wonderful building inside. Today's meeting was in one of the six committee rooms, but I walked over and had a look at the big assembly room one sees in pictures in the news – a most lovely building inside, beautifully laid out and most comfortable. My Foreign Office friend introduced me to the private secretary of the President of the U.N, the Australian Dr H.V. Evatt, who offered to get me the required ticket for any special session that might come up in the near future.

[15 October 1948] At 6.30 I'm going for a few cocktails to the house of an interesting English couple I met at the bus stop: he is also in the Foreign office and has a house here in Neuilly. They have some white Russians coming to dinner this evening, and thought I would like to meet them. I most certainly shall.

[16 October 1948] Dear Audrey, There is a great flap on in the Bulgar colony here since the news that I might be going to Sofia – all are scared that I might unsuspectingly mention one of their names to a Bulgarian when I get to Sofia and thereby cause their relations to be sent to jail! I'm getting fed up with being told to forget that I ever met them when I get to Bulgaria. As if, when I get there, I'm going to say to the population: 'Oh yes – Gospodeen' so and so is doing all he can in Paris to fight against the present regime here in Bulgaria!' I know as well as they do the dangers of mentioning names, and will be equally careful. What I like about old Kiroff, he never says a word to me, knowing full well, of course, that I shall not say anything: for that reason, I have not mentioned to either Pinto or Kusseff the name of the person I'm staying with. I hear things in Bulgaria are almost unbelievable. However, have no fear, they cannot do that to anyone but their own people, and even then they won't stand it indefinitely.

On 20 October, in the coal mining area of North France demonstrators put barricades up at the entrances to the mines, having occupied the shafts and the winding gears. The Communist Deputy was arrested, as were hundreds of miners. French soldiers with armoured cars were recalled from Germany to regain control.[34]

> [22 October 1948] Dear Audrey, I have been in the UNO today. I had to get away from Mme Kiroff . . . the wretched woman is lying prostrate in bed groaning . . . I feel it is to do with her mental state – I told you she is scared stiff for her relations in Bulgaria, but for the life of me I can't think why, for as long as they behave themselves, I can't imagine anything happening to them. Today, I regret to say, was a wasted day in UNO. I went because the Berlin question was tabled, but all that happened in the morning was that the United Nations Assembly (58 nations) voted for 5 new presidents of sub-committees. This was a long and laborious procedure, and when the votes were taken from the ballot box and counted, it was found that only three members had received the required number of votes to make them eligible to be presidents, so the whole procedure had to be done over again to obtain two presidents!! However, as it had gone midday, Shishmanoff and I beat a rapid retreat into a Committee room where, for half an hour, we heard a very interesting debate on 'how to suppress the white slave traffic throughout the world'. There are six committee rooms, and usually there are interesting debates going on in three or four of them, example: the first time I went was when I sat near the Soviet delegation when they discussed 'disarmament'. Then there are committees on 'Atomic Warfare', 'International Trade', etc. At all these committee meetings there are represented members from all the 58 countries. This morning I watched the United Nations in action (voting) – the UN is when all nations assemble in the Grande Salle and on the stage are only the President (Dr Ewatt), the Secretary and one other. All delegates sit in the 'stalls' of this ex-theatre (in the 1/- and 1/6 seats!) with lighted tables in front of them, and the spectators in the 'rear stalls' (or 2/- seats)! The balconies and side boxes are occupied by the six translators, the Press, lighting experts, electrical technicians, etc. This afternoon, the Berlin question was tabled for the Security Council – that is a special Council of eleven nations (five permanent members, the victors in WW2: Britain, USA, France, USSR, and China, plus six temporary members) who decide questions of World Peace. They all sit on the stage in a half moon facing the auditorium, where again all are seated.

[24 October 1948] One of my Bulgarian friends phoned today to say that the British Officer Loder was leaving for Sofia this evening and wanted to meet me before he left, so I will see him at 6pm. So long as I chat to him for an hour this evening, that's all that matters.

[25 October 1948] I met Loder last night at his hotel in Paris for a couple of hours before he set off for Bulgaria. I was very interested to hear of all that goes on behind the IC. He loves it there but said it was even more expensive than Paris as the exchange rate is so bad. He doesn't think I will get a visa until later in 1949 when he and the Major return. So I shall probably return from here at the beginning of February, take the exam there, and start a job in Military Intelligence at the War Office. Personally this will suit me very well.

Loder said Bulgaria is a lovely country, and they are able to travel about quite a lot in the mountains etc. and everyone in the 'Western Colony' enjoys it very much. For us there is almost anything available in the shops if one can afford to pay for it and the servant situation is very good. In fact one has to employ a maid, batman and chauffeur. During the winter, they have the most wonderful skiing in Sofia, and in the summer the mountain streams and valleys are glorious. He told me lot more about the place, which I cannot write here, but will tell you all about when I get home.

Today I managed to find time to go down to the Latin Quarter to look for a Bulgarian lady (married to a Frenchman) who Pinto told me to look up one day as she was a useful person from the point of view of meeting more Bulgars. Pinto gave me the wrong address: it was a warehouse. Pinto incidentally hopes to go to Bulgaria for a year to study the language, as 'guest of the Bulgarian Government'! I've no need to tell you how he gets such a distinguished invitation. However, there is no fear of him mentioning us, for that would ditch his chances straight away – on the contrary he is scared stiff we will mention that he taught us!! If he goes to Bulgaria the poor students will be left with only Kusseff to teach them – poor devils, what an outlook!!

I am sending you a very perceptive article written by Sir Esmond Ovey to the 'Continental' *Daily Mail*:

Sir, We have wasted too much time inviting the Russian Bear to dance with us around the maypole of international amity . . . There is more horse-sense in any one of Aesop's fables than in

> all the doctrines of Karl Marx and in the sturdy Roman saying, '*Si vis pacem, para bellum*', than in all the highbrow theories. The Bolshevik believes that, by making Bolshevism universal, there will eventually be no Iron Curtain at all. We must make ourselves strong enough morally, physically and militarily to live independently and 'let the best side win' the peace. The USA are the trustees of our security. They possess not only immovable mass, but irresistible force. God grant that the atomic bomb may never have to be used again but this force is our capital reserve . . . Is this a policy of war? No. Horse-sense.

On 28 October 1948 British and US Intelligence received a major setback when the ability of their signals intelligence operators to decipher Soviet traffic was abruptly curtailed. William Weisband, an US Army Security Agency cipher clerk, had revealed the secret that Western intelligence had been reading Soviet military communications for years, and especially gathering the important 'Venona' intercepts, which had exposed the US 'atomic bomb' spies. As a result of this betrayal, a totally new one-time cipher pad system was introduced in the Soviet armed forces. Moscow also introduced two radical changes to their signals communications, by moving away from wireless communications to landlines, as well as changing their radio procedures and encoding procedures. In Berlin in early 1954 a major listening tunnel GOLD would be constructed under the Soviet sector to tap into Soviet landlines.[35]

JBS:

> [29 October 1948] Dear Family, No doubt you read in the papers the other day of the charges of espionage preferred against certain diplomatic personnel in Romania – including our military personnel there. Strictly between you and I, these charges are always 'trumped up' by the government in question in order to get rid of officers who are either too well known in these countries, or who have a good knowledge of the language and can therefore converse with the local populace. The procedure is simple – a few secret police come up to the officer in question in the street, plant information on them, and then arrest them, and thereby have them evicted from the country! Whereupon they then refuse to grant visas for their replacements. I am only telling you this to point out how unwilling they are to have any military personnel whatsoever in their countries, and for that reason the war office are having difficulty getting a visa for me. There are

already three military officers in Sofia – you see I am in a position to appreciate the difficulty even more than the officials in London who are applying for my visa. I met the present assistant Military Attaché from Sofia in Paris the other day, and he tells me his job ends in May next year, together with one of the two officers there, so I have a good chance of getting one of these vacancies next year. I am certain the training I am having here will be of great benefit to us later on. Apart from that, life everywhere in the world is very insecure, and I am sure that when these post-war troubles sort themselves out, things will begin to get back to normal again, but I very much fear that there's no hope of that until we solve the communist problem. I console myself in the thought that at last America and ourselves have realised that there can only be peace as long as we are strong, and I am very hopeful that Russia will 'climb down' to American threats of war that are bound to come next year.

Next week two more chaps are arriving from England to join the 'merry throng' – learning what I originally intended to learn [Russian]. The Military Attaché asked me to find them accommodation, so I rang up our friends in the Chateau of Marly-le-Roi. They said they are only too happy to do something for them.

Our party for the Bulgarians was a great success last night. They enjoyed themselves so much they didn't go home for dinner, so as the evening rolled on, we had to search frantically in the cupboard for the remains of any food left over. I found a big joint of cold veal and carved it up most expertly and everyone had enough. I was OC booze, so you can imagine I was fairly busy shaking cocktails the whole evening. Like everyone else I got gradually merrier and merrier! By 11.30 we were all singing Bulgarian songs, and for the next hour I imagine we kept the whole block of flats awake! Peter got very tight, I thought, and became rather 'morbid' because his girlfriend didn't seem to pay him much attention! I feel sorry for him as he has not got a clue. If I was a girl, I would find him a complete bore. However that's his character and I'm sure nothing will change him. I shudder though to think what he will be like in 30 years time!

[2 November 1948] Dear Audrey, Incidentally don't tell anyone about your prospective move apart from members of our family and close friends, and even to them, I am no longer in the Army and am transferred to the Foreign Office as a civilian, and as

> such will travel as any ordinary member of the Foreign Office with, of course, full diplomatic rights. If we go, we can expect to be back next birthday in August – that is if I have not managed to work myself into the job that I am really after there – i.e. Assistant MA.

Plans for secret SIS incursion in the Balkans, meanwhile, were underway. The author Stephen Dorril notes that in November 1948 the Cold War Sub-Committee met to consider a paper, 'British policy towards the Soviet Orbit in Europe'. It was produced by an assistant under-secretary who suggested a policy of going on the offensive, but stopping short of a 'hot war'. Another senior FO official proposed starting a civil war in Albania, as the Russians had instigated in Greece. Lord Tedder said: 'we should aim to win the Cold War (i.e. overthrow the Soviet regime) in five years' time'. SOE optimistically believed that: 'well-trained agents could organise a guerrilla-backed operation . . . supplied by airdrops . . . what if the anti-communist revolt in Albania sparked off others throughout the Balkans? The whole basis of the Russian satellite empire could be shattered by an uprising that had its birth in one small guerrilla operation.'[36]

JBS:

> [12 November 1948] 126 Rue Perronet, Neuilly.
>
> Dear Audrey, I was feeling disconsolate reading the daily paper, as there was scarcely a word that did not imply a future war – I think everyone has gone mad darling, to even contemplate a repetition of the two previous shows, and yet according to the news on Nov 11th – a day when people should be thinking of peace rather than of starting another war – the papers seem full of the most disheartening talk. It makes me wonder if our children will ever live in peace? I think one must just hope that through strength of character and arms, we shall be able to frighten off the communist menace which is growing daily all around us.
>
> [13 November 1948] Dear Audrey, I went to the Embassy at 11 o' clock for our weekly meeting with the Military Attaché: it lasted an hour. I am going out to dinner tomorrow night with Peter G. and one of his Bulgarian tutors, and there again, I shall be known as J.W.!! I'm getting quite used to it now! So if ever I introduce you as Mrs Wilkinson you should not look as though I have gone quite mad! Yesterday evening, Bimbo and I went to the room of a Bulgarian university colleague of his and we sat chatting for half an hour before two other students (Americans) arrived. Our host then spent half an hour talking to his parents in Bulgaria

on the telephone, and from then onwards the conversation was mainly in French, except for occasions when they broke off for a moment to explain something to one another in Bulgarian or English. It was interesting talking to them. I took part in the discussions as far as my language skills permitted and also took part in a little solid drinking, but not enough to make my head hazy. The Americans were quite unpretentious and I liked the Bulgarians very much. Bimbo introduced me as John Wilkinson, since the Bulgarian's father is a Communist – although he himself is far from being one!

Madame Kiroff has a spell of misery from time to time over the loss of income that that will be sustained if I leave at the end of the month. I have had enough of living here and am beginning to get bored with trying to make conversation all day long – if only there were a few young people living with the Kiroffs, it would be so much more interesting, instead of having to put up with a miserable disheartened female, and her long-suffering old husband!

[16 November 1948] The most enjoyable part of today was reading an account in the newspaper of the BOT inquiry into corruption in John Belcher's branch of the Bank of England. They appear to have been going in for it in a big way – this will not further the Labour cause very much! To my mind it could not be more obvious that Belcher and his pals are up to their neck in troubles!

Sidney Stanley, né Kohsyzcky, a fraudster had been able to get preferential treatment in return for money bribes. Belcher resigned after an inquiry.[37]

JBS:

[18 November 1948] Dear Audrey, When I returned to Neuilly I was amazed to see hundreds of police lining the roads, and surrounding the local town hall! It was obvious that some high personage was about to visit the Mayor and the Corporation, and, on enquiry, I learned it was to be General de Gaulle. So I hung around for three-quarters of an hour with a small crowd of excited women and children until he arrived. I scarcely realised it was him when two very ordinary French cars drew up in front of the town hall, but there was no mistaking the tall figure of the general, in spite of the numerous feminine cheers of 'Vive de Gaulle', 'Vive La France', etc. I stress 'female' because the men were either in the cafes or at work (probably the former) and it's really the women of France, more than the men, who support the General and believe it or not, I'm told it's because of his tall and handsome figure! He certainly looked a cut above the average Frenchman as he stepped from his car, walked up the town hall steps, and turned to the crowd with raised hands rather as though he was bestowing his blessings upon them. Did you read his press conference report in the papers today? I must admit to sympathising with him, and in fact all French statesmen who have fears about the future control of the Ruhr by the Germans. Whatever one might fear about the immediate necessity to gather together all the Democratic countries in defence of the Communist menace, I feel we want to be most careful how much rope we allow the Germans, for I would not trust them an inch, and although they are a powerful potential military ally, they can easily become, together with the Russians, an almost indomitable menace in the near future to any country that opposes them. I'm certain most military leaders in Germany, if offered by the Russians a chance of regaining their lost glory and present humiliating position, would join with the Russians in a search for world conquest without the slightest hesitation, and in this fear, I am sure the French are right. I only hope our politicians bear this in mind sufficiently. They certainly seem to be doing everything they can to anger the French, which is bad politically, whatever we might think of the French! For instance, was it necessary to announce on 11 November their intention to hand over control of the Ruhr to the Germans, knowing it would anger the French? Surely any other day would have been more appropriate.

[21 November 1948] Old Kiroff called on me to warn me to put on my best suit as some of his Bulgarian friends had just come back from Switzerland, and were coming to dinner. They arrived, an almost identical couple to the Kiroffs, and a young Bulgarian of my age, but practically twice the size! I thought them quite pleasant, but I could not imagine how the older one had been a Bulgarian minister for years before, and during the war in Romania. However, he had indeed been a minister, and spoke Romanian like a Romanian, as I was to discover later in the evening. The young chap apparently owned a large factory or shop in Bulgaria and was considered very wealthy there. But, of course, when the 'Reds' arrived Bulgaria was no place for him, and he commenced his travels through Europe with the aid of a large car and ample stacks of dollars, Swiss francs, pound notes and what have you! For the past three years, he has been moving from one country to another just before the Iron Curtain fell on each country. The first country to go completely 'Red' was Bulgaria so he was able to live in Romania for some time, before he had to move to Hungary (you remember they did not sling King Michael out until some time after the Communists took over). However, the inevitable eventually happened in Hungary and he had to move on again, this time to Germany and then to Czechoslovakia: and now Switzerland. During this time he had to sell his car, and has decided he cannot afford to live any longer in Switzerland, and is thinking of living here. His father was beaten up and killed by the Communists, and to save his own life he had to leave his elderly mother in Bulgaria. It truly is a tragic world. The awful thing is that he is only one of millions. I have met so many of them here in Paris, and although they try to keep cheerful, I know how hard they have to work to keep going. Of course, I don't mean the ex-diplomats I have met: they all seem to have an inexhaustible supply of dollars or Swiss francs, and how they live is a complete mystery to me! The only hardship they are having is that they cannot live on the grand scale in which they were living before the communists came to power. Over dinner we chatted about life before the war and about life after the closing of the Iron Curtain.

When we had finished, the Romanian minister announced we were all invited to a cabaret at his expense. Around 10pm, after a phone call had been made, we all set off for an hotel, where we met the remainder of our party – ten Romanians and a more peculiar bunch of men I have never yet accompanied out for the evening!! Their wives were quite sweet though! All fifteen of us piled into a couple of taxis, and off we went to the famous 'cabaret' night club called 'Tabarin'. I was most pleased at the thought of a free evening at such a renowned place, even with a bunch of half-canned Romanians!! Our table for sixteen was right up near the stage, which stretched into the centre of the night club. The lower 'floor' opened out at various stages of the evening, and artists, trapezes, and stage equipment appeared on a lift from the bowels of the building. The whole programme from 11pm until 2am consists of a series of cabaret turns, the likes of which I have never seen before – I couldn't count the number of naked females with only a fig leaf below, that appeared and danced about the lower stage at various periods of the evening! However, they did not interest me nearly as much as the chorus who did the Can-Can perfectly – this night club is famous throughout the world for its Can-Can and I must admit it's an interesting spectacle! So typically French! The scantily clothed females appeared so regularly that in the end one became quite blasé about the whole thing, and I remember thinking that if, in the future, women's bathing costumes turn into trunks only, they would probably cause very little more of a sensation that when men discarded the old swimming costume not long ago.

There was a strong man act (presumably for the benefits of the ladies!), a rather good ballet dancer, comedians, etc. After each turn, the band played for dancing, when the floor packed with people doing a night club crawl. We did not drink much during the evening – our hosts bought champagne – one has to buy at least one bottle on each table – so the women had the champagne and the men ordered a brandy each, merely to get a glass in to which we could pour brandy from the bottle which one of the Romanians had in his pocket!!

At 2 a.m. the show closed down, and we all walked to a nearby restaurant, where we had either oysters, prawns, snails or soup. Some of our friends were very tight, and everyone jabbered away in Romanian, and apart from the odd conversation I had with Kiroff, I merely sat listening to Nina Kiroff and another woman singing Romanian folk songs! (The next day she had a nasty hangover.) The Kiroffs and I found a taxi for which I paid 200 francs (4 shillings) – the sum total of my expenses for a very amusing evening! The Kiroffs remarked on our return that they were very pleased with my Bulgarian and that I had been talking nearly all evening and scarcely made any mistakes. I did feel that perhaps some of what I had been learning had sunk in!

[26 November 1948] Being Sunday I was sitting firmly in position in 'La Rue's' at 11.30 a.m., watching all the world go by, and reading my 'News of the World' which I had bought from a passing 'newspaper boy' (aged 90!). Sipping a fresh cool ale, I was soon joined by fellow officers in Paris. Peter G. said he was going to hire a car for a day for a trip. He must have had a reason for being so extravagant, so I asked him what her name was! He replied that she was too angelic to even mention her name! Kiroff later informed me that the young lady in question was indeed of unusually good appearance, young and well-off. No wonder Peter was interested! The fact that she is Bulgarian, however, would make me very careful in my relations with her, and I only hope Peter does not make a fool of himself. Bulgarians with money might be quite different from the usual run of Bulgars!

Later we had twelve people to drinks after dinner and the session went on to well after midnight, with four solid hours of talking Bulgarian. Mr and Mrs Ruskov (who said they had thought you '*mnogo simpathechna*' – 'very nice') were there together with Mrs Marinova (the wife of a Bulgarian General). She speaks fluent English as well as you and I. Mr and Mrs Shishmanov (who was one of the prettiest women in Bulgaria and is still only 35 years) were there too, as well as Old Tuckvoria, the Frenchman in the tobacco trade and his attractive Bulgarian wife. They have a splendid appartment not far from L'Etoile. As usual, he did all the talking! Like all Frenchmen, he has the answer to <u>all world</u> problems, none the least being their own!

One day, if there is a Military Attaché vacancy, I will have a diplomatic appointment in foreign lands, where your presence will be equally as important as mine, and I know you will be a great success with everyone. Perhaps you could brush up your French so that if we go to Bulgaria you would not be lost for a language – as you know French is the generally accepted diplomatic language? John

[29 November 1948] I had to venture into Paris again this afternoon to visit the American Consulate on behalf of Mr Batchinski who had heard the discouraging news that, as he came out of Austria into France, he is no longer a Displaced Person, and will have to wait over two-and-a-half years for his immigration papers to come through for America. (I was insulted by the French female on duty). Poor old chap was heartbroken, and I'm not looking forward to seeing him again tomorrow for my lesson, for the position is indeed not very bright for them. Apparently America is not willing to admit too many DPs at the moment, for many of them are old and unable to work, and, in the event of trouble, they would only be a liability for the country which I can easily understand: its hard on the DPs.

[30 November 1948] The Kiroffs have gone into the deepest gloom at my prospective departure – or rather Mrs K. has. Old Kiroff never complains, and is pleased, for my sake, that I will

> have this opportunity. I like him very much. I feel so sorry for them, and don't know what they will do in the future – their limited funds can't last forever! Batchinski came today to give me my lesson and every time he comes I feel convinced that I know Bulgarian better than he does! However, what can I do – he can't find any work?

A. Beevor and A. Cooper wrote that the Marshall aid was turning out to be much more effective in improving the French economy than had been expected. When General Marshall visited France in 1948, attitudes were already changing. With the end of the crippling strikes and the Monnet plan in implementation, despite the damage caused by years of war, the country was poised for economic recovery. 'The priorities [of] steel, coal, hydroelectric power, tractors and transport had been established.'[38]

In Bulgaria the Sandersons would become good friends with John Blakeway who had also met Bulgarian students in Paris. In 1937 the two friends John Blakeway and Bob Conquest had been travelling around Europe for nine weeks, including north-east Bulgaria. Conquest was educated at Oxford University (gaining a doctorate in Soviet history) where he was an 'open' member of the CPGB (Communist Party of Great Britain). A British Army officer in the Second World War, he was posted to the School of Slavonic Studies where he studied Bulgarian for four months. In 1944 he was posted to Bulgaria as a Liaison Officer with the Bulgarian forces, fighting under Soviet command. In 1945 he joined the FO and returned as a diplomat in the British Legation in Sofia. This experience opened his eyes to the true face of Communism and he left Bulgaria in 1948 (just before John Sanderson's arrival in Sofia in December 1948) to join the FO's 'Information Research Department' which gathered and distributed information on the wrongdoings of the Soviets and Communists. As a freelance author, Conquest wrote, amongst other anti-Communist books, the classic *The Great Terror: Stalin's Purges of the Thirties*, in which he described the series of show trials of disgraced Russian Communist leaders who had 'confessed to their crimes' and were subsequently executed. Conquest also drew attention to the vast and underestimated millions killed in Stalinist purges.

Conquest described his travels with his friend John Blakeway:

> When we arrived in Paris I was met and whisked off by my girlfriend. John Blakeway left alone, saw some students begging in the gutter in the Rue de la Sorbonne. Pretty broke himself, he joined them. They turned out to be Bulgarians, and we soon

> became friendly with them, in particular with Ivan Ranchev – little guessing that this friendship would be renewed in Bulgaria, where John would eventually join us, and from which Ivan would eventually escape. After a short course at the School of Slavonic Studies in London, I was flown into Bulgaria in 1944.[39]

Conquest was based in Bulgaria for three-and-a-half years. In 1993 he returned to Sofia on a cultural visit and was photographed in front of the statue of 'Tsar Alexander II, the Tsar Liberator', some fifty years after his previous snapshot there.

John Blakeway would work with John Sanderson in the Press Section of the British Legation in Sofia in early 1949, before his expulsion in August. An SIS colleague of John Sanderson, Major Anthony 'Tony' M. Brooks had been posted to Sofia in May 1947 to open one of the first SIS stations behind the Iron Curtain. Brooks, a former member of SOE, had been parachuted twice into France at the age of 20 to organise the 'Pimento' resistance circuit that operated in a vast expanse of southern France, with HQ in Lyon and Toulouse. Brooks had attempted to remove the explosive charges from Lyon bridge when the Germans left and he had led the first US Army patrol into the city.

Keith Jeffery, whose book is based on his unique access to, and examination of, reports in M16 files, described Brooks' Bulgarian experience in the context of the 'difficult and unrewarding effort which SIS had to mount in Eastern Europe, well illustrated by the experience of postwar Bulgaria'.[40] Brooks and two female secretaries spent five days in the train between Paris and Sofia, with long spells in Balkan railway sidings. Their luggage was stolen in Italy. Brooks was inhibited in his important SIS work by the British Minister Bennett who, afraid that SIS would compromise his mission, insisted that since he had a diplomatic cover Brook should undertake legation work. The disappointing result of Brooks' work over the first three months in Sofia was nine main sources, three of whom were British. In five months Brooks filed fifty reports. Of the four grade 'A' reports he filed, two were from the Sofia military mission. The minister then ordered Brooks to stop all SIS activities. In January Brooks found that the 'only three individuals [who] seemed remotely suitable were a Bulgarian, who could have been an agent provocateur, and two Americans who were terrible social gossips'.[41]

Professor Jeffery's examination of the secret files reveal that back in London A. Halford of the FO confirmed to Brooks that Bevin desired 'that every effort was to be made to penetrate the Iron Curtain and that 'pressure would now be brought to bear on Bennett to lift his ban on SIS activity'. The MI6 files revealed that in July 1948 Brooks reported that 'all normal procedures for collecting intelligence are barred'. The British and US legations, he wrote, were being targeted by the Bulgarians and a junior member of the US Legation had been caught red-handed giving money to a Bulgarian for information, while a clerk of Bulgarian origin at the British Legation had evaded a similar fate after a car chase through the streets of Sofia. He was later expelled by the Bulgarians, accused of spying. Brooks offered, amongst other schemes such as posting letters and dead letter boxes, to prepare special operations plans, by 'selecting landing grounds and dropping zones' and scouting locations for wireless sets and other stores. These were impractical in this political climate.[42]

A new Minister had arrived in February 1949 and appeared to want to close the SIS station completely. Brooks stayed in situ until the end of 1949, keeping his position active for his successor. The Bulgarians tightened the pressure on the legation threatening to close down their wireless sets in August, intermittently harassing the staff and accusing the British, US and Yugoslav missions of being 'nests of espionage'. Instructions from London advised Brooks of the steps to be taken if he had to close the station down; destruction of papers and the return of SIS cyphers 'by confidential bag forthwith', depositing the gold with the caretaker officer and local currency left with the mission, both in return for receipts. Cameras and photographic equipment had to be returned to London and secret-ink material to 'be destroyed on the spot'.[43]

After three years in Sofia, and having operated for SIS in Paris and Belgrade, Brooks returned to Britain in 1950, 'where his considerable experience of clandestine work was fully utilised by the training section'. Brooks left SIS temporarily in 1952 but rejoined to take part in Operation MUSKETEER in 1956 with the Suez Crisis. Afterwards, Brooks was based in Cyprus on counter-terrorist operations.[44]

According to Nigel West, Tony Brooks 'had transferred more recently to MI5 where he was to score some impressive achievements, which were to include the recruitment of the KGB's Oleg Lyalin'. After George Blake's escape from Wormwood Scrubs prison, Brooks, as a 'veteran intelligence officer', gave expert advice in secret at Earl Mountbatten's review of prison security. This was to protect his identity.[45]

Keith Jeffery noted that in March and April 1949, 'the Athens S.I.S. station managed to assemble an undoubtedly brave and determined team' of anti-Communists who crossed into Bulgaria from the north east of Greece and reported back on troop deployments and Bulgarian support for the Greek Communist rebels. By the end of 1949, however, the SIS station decided 'that our customers (the Greeks) do not seem to be particularly interested in south Bulgaria any longer'. The Greek civil war was over. An earlier operation, codenamed CONTEMPLATE, involving close liaison with the Greek Air Force and using a specially equipped Spitfire to fly across the borders of Albania, Yugoslavia and Bulgaria to take reconnaissance photographs, was blocked by a Greek minister.[46]

The Cold War was now mainly confined to Europe. The war in Korea would lead to a very hot war between the Cold War rivals. For his next posting Captain John Sanderson would be 'de-badged' and travel as a civilian to Bulgaria under cover as a journalist, an Assistant Press Attaché.

Chapter 16

Behind the Iron Curtain, Bulgaria, 1949

> Owing to the all-seeing eyes of the aeroplane, manoeuvre by night has become of increasing importance, and the soldier must learn how to find his way about in the dark. He may first be taught in the day-time with the aid of night glasses, and then he will be taken out at night and shown how to ape the cunning and the silence of the poacher or the cat-burglar.

This passage was set for Sanderson in his interpreter's exam for translation into Bulgarian and has an element of direct operational relevance. In 1961 Sanderson would require the cunning and silence of the cat-burgler when exiting his CIA colleague's car at speed at night-time outside a military airbase.

Audrey Sanderson:

> My husband spent four months in Paris and then returned home for leave: but on December 17th, after only two weeks holiday, he left England once again, this time to take up his duties as a Press Attaché at the British Legation in Sofia. It was very sad that his daughter had her first Christmas without her father, so everyone was especially kind to her. Twelve people sat down to Christmas dinner and everyone, including baby, wore paper hats.

The first cross-border CIA–MI6 operations into Bulgaria took place in 1948 and others followed during the next two years (including 1949 when John Sanderson was in Sofia) with military OB (Order of Battle) information as the principal objective.[1] In 1949 the Communist parties of Eastern Europe began purges, with the victims being 'home' Communists, distrusted by Stalin because they had been in wartime Communist resistance groups or had come into contact with Westerners and thus been politically 'infected'. In Tirana the Minister of the Interior was tried and executed. In Budapest, Hungary, there were show trials with fabricated evidence of a coup planned with Yugoslav help.[2]

Captain John Sanderson arrived in Sofia in December 1948, sent by SIS under cover as a Reuters journalist, with articles later published in *The Times*. As Mr Sanderson, an Assistant Press Attaché at the Embassy, he was to observe and to report on the Communist show trials of Christian Church leaders. These Eastern European purge trials were the echo of those Stalin ordered in the Soviet Union before the war.

JBS:

> [23 December 1948] Sofia. My dear Audrey, At last I am able to sit down and drop you a line. I am very happy with the prospects here – I am in a comfortable flat. I have met practically everyone in the Legation, and I must say they are as nice a crowd of people as one could hope to find anywhere. The chap I work with in the Press section John Blakeway is a grand chap (married to Jasmine) and we have discovered that we served in the Indian Army together during the war, and were even in the Arakan together! So we have quite a lot in common. You will love it here. Sofia is a grand town, and the more I see of the Bulgarians, the more I like them. I travelled up in the train from Belgrade to Sofia in a crowded 2nd Class carriage (no sleeper to Nis!) and thoroughly enjoyed chatting with the locals, sharing my cigarettes and the remainder of my rations with them. All the people in the Legation like them very much, and we only feel sorry that we do not have more opportunity of meeting more of the locals. I am starting off tomorrow by writing my first summary of all the newspapers – I rather dread the thought, but expect it will come to me fairly quickly. Hope so! John

On 29 December Audrey Sanderson wrote: 'I have a great surprise, for John telephoned from Bulgaria and asked me if we could possibly set off for Sofia on the following Monday, with the baby of course. I felt rather dubious about being able to prepare for a complete move in four days – what a scramble!'

Denis Greenhill: 'Our departure from London at short notice precluded any adequate briefing and any rush language courses. Indeed, at that time, the Foreign Office was not organised properly to equip people before they left for new postings'. The only way for a family to reach Sofia in 1949 was by train. The weekly diplomatic bag left London on a Friday night under the care of a King's Messenger and an armed guard companion. They usually returned from Sofia on the Friday night with the British Legation's London mail. The Orient Express, with only one sleeping car and no restaurant car, stopped at most railway stations after Venice. Repairs to the line and the wartime damage to bridges, meant that, after Ljubljana, the train moved at a snail's pace. Snowstorms often stopped the train in its tracks. At stops within Bulgaria, peasants would often board the Orient Express, loaded down with vegetables they planned to sell in the Sofia markets.[3]

Denis Greenhill was in post as Head of Chancery at the British Legation in Sofia, at a time when the politics of Bulgaria were in turmoil. The country had entered the war late, having been an unenthusiastic ally of Germany. Major Frank Thompson, of SOE and the brother of the historian E.P. Thompson, had become something of a legend in Bulgaria, with a village named after him. A member of the CPGB, like his friend Iris Murdoch, Thompson had studied at Oxford in 1939. Trained by the SOE in Egypt, in 1944 he was parachuted as a Liaison Officer into Macedonia, before crossing into Bulgaria to fight alongside the Communist partisan movement. Sadly, his luck ran out. He was finally wounded, captured and executed.[4]

Greenhill wrote that the first priority of the Bulgarian Communist Party was to eliminate all domestic opposition by executing non-Communist party leaders, imprisoning them or forcing them to leave the country. The 'Fatherland Front', with false democratic members, was in reality a total Communist dictatorship. The Western Powers' vain hope that democracy would flourish was dashed in a country under the yoke of an oppressive Russian influence. British military and diplomatic missions were established in Sofia when the war ended, and the British hoped there would be some form of democracy. At the Yalta Conference in February 1945 Stalin and Churchill had discussed an arrangement whereby Russian influence in Bulgaria would be set at 75 per cent with the influence of 'the others' (the Western Allies) less at 25 per cent. This was a crude yardstick and evidently unworkable in practice. As an indication, however, of an acceptance by Stalin of the post-war majority influences of the former wartime allies in countries in the Balkan region, it had some purpose: Stalin accepted that the Western Allies would have the greatest 'percentage' influence in Greece. His main focus was on consolidating his hold on his central European satellite states.

All Bulgarian ties with the West, however, were broken. The country turned in on itself and forbad all friendship between Bulgarians and

Westerners. The isolation of the members of the Western legations drew them closer together, the British and US diplomats being the closest. Greenhill did not get on well with Bob Conquest, 'who was permitted certain favours by the Bulgarians and succeeded in removing a local girl out of the country'. Greenhill was not disappointed when Conquest left. Conquest's wife was very unhappy there.[5] Greenhill: 'Sofia was a sad city, still recovering from the war and bewildered by political developments and offered little recreational or cultural activities. One felt very isolated in Sofia. Papers from home were late. The BBC Overseas Radio Service had poor reception.'[6] Then, as Greenhill explained: 'After this an entirely different blow fell which changed everything.' The Bulgarian government began to persecute the Christian churches as other Soviet bloc states were doing. In the Orthodox Church, a respected exarch had been replaced by a more compliant figure.[7] Denis Greenhill and John Sanderson became good friends. The two men learned that they had both been in India in 1945. Greenhill described an encounter with Lord Mountbatten:

> I saw little of Mountbatten, except on one occasion in Burma . . . we were told that the Supreme Commander would shortly pass that way and say a few words. There were mutterings. Most felt that the war had gone on long enough and the time of pep talks was past . . . Preparations were being made for the seaborne liberation of Rangoon and ultimately for landings in Malaya . . . In the event the brilliant success of the 14th Army led to the freeing of Rangoon by land.[8]

John Sanderson would have reminded Greenhill that his Parachute Brigade was also involved!

JBS wrote to his parents-in-law in London:

> [2 January 1949] I am hoping Audrey will be leaving to join me tomorrow evening. You will be equally anxious for your daughter's journey to the Iron Curtain. I have done the journey and found it very interesting and comfortable. At the moment we are having the most awful fog Sofia has experienced for several years, and I do hope it will have lifted soon. It is not as thick as London fogs, but one-hundred times more dirty. It's impossible to keep one's linen clean for more than half a day, and the dirt seeps into the house through double windows, making curtains filthy! As I told you in my last letter, it's the coldest winter this year than they have had it for years.

It must be difficult for you to picture the town of Sofia – one thinks of a dirty, semi-Eastern town of half dilapidated buildings, with the streets full of beggars and stray dogs, but in actual fact, it's entirely the opposite to that. There are no such things as beggars here, and one rarely sees a dog as the population have not enough to feed themselves, let alone animals. In any case, the militia patrol the streets from morning to night, and pick up any stray dogs they find and, if they are not claimed within three days, they are then destroyed. Without doubt, that is one of the very few good things I can say for the present administration. Regarding the buildings and the town, one cannot say enough in praise of the layout, design and general convenience of everything. The standard of workmanship here is far below our standards. They go in a lot for bricks haphazardly thrown together, relying on concrete, marble, etc. for covering up the poor quality of the work, but the effect is far superior to anything we have in the provincial towns of England. There are some really lovely buildings here, and the average flat in the town – everyone lives in flats – would be classified as a luxury flat in London.

Regarding food, we have to rely mainly on tinned food, as there is absolutely nothing to be bought in the shops. How the Bulgarians live, I cannot imagine – it really is tragic. We have special diplomatic ration cards allowing us to purchase from the shops – this is about twice the Bulgarian civilian ration, and since I have been here the sum total of my civilian ration has been about three loaves of bread, two ounces of margarine, and about 4 ounces of meat. That is in two weeks! I think the population lives solely on potatoes and bread. There are no vegetables in the shops at the moment, but that's understandable, as everything is frozen. We can, however, buy eggs at one shilling each and black market meat at ten shillings a pound. Strangely enough, I miss fresh fish here – for some unknown reason, the government seem incapable of providing a single piece of fish to the starving population!

They tell me if one lives here for a long time, the present atmosphere of ill-feeling between the Communists and the Monarch Fascist Imperialists (!) gets one down in the end. There is literally no contact whatsoever with the population. The Communists won't speak to us, and the pro-Western sympathisers are frightened to death to say a word to us, or in favour of us, even to their own relatives, in fear of being shot or sent to join the 19 million people in labour camps in Siberia. It is unbelievable that such a gang of thugs could possible get a hold on the population. This hold on them is practised down to the smallest degree: every block of flats has a 'communist' leader who guides the 'social and cultural' life of the inhabitants of his block. He reports on all his 'charges' from time to time – where they go, the visitors they have, the food they eat and the goods they buy. If the government calls for a parade or manifestation in honour of some party conference or anniversary, a notice is posted up by the leader of each block of flats to the effect that every person is expected to attend. If they don't, the fact is reported and very shortly that person disappears. Our maids have to report to the militia on our guests, on what we eat and what we talk about, and for that reason, one dare not invite any Bulgarian to our flat for a meal – for one thing they would not come unless they had the permission of the party.

In spite of all this, it's wonderful to see the heavenly countryside and have the opportunities of seeing new faces and customs, and to have the joy of going to friends' houses to hear laughter and dance music (this is considered by the new regime to be an occupation solely of the non-cultural imperialists!) as well as free political discussion and the lack of fear. These are the pleasures of Sofia.

As you can imagine, I am learning a lot of the ways of Communism from the daily papers I read each day, and the more I read, the more I become convinced of the cruel, cunning, cold-blooded extortion of the whole system. A system of rule by a bunch of ruthless, generally uneducated people who are out to get all they can for themselves, without the slightest interest for welfare of the population. Their only objective is the rule of the Kremlin, and their one aim in life is to save their own necks and make as much as they can out of their jobs.

It's a sad thing to see a population that literally has nothing to live for, with no hope of the future – other than a war, which most of the population want in order to be freed from subjugation. They see the much publicized five-year plan coming and going, each one bringing less economic stability and more enslavery. They realise this system cannot succeed, with half the population wearing a uniform of either the Army, the Militia (Police), the secret police and the frontier guards. One sees more people in uniform in every town of this country, than one sees in Aldershot

> or Salisbury. Where it will all lead, I cannot say, but I have a fairly good idea. But may God grant us and them some other solution.

Audrey Sanderson's handwritten account describes her first journey by train to Bulgaria:

> On 3 January 1949 at 9.30 hours, my daughter and I steamed out of Victoria Station on the 'Golden Arrow'. The sadness of saying 'goodbye' to my family mingled with the happiness at seeing my husband again.
>
> The journey to Paris seemed to pass quickly as my daughter was a model baby. When we arrived at the Gare du Nord, Peter Greenhalgh was waiting with one of the embassy cars, and we all 'piled in' amidst a mass of luggage including the pram. Peter and I had dinner together and then we weary travellers were safely installed in our sleepers on the Simplon–Orient Express which departed at 21.30 hours We were soon asleep, myself in a bed and my daughter in a cot beside me. Waking the next morning at Montreux, we found the sunshine was sparkling on Lake Geneva and reflecting a pink glow on the snowy mountain summits. The sun continued shining all day on the magnificent scenery of Switzerland and Italy but my daughter slept all the way, only waking for her food. The train missed the Sofia connection at Milan and we had to wait four hours in the station. The platforms were crowded with people, with trolleys laden with fruit, wine, chocolate and luncheon baskets. It was amazing how quickly Italy, a defeated country, had recovered from the war.
>
> The train was eventually reformed and the journey continued to Venice and Trieste. As one entered, and passed through, the 'Iron Curtain'; the contrast with the West was startling, and somewhat frightening – all the stations were crowded with men in uniform, the civilians shabbily dressed, and their grim expressions, all created an unpleasant atmosphere of preparation for war. All night long we were disturbed for passports and customs. After an unpleasant night in a sweltering compartment, we awoke to find ourselves in Yugoslavia. The restaurant car had been unhitched in Trieste, so I made my daughter's feeds and brewed a cup of tea over my tiny spirit stove – in secret, as it was forbidden. However, a new drunken Yugoslavian attendant had joined us and he really didn't seem to care. Wild, desolate rocky scenery passed by and then the uninteresting plains of Yugoslavia.

> After Zagreb, the scenery became dreary, the skies grey and we looked out on squalid little huts and villages everywhere. The journey had seemed very long when the Bulgarian frontier was reached at about 10.00 hours on 7 January 1949. All sorts of officials boarded the train, and examined our luggage, passports. Heavenly! Only five more hours to Sofia. The scenery continued in colourless monotony. I felt very tired, although my baby had been marvellous throughout the whole trip. I could not contain my excitement though, for the train was slowing down and entering Sofia station, a very dirty station, where my husband stood waiting for us on the platform, wreathed in smiles.

JBS described meeting her:

> Both arrived safely at the station yesterday afternoon at 3 o'clock, and their carriage drew in right alongside where I was standing. It was so wonderful to see them again, and both were looking so remarkably well that I could not believe that they had spent four days in a train. Audrey looked lovely in her new hat and coat and the baby seemed very thrilled (and unperturbed) by her new surroundings.

Audrey described her first experience of Bulgaria the following morning:

> After unpacking, I peered through the window. There was a crowd of young people gathered on the pavement opposite. It looked like a strange shop at which they were queuing but I saw huge red banners and pictures of Stalin and Georgi Dimitrov in the window. The cook said it was a Communist Club. Several companies of soldiers marched by singing National songs in unison, very beautifully, I thought. Apparently here it is a crime to run water on certain days of the week. If one dares take a bath on a Thursday, one would surely be disturbed by an armed militiaman hammering on the door!

Greenhill described how, at the end of 1948:

> we got news that fifteen Protestant Pastors in Bulgaria had been arrested and that a show trial was impending. Questions were asked in the Westminster Parliament. Gossip in Sofia suggested that members of the U.S. and British Legations would be implicated

> in charges of espionage. We pressed for representatives at the trial but were refused. A strange British clergyman arrived suddenly in Sofia to 'observe' the trial.

Greenhill, for obvious reasons, omitted to mention in his autobiography that actually a member of MI6 had arrived in the guise of an Assistant Press Attaché, a colleague called John Sanderson.

On 25 February 1949 Audrey Sanderson wrote to her parents:

> John left for the Legation early, as he is very busy attending the Trials of the Pastors. It makes me sick because, of course, the whole thing is a put-up job. Last night we went to a concert of folk dances and an operetta. All very amateurish. The operetta was frightful, all propaganda, with little children carrying the Red Flag around and saluting. It made us so sick that we left before the end. We went to the Hotel Bulgaria for dinner. It was empty except for a few fat communists.

During this first stay in Bulgaria as an Assistant Press Attaché, working for the FO, John was deeply affected by the public 'show trials' of Protestant pastors. The foreign press had received the text of the confessions of the accused before the trial had actually taken place. So effective were the Communist brain-washing techniques that, for several hours, the pastors confessed their supposed crimes in court, reciting from memory, word for word, the exact text that had been distributed previously to the press.

JBS' typed trial report reads:

> The trial took place in the Palace of Justice, one of the most imposing buildings in Sofia. The courtroom, with a seating capacity of about 250 persons, was well lighted, ventilated and clean, but not sufficiently well heated to permit the Chief Prosecutor, Defence Counsel, several of the accused and most of the spectators to discard their overcoats. A large mural of the blindfolded statue of Justice, holding a pair of scales, perhaps gave the accused added confidence when so freely admitting their crimes. Seated on a raised platform facing the courtroom were the President and the two members of the court (Judicial Assessors). On their right sat the two prosecutors and on their left, an apparently newly cast bust of Georgi Dimitrov was prominently placed on a six foot stand. The fifteen accused sat on five benches in front of the spectators, each separated by a militiaman. Spectators were

admitted by ticket only, and appeared to be mainly friends or relatives of the accused or persons who had obtained a ticket from the President of the Sofia District Court. Members of the Press occupied the gallery. The Court was the normal Sofia District Court. The President, K. Undjiev, appeared to be a man of about 45 years of age, clean-shaven, efficient, educated and extremely self-possessed. The two Judicial Assessors, summoned for fifteen days, were both reported to be qualified lawyers. They took no active part in the proceedings, apart from showing an abstract interest in the evidence. Neither uttered a word nor made a single note throughout the whole trial. All the accused appeared to be in good health, were well dressed and groomed. They gave their evidence from a small dais just below the President in clear, almost monotonous tones for periods of up to six hours. Scarcely a detail was omitted. All the accused used notes, but it was obvious that the testimony of each witness had been well-rehearsed prior to the trial, for they followed almost exactly the original 'confessions'.

A microphone was installed for the witnesses and the Prosecutor, but the loudspeaker system broke down at frequent intervals, making it practically impossible at times to hear the evidence. This was, however, not considered to be intentional! Correspondents were treated with respect and granted ample facilities for telephoning the news out of the country. A refreshment bar was provided for their use. The Chief State Prosecutor, D. Georgiev, had a most brusque manner when questioning the witnesses, and spoke with a distinct Russian accent which even the witnesses found difficult to understand clearly. It was reported that he had spent nearly ten years in Russia. The Assistant Prosecutor, F. Taskov, could not have been more efficient in conducting his part in the Prosecution, i.e. that of the eleven minor defendants. The Defence, except in a few instances, was virtually ineffective and was obviously considered by the Court and the Prosecution to be a waste of time – which indeed it was. However, the advocates pressed home their pleas in mitigation in spite of the cynical smiles from the Chief Prosecutor and signs of exasperation from the President, who ran his hands quickly through his hair at frequent intervals.

Most of the substantial Prosecution witnesses were under arrest and 'freely' gave all the evidence required of them. Defence witnesses, without exception, would not commit themselves.

> Even Andreichin and Kolishev, who were in a position to defend Ziapkov's activity in Paris, were only prepared to say that they had heard that he had done good work, but as he was not a member of the delegation, they were not prepared to say more. The prosecution witnesses under escort were not nearly so neatly attired as the fifteen accused, and were escorted into court either by plain-clothed guards, uniformed guards with rifles, or in the case of Christo Stratev, a uniformed guard with an automatic weapon.
>
> When the sentences were pronounced, all the accused were given the opportunity to appeal but waived this right and expressed their satisfaction with the sentences passed. They showed no surprise, and indeed it would appear that they were previously informed of what the sentences would be.[9]

During the show trial, Denis Greenhill was surprised and perplexed by false allegations that he had recruited the most senior pastor of the fifteen on trial to spy for him. The Bulgarian press quoted 'verbatim' remarks that Greenhill was supposed to have made. Ziapkov had been 'set up' by the evidence of a young man who had posed as his daughter's fiancé. Greenhill had on two occasions met Ziapkov, whom he was alleged to have tasked, in spite of his very poor eyesight, with swimming out into the Black Sea near Varna and counting gun emplacements on the coast. Pastor Ziapkov was sentenced to twenty-five years in prison, eighteen of which he served. A letter from Lord Vansittart in *The Times*, critical of the Bulgarian government, precipitated Greenhill's expulsion from Bulgaria, much to his chagrin and anger.[10]

The PUSD (cover name for SIS) was a department created in about 1948 to coordinate intelligence and covert political action under FO supervision. In 1973, when Lord Greenhill was PUS at the FCO (Foreign and Commonwealth Office) and Chairman of the JIC he was surprised to receive an invitation for his wife and him to visit Bulgaria at the government's expense. It must have been a strange experience to return to Sofia, this time as a welcome and honoured guest.[11] John Sanderson always planned to return to Sofia, after the fall of the Berlin Wall, to request his Bulgarian secret service file but he never did. Interviewed in 1996, Lord Greenhill looked back to the old days of the FO: 'What was pleasant and attractive in the Foreign Office [then], that I believe is nowadays being destroyed or driven away [was that] you knew so-and-so and his wife and children and you meet them now. There was a sort of camaraderie which was genuine and worthwhile.'[12]

Whilst his wife was abroad in Sofia with their family, John Sanderson returned to sit his interpreter's language exams in London, alongside Peter Greenhalgh. In Sofia Audrey Sanderson was discovering the Bulgarian way of life. She came to admire the simple, generous Bulgarian country people:

> We went to Charo Krea last weekend with John and Jasmine Blakeway, travelling in a truck. The weather was just beautiful the whole time. In the afternoon of the second day we drove to a heavenly spot high in the mountains and lay all afternoon amongst the flowers, admiring the view. We had brought everything to make tea, and then realised that we'd left the kettle of water behind. Miles below we saw a village and, being typically British, we had to have our tea. So down we went. Eventually we met a young man who took us to his home. This was a small farm, not very clean but like a musical comedy with balconies and pigs and mud underfoot. The grandmother and the man's wife came to meet us both dressed in spotless national costumes. They were so kind and brought us a table and chairs. Then they put a large bowl of sour cream on the table and gave us a spoon each. Then one plate of cheese and a fork each and a piece of black bread each. Eventually the tea arrived in a large pan with a ladle. So the British had their tea after all. They wouldn't charge us a penny. The man had caught some small trout which we bought from him. Jasmine and I cooked these for supper and afterwards we sat around the fire, as it was quite cold by night time. Charo is 9,000 feet high. It is interesting to see the village life where women and men in national costumes draw the water from the village pump into quaint coloured water carafes. Everywhere are oxen carts and these are drawn by water buffalo.

But Sofia had its darker side.

> BULGARIAN MURDER SQUAD EXPOSED. *DAILY TELGRAPH* 31/07/2010
>
> A secret Bulgarian unit known as 'Service 7' was set up to 'execute death sentences' on opponents of the Communist regime including Georgi Markov, who was killed by a poisoned umbrella tip in London thirty-two years ago. The existence of the death squad, long denied by former officials, came to light after a British journalist discovered that intelligence service files had been declassified under a new (Bulgarian) law.[13]

This was the September 1978 assassination of the celebrated Bulgarian dissident playwright and novelist Georgi Markov, who had defected to the West in 1969. Markov became a journalist for the BBC World Service: his broadcasts were said to infuriate the Bulgarian dictator Todor Zhivkov. Markov was killed, according to the *Daily Telegraph*, by a secret assassination unit called 'Service 7'. Newspaper reports at the time identified the cause of death as a miniscule pellet containing the chemical ricin, in all probability, fired into his leg by an 'umbrella gun'. C. Andrew and O. Gordievsky described how the assassination was planned. Todor Zhivkov was determined to silence Markov. He turned to the Moscow Centre who offered the resources of the ultra-secret KGB laboratory, attached to their Technical Directorate. Here they produced poisons which they could supply to the Bulgarian DS (Bulgarian intelligence and security service). Sergei Golubev, who ran Laboratory 12, visited Sofia on several occasions in 1978 to help plan operations against 'troublesome' émigrés. He had a special poisonous jelly that could be smeared on objects and which induced heart attacks. Poisons could be put in drinks, he said. The KGB advised that it would kill the victims without leaving a trace, when absorbed into the skin. Golubev instructed the Washington embassy to buy umbrellas which were then sent to the Moscow Centre where their tips were fitted with a mechanism to inject very small pellets containing ricin, an extremely toxic poison. Golubev delivered the umbrellas to Sofia for the DS assassination squad to use on Markov.[14]

Nigel West revealed that the prime suspect in Markov's death was a Danish assassin. West also noted that a Romanian defector to the CIA had identified plutonium being employed as a method of assassinating journalists of the Munich Free European Radio, the radioactive substance being left in desk drawers. The resultant exposure caused lung cancer. This ties up with John Sanderson's disclosure of the Western diplomat in Sofia developing cancer after a radioactive substance was secreted under his bed.[15]

Bob Conquest described how he had 'spoken with Markov, who had earlier been the white hope of Communist literature, a year or two before his death and he had told me that he knew himself to be in particularly bad odour because of his firsthand accounts of Zhivkov over the BBC'. These included his telling how Zhivkov, his host at the former royal chalet at Chamkoria, had said to him in awed tones: 'Tonight you sleep in the bed of a king!' Conquest's musician friend Pashanko Dimitrov, who afterwards escaped to London, had apparently committed the offence for which the Secret police had arrested him – he had attempted to blow up a statue of Lenin.[16]

On 4 March 1949 Stalin removed Molotov as Foreign Minister and replaced him with Andrei Vyshinsky. Andrei Gromyko described Vsyhinsky's obsequiousness when Lavrenti Beria telephoned: 'As soon as he heard Beria's voice, Vyshinsky leapt respectfully out of his chair . . . Vyshinsky cringed like a servant before his master.' The turn of the screw would tighten on Beria himself later.[17]

Audrey Sanderson wrote to her parents:

> [1 April 1949] Sofia. Dear Mother and Father, We had a big 'do' last Saturday. John was going to invite two Bulgars to lunch but, in the end, we invited all our Bulgarian office staff from the British Legation and, just to show that it wasn't an espionage meeting, several Communist press men besides. 25 people at least! Our flat lends itself beautifully to parties with its large rooms and parquet flooring. We opened the folding doors and had a buffet supper of cold chicken, lamb, salads, jellies, fruit salads etc. We had cocktails and snacks first. So we really 'did them proud'. We borrowed a radiogram and danced, then had games and ended with a sing-song. They must have enjoyed it because they stayed until almost 3 o'clock in the morning! Several people told me next day that our Bulgarian guests had said, with tears in their eyes, that it was the best party they'd had for years. They are afraid to have parties or get together.

In the West, Europe was preparing to defend itself. On 4 April 1949 the NATO alliance pact was signed by twelve nations. The essence of the agreement was Article 5 which defined the *casus foederis* ('case of the treaty') which commits each member state to consider an armed attack against one member, in Europe or North America including Canada, to be an armed attack against them all.

Unknown to the signatories, the Fifth Cambridge spy John Cairncross had previously passed over to his Russian handler Modin a complete collection of papers for the future structure, financing and composition of NATO, before it was created. Cairncross was a gifted linguist who had also studied at Glagow University and La Sorbonne. The journalist Tom Boyer, in his obituary on Cairncross in the *Independent*, wrote a lively account of Cairncross's effectivevess as a Russian agent both during the war and after. Cairncross was recruited by the Marxist James Klugman. At the outbreak of the war, he was posted to the Cabinet Office as Private Secretary to Lord Hankey. He handed over reams of top-secret Cabinet papers to the Russians. In 1941 he was posted to GCHQ at Bletchley Park, where he mined a treasure trove of intelligence for the KGB. In February 1943 he handed over intercepts with full details of the Wehrmacht's summer offensive along a 1,200km front, which would climax in the

Battle of Kursk. The Soviets made pre-emptive strikes, using Cairncross's information to develop a new anti-tank shell capable of penetrating the new thicker German tank armour. Cairncross was awarded the Order of the Red Banner for his espionage but deluded himself that he was not a traitor since he had never passed across any intelligence harmful to Britain: he saw himself as helping the then ally Russia. In 1944 he moved to SIS in the Broadway H.Q.

When Burgess defected to Moscow, MI5 found hidden in a guitar in his flat a secret FO paper with an attached, unsigned note in Cairncross's handwriting. This evidence eventually led MI5 to Cairncross and he was placed under surveillance. Followed through the London Underground, he was observed nervously smoking, whilst waiting for someone. His handler Modin, though, had spotted the three MI5 watchers and left the rendezvous without making contact. Knowing that Cairncross was a non-smoker, MI5 pulled him in for questioning. Confronted with the evidence, he did not confess, as MI5 had hoped, but would only admit to having Communist leanings and an innocent friendship with Burgess. MI5 regrettably had insufficient evidence to prosecute. As Cairncross now had no job or funds, the KGB paid for his travel to Canada where he became a professor of French literature. Some years later, the dogged ace MI5 interrogator Arthur Martin visited Cairncross in Canada and managed to obtain his full confession. Cairncross revealed to Martin that Anthony Blunt was a spy. Cairncross then moved to work in Rome, where in 1979, he revealed to an investigative journalist that he was indeed the 'Fifth Man', this confirmed a decade later by Oleg Gordievsky.[18]

John Gaddis, the Cold War historian, described the creation of NATO as a European initiative which accepted the reality that the USA was the major military power in the Western camp, positioned in the heart of Europe and assuring security in the face of Soviet threats. Washington agreed to the NATO alliance on the condition of the creation of an independent West German state, which they viewed as a future NATO ally, rather than a defeated enemy. As General Clay succintly remarked: 'Forty-two million Germans in the British and American zones represent today the biggest outpost against Communist penetration that exists today.' There was felt to be a real threat of a Russian invasion. It was estimated that the Soviet bloc would soon have a collective conventional force of 175 divisions, facing a paltry 12 Western divisions. Although the French experience of a wartime German occupation made them reluctant to accept a rearmed Germany, they did see NATO as a 'double containment' of both the Russians and the French. The new FRG (Federal Republic of Germany) would have no independent army: its military would be integrated into NATO defence forces.[19]

The three Sandersons took a memorable trip to Varna:

[9 June 1949] Sofia c/o Foreign Office, London S.W.1

Dear Mother and Father, We arrived back in Sofia last night after five days in a small place on the Black Sea called Varna. We caught the train there and were met by a car run by the Balkan Tourist Association and driven about six miles to their new hotel which was opened only two weeks ago. It is right on the edge of a beach but raised about fifty feet on a hill, so that you look through trees down to the sea. It was very lovely, with beautiful views – rather like Cornwall. When we arrived, we were told that there wasn't a room free as a large group of 400 Czech workers were there, as a reward for their good work in Czechoslovakia. However, they eventually found us a single room. There was a 'Horomag' (People's Shop) and we ate there, surrounded by workers! The food wasn't very good, masses of meat but nothing to eat with it. No vegetables or potatoes. Every so often they gave propaganda talks and news items such as the Railway Strike in Britain which they all cheered! One evening was very interesting, the peasants came in their national costumes to dance and sang for us. The dancing was really very exciting to watch, with the speed of their footwork and the gay colours of the costumes. There was a very good band and dancing overlooking the sea. It would have been heavenly but of course the rough workers rather spoilt the atmosphere. The Belgian Minister was staying there with his wife and children and you can imagine he felt a bit out of it amongst all the work people. The country people we met on our walks all said they liked the English and at one little cottage the peasants made us sit down and brought us hot doughnuts and cherries to eat. On the plane back to Sofia I had my first flight in a plane. We left at 2.30 pm and arrived in Sofia 3 hours 15 minutes later, having landed at two places on the way, stopping fifteen minutes at each. It was a very old German Junkers and John says the noisiest he has ever flown in. It was interesting to look down on the countryside with fields and mountains, but the plane was so smelly and old that I was ill. Audrey

JBS:

[10 June 1949] Sofia. We had a nice garden party yesterday on the occasion of King George VI's birthday. Over 300 guests attended, and I spent 4 solid hours using my Bulgarian. Every legation was represented, even the Russians came. The weather was kind to us and it was held in the garden of the residence. Afterwards I gave a film show to four of our American friends in our flat: the *Winslow Boy*. Each week we get a 16mm film from Trieste, and anyone can give a private showing in their flats, if they so desire. We have the equipment in the legation, and each person operates it himself. John.

In July 1949 the Bulgarian Communist leader, Georgi Dimitrov, in power since 1946, was resting in a sanitorium near Moscow when he died, suddenly and mysteriously. According to the Bulgarian writer Kapka Kassabova, when Dimitrov's brain was tested in 1999, there was evidence of mercury poisoning, no doubt administered on Stalin's orders. Dimitrov was returned to Sofia and installed in a huge mausoleum, his body preserved on display, like Lenin's in Red Square, and spruced up chemically every year. Soviet-trained embalming experts would lower his body into 300l of embalming fluid and afterwards install him in a new suit. The mausoleum edifice also served as a nuclear bunker, connected to the Communist Party HQ, demonstrating that during a nuclear attack, some workers were more equal than others. After the fall of Communism, the structure was blown up by the army and the empty space was renamed Prince Albert of Battenburg Square.[20]

JBS wrote home about his friend John Blakeway:

Sofia British Legation. Dear Mother and Father,

You will have read in the papers, by the time you receive this letter, of the sad news of our Press Attaché, John Blakeway, being declared *persona non grata*. It will be a great loss to the legation, for he is an expert on Bulgarian affairs and speaks the language fluently. He has been here for over two years (of course, this is precisely why he has been declared PNG). Both he and his wife are a very popular couple, not only amongst the Diplomatic Corps, but also amongst the Bulgarians themselves. Naturally, he has done nothing to warrant this action, and we shall have to take reprisals, which can only go to worsen relations between our government and the Bulgarians. The latter, of course, are continuing their policy of making life as difficult as they can for us and they have picked on John Blakeway because he knows too much about the country. I'm sure if I had not let it be known that I was leaving in September, I would have been asked to leave as well, simply because I can speak to the man on the street and

> learn the truth of what really does go on in these countries – and I don't have to tell you that it's not pleasant listening. John

The Australian *Canberra Times* reported the Bulgarian government's expulsion in August 1949 of John Blakeway, who, like John Sanderson, had arrived in Bulgaria as a Press Attaché. In a tit-for-tat reprisal, following Blakeway's expulsion, the British government demanded the recall of Boris Temkov, a Press Attaché at the Bulgarian Legation in London. In Hungary a complicated chain of PNG expulsions arose. The British government accused the Budapest Police of having kidnapped a Mr Wallace Harrison, a former British Legation employee in Budapest, and of having attempted to force him to become their agent. The Hungarian authorities replied that they were in possession of a recording which they said proved that Mr Harrison had volunteered to work for them in exchange for the release of a British Legation telephonist arrested by the police. When the British then expelled a Hungarian diplomat in London, the Hungarians ordered a British official at the Budapest Legation to leave the country.[21]

On returning to Britain, *JBS* penned his feelings about his past posting:

> In October 1949 the Sanderson family was back in England, more with relief than regret to have left Bulgaria. The only regret was leaving very good friends at the American and British Legations – without them life in a Communist country, where members of Western missions have absolutely no contact with the population, would have been intolerable. The few Bulgarians who dare to show their friendships towards the British or Americans have long since been arrested. The relief on leaving the country is no way due to poor living conditions, for diplomatic personnel from Western countries are still treated with a little consideration in this respect – simply for fear of reprisals! It was the depressing dictatorial atmosphere, the widespread unhappiness of the populace and the strained relations between East and West that made a prolonged stay in Bulgaria unpleasant.
>
> The misery and destitution of the people, the hopelessness of their cause and their touching hopes that in some manner the Western Powers could help them was, in these days of comparable peace, a moving spectacle. It demonstrated the depths to which Communism will lower a country to achieve its own ends.
>
> A forbidden zone of some 50 miles along the frontiers of the country allowed little scope for travel. Apart from a five-day holiday at Varna, on the Black Sea, a trip to the town of Plovdiv and

> several weekends at the villa in the mountains, the time was spent in the capital. My baby daughter experienced her first journey by air on returning from Varna to Sofia. The plane was an old German Jünkers with twin engines and an all-metal body. The vibration of the 90mph journey caused her to be exceedingly sick and her mother to pray that she never has to take 2ft off the ground again!
>
> Thus lived my young child in Sofia whilst the children of Bulgaria were being taught that Christ was a mythical leader of the oppressed classes and all around her were political meetings, manifestations, purges, mass arrests and forced labour. With this background to the artificial life of the diplomat behind the 'Iron Curtain', the days passed quickly by. On 3 September 1949, exactly ten years after the commencement of the Second World War, the train from Sofia set off on a journey through a Europe, once again overshadowed by a dark and fearsome cloud.

This 'dark and fearsome cloud' was the Soviet atomic bomb, exploded on 29 August 1949, five days before the Sandersons' departure by train from Sofia. FBI Director J. Edgar Hoover said that Soviet espionage rings in the USA had 'stolen the most important secrets ever known to mankind and delivered them to the Soviet Union', but, according to Phillip Knightley, this was an exaggeration: Soviet physicists developed it themselves. The atomic spies such as Klaus Fuchs may have only advanced the date of the first Russian atomic bomb.[22]

In Bulgaria the repression continued after the Sandersons' departure. Interestingly, an article in *The Times* described a former 'Western' Military Attaché who had spoken Russian in an attempt to gain intelligence on Bulgarian military bases:

> BULGARIAN SPY SCARE CAMPAIGN. *The Times*
>
> The Bulgarian authorities are accompanying the trial of Mr Ivan Gheorghiev, a former Bulgarian diplomatist, who is accused of working for American intelligence, with a spy scare campaign 'Beware of Russian-speaking strangers', Radio Sofia has warned its listeners. 'They may be Western spies posing as Soviet citizens'. A former Western Military Attaché is said to have tried to penetrate military units pretending to be a Russian, whilst another, unspecified Russian-speaking agent, having introduced himself as an applicant for a job, walked into a Government department, listened to conversations and, having learnt many state secrets, went off to write a five-page report.[23]

Daphne Park, the plucky female MI6 officer posted as Second Secretary to Moscow in the mid-1950s, showed her initiative in an opportunist event similar to the above. On a trip to Kalinin with the Assistant Air Attaché they had found the local KGB offices and had the effrontery to walk boldly through the open door and up to the first floor, where they proceeded to carefully note down the names and positions of the officials displayed on the doors. Realising they were being observed, they calmly donned swimming costumes and swam across the Volga with their information. She would later enter the House of Lords as 'Baroness Park of Monmouth'.[24]

A year after John Sanderson's wife and little daughter's January 1949 journey out to Bulgaria on the 'Orient Express' – and the very month that John Sanderson qualified as an interpreter in Bulgarian in London – the following macabre incident occurred on an Orient Express train in Hungary. The diplomatic immunity that Military Attachés enjoyed as diplomats in Eastern bloc countries did not always guarantee their safety and security, if they invoked the displeasure of their hosts and the Communist security services.

> *CANBERRA TIMES*, 27TH FEBRUARY 1950
> VIENNA Sunday. The Austrian authorities said that the death of Captain Eugene carp, American Naval Attaché in Bucharest, was the result of foul play. Karp's battered body was found on the railway line in a tunnel on the route used by the Arlberg–Simplon Express.
>
> On 24 February 1950, it was reported in the international press that Austrian police had discovered the headless body of a man lying along the rail track used by the International Arlberg–Orient Express, to the south of Salzburg. Unrecognisable, the man could only be identified by his identity papers. It was Captain Karp. The diplomat, who worked for the American secret service, had just been implicated in a spying affair, for which one of his compatriots and friends Robert Vogeler had been sentenced to fifteen years in prison by a court in Hungary. Karp evidently had wanted to get back to the west. It is known that he visited Vogeler's wife two days previously, no doubt to collect important documents. Then he climbed aboard the Orient Express for Paris. He had reserved a single bed in a sleeping compartment. The police reported that he seemed anxious. After this his trail went dead. The steward responsible for the wagon lit was found drugged and Karp's bed sheets undisturbed. No doubt pursued by two Romanian agents, the American had been thrown out of

> the train in the middle of the night when the train passed through the Luz tunnel. His body was smashed against the walls of the tunnel. A spectacular crime which, in a legendary train, is an example of the implacability of the Cold War.[25]

The dangers were equally real in Russia for those that stepped out of line or questioned too much. Stalin had cleverly exploited Russian patriotism to foster a cult of a benign leader and to propagate the idea 'that their destinies were guided by a father figure'. In December 1949 the overblown celebrations of Joseph Stalin's 70th birthday 'reached a climax (when) . . . his image appeared in the night sky above the Kremlin, suspended from a balloon and illuminated by searchlights'.[26]

In June 1950 the Cold War suddenly became hot and even more dangerous, when North Korea invaded South Korea and threatened to destroy the US Army. However, only five years had elapsed since the end of the Second World War and the USA was able to respond and mobilise reserve troops with combat experience from the Second World War: its economy was still geared to produce war materials.

After the Korean War, more than sixty US Army National Guard and Reserve Units from thirty states, mobilised for the Korean War, were sent to France, most being all-black enlisted troops. France provided ocean ports that served a complex network of US Army depots spread right across France, far from the Soviet satellites. In 1951 General Dwight D. Eisenhower returned to Paris as the first Supreme Commander of SHAPE HQ of the recently formed NATO. From 1952 to 1962, over fifty discharge exercises were held to practise landing cargo and troops on French beaches from the border with Spain up to Quiberon in Brittany. To support combat forces in Germany, more than 400 installations were built across France, from Bordeaux in the south west through the Loire Valley and Paris regions to Alsace-Lorraine in the north east. By 1958 the US military would employ the third largest workforce in France. By 1961 there would be more than 100,000 US military and family members in France.[27]

In 1954 Sanderson would be posted to Egypt and stationed on the Suez Canal. In 1956 he would take part in the Suez invasion. The British bases in Egypt were unpopular with the Egyptians and Nasser was flexing his muscles. The journalist Alan Whicker, the former officer cadet who trained at Barmouth 162 OCTU with John Sanderson, recalled his time in Egypt in 1951:

> In 1951 the Wafd party had been struggling for a year to drive the British out of the Kingdom of Egypt . . . The British Army

had withdrawn its 80,000 men behind the garrison defences of the Canal Zone base. . . . The World's Press was converging upon Cairo for the Egyptian angle and the political story. An unknown Major called Nasser had told the *New York Herald Tribune*: 'Not formal war. That would be suicidal. It will be a guerilla war. Grenades will be thrown in the night. British soldiers will be stabbed stealthily. There will be terror.' . . .

Snipers within the Casbah would fire across at military transport using the road, which we called Murder Mile. When the terrorism became insupportable the [British] Army reacted. We followed Centurion tanks into Ismailia. Their 20-pounders blew junks off the Egyptian Police HQ, where the action was being organised, killing 46 and wounding 60. . . . revolutionary ardour cooled quickly. For a short while afterwards fewer British soldiers were ambushed and murdered.[28]

Chapter 17

Clandestine War Behind the Iron Curtain

O Rose thou art sick!
The invisible worm that flies in the night,
In the howling storm,
Has found out thy bed of crimson joy,
And his dark secret love
Does thy life destroy.

William Blake[1]

The Clandestine War Waged by M16 and the CIA Behind the Iron Curtain in the 1950s

Much has been published in recent years about the operations that the West sponsored and organised behind the Iron Curtain, usually with the involvement of trained and armed exiled groups. The aim was to have strong resistance in place in case of a Soviet thrust south to the Mediterranean or a Soviet invasion of Western Europe. Obituaries and other sources have described such operations in Albania, Poland, Hungary, Ukraine and the Baltic States. Less information is available on operations into Bulgaria.

A 'TOP SECRET' report entitled 'PROJECT BG/FIEND' was approved on 22 June 1949 after discussions between the USA's Department of State with the JCS (Joint Chiefs of Staff) and Britain's FO with the SIS. The main objective was the overthrow of the Albanian government, with the secondary objectives of a) eliminating support for the Greek Communist guerillas, b) denying the Soviets a Mediterranean base for land, air and naval forces and c) a psychological stimulus to Iron Curtain countries to overthrow their dictatorships. To achieve this they proposed to covertly establish an Albanian National Committee representing émigré groups, to organise and train Albanian patriots outside Albania and lastly to create a provisional government to take over Albania after a *coup d'état*. In August 1948 the creation of a National Committee was announced in Paris, composed of three Albanian political parties to participate in covert operational matters (it was later excluded from knowledge of covert operations due to Soviet infiltration).[2] At a NATO council meeting in Washington in September 1949 the Foreign Secretary Ernest Bevin had proposed instituting a counter revolution in Albania. The US JCS knew from intelligence reports that Soviets had plans to make the harbour of Valona a Soviet submarine base and saw it as a possible forward base for the US fleet in the Mediterranean if Albania could be 'liberated'. Hundreds of staff were now involved in the planning and training of émigré fighters.[3] Following the NATO meeting in December 1949 the objectives were reconsidered. New policy aims were to harass the Hoxha regime, and to create and support a skeleton Albanian liberation resistance movement with a pool of 500 trained men. A new psychological warfare policy was planned with a) black propaganda broadcasts in the Albanian language (a covert radio station was set up near Athens, after broadcasts from a boat proved ineffective) and b) a programme of dispatching letters and parcels to individuals in the Hoxha regime to cause embarrassment amongst regime politicians. The correspondence would use Swiss Bank letterheads for non-existent accounts or would be supposed replies to enquiries to open bank accounts. A few small parcels of luxury goods would be sent to wives of prominent communists in response to fictitious orders.[4]

Meanwhile, training continued in Malta and a special school in West Germany for Albanian refugees recruited in DP camps. Explosives and weapons were sourced without identifying markings to aid denial. The Greek government was applying pressure on the US government to act over Albanian support for rebels.[5] On 3 October 1949 nine Albanians climbed off a Greek caique, *Stormie Sea* (fitted with a powerful British engine), into rubber boats and were rowed ashore. Five days later Philby arrived in New York for his new post as First Secretary at the embassy, in reality as the Liaison Officer with the FBI and CIA in Washington. Stephen Dorril pointed out that Philby, after returning from his Turkey posting in September, had met Jack Easton, who was deeply involved in Operation VALUABLE. The update that Easton must have given Philby would have been promptly passed on to Philby's KGB handler, 'Max'.

On 10 October a second landing of Albanians was made on a beach north of Valona. The two operations were doomed. Philby in Washington was a member, as a joint commander, of the committee that ran the Albanian operations and was briefed daily.[6] On the 12th a first-team member radioed that Sigurimi (Albanian Security Service) were waiting for them, that the army had the area surrounded and that three had been killed, one captured and one missing. The remaining four and all of the unsuccessful team made it to Greece. They reported that their handlers had completely exaggerated the counter-revolutionary spirit of Albanians. They thought their mission had been leaked. One of their number later assisted the Albanian Intelligence in organising a 'double-cross operation'.[7] OPC and MI6 were at this time running a similar infiltration operation into Bulgaria. The details of this were passed on to Moscow by Philby in Washington. During the winter of 1949/50 the *Stormie Sea* was involved in carrying 'mysterious cargoes to agents in Bulgaria through the Black Sea'.[8]

With the treacherous Soviet mole Kim Philby deeply burrowed in the heart of British Intelligence, and betraying his country so effectively, many of these missions were compromised from the start. Many brave men were needlessly sacrificed for minimal reward. These infiltrated émigré agents were different operatives from the 'illegals' and 'sleepers' who were placed in a country (according to John Sanderson), often from a young age, and proceeded to progress inside the target society, always remaining faithful to their 'base' country. Philby was in this category of a 'long-term' agent who had skillfully manoeuvred and positioned himself to obtain the maximum of secret intelligence and to inflict maximum damage to his country. Philby was the consummate 'cameleon': he blended in perfectly within his chosen intelligence environment. His lack of personal scruples about his daily acts of treason were matched by his idealistic devotion, almost on a par with a religious zeal, to a Communist system that was evidently oppressing millions. The Russians were quite prepared to patiently wait for Philby's career to flourish: the eventual rewards and operational advantages for their intelligence services were incalculable.

Evan G. Galbraith (later a director of Morgan Stanley and the US Ambassador to France from 1981–5) was involved in this secret war, as a naval officer posted to the CIA and assigned to the security of operations in Bulgaria and Albania. Galbraith described his experiences in an article entitled 'Hot Spots in the Cold War'. (John Sanderson discussed only one operation with the author. It was all too secret. He did, however, retain four copies of Galbraith's article, with the Bulgarian incursions highlighted, as a record of SIS operations into Bulgaria with which he was undoubtedly involved during his posting to Turkey from 1951–2 and, afterwards, to Sudan, Egypt, Cyprus and Bulgaria in 1960. As a trained parachute officer, his experience was extremely useful.) Galbraith was involved in the post-mortem on the unsuccessful Operation GRAPE to introduce eighteen Albanians agents into their homeland. The CIA had shared their planning with M16. Philby's treachery gave advance warning, through the Russians, to the Albanian authorities with the result that the Sigurimi captured, interrogated, tortured and executed the unfortunate, captured agents. The Americans and British had broken off diplomatic relations with Albania in 1946. Galbraith explained:

> There was also blood from other operations on Philby's hands... GRAPE was one of hundreds of cross-border operations, by land, air and sea, launched by the CIA into Eastern Europe in the 1950's . . . . It was an heroic, high-risk effort. After the Communist attack against Korea in June 1950, much of Western Europe was demoralised and convinced that the Soviets would attack . . . the reports of bloody oppression by the Bulgarian and Albanian governments created a desire to fight back. Yugoslavia, a crucial element in the defence of Western Europe, after Tito broke with Stalin in 1948, was faced on four sides by hostile Communist forces which mobilised 35 divisions with significant firepower 1950–51. Pre-emptive destabilising action against Bulgaria, Albania, Rumania and Hungary in the defence of Yugoslavia was unanimously accepted within the Truman Administration.
>
> The first cross-border operation into Bulgaria took place in 1948 and others followed during the next two years, with military information [OB] as the principal objective. Typically, teams of three to six armed agents crossed a remote area of the frontier and returned, if successful, after about ten days. In one case, three agents from one team were killed in a firefight with the DS and the surviving agent had to spend two months living in a shallow cave.
>
> The idea was to have a strong resistance force in place in the event of a Soviet attack on West Germany. The cross-border operations in Bulgaria continued until 1958. They numbered perhaps 150–200.

John Sanderson, who was involved in this clandestine war into the Soviet bloc as a member of MI6 and who was by nature and necessity discreet, did mention one particular operation which he had been running, probably organised from the Edirne Station in Turkey, into both Bulgaria and Hungary. *JBS*: 'One of the operations in which I was involved, was sending veteran Polish pilots into Hungary in bombers to drop propaganda leaflets.

These reckless Poles took great delight in antagonising the Communist authorities: one flew his plane under a central bridge in Budapest, not an easy feat by any means.'

Galbraith continues:

> CIA incursions into Romania and Bulgaria drove the Communists crazy. Our planes flew in low under the radar in Second World War B-25 and B-26 bombers. The pilots were usually Polish RAF . . . In one case, a Polish pilot flew his B-26 down the main street in Bucharest under the trolley wires. The Communists were seriously stung by these invasions and by the furious firefights, the ambushes, and the acts of revenge. Also we had leaflet drops from planes and balloons. Sometimes these leaflet missions were a diversion for an agent air drop elsewhere: sometimes they were straightforward propaganda. It is estimated that 21 million leaflets were sent into Bulgaria between 1950 and 1960. . . .
>
> The men who went in, hundreds of them, are genuine heroes of the Cold War, men who knowingly faced death under gruesome conditions to liberate their countries.[9]

In Evan Galbraith's view, the sacrifices were necessary.

Whilst John Sanderson was based in Turkey, his colleagues in the WO would have been examining images from secret overflights over Russia, permission for which had been recently cleared by Churchill after a previous ban. The Cold War was in a dangerous phase. A JIC paper of 1947 had outlined the expected threat over the next decade:

> The Soviet armed forces, despite certain deficiencies, could embark on a land war at any time, and would, at least in the early stages, have the advantage of numbers against any likely combination of opposing forces . . . It seems likely . . . that, while doing all she can to develop the atomic bomb, she will at the same time devote special attention to the rapid development of biological weapons.[10]

The US Military Intelligence in Germany in 1945 had urgently sought out Luftwaffe documents with information on flight paths which designated routes for the bombing of Soviet military and industrial targets. Truman had given the green-light in 1947 for USAF and Navy reconnaissance flights over Soviet territory, most leaving from Alaska and Germany.

David Stafford explained that there were 50,000 American personnel on 40 American bases in the south of England. From here reconnaissance flights were planned in 1951 to identify Russian targets and radar defences. He described how in April 1952 three RB-45 'C' USAF Tornado bombers, with RAF markings, took off from Norfolk on the first of many highly secret high-altitude missions over the Soviet Union, staffed by US and British pilots and navigators. Fitted out with complex radar, the aircraft were refuelled mid-air by KB-29 aircraft on their way out. Over Soviet airspace, the reconnaissance flight split up, the first heading north over Leningrad, the second flying almost to Moscow, and the third heading south over Belorussia and the Ukraine. The Tornado crews photographed their objectives, whilst airborne aircraft and ground-based listening posts electronically recorded the triggered Russian radar signals and air defence responses. All three aircraft returned safely, making their rendezvous successfully with their refuelling aircraft on their return flights.[11]

From the mid-1950s the USA took over the responsibility for the defence of Turkey and Greece from the British, who could not afford the high costs involved.[12] Resistance to the Soviet post-war occupation of Ukraine was very strong. Ukrainian partisans' resistance operations, 1945–53, and M16's support for them was outlined by Askold Krushelyncky:

> The UPA (Ukranian partisan group) fought the Nazis occupying Ukraine and later attacked the Russian Communist forces whom they also saw as invaders. The UPA numbered about 100,000 men and women mostly operating in the hills and forests of Western Ukraine, in the Carpathian Mountain area. MI6 acted as a go-between with the Ukranian nationalist émigrés in the West and with Western governments. MI6 gave some parachute training and unmarked RAF planes, taking off from bases in Cyprus and Malta, parachuted them into Ukraine. Sadly, the traitor Kim Philby, having detailed knowledge of the operation, alerted the Soviet security forces about the planned drops. Scores of guerillas were intercepted and executed. The UPA was broken as a fighting force by 1953. The Soviets carried out vicious reprisals against the civilian population. Thousands were murdered or sent to the Soviet Gulags.[13]

Stephen Dorril estimated that the war inside Ukraine killed 35,000 of the Polish and Russian secret police and troops in the 2 years after the war. However, after 1946 guerilla morale soon declined. Operation VISTULA took brutal measures to eradicate the UPA, together with mass deportations. MI6 continued to back émigré groups, with the Vatican lobbying support. Eventually many of the remaining guerillas broke out over the mountains to Austria and Germany, although many died on the 1,500-mile trek.[14] Phillip Knightley noted that the CIA carried out their own drops with a variety of émigré nationalities: Lithuanians, Estonians, White Russians, Ukrainians and Armenians whom they transported in two CIA planes, piloted by a Hungarian pilot crew and a Czech pilot crew but with USAF ground support. They crossed the borders, were tracked by Soviet radar and shot at but never shot down.[15]

Tony Northrop (1922–2000) was a former SOE wartime operative and MI6 officer. His obituary in *The Times* described how, during the Second World War:

> he spent a year in occupied Albania fighting alongside partisan guerrillas, and later drew on that experience for the first Cold War attempt by British Intelligence at rolling back Communism through covert force . . . he was recruited by MI6, his integrity and quiet modesty, as much as his wartime experience, making him an ideal candidate for that type of work . . . Between May 1950 and the end of 1952 he instructed Albanian émigrés in skills of sabotage and guerrilla warfare prior to their being sent back to Albania, where MI6 and the CIA hoped they would stir up trouble for Enver Hoxha's Communist regime.[16]

Next Wisner appointed to OPC a tough intelligence officer named Gratian Yatsevich, a former Military Attaché in Bulgaria from 1946–9, as the new commander of operation FIEND, with Kim Philby. At this stage of FIEND, OPC used Polish ex-RAF pilots, organised by Air Force Colonel Rudkowski, to parachute in Albanian émigrés in small groups. H/Turkey (the SIS Head of Station) in Istanbul after Philby, Rodney Dennys, thought this was a mistake as overhead aircraft drew attention to the operations.[17]

In January 1951 a sizeable battle lasting several days took place in north Albania when forty-three guerrillas landed by boat and parachute; twenty-nine guerrillas were killed and fourteen captured. In spite of these setbacks, the Albania operations continued in the summer of 1951 but still met with failures, as a result of an Albanian 'double-cross'. The Albanians, advised by the Russians, had forced a radio operator to send an all-clear signal to his MI6 base in Cyprus. When he requested that further agents be parachuted in to meet up with dissidents, they too were seized in a trap. John Dulles, the US Secretary of State from 1952, commented: 'At least we're getting the experience we need for the next war.' The Albanian leader Hoxha, who survived until 1985, boasted: 'The bands of criminals came like lambs to the slaughter.'[18]

John Dulles would remark on operations to rollback Communism in Berlin, Korea, the Middle East and Europe: 'We are not dancing to any Russian tune.'[19] But Wisner, now under the CIA, was less upbeat and was beginning to think there was a traitor in their organisations, and he thought Philby could be the source of the failures of so many MI6/CIA operations. In MI6 doubts were being expressed about the wisdom of 'rolling back' the Iron Curtain in peacetime. In May 1951, after Burgess and McLean had disappeared, William Harvey of the CIA produced a damning report that listed Philby's appointments and his network of contacts. This document was sent on by the Director of the CIA to 'C' in London with a demand that Philby be sacked. The assistant chief James Easton considered the US charges against Philby to be accurate but he found himself ostracised by Philby's supporters for his views. In January 1952, John Sanderson's colleague John Bruce Lockhart was sent as the official MI6 representative to Washington, to pour oil on the troubled waters.[20]

The infiltrations behind the Iron Curtain into Bulgaria had evidently struck a nerve within the KGB. C. Andrew and O. Gordievsky noted that over three decades later, in April 1985, the KGB Chairman Vladimir Kryuchkov declared that a series of explosions in Bulgaria in August and September 1984 were caused by sophisticated devices, evidence of the involvement of Western 'special services'. Kryuchkov was concerned that the use of Bulgarian émigrés to commit terrorist acts might indicate such acts were possible in other satellite countries.[21] The KGB leaders had long memories and the early clandestine operations had not been forgotten.

Chapter 18

Edirne Intelligence Centre, Turkey

The Cold War up to 1949 had been mainly confined to Europe. The outbreak of war in Korea from June 1950 lead to a very hot war between Cold War rivals that lasted three years. Experienced Second World War Soviet aces would battle US pilots in fighter jets above the Korean peninsula. J. Hughes-Wilson revealed that the Attlee government, in seeking to improve trade relations with Russia, had unwisely passed over the latest technology of Rolls-Royce engines to the Soviets. These engines was used to power the new fast MiG-15s (Soviet jet fighter plane) that attacked the slower USAF F-80s and F-84s over Korea. In October 1951 100 hundred MiGs attacked B-52 bombers, escorted by US F-86s fighters, which were heavily outnumbered. Daylight US raids were stopped after eight US bombers were shot down. Twenty-four Soviet Air Force Regiments were rotated over Korea to give the Russian pilots combat experience.[1]

In 1951 Winston Churchill was back in power after the Conservatives won a majority of twenty seats in the general election. Anthony Eden returned for his third time as Foreign Secretary.

On 13 October 1951 Captain John Sanderson was SOS ('Struck off Strength') of the WO on reliquishing GSO3 MI4 (General Staff Officer on German and Eastern European desk). After leaving his post at the York and Lancaster Depot on the 28th, he was posted to the Intelligence Corps Centre. His posting Special Instructions read:

> To report to M.I. Directorate, War Office for Briefing from 5–7th November.
>
> To relieve Major P. Greenhalgh.

On 1 December 1951 the Sanderson family took off for Turkey, where they moved into a house on the European side of the Bosphorus straits in Istanbul. The new year of 1952 would be significant for Turkey: on 18 February the country became a member of the NATO alliance.

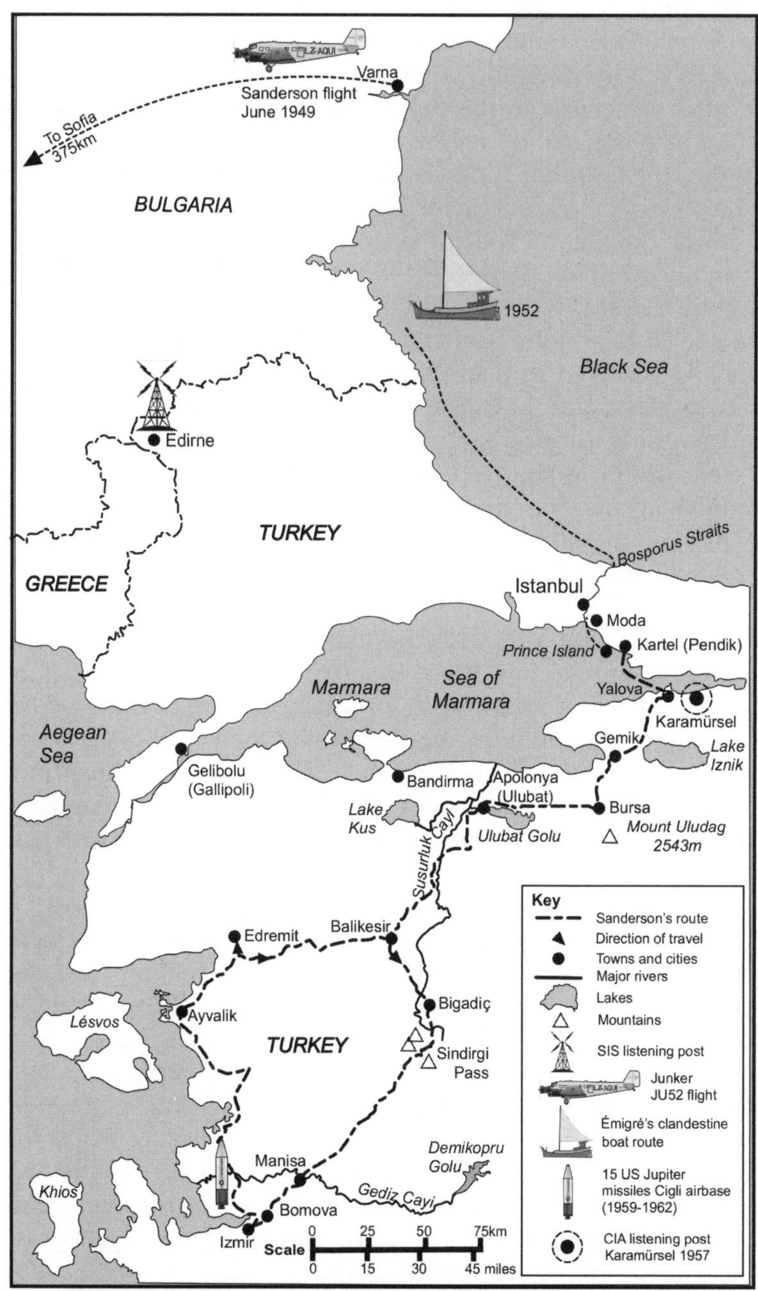

Map 9 **JOHN SANDERSON'S M.A. RECONNAISSANCE TRIP OF WESTERN TURKEY BY JEEP, APRIL 1952 AND SIS OPERATIONS 1952**

When Sanderson took up his new post as the Commandant of the Edirne Intelligence Centre, Sanderson's Paris colleague Major Peter Greenhalgh was the outgoing Commandant. The Edirne SIS station, which was located very close to the Bulgarian and Greek borders, housed an important listening station for eavesdropping on radio communications behind the Iron Curtain. Turkey was in the front line of the Cold War at this time, being the main base for MI6's intelligence work in the Balkans and Central Europe, as well as operations directed against the Soviet Union and its southern borders.

Istanbul had always been a city renowned for spying, at the junction of Asia and Europe. John Sanderson, with his fluency in Bulgarian, was occasionally involved in debriefing refugees crossing into Turkey from Bulgaria to glean any intelligence useful to MI6. At this time, refugees fleeing from Bulgaria afforded valuable intelligence and John's linguistic skills were useful in the respectful questioning of possible infiltrating Communist agents and those who might be willing to share useful information on the current political and military situation in Bulgaria.[2]

Stephen Dorril wrote of interrogations when Philby was in Turkey:

> Unfortunately for MI6, while the exile groups with spy networks in eastern Europe and the southern flank of the Soviet Union supplied the local station with information, most of it turned out to be fake . . . Kim Philby recalled 'it was their way of garnering finance to keep themselves and their dreams going.' MI6 officers had to spend much of their time 'devising means of smoking such operators into the open, so we could judge what price to put on their work'.[3]
>
> Many refugees from communist countries made their way to Turkey, where they were debriefed by the efficient Turkish secret service, whose head, Colonel Peredzh, had worked for the Royal Yugoslav Intelligence. He was also employed by MI6 on a monthly retainer to supplement his meagre salary. The refugees all had to provide detailed documentation, including photographs, to get a visa . . . the authorities were well informed as to where everyone was and quite often, what they were doing, 'unfortunately, whilst this should have been an excellent source of information on what was going on inside Soviet-controlled Eastern Europe, the intelligence passed on to MI6 was low quality owing to poor interrogations'.[4]

Between John Sanderson's posting to MI Directorate in October 1951 and his departure for Turkey on 2 December, the extraordinary news broke in

November that his SIS colleague Kim Philby had been sacked by 'C'. He was under suspicion after the sudden disappearances abroad of Maclean and Burgess in May that year. (It would not be until 1954 that a defector in Australia, Vladimir Petrov, would confirm that the diplomats had been long-term spies, recruited at university. In 1956 Maclean and Burgess held a joint press conference in Moscow.[5])

Kim Philby had been posted to Turkey as H/Turkey, station chief of SIS, from February 1947 and stayed two years, until he moved to Washington as British Liaison between MI6 and the CIA and FBI. His cover at the Istanbul Consulate-General was First Secretary. He had been told to concentrate on Russia, not the Balkans, which was still an SOE active area (the disbanded Long Range Desert group refused to get involved: they were sceptical about this counter revolution).[6] Phillip Knightley noted two reasons for his move there: 'Turkey was in the front line of the rapidly deepening Cold War and an ideal place from which to run operations into the Soviet Union's southern flank: and Philby . . . had little experience in the field'.[7] Philby:

> When I heard from Sinclair that I had been chosen to take charge of the SIS station in Turkey, with headquarters in Istanbul, I felt that things might have been very much worse. Istanbul was then the main southern base for intelligence work directed against the Soviet Union and the Socialist countries of the Balkans and Central Europe . . . In preparation for my overseas tour of duty, I was attached to the training section of one of the officers' courses. The training staff consisted in the main of officers drawn from SOE, and their tuition was conditioned by their experience of SOE in wartime.[8]

The historian Philip Davies noted the experience of Anthony Cavendish, an SIS operative, who described in his book *Inside Intelligence*, the course run, since spring 1946, by experienced SIS and SOE agent runners, called back to the Training Section, to initiate new recruits in 'handling human sources':

> I was sent on an intelligence course . . . (General Trade Field Craft), which lasted eight weeks. It was held in an old building in Palace Street . . . Our course director . . . explained that we were divided into syndicates and that in . . . exercises, the syndicates would be pitted against each other . . . Some of our exercises involved shadowing or being shadowed through the streets of

> the West End . . . There were also exercises in making contact with an 'agent' at a given rendezvous and at a given time, with necessary signals and passwords . . . We had long lectures on famous examples of agent handling and innumerable discussion sessions, in which problems were raised and we were invited to solve them.[9]

JBS had undertaken the same field craft course: 'I was sent on an SIS course in London. By entering an old style red British telephone box, and simply removing the overhead light bulb, and then fitting in a plug with a wire, I was astounded to be able to clearly hear telephone conversations in the adjacent building.'

According to Peter Wright, there was a Post Office Special Investigations Unit near St Paul's where a Major Denman handled mail interceptions and the installation of telephone taps on the authority of PO warrants. 'Denham . . . was terrified in case the PO role in telephone . . . intercepts was discovered . . . The Home Office was always highly sensitive on the issue of interceptions, and they were always strictly controlled.'[10] In Russia people would soon be using the street phone boxes to make private calls: their homes could in all likelihood be 'bugged'.[11]

Harold 'Kim' Philby and John Sanderson had in common their childhood upbringing in India (Philby was born in the Punjab). St John Philby, Harold's Eurasian father, had started his career in the colonial service in India. G. Corera noted that: 'when his young son Harold talks to the locals in India, the father said of him, "He's a real little Kim", after the Rudyard Kipling spy-boy who could blend in with the locals'. The nickname stuck with Philby thereafter.[12] Murray Sayle, the Australian journalist, 'formed his own assessment of Philby and found him a charming, entertaining man with a great sense of humour'. Sayle astutely noted: 'Espionage is a strange kind of adventure, of being semi-criminal but with official backing. It's a mixture of the courageous and the deceitful, or whatever the exact mixture comes down to – you have to be a spy to sense it.'[13] In these three qualities, on reflection, Philby had much in common with Captain Sanderson who followed him to Turkey as a head of Edirne LP. Both men had strong views and an affable exterior that concealed a very tough and determined interior. In their loyalties, however, they were the opposing faces of the coin, one being an individual with a misplaced loyalty to an outdated political ideal and the other a confirmed patriot, dedicated to the security and safety of his King and Country above all else, and with a balanced home life and strong roots.

Philby admitted, when reacting to the charge that he was a traitor, 'I never belonged. To betray, you must first belong.'[14] Another apposite description of Philby was given by Captain Henry Kirby MP who had worked in SIS in the 1920s: 'I had got to know Philby towards the end of the war. He was a weird mixed-up character, nervous and jumpy, and could really knock it back. He gave the impression he was going places and knew it. Personally, I thought he was a shit.'[15] Philby had written:

> Each country was now given a symbol consisting of three letters of the alphabet. Turkey was BFX-land. Thus as head of the SIS station in Turkey I found myself . . . BFX/51 . . . I found a delightful villa on the Asiatic shore of the Bosphorus, a place of such loveliness that I agreed without demur to pay an exorbitant rent. It was next door to the landing stage, and for three years I was to commute daily between Asia and Europe . . . The old Turkey hands were aghast. I had no cause to regret the choice of my remote Asian hide-out. Indeed, my example was soon followed by some of the more imaginative spirits.[16]

Phillip Knightley wrote that 'Philby found a charming villa in Beylerbeyi . . . whose garden and orchard ran nearly down to the water', and from where he could see from 'the minarets of Hagia Sophia in the distance to an ancient fortress on a bend of the Bosphorus'. His villa gave him rights to fish lobsters out of the straits. Knightley noted that Philby's wife 'Aileen and the four children joined him . . . The children found life in Turkey one long holiday.' They played in the garden and swam in the Bosphorus.[17]

Sanderson's daughter recollected her own similar experiences of living on the Bosphorus when her father was working there with SIS:

> As a child I was lucky enough to travel with my family to many exotic destinations and I can look back and see how they enriched my life and brought so many happy memories. That time has passed and these places will never be the same again. When I was four years old, we lived on the first floor of an apartment in a small building on the Asian side of the Bosphorus in Turkey. We had a large balcony overlooking the sea and there was a lawn leading right up to the waters' edge with wooden steps directly into the sea. My mother used to take my younger brother and myself under each arm and wade waist deep with us through the sea to visit our neighbour, who was an Egyptian princess and

> had a higher house next to ours with a lot more wooden steps to reach! I found this very exciting. Once we reached our destination I would play happily in a sandpit while my mother chatted.
>
> On another occasion I remember my parents returning home in the early hours with a haul of lobsters obtained from the harbour and the Turkish fishing boats that had been out at night in the strait and cooking the poor things in a large pan in our kitchen! I remember my father swimming across the Bosphorus from Europe to Asia and my mother being there to greet him with a cooked breakfast. There was the trip in our jeep to some beautiful mountainous countryside, where the people had never seen westerners before. I slept alone in a little tent only to awake one morning to find fascinated strangers peering in at me while I was sleeping. I was only four years old and was not at all afraid. They were just very friendly farmers unspoilt by politics. To this day I will never forget the delicious smell of cooking over an open wood fire and the lush greenery and pine trees surrounding us.

Philby had worked closely with Arthur Whittal, whom John and Audrey Sanderson were soon to befriend. He was part of an old established English family living in Turkey and an SIS representative, not part of the diplomatic corps but working for the FO:

> There was the Passport Control Officer who was . . . responsible to me for his intelligence duties. So far as I was concerned, he acted as liaison officer with the Turkish services. He was an old Turkey hand, bearing the honoured name of Whittal: he spoke fluent Turkish: but he was far too nice to liaise with the Turks. The Turkish services were known as the Security Inspectorate, and our relations with them conditioned almost all our intelligence activity in Turkey.[18]

One idea that Philby had taken up whilst in Istanbul, was to infiltrate behind the Iron Curtain by sea. Philby had returned to London in 1949 where he met Commander Anthony Courtney of Naval Intelligence, a Russian speaker and former diplomat in Bucharest, who had the idea of using fast naval boats or submarines, working with MI6, to organise diversionary operations by sea, an idea that the Turkish Secret Service supported wholeheartedly. Attempts were made to recruit agents amongst the expatriate community in Paris but this was unsuccessful, producing only two likely recruits.

Stephen Dorril noted that infiltrations, suggested by Philby, began in 1949 after he left Istanbul and 'were based on Prince's Island, in the Sea of Mamara, from where agents were sent by boat across the Black Sea and landed in deserted spots in the vicinity of Sukhumi, Sochi or further north towards the Crimea. Caucasian anti-communists were recruited in Istanbul by the North Caucasian Emigration Society – another MI6 front organisation'. Once again these operations failed entirely, infiltrated by the Russians and no doubt betrayed, without a moment of remorse, by the traitor Kim Harold Philby.[19]

The Sanderson family formed a close friendship with the Whittals, who were related to the wartime SIS head of station Harold Gibson. Arthur Whittal was the Passport Control Officer, an SIS cover position which did not give diplomatic immunity and was the MI6 liaison officer with the Turkish secret service. Kenny Whittal, the son of Edwin who owned a large wooden house on the Bosphorus in Moda, often took the Sanderson family, including the author as a child, sailing on his large yacht *Bati* along the Bosphorus and into the Sea of Marmara. This was the yacht that was most probably used for infiltrations into Bulgaria or southern Russia. The friendship continued after the Sandersons had returned to London, with Whittall writing to ask after the children and enquire when they would all be able to meet up again. The Whittals' fluency in Turkish and their deep knowledge of the country was very helpful to Sanderson, and His Majesty's government.

Nigel West noted that Monty Woodhouse reopened the SIS Athens Station, later joining SIS's post-war War Planning Directorate, preparing stay-behind networks across Europe in preparation for a Soviet invasion. In 1951, as head of the Tehran SIS station, Woodhouse had briefed Anthony Eden on Operation BOOT, a plan to remove the Iranian Prime Minister Mussadeq from power and put Reza Shah Pahlavi on the Peacock throne (taken by Nader Shah from Delhi as a war trophy in 1739). Eden gave his approval and in August 1953 Woodhouse, based in Cyprus, would organise the successful coup that brought the Shah back from Rome. Iran would then be the location of an important Western listening station.[20]

Back in 1951, as part of a tour of the Middle East SIS stations including Egypt, Cyprus and Lebanon, undertaken before his arrival in Tehran, Woodhouse visited Turkey to, as he put it, 'acclimatise myself afresh'. Cyprus is situated only 50 miles off the coast of Turkey.

Monty Woodhouse described in *Something Ventured* how on 7 June 1951 he was in a club in Cairo when he heard tales of the drunken and boorish behaviour of one Donald Maclean, the late Head of Chancery.

Woodhouse noted that although Maclean had been repatriated with a 'nervous breakdown', following his undiplomatic antics in Egypt, the FO had surprisingly seen fit to appoint him head of the American Department. By coincidence, when Woodhouse was leaving the Cairo club, the ticker-tape board in the entrance reported that two members of the Foreign Service had disappeared. 'One of the names was familiar and notorious: I could believe anything of Guy Burgess', Woodhouse wrote, before realising that the second name, Maclean, rang a bell. It was that of the diplomat he had just been discussing. 'For the next few months I was to hear of little else. Both names came up again in Istanbul, where I was staying a month later with the Consulate-General.'[21]

Donald Maclean had held important posts in Washington: First Secretary and Acting Head of Chancery. Not only had he betrayed confidential discussions between Churchill and Truman to Stalin but he was in 1947 Joint Secretary of the Anglo-American Atomic Energy Committee. He would be trapped by two pieces of luck and much hard research. The first piece of luck was the retrieval on a Finnish battlefield of a charred Soviet code book, containing Russian words and corresponding numbers. Next, between 1943 and 1945, US codebreakers had been able to analyse the 'VENONA decrypts' from NKVD radio traffic, sent from the New York Soviet Consulate. When combined with a repeated set of code numbers sent in error, and plain text messages photographed at the Soviet Purchasing Commission in an FBI break-in, a way was found into part of an 'unbreakable' Soviet code, partially opened up through years of meticulous graft. A legendary cryptoanalyst Meredith Gardner and his team were able to decipher only a fraction of the KGB messages.[22]

However, the net was closing in on several Soviet agents including Maclean, codenamed HOMER, the Rosenbergs and another spy codenamed REST and later CHARLES. The latter was Klaus Fuchs, a British scientist working at Los Alamos on the Anglo-American atomic bomb project and later at Harwell. Fuchs confessed in England and was sentenced to fourteen years. Kim Philby (OBE in 1946) was watching the seven-year molehunt trail lead ever closer to incriminating Maclean and eventually himself, codenamed STANLEY, by association. It was only a matter of time.[23] Woodhouse describes Philby's Jeep (used by John Sanderson and his wife nine months later for their coastal reconnaissance):

> He drove me around in a jeep inherited from his predecessor, Kim Philby. Philby's name had not yet become famous, but the

> jeep was already a link in the Great Spy Mystery, for attached to the dashboard on the passenger's side was a short length of rope on a strong metal hook. It had been fitted there, I was told, when Burgess was visiting his friend Philby, so that he could hang on it when rounding corners, for he was seldom sober. It would be interesting to know what Philby and Burgess talked about in their days together in Istanbul. Perhaps they chuckled over the fate of the British agents whom they had betrayed to the Soviet Secret police. Later they were to meet again in Washington, where Philby gave the warning of impending discovery which enabled Burgess and Maclean to escape. By the time I grasped Burgess's length of rope on the jeep in Istanbul, he was already in Moscow.[24]

In *My Silent War*, Kim Philby described his time in Turkey from 1947: 'I put in for two jeeps, lightweight tents, miscellaneous camping equipment, compasses etc.'[25] In the summer of 1947 Philby undertook a reconnaissance of the eastern frontier of Turkey with Russia to look for a place to infiltrate agents:

> The topographical survey was of interest to SIS for different reasons. Our War Planning Directorate, thinking in terms of global war against the Soviet Union, was busy with projects for setting up centres of resistance in regions which the Red Army was expected to overrun and occupy: Turkey was one of the first countries to be considered in this respect.

Philby, in what he named Operation SPYGLASS, infiltrated Georgian volunteer émigré agents, sent from London, across the Georgian border: 'The two agents had been put across . . . so many minutes later, there had been a burst of fire, and one of the men had fallen – the other was last seen striding through a sparse wood away from the Turkish border. He was never heard of again.'[26]

C. Andrew noted that in 1953 the Lubyanka KGB HQ in Moscow had a display of equipment (arms and radio transmitters) captured from émigré CIA and SIS resistance groups in Ukraine, Poland, the Baltic States and other border regions.[27] Marmara Island is located off the coast of Bursa and is in exactly the area where John Sanderson carried out his reconnaissance by Jeep with his wife. One of the objectives of the trip would have been to look for locations for arms and stores dumps, needed for stay-behind agents if the Soviets should invade Turkey. The defector Vasili Mitrokhin would reveal in 1992 that the Soviets had similar plans: across the USA and Northern Europe the KGB had hidden radio and arms caches with mines, explosives and detonators to create havoc during an invasion.[28]

In April 1993 Radio France and Reuters reported that the KGB had lost $200,000 under a French highway. It appears the road was built over a cache of money left in Grenoble in the 1960s by Soviet agents for use in wartime. Radio France, quoting ex-KGB Colonel Igor Previn, reported that Moscow had arranged to hide money and radio sets in several Western European countries. Previn said KGB agents visited all the caches at the time of detente in the 1970s, but all they found at Grenoble was a new highway to Lyon.[29] There were other secret preparations to resist behind an advancing Soviet invasion in NATO countries – Norway, Begium, Italy and Holland – as well as the neutral countries of Austria, Switzerland and Sweden.[30] During 1950, the Russian MGB had begun a secret cartographic reconnaissance programme in Britain that would last for over three decades. In contingency planning for a Soviet invasion of Britain, Russian intelligence officers would travel extensively throughout the British Isles secretly measuring and mapping significant cities, towns, bridges and military buildings with precise accuracy, in greater detail than British Ordnance Survey maps. Alexander Kent and John Davies described the extraordinary post-Soviet era discovery in Latvia of thousands of Soviet maps of Britain. A 1982 map of Chatham Dockyard, where British nuclear submarines were constructed and serviced at the time, was drawn in surprising detail. Soviet ships secretly carried out soundings of British rivers to produce very accurate maps of the riverbed depths and contours of the Thames, the Mersey and the Forth. In the Soviet Union whole towns making armaments like rockets did not appear on any Russian maps.[31] SIS, for their part, were examining the lay of the land in case of a Soviet invasion of Turkey.

The following are extracts from the John Sanderson's reconnaissance trip around western Turkey in March 1952. His report would have been filed at the FO in a similar way to Philby's report three years previously. John and Audrey Sanderson wrote up a detailed account of this trip which was made by Jeep. John was armed with a pistol to meet any eventualities in the wild. This was the German Luger pistol that he had acquired in Germany in 1946 and carried with him to foreign postings and missions until his retirement from the TA in 1984. The tour started on the shores of the Sea of Marmara at Kartel from where the Sandersons took the ferry to Yalova. In 1957 the Americans would build a huge listening station at Karamursel nearby.

JBS:

1st Day: The day was bitterly cold as we set off in our open Jeep for our trip to southern Turkey. The jeep was loaded with jerrycans full of petrol, a tin trunk of food (padlocked to the floor), bed rolls, and a loaded Luger revolver in case of bears or brigands.[32]

2nd Day: We were up early and after a wash at the cottage pump, brewed up some tea and were soon on the road to Bursa. It was a glorious morning but still cold. As we sped through Yalova the villagers were obviously amused at the very old Jeep so heavily laden. The run from Yalova to Bursa takes about 2 hours and is through mountainous scenery. Deep valleys with rushing rivers, emerald fields of young corn with the Judas blossom making magenta splashes of colour. We only passed through one large town, Gimlik, and this was about the size of a Cornish fishing village. We stopped for a glass of cay [tea] and watched the men pulling in the nets; the sea was shimmering silver with thousands of live sardines. Their colourful boats were pulled up on the beach and were the same in design as old Viking boats: they were painted in bright blues, yellows and reds. The best view of Gimlik was from the hill as we left the town – the huddle of white buildings against the steep mountains and the Marmara's brilliant blue. Bursa is a holiday resort, lying at the foot of the Uludağ [*dağ* – mountain] still topped with snow: it is famed for its natural hot springs and boasts several original Turkish baths dating back 500 years.

3rd Day: Apolonya. We were on the road at first light heading west out of Bursa and were soon skirting the northern shores of Lake Apolonya (now seems to be called Ulubat Gölü [*göl* – lake]). The faint mist hanging over everything gave it an unreal appearance: a painting with the touch of Jean-Baptiste Corot. We decided to visit the village of Apolonya and turned off the main road along a cart track through marsh land for about 4 miles. The village is built on an island joined to the mainland by only a narrow wooden footbridge, so we abandoned the Jeep and walked across. We were met by a polite old gentleman in the traditional baggy trousers and scarlet striped sash. He shook our hands solemnly and led us off on a tour, through the narrow cobbled streets and miniature bazaar under balconies of old wooden cottages which seemed Gothic in design, into a tiny mosque with its quiet carpeted floors and cool whitewashed walls –

on into the little school, where the master conducted us into the classroom where the children – girls and boys alike – were all clad like Dickensian characters in black tunics and enormous stiff white collars. After the school, he led us to the shores of the lake where traces of ancient Greek remains could still be seen, tumbling down with huge stones into the sea. Here the sun broke through. The old man and I smoked a pipe – no one spoke – it was like something out of a forgotten world. The colours of the mountains on the southern banks of the lake contrasted brightly in the sunshine. The many islands were even now inhabited by strange religious sects. The water gently lapped – a heron skimming across broke the silence – we were sad to leave Apolonya – the peace was indescribable. But, once again, we set off across the dusty plains between olive groves and fields – every inch cultivated with peasant men and women, forever toiling – and so to Balikesir for the night, a small attractive agricultural town.

We find the Turkish peasant a far more serious character than his opposite number in Bulgaria. One rarely finds them singing and dancing in the evenings, as is the custom in the Balkans. On the other hand, they are most friendly people and out to do all they can to help. If one halts by the roadside for the most obvious pretext, every single passing vehicle will draw up and enquire whether all is well. On other occasions, when we decided to set up camp, the locals appeared from nowhere and sat around fascinated by the proceedings until, in the end, we began to feel rather annoyed by their curiosity and endeavoured to find places many miles from any sign of habitation. The same thing would happen in the small restaurants – one was never at a loss for advice on what to eat and they would always stop to make sure that you enjoyed your meal. Moreover, the word would get round the village that two strangers accompanied by an unusual looking dog, were eating in the cafe and long before our meal was over, dozens of inquisitive little children would throng round the Jeep waiting to see us emerge and speed on our way. They must wonder what goes on in those strange lands across the seas.

4th Day: We set off from Balikesir early with the object of reaching İzmir, 130 miles away, in time for tea. 25 miles out of Balikesir we passed through the first village of any size named Bigadiç, which had to be approached over an intervening range of hills. More hills lay to the south until the road crosses the Sındırgı Pass, the most lovely piece of scenery of the whole trip. The top of the pass is over 2,000ft high and marks the watershed between the systems of rivers flowing into the Sea of Marmara and those entering the Aegean. Hitherto, we had been in the Marmara catchment area and travelling up the Sinav Cay (*çay* is the Turkish for 'river') basin, but once over the Sındırgı Pass, the streams flow into the Gediz Cay, which periodically brings floods to the Manisa and Menemen plains, and reaches the sea just north of İzmir.

The road winds up the pass through pines and beech trees: there is a wonderful view of the valleys below. The green grass and multitude of wild flowers brought back memories of similar scenes in Switzerland and only the loose gravel Turkish road, with the consequent cloud of dust which follows every vehicle, reminded us that we were in Turkey. But the lure of hot weather to the south led us on down the other side of the pass and into the plains again. This plain stretches for 40 miles: it gives one a view of the great wall of the Manisa Mountains rearing up behind the town. This wall of mountains makes a most impressive sight as one approaches Manisa: it rises with great steepness 5,000ft above the plain.

Beyond Manisa is a vast chasm or cleft which is readily accessible from the road. The view of the plains is very impressive. On the west of the chasm are rugged slopes, culminating 1,000ft above the road in a carved and hollowed-out platform of rock called 'Pelops' Throne'.

5th Day: Easter Sunday. İzmir is one of the oldest cities in the world. It derives its name from the Amazon 'Smyrna' and this, in fact, was the name of the city before the era of Ataturk reforms. But İzmir today gives one the impression of being an extremely well designed and modern city. It has the advantage of a very lovely setting in the most perfect climate. It lies at the head of a gulf and the Aegean reaches right up to the Ataturk Boulevard, which runs the whole length of the new city. On one side of the road are all the hotels, consulates, private houses and business premises and on the other the sea, with countless berths for the largest ocean-going vessels. A breakwater over half a mile long protects a section of the shore.

In the morning we drove out to Bornova, a residential area about 8 miles out of the city, where most of the British inhabitants live and there we called on the Consul General. We returned to Bursa by the coast route from Pergama to visit the town of Ayvalık, which we had been told was one of the most attractive on this

> coast. It lies on the shore of a large, circular bay enclosed by low hills covered in pines. A very narrow entrance to the bay gives it the impression of being a large lake and the many islands which cover the entrance afford protection from sea gales and tides. The harbour is constructed from local stone blocks and forms a most attractive picture with the innumerable fishing boats and 'kayiks' painted in soft shades of blue, yellow and green. The sun was warm and the sea very blue; we could not help a feeling of envy as we watched the fishermen going about their work in such a peaceful and lovely spot. We motored along the front to the cool of the pines and sat amongst hundreds of wild rose bushes freshly in bloom and wished that the water had been hot enough for a bathe.
>
> The camp on the 9th day was by a river at the foot of a pass though the mountains half way between Fdremit and Balikesir. The dachsund Santa slept at the door of the tent to warn of any approaching strangers. He was fascinated with a large grasshopper which jumped away every time his nose came close to it. Finally, in desperation, he swallowed it whole and spent the entire night trying to cough it up – and succeeded!

JBS described Istanbul traffic:

> The constant blare of horns from the innumerable large American cars, mostly taxis, which roar around the town is appalling. They were banned in Turkey this year. The Turkish taxi driver lacks the good common sense of his counterpart in London. Consequently, he drives like a child with a new toy, the most fascinating feature being the klaxon which is scarcely quiet for more than a few seconds. The result is most shattering to the nerves and highly dangerous because the drivers rely on their horns to clear the busy, and badly constructed, roads of all opposition.

On 22 July 1952, catching SIS by surprise, General Mohammed Neguib with 3,000 soldiers and 200 young officers seized power in Cairo. Gamal Nasser had inspired the revolution and was the real driving force behind the revolution as leader of a small group of anti-British officers. King Farouk left on the royal yacht for Italy, carrying aboard gold from the country's reserves.[33] In the same month Archbishop Makarios, leader of the Greek Orthodox Church in Cyprus, met Colonel George Grivas in secret in Athens. During the war Grivas had organised the Greek right-wing resistance movement 'X' to fight for Cyprus to achieve enosis, a political union with Greece.[34]

A month before John Sanderson relinquished his post at Edirne, in November 1952 the 'trial' and interrogation of Philby was held at MI5 HQ in Curzon Street, Mayfair.[35] It had been seven years since Philby had foiled the defection of the KGB officer Konstantin Volkov in Istanbul, the latter having revealed to the SIS station there that there was an NVKD source 'fulfilling the duties of a Head of Department in British Counter Intelligence'. By luck, Philby had contrived to arrange for himself to fly down to handle the situation. By the time he arrived, after a delayed journey, his tip-off to Moscow had led to the unfortunate Volkov being forcibly repatriated. It had been a close shave for Philby.[36] In January 1955 a certain Colonel Oleg Vladimirovich Penkovsky was posted to Turkey as an AMA and acting head of the local GRU network. Penkovsky would later prove to be a top-level agent for Western Intelligence and to have a crucial role in the Cuban Missile crisis seven years later. He would describe himself in his signed oath of allegiance to MI6 as a 'soldier of the free world fighting against Soviet tyranny'.[37]

Chapter 19

Cyprus–Egypt Intelligence SIS Course, 1953

When Stalin died from arteriosclerosis on 5 March 1953, there was a public expression of grief, although with reservations. The writer Constantin noted: 'We have lost a great man. But,' he later added, 'it might have been better to have lost him earlier.' In the gulags there were 'zeks' (Russian slang for a forced labour prisoner) whose hearts lifted at welcome news of the tyrant's demise.[1] Joseph Stalin had been leader of the Soviet Union for 10,636 days, from 1924–53. Khrushchev would be Party Secretary for 3,536 days from 1955–64.[2]

Geert Mak wrote that since 1951 Stalin had become more withdrawn and isolated. Khrushchev had heard him say: 'I am finished. I don't trust anyone anymore, not even myself.'[3] An influential Polish Communist Wladek Matwin recalled meeting Stalin: 'He spoke Russian with a horrible Georgian accent. But I'll never forget his eyes; not brown, not blue, not dark, not light; the eyes of a tiger . . . Stalin was a villain, a major criminal . . . The entire pre-war leadership of our party turned out to have been murdered by the Soviets.'[4] Everyone had feared Stalin. Those surviving politicians around him who had managed to save their necks were stunned but happy that he had died. Lavrenti Beria confidently saw himself as Stalin's successor. Too soon, for his enemies soon moved against him. Khrushchev, Malenkov and Molotov, when they had breached the subject carefully, realised they all wished for Beria's disappearance. They had to move carefully. Beria had all their homes bugged and controlled several hundred thousand security troops. Khrushchev's Presidium colleagues had underestimated Khrushchev's 'peasant cunning'. Lacking education, he made up for it in intelligence. He took the lead in arresting Beria. Professor Archie Brown described how Khrushchev accompanied Beria home the previous night, shaking his hand warmly to reassure him. Khrushchev recalled thinking: 'All right you bastard I'm shaking your

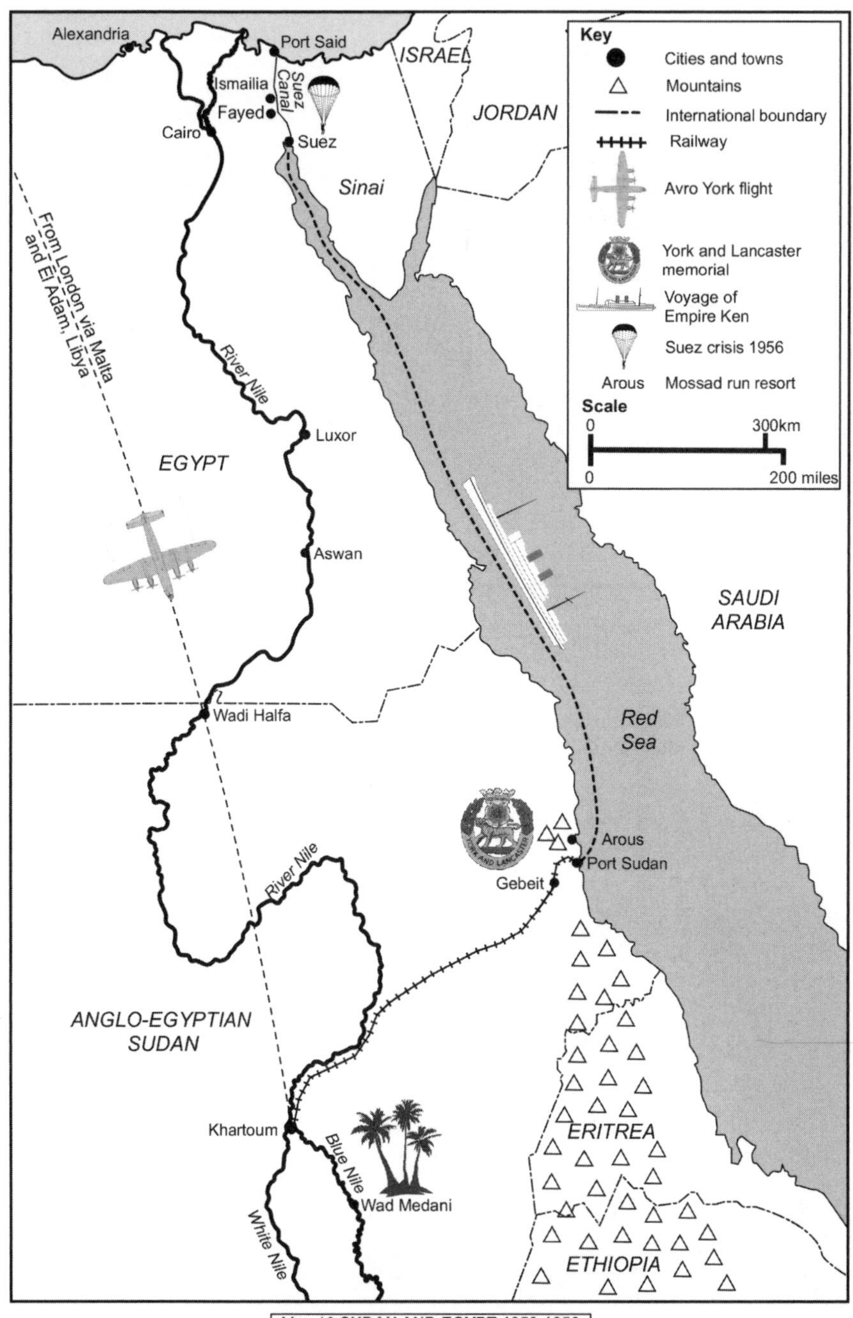

Map 10 **SUDAN AND EGYPT 1953-1956**

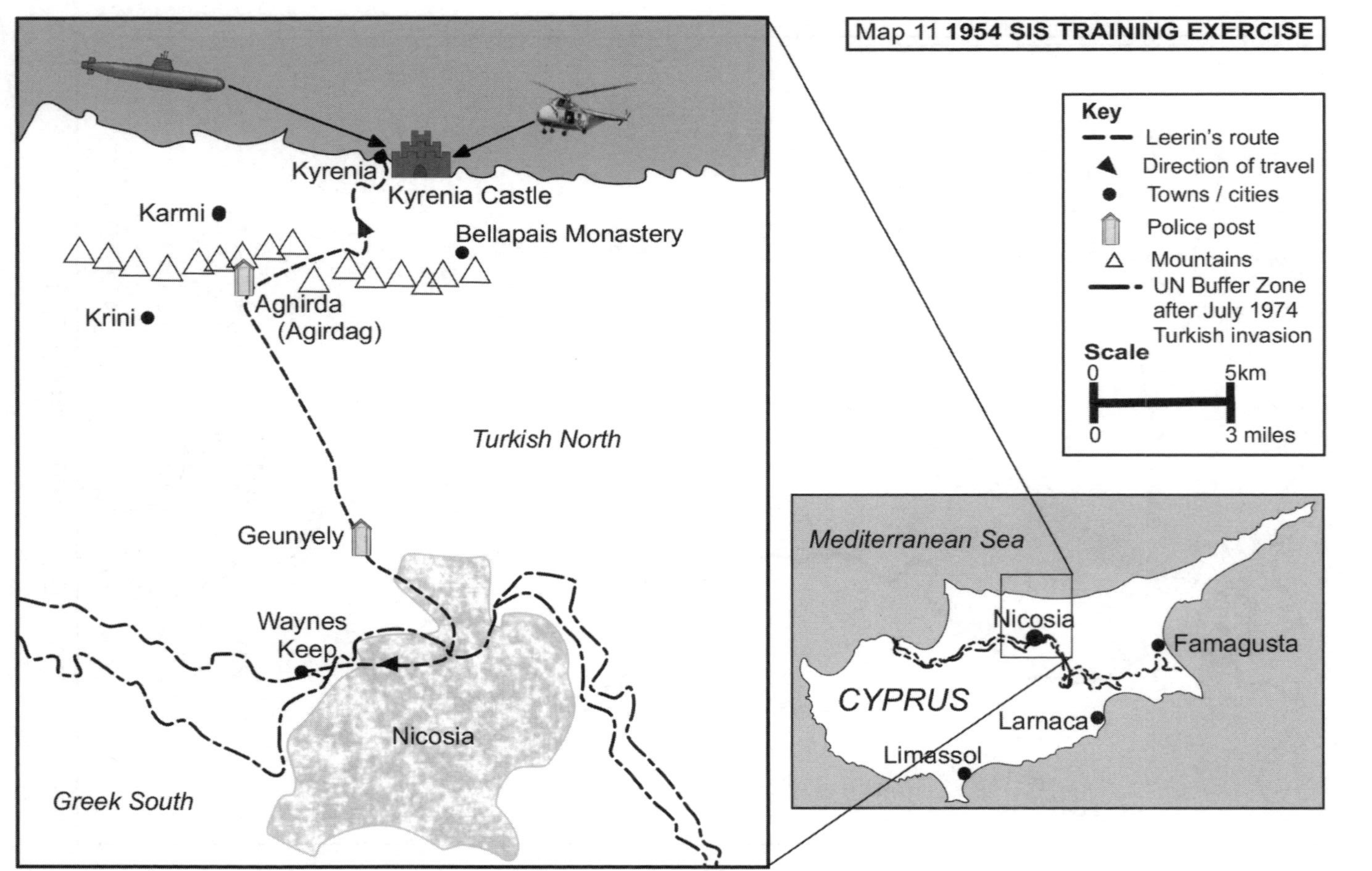
Map 11 1954 SIS TRAINING EXERCISE
Kyrenia
Kyrenia Castle
Karmi
Bellapais Monastery
Krini
Aghirda
(Agirdag)
Turkish North
Geunyely
Waynes
Keep
Nicosia
Greek South
Key
Leerin's route
Direction of travel
Towns / cities
Police post
Mountains
UN Buffer Zone
after July 1974
Turkish invasion
Scale
0
5km
0
3 miles
Mediterranean Sea
Nicosia
Famagusta
CYPRUS
Larnaca
Limassol

hand for the last time . . . tomorrow, just in case, I will have a gun in my pocket'.

They took Beria by surprise by using the army at a Presidium meeting. Beria's Kremlin Guard Commander had been sent out of Moscow on a pretext. Malenkov pressed a button and Zhukhov rushed in shouting at Beria that he was under arrest. Beria was accused of criminal anti-state activities and even the heinous invented crime of being a British spy and imprisoned. From his cell, Beria wrote pleading letters to his old colleagues asking for 'the smallest job'. In vain. He was handcuffed, and hung from a wall hook, before receiving the usual bullet in the forehead. The man whom Stalin once called 'my Himmler' had been tried by a secret court and executed on the same day. His family was also arrested. Beria had once been a powerful individual who had organised the vast project of building the Soviet 'A' bomb. An army of slaves had been mobilised and billions of roubles invested in associated technological, power and mining industries. Beria became a non-person after his death: collectors of the *Great Soviet Encyclopedia* were sent a special article on the Bering Sea to replace the entry on Beria, with instructions on how to cut it out with a razor blade or sharp knife. Beria the man had been removed and replaced with equal precision. When Khrushchev was himself replaced in a Presidium coup, aged 70 years, he too would became a non-person, his demise noted in small print in the newspaper as 'the death of a pensioner'. Such was Soviet life.[5]

As a reward for Zhukhov's help in arresting Beria, Khrushchev made him Minister of Defence two years later and a member of the Presidium in 1956. He was perceived as becoming too arrogant, however, and in 1957 accused of planning to seize power with a secret commando unit. General Zhukhov committed the cardinal error of remarking that the KGB was the eyes and ears of the army, which drew a furious response from Khrushchev that the KGB served the party. The Politburo ousted Zhukhov in October 1957, after he was summoned for the usual condemnations.[6]

On 9 March 1953 Major Sanderson left the Seaforth Barracks of Liverpool with the 1st Btn York and Lancaster Regt and embarked on a two-week voyage aboard HMT *Somersetshire* (Her Majesty's Transport), via Port Said, for the Red Sea and Port Sudan. *JBS* wrote home from Khartoum to his wife:

> Dear A, Don't get too upset about what's going on in Egypt as far as your passage is concerned – it makes not a scrap of difference to your coming out here and I don't think that it is only you that is delayed. More likely most of the RAF planes are being used

> to shuttle people in for the Coronation from all over the world and they cannot be spared for the Khartoum run. There are plenty of planes coming into Fayed, but not into here, and they don't generally fly families via Fayed. You will be put on a plane coming here direct. John

From Khartoum the regiment was posted to Gebeit, in the hills above Port Sudan, for military training and exercises. In April *JBS* wrote to his wife explaining how his regiment kept their recruits:

> I have got to write to every wife or mother of every man of 'C' Company who came out with me – over 60 letters. It's quite a good idea and the parents do appreciate it and write back. Then, in six months time, I write again and say what a good boy Johny has been and suggest that it would be a very good idea if he signed on for a regular engagement. You would be surprised how often it works!

In May *JBS* wrote again:

> It is not too hot in Gebeit, and a pleasant breeze is blowing throughout the day and, of course, the evenings are perfect. Every night the sky is a galaxy of stars and when there is a full moon, one can almost read by the light. I may be able to travel up to Khartoum to meet you. . . . You need have no fears whatsoever about travelling out here in the Sudan. The Sudanese are a very likeable race. They are thoroughly honest, law-abiding and helpful and, unlike Turkey, a European male or female can travel anywhere in the Sudan (even alone) and be quite safe and looked after.

In London the Sanderson family (the author was accompanied by his sister and mother) met up with Major John Sim MC (who had parachuted into Normandy on D-Day). He took them under his wing, with his own family, for their long and exhausting journey to Sudan. John's son Richard Sim, later a York and Lancaster officer himself, recollected in 2018:

> I was eight years old at the time. Our departure was delayed because military aircraft were being used to ferry Commonweath troops back to their countries after the Queen's Coronation. Our two families finally took off in an Avro York, the civilian version of the Lancaster bomber, from Stansted Airport to Malta, where

> we were not expected. The next day we flew on to El Adam, just south of Tobruk in Libya, where we refuelled and continued on to Khartoum. The weather was very turbulent, children were vomiting and the pilot took the aircraft up to 12,000 feet, 2,000 above normal and the highest he said he had ever taken an Avro York. We were in Khartoum for a year, our families living in the barracks north of the Nile river bridge, just below the railway line embankment, with the regiment in barracks across a girder bridge on the south side. Our houses had spacious rooms with large fans rotating continuously on the ceilings.

In 1953 the Anglo-Egyptian Agreement secured independence for Sudan, beginning the process of self-government. Elections would be held in 1954. Sanderson's daughter described her memories of life at this time:

> I was four years old. The Battalion was sent on detachment for some weeks to a remote camp at Gebeit, near the Red Sea coast. My mother, brother and I left with the soldiers by train on a long journey across the desert, through flat, barren scenery, passing the occasional nomads on camels on the way. The camp consisted of a few huts to house the troops and the officers' families, a cookhouse and a large water reserve tank, in which we used to swim to cool off. In Sudan the showers were run off water tanks on the roof, which were heated by the blazing sun: it was often 40 degrees Celsius in the shade. Nothing else for miles. We were the only white children for hundreds of miles. There were some goat herders living in wooden huts on the fertile mountain side and they let me befriend their goats. One day word came through that the regiment out on an exercise in the mountains required water urgently, so my mother and I accompanied a soldier driving a truck loaded with jerry cans of water. To keep the soldiers occupied, each regiment had laid out huge cap badge designs on the hillside, using different coloured rocks. They all stretched across the slopes of the mountains. They are there to this day. It was very impressive. Gebeit was the most enchanting place I have ever lived. I will never forget sitting on the veranda watching the most spectacular thunderstorms. We acquired a young tame deer that slept by our beds.

Not far north of Gebeit and Port Said on the Red Sea coast, was a place called Arous. Twenty years later, it was the location for a secret base for

Israeli agents, disguised as an idyllic holiday diving resort isolated on the edge of the Sudanese desert. At the time Sudan was seen as an 'enemy' Arab country by Israel. However, the secluded resort was leased from the Sudanese and run by Mossad as a cover for a secret humanitarian missions to rescue 'Beta Israel' Ethiopian Jews, trapped in Sudanese camps. The refugees were collected and driven on an 800km journey to Arous, where Israeli navy special forces took them off the beach in Zodiac dinghies and transported them for 90 minutes to a waiting Israeli naval vessel for evacuation to Israel. When the Sudanese customs almost stumbled on the operation in 1982, the Israelis switched to driving refugees to secluded Sudanese desert areas, from where C130 Hercules planes airlifted them out. An abandoned British Second World War airstrip near the coast was later used in pitch darkness for clandestine rendezvouses. One refugee recollected: 'I'd never seen an aeroplane in my life. I felt like Jonah the whale going into the belly of the whale and three hours later I was in Zion.'[7]

While in Sudan John Sanderson was also responsible for helping a young Eritrean man to find a new life abroad. Mario was employed to help around the house, and the Sanderson family were all very fond of him. When the family moved to Egypt, he was told he would have always have a job with them. He took them at their word for no sooner were they settled in their new home, than he came trudging up the dusty road with his battered suitcase. Mario had hitched a lift on a lorry from Khartoum and resumed his family life with them. When the time came to leave Egypt, Sanderson found a job for him with an English officer on Cyprus and paid for him to go there. Some weeks later Mario contacted him to say that he was very unhappy in the officer's home. Once again Sanderson arranged a new job for him – this time with an American commander. This second position obviously worked out well: several years later Sanderson was surprised to receive a letter from Mario with an American stamp. Inside was a photo of Mario with a wife and child. It said that he was very happy running his own restaurant in New York and that he had now owned a Cadillac. The invitation was there to come and eat in his restaurant whenever he wished – but Sanderson never did make it.

In the autumn of 1953 Major Sanderson left for Cyprus, on SIS intelligence duties. Cyprus had been a Crown colony since 1925. Britain had rejected the Greek Cypriots' calls for enosis, a uniting of the island with Greece: the island was a vital strategic outpost with sovereign bases, and a valuable SIGINT listening station at GCHQ Agios Nikolaos. Britain saw trouble brewing between the Greek Cypriots and both the British authorities and the Turkish minority population, who wanted taksim, a partitioning of the island. SIS played a role in interdicting supplies of weapons to EOKA (National Union of Cypriot Combatants). In November Sanderson flew to Egypt for a war course. Below is part of the Middle East Staff exercise that Sanderson attended. This 'restricted' sheet, retained in Sanderson's archives, gives a unique insight into 1950s military thinking. Most probably no other copy survives. The third world war game scenario outlined in this 1953 exercise proposed a Soviet invasion of the Middle East, with the name 'Fantasian' being used as an alias for the Soviets. Exactly twenty years later, a similar exercise scenario called Able Archer 83, a supposed Soviet invasion of Europe which also involved Turkey and the Middle East, took the world to the brink of a nuclear Armageddon. A paranoid and scared Soviet leadership believed the 1983 exercise was a pretext for actual war, a first strike on the Soviet Union and were on the point of launching their own pe-emptive nuclear strike.

RESTRICTED
1953
Middle East preparatory Course
APPRECIATION EXERCISE 1 – EX 'HILARION'
maps: CYPRUS 1/50,000 Sheets 7 and 8

OPENING NARRATIVE
It is 1954. World War III has been running for some 6 months. Fantasian forces had some remarkable early successes in the MIDDLE EAST, and rapidly overran IRAN, IRAQ, PALESTINE, SYRIA, and Eastern Turkey. CYPRUS, which we had decided not to re-inforce, was captured by an AB attack. The Fantasians have now been held for nearly three months in TURKEY and in Southern PALESTINE, and for the moment their effort seems to be spent. Our build-up is proceeding apace.

NARRATIVE ONE
The Fantasians are holding CYPRUS with a weak div[ision], of which it is reported that one b[riga]de is at each of LIMASSOL, LARNACA, FAMAGUSTA and KYRENIA. The Greeks in CYPRUS, deceived by enemy propaganda, are passive or even acquiescent in their attitude towards the Fantasians: the Turks, on the other hand, are strongly pro-BRITISH, and are running a promising resistance war on the western end of the island.

On Fri 13 Nov, you are back on leave from PALESTINE, and are enjoying some high life in the great Allied base at FAYID, when you are unexpectedly sent for by the C-in-C. He tells you that you have been selected to lead a raid in CYPRUS to capture an enemy VIP, one LEERIN, the head of the Secret Police, who is visiting there. It is a matter of great importance, as experience has shown that captured enemy high-ups are often quite prepared to 'talk', and LEERIN, who is one of the Big Five in FANTASIA, clearly knows much of their plans. Although the enemy has air superiority over the CYPRUS area, his radar screen is defective in some respects, and it is thought to be possible to fly in a helicopter at a very low level without being detected.

Much flattered you withdraw to receive an elaborate briefing, contact your henchmen whom you intend to take with you, collect a load of weapons and, on the advice of a sapper friend, two sackfuls of the new 'bootpolish tin' A pers[onnel] mines. The next night you all embark on a submarine. Twenty hours later the submarine surfaces and you take off in a helicopter and land in the woods on the WEST end of CYPRUS. Here you are met by a Turk called SAMMY HABZI, who is headman of KRINI 9281. SAMMY is head of the partisans in the KYRENIA-NICOSIA area and this is what he tells you.

'LEERIN is living in the strongly guarded KYRENIA CASTLE 0087. He appears to be interested mainly in a big wrs sta [wireless station] being built in KYRENIA. Twice a week (Thur and Fri) he drives into NICOSIA at about 1100 hrs to visit Gen[eral] N. the military governor, who lives in the great Brit fort at WAYNES KEEP (approx 9770). He usually returns home just before dark. Rumour has it that LEERIN is leaving the island in a week's time. On all these visits to NICOSIA, LEERIN is always escorted by two trucks full of soldiers, but he likes to drive himself, and does so extremely fast in a big CADILLAC, often arriving at his destination over a mile ahead of his escort. He apparently feels quite safe as NICOSIA and KYRENIA, besides being full of tps [troops], are predominantly Greek and friendly to the Fantasians.

There are a few Turkish villages about, however, notably
KRINI 9281 AGHIRDA 9582 KARMI 9484 GEUNYELY 9873

The rd [road]) KYRENIA–NICOSIA is also patrolled regularly with armed Cs, and there are police posts at GEUNYELY 9873 and AGHIRDA 9582.'

Armd [armed] with this info, and some good maps, you arrange with SAMMY to move to a lying up place in the KYRENIA range just NORTH of KRINI (9281) village on the night 16/17 Nov.

> During the morning of 17 Nov you see as much of the country as you can; in the afternoon you make your appreciation.

In the year of the imagined world war three Fantasian exercise, the Cold War entered an even more dangerous phase. On 1 March 1954, a new terrible weapon was added to the world's destructive arsenal. The author John Gaddis described the American testing of the world's first hydrogen bomb. The 15 megaton thermonuclear device exploded in a fireball that spread miles from the detonation site, sending a blastwave out over 200 miles to all points of the compass and leaving a crater a mile wide and 250ft deep. The radiation spread throughout the world, leading Khrushchev to remark that with the wind blowing the radioactive dust, nobody was safe. Gaddis describes an eyewitness account: 'The impact of it . . . transcended some kind of psychological barrier'.[8]

In March 1954 in Khartoum the first parliamentary elections took place, with the pro-Egyptian National Unionist Party winning a landslide victory. Nasser had taken over in Egypt the month before as Prime Minister. On 1 March, the President of Egypt, General Naguib (who was born in Khartoum), arrived on a state visit for the opening of the new national Sudanese Parliament.[9] The event was disrupted by violent protests by huge crowds of Ansar, demonstrating on behalf of the anti-Egyptian opposition Umma Party. The Ansar were Sufi followers of Muhammad Ahmad (1844–85), the self-proclaimed Mahdi. In January 1885, it was the Ansar, Mahdi's men, who had attacked and destroyed the British garrison of Khartoum, killing General Charles Gordon at the Governor-General's Palace. They had managed to find a weak point in the defences where the Nile was low.[10]

Audrey Sanderson, her children and the Sim children were in the Khartoum North Barracks whilst the violent unrest was taking place in the streets. Mrs Sim had left to deliver a car to Wad Medani and later returned by plane to be met at the airport by an armoured car for protection and escorted back to her children in the barracks. Ten policeman and the British Police Commandant Hugh McGuigan were killed that day in the riots. (McGuigan's sister was married to a regimental officer.) The York and Lancaster soldiers were called to arms in case the situation deteriorated.

The same month Nasser contacted the British Embassy in Cairo seeking a rapid agreement for the pull-out of British troops from Egypt. An embassy official noted: 'We are on the decline as a Great Power, they have a real hatred politically of us in their hearts. No amount of concession or evacuation on our part will evoke the slightest gratitude in return.'[11] Soon afterwards, the regiment left by rail for Port Sudan. The carriages had no air conditioning, so the army used their ingenuity. Before departure, they filled hay boxes with large blocks of ice. The windows and doors of the compartments were opened to create draughts and the blocks of ice, wrapped in towels, were hung in the windows to provide refrigerated air. From Port Sudan on the Red Sea, they embarked for Egypt on the ship HMT *Empire Ken*, a U-boat depot ship during the Second World War before becoming a German hospital ship in 1945, and then finally a British troopship. In Fayed the families lived on the military base in married quarters near the Officers' Club, on the west bank of the Dead Sea. The children travelled daily to the Fayed Junior School, a 5-mile journey in a converted 3-ton army truck fitted out with a metal wire cover and guarded by a British soldier with a loaded rifle. During one family trip to Ismailia Mrs Sanderson was arrested by the Military Police for driving into a 'No go area' but was let off with a caution.

During 1954, with Major Sanderson back on intelligence duties in Cyprus, the Sanderson family moved for two months to Kyrenia, on the Turkish north coast of the island, where they hired a whitewashed house on the harbour waterfront. They were joined on holiday by the Sim family for a visit to the thirteenth-century Bellapais Abbey. Soon afterwards, the Anglo-Egyptian Treaty of 27 July 1954 ended seventy years of British occupation of the Canal Zone. The British would agree to withdraw British troops in stages until a final pull-out in June 1956. The families embarked with the regiment from Port Said, on the troopship HMT *Lancashire*, heading back to England and to their fathers' next posting in Dover. The British retained the large military base at Ismailia, in case of future hostilities. The 1st Btn the York and Lancaster Regt, however, would return to Suez in 1956 during the Suez invasion. The Sudanese government would welcome Osama Bin Laden in 1990.

In Cyprus in early 1955, the Greek-Cypriot EOKA organisation began an armed insurrection against the British, led by Colonel Georgios Grivas, a Greek Army officer. In a typical terrorist operation in October, a young Greek-Cypriot gunman called Andreas Antoniades lay in wait in a Turkish pine tree in the Troodos mountains. His target was Stanley Holloway, believed by the EOKA rebels to be an undercover British 'Chief of Intelligence'. When Holloway drove his Land Rover up to his house and stepped out to admire the view, Antoniades lined up the sights of his rifle and shot him. In spite of this crime, this hitman, nicknamed Keravnos, or 'Thunderbolt', was later interrogated and turned by British Intelligence. He went on to become an important spy, informing for decades.[12]

Nigel West wrote that the go-ahead was given 'for the elimination of Grivas . . . a potential solution to the crisis . . . In the event, although an SIS volunteer was dispatched to the island, a settlement was reached before Grivas could be found.' Cyprus eventually became independent in 1959 under President Archbishop Makarios. The Greek Army colonels, who seized power in Athens in 1967, had been funding EOKA through KYP (Greek intelligence service) for years. In 1974, with their support, the mainly Greek National Guard organised a coup against Makarios, who narrowly escaped to Malta. The colonels had hoped that the Americans would approve their coup, with the Sixth Fleet anchored in Greek ports. But Washington was loath to alienate Turkey, with vital CIA listening stations on the Turkish Black Sea coast monitoring Soviet missile tests at Tyuratam and Kapustin. The British had their listening station at Edirne. CIA and SIS stations in Cyprus, Turkey and Greece failed to provide prior intelligence on the subsequent Turkish invasion of the north of Cyprus on 20 July 1974. By the end of August the Turks had achieved their long-desired taksim partitioning with 30,000 Turkish troops occupying a third of the island from Kyrenia to Nicosia. Britain had guaranteed Cyprus' independence under treaty but had insufficient military and naval forces based in the Eastern Mediterranean to enforce it. As Nigel West pointed out succintly, SIS escaped censure in the following Foreign Affairs Select Committee investigation because, officially, it did not exist.[13]

Chapter 20

Gold Tunnel, Berlin, 1953–6

The tunnel in Berlin was an incredible project to tunnel from the American zone under East Berlin to access Soviet signalling traffic. It was a great source of pride to British Intelligence but a real blow when it was betrayed by George Blake.

JBS

After the war, John Aldwinckle, who had been based in Brindisi in 1944 flying special operations for SOE (see Chapter 6), returned to the UK to study French and German at the Queen's College, Oxford. He subsequently re-joined the RAF in 1949 in his wartime rank of flight lieutenant and was immediately seconded to the JIB, the forerunner of today's Defence Intelligence. Aldwinckle's training in languages followed a similar path to Captain John Sanderson's. At the time, SIS was desperate for Russian speakers and Soviet specialists. As a foreign languages graduate, Aldwinckle was sent to the School of Eastern and Slavonic Studies at London University to learn Russian. Then, in 1952, he moved to Paris for six months (as Sanderson had in 1948) to live with a Russian émigré, and within the large Russian émigré community there, to perfect his Russian and immerse himself in the culture.

Returning to London, Aldwinckle was seconded to the SIS, and in 1955 was sent to Cologne as part of the British Control Commission for Germany, where he was involved in setting up a network of German 'stay-behind' agents. These were to form the nucleus of a resistance movement should Western Europe be overrun by Soviet forces, which some considered to be a very real threat throughout the 1950s.[1] Tony Geraghty noted that the British mission in East Germany was working flat out in October 1953 to deduce Soviet military intentions. They completed sixty team tours, driving an incredible 25,000 miles around the GDR (German Democratic Republic), collecting the intelligence to recreate a complete Soviet battle exercise. This evidence enabled MI3 (operational side of intelligence) gathering technical teams to understand that the 'battle' had involved the 9 million Warsaw Pact soldiers fighting without artillery, nuclear weapons or artillery. It was the time of detente in Europe. All this information would have been relayed to NATO HQ at Rocquencourt, near Versailles, where in 1962 Lieutenant Colonel Sanderson and Squadron Leader Aldwinckle would be based in the Intelligence Division of SHAPE during the Cuban Missile Crisis. Both officers would no doubt have attended the half-yearly Warsaw Pact Intelligence Conference, held in London and run by MI3. It was later called MI or DI (Defence Intelligence) 60 Land Warfare Technical Intelligence Conference attended by the military intelligence officers of Australia, Canada, Britain and the USA (AUSCANUKUS group).[2]

During the 1950s British and US Intelligence set up 'stay-behind' networks across Western Europe, with the cooperation of the NATO countries of Italy, Belgium, France, Greece, West Germany, the Netherlands and even with neutral Switzerland. If Russia and the Warsaw Pact had invaded, these paramilitary networks would have been activated and have uncovered concealed secret weapons depots, before resisting enemy occupation. The exposure of an underground network 'P-26' in Switzerland would create a furore in 1990: Switzerland was a supposedly 'neutral' country and outside NATO. A subsequent 1991 Swiss public inquiry would reveal that around 900,000 Swiss citizens had been under 'P-26' surveillance. Furthermore, in January 2018, it was revealed that secret appendices of 'P-26' files held in Swiss national archives had disappeared with the Swiss secret services suspected of removing these sensitive files.[3]

In 1954 Aldwinckle was sent to the epicentre of Cold War espionage, Berlin, where, under the cover of working for the Political Intelligence section of the Control Commission, and by now a squadron leader, he became one of around thirty SIS officers working in their Berlin station, located next to the Olympic stadium built by the Nazis for the 1936 Olympics. (John Sanderson immediately after the war had also used the SIS offices located in the north-east part of the Olympiastadion). So prolific was the espionage in Berlin that it gained a particular description of Agentssumpf, meaning a 'swamp for spies'.

As John Aldwinckle and his wife Helene now had four children, aged 8 years and under, he was assigned a large house in the smart Dahlem district of West Berlin in the Grunewald, Berlin's forest where West Berliners liked to go for walks on Sundays. They had two live-in maids and a children's nanny. The nanny's husband was their gardener. All were German and all were almost certainly paid by the Russians to spy on the family. The house had previously been occupied by the Governor of Spandau Prison and had been requisitioned from the famous German soprano Erna Sack, known as 'the German Nightingale' for her high vocal range.

Their house was a short drive to the Olympic stadium, from where Aldwinckle would set out each day in his black Volkswagen to find and nurture agents. Tens of thousands of migrants were making their way into West Berlin to escape the privations of the Communist East. Many would recommend contacts in the East who might work for the Allies. All the SIS officers were provided with an identical car, as were the CIA heading to their clandestine rendezvouses in their VWs. Every so often, in true cloak and dagger style, Aldwinckle would stop in a quiet part of the Grunewald and change the car's number plates, as all SIS officers were encouraged to do, to confuse the Soviet-controlled agents who were keeping tabs on him. (He later learned that the Russians had an agent posted in a building across the road from the Stadium's entrance, whose sole job was to note down the driver and number plate of every Volkswagen arriving and leaving, so this probably made little difference.) In the middle of 1946, SIS had begun to establish undercover agents and contacts in Berlin and across Germany. German hatred for the Communist occupiers and the appeal of food were the prime motivation for those who took up the offer.

The SIS Berlin Station was run at this time by Peter Lunn, a quietly spoken Old Etonian who had captained the British Winter Olympic skiing team in 1936 and whose father, Sir Henry Lunn, had founded the travel business Lunn Poly. Lunn was previously SIS's Head of Station in Vienna, where he had successfully masterminded an eavesdropping operation called Operation CONFLICT. This involved building tunnels to tap into underground telephone cables carrying communications between the occupying Soviet Kommandatura Army HQ and its operations in their zone of occupation. Lunn kept all the German agents recruited by SIS on a card index system, which made it all the easier for Blake to provide lists of names to his controller in the Russian sector.

At a meeting in London in December 1953, SIS and the CIA met to discuss developing a similar eavesdropping arrangement in Berlin, to be codenamed Operation STOPWATCH by SIS and Operation GOLD by the CIA. This involved digging a secret tunnel, 1,800ft long, from underneath a disused house in a suburb of the American sector into the Soviet zone, enabling the telephone cables to be tapped from the Soviet military command in Zossen-Wünsdor, East Berlin, to Moscow and other Warsaw Pact countries.[4] The main aim of the Berlin project, was to give prior warning of a possible Soviet attack on the West. The 6ft-wide tunnel was nearly half a mile long from Rudlow in the US zone, extending under the Soviet zone to intercept a Soviet cable beside the Schönefelder Chausee.

A shaft was sunk beneath the cover of a radar station and the tunnellers broke into the target junction box in three weeks. British telephone engineers installed 25 tons of equipment with banks of tape-recorders. In London 300 linguists, proficient in German and Russian, worked around the clock translating the traffic intercepted. The eavesdropping continued for almost a year.[5]

The building of the tunnel and its operations were handled by one of four groups in SIS's Berlin Station. Another dealt with scientific intelligence, a third aimed to gather information on Soviet and East German forces, and a fourth group was responsible for collecting political intelligence and penetrating the Soviet HQ in Karlshorst in East Berlin.[6] Karlshorst contained the well-protected SMA (Soviet Military Administration) where Marshal Zhukov had been based in early 1945, together with the GRU General Ivan Serov, who would be dubbed 'the hangman of Hungary' for his organisation of the ruthless 1956 suppression of the 1956 revolution. Serov would finally came to grief in 1960 over his friendship with Colonel Penkovsky, the MI6/CIA agent for whom he would write a letter of support to the 2nd Chief Directorate Head. As a result, Serov would apparently shoot himself in the back of the head whilst drunk, although this official explanation sounds highly unlikely. The historian John Gaddis noted that, from 1945, 2,000 staff worked in the NKVD Karlshorst base which covered the Soviet zone regions, each with an NKGB HQ, further split into districts run by security groups that exercised surveillance of political parties, trade unions and churches.[7]

Aldwinckle would travel to clandestine locations in East Berlin, usually in the evening or at night, to rendezvous with agents. On one occasion he met an agent who worked alongside a military airfield in the Russian sector, from where she could monitor details of flight movements and pass these back to John. She ran a kennels and, perhaps as a way of being able to pass her a large sum of money without arousing suspicion, John bought a pedigree long-haired dachshund puppy from her, which he took home to become the family pet. Around two weeks later, the dog disappeared (as had the dachshund of John Sanderson when he was based in Berlin). It was probably stolen by someone who recognised its value. His children were distraught, so Aldwinckle returned to the agent to buy another puppy from the litter, no doubt with his own money this time, which the family called Fritzi. SIS officers operated independently, and it was understood that you did not attempt to recruit or contact each other's agents. On one occasion, when Aldwinckle was meeting one of his agents at night in an apartment, he was suddenly aware that he and his agent were not alone. In a glass window he could make out the reflection of a man, lurking in the semi-darkness. After a short while he recognised the shadowy figure. It was his fellow SIS officer George Blake. Aldwinckle returned home puzzled and shaken, wondering why Blake had been there and whether he should report it. If he did, the chances are he would have been told by Lunn not to worry, since Lunn considered him to be the best agent runner he had.[8]

Blake, Russian codename Agent Diomid, was later to admit that he 'passed a great deal of information on the structure of the Berlin station, on the aims of the Berlin station, and on the make-up of the "order of battle" of the Berlin station. They got a good inside view of how it operated'.[9] He claimed not to concern himself with the (agent) networks. Aldwinckle's experience suggested otherwise. Blake handed over to his contacts in Karlshorst the names of all SIS officers, as well as the agents SIS employed in Germany. In 1955, the first year that Blake was in Berlin, 772 agents were arrested in the GDR, including at least 105 SIS agents; 679 were arrested in 1956 and 582 the following year.

In the early 1950s Moscow needed new recruits after the breaking up of the Cambridge spy circle. There were suspicions about the 'Third Man', Kim Philby, from both sides of the Iron Curtain. SIS at this time was having little success with penetrating the Soviet Union and defectors were thin on the ground. A new department, Section Y, had been created and it had been hoped to obtain the shortfall in intelligence through technical telephone interceptions.[10] Blake had told the Soviets about the Berlin tunnel, having been the note-taker at the original CIA meeting in London in 1953 where the scheme was laid out. He had then passed the details to his controller in London, although a full report was not conveyed to Moscow until February 1954, when the work had just begun.[11] The tunnel had been compromised before it was even built and when it was 'accidentally' discovered by surprised workmen in April 1956, eleven months after it became operational, it must have aroused suspicion there had been a leak. MI6 were still transcribing the vast volumes of material gathered seven years later when they discovered George Blake had betrayed the tunnel.[12] The communications needing transcription were significant since all Soviet telephone traffic from Warsaw and even Bucharest was routed through Berlin to Moscow. In all, 40,000 hours of telephone conversations and 6 million hours of teletype traffic were recorded.[13] In 1951 the Soviets had shifted their wireless communications to encrypted land lines for military traffic. The tunnel interceptions had succeeded for this limited period, despite Blake betraying it before the first spade had been kicked in the ground. The KGB decided not to close it down to protect their valued agent. They did not pass information on its existence to their 'neighbours'

(KGB parlance for the GRU) or the Stasi (GDR state intelligence and security service).[14]

The conclusion in the end was that there was no planned disinformation action by Soviet Intelligence to feed false information to the Allies, so that the intelligence gleaned was genuine. To have done that would have been just too complicated and too hard to conceal, with Blake's cover most definitely blown as a result. Sergei Kondarashev, Blake's handler, later confirmed that to protect their major agent, Blake, the KGB had permitted Western experts to listen in to the unrestricted flows of Red Army telephone communications. Blake's treachery was eventually exposed in 1961 by a Polish defector.[15] The technical feat and imagination of this project was admired widely in the Western press at the time and its discovery was not the propaganda coup the Soviets had envisaged.

Although Aldwinckle always thought Blake was 'a bit of an oddball', Blake and his wife Gillian were well liked amongst other officers in the intelligence community and their wives, and took an active part in its social scene. John's wife Helene remembers him as being very polite, attentive and kind towards her children and her partially disabled sister when she came to visit.

In November 2012 George Blake celebrated his 90th birthday in his Russian dacha near Moscow, two weeks after the death of his former SIS colleague Wing Commander John Aldwinckle. Blake, still alive in 2018, is quoted as saying he had no cause for anguish for what he had done, that he considered himself 'happy and lucky' and that 'looking back on my life, everything seems logical and natural'.[16] In 2015, an article by a *Financial Times* journalist suggested that treachery didn't quite apply to Blake and that he 'didn't betray his nation because he was hardly British'. Wing Commander John Aldwinckle's son Richard wrote a letter to the newspaper which was published it full.

> Blake was not only a British subject from birth, he was a second generation immigrant. He may have spent most of his childhood outside the UK but that does not exonerate his treachery. Don't be fooled by Blake's gentle voice and innocent demeanour. He knew exactly what he was doing when he betrayed, by his own admission, 500–600 British agents to the KGB, and knew perfectly well that the KGB or Stasi would summarily execute most of them. As well as sentencing them to death by his actions, his treachery also compromised the difficult and dangerous work of SIS officers in Berlin in the 1950s, including my late father, whose careers he either destroyed or damaged.[17]

Nigel West noted that, after a hostile penetration by a mole such as Blake, a damage control assessment was undertaken to try to withdraw agents. Any intelligence personnel who had worked with Blake were judged to have had their cover blown. 'When, in January 1961 George Blake confessed to espionage, SIS undertook an immense exercise, code-named CRUET, to mark the personal files of everyone known to Blake, and therefore likely to have been compromised, with a traffic-light symbol of red and green colours to indicate the level of danger.'[18]

In 1957, John Aldwinckle and his family returned to the UK. They were given very little time to pack up their house, say their farewells and find a home for Fritzi the dog before leaving. John and his two youngest children flew back to the UK on an RAF transport aircraft; Helene and two eldest children left by train to Hamburg and then to Harwich by ferry. It is not known why their departure needed to be so hasty but it may well have been because John had discovered his cover had been 'blown' and he had to leave quickly for security or safety reasons. Once back in the UK, he was debriefed then waited to receive details of his next posting. In the RAF, unlike the British Army, there was not a dedicated Intelligence Corps. Instead it is part of the Administrative branch. His next post was not in Intelligence and it was a few years before he was asked to take on another intelligence role, in Cologne again, in 1960. He often felt his agents in Berlin had never really produced much that was worthwhile and in 1961 he discovered why, when George Blake was arrested.[19]

The GOLD tunnel was not the only tunnel excavated between the Russian and Western sectors of Berlin. Over seventy tunnels were excavated from the opposite direction, by East Germans attempting to escape to the West. In the early 1960s over 300 people managed to crawl to freedom through 19 tunnels. In 2018 German engineers discovered an 80m-long tunnel, built in 1961. After a 5m-deep shaft, the wood-lined tunnel headed under wartime anti-tank defences in the Mauerpark towards the Berlin wall, where it stopped 'tantalisingly close' to the cellar of a house in the Western sector. An informant had revealed the tunnel to the Stasi Secret Police. The tunnel was boarded up and flooded.[20]

Chapter 21

Suez Invasion, 1956

On 4 April 1955 Iraq, Turkey and Jordan signed the Baghdad Pact, joined later by Britain, Pakistan and Iran. This was a defence pact, sharing intelligence on Soviet activities, joint military exercises and planning of stay-behind networks in case of a Russian invasion.

JBS told the author three decades ago that: 'The Egyptian army were poorly supplied with tanks themselves. After the Second World War the Americans had sold them British tanks that were surplus to requirements but withheld the spare parts and ammunition that they needed to operate them.' As the historian Stephen Dorril pointed out, the newly elected Anthony Eden's policy led Nasser to agree his first arms deal with Czechoslovakia. The British refusal to increase the quantity of weapons supplied to the Egyptian Army, including shells for its Centurion tanks, 'effectively drove Nasser straight into the arms of Moscow'. Czech weapons were secretly shipped to Cairo. Dorril noted that the vast arms deal included 150 tanks, 80 MiG-15s and 45 Ilyushin-28 bombers.[1]

In July 1955 at the Geneva four-power summit meeting both sides had fixed positions. Dwight Eisenhower proposed an 'open skies' initiative to Khrushchev that would allow military over-flights of each others' territory to observe key installations, together with the exchange of technical blueprints. (This would later form the basis of Reagan's 'Trust but verify' policy.) The historian Hughes-Wilson noted that Khrushchev, a quick-witted man, found Eisenhower's proposal highly amusing, joking: 'Nyet, nyet, nyet, you're just trying to see in our bedrooms!'[2]

In London, Philby was under the spotlight and serious suspicion. In the furore surrounding the precipitous defection to Moscow of his fellow Soviet agents, he held his nerve. His suave manner and apparent self-confidence hid inner turmoil. He knew the lack of evidence strengthened his position. He called a press conference in November 1955 to demand an apology from a Labour MP who had named him in Parliament as a spy. The accuser was forced to retract. Not only that, the

Prime Minister himself announced in Parliament that he had 'no reason to conclude that Mr Philby has at any time betrayed the interests of this country'.[3]

After several minutes of flash photography, Philby brazened out the questioning of his association with the defectors Maclean and Burgess, now in Moscow and revealed as Russian spies.

> Mr Philby, Mr Macmillan, the Foreign Secretary, said there was no evidence that you were the so-called Third man who allegedly tipped off Burgess and Maclean. Are you satisfied with that clearance that he gave you?
>
> A. Yes, I am.
>
> Q. Well, if there was a Third man, were you in fact the Third Man?
>
> A. No, I was not.
>
> Q. Do you think there was one?
>
> A. No comment.
>
> I am debarred by the Official Secrets Act from saying anything that might disclose to unauthorised persons information derived from my position as a former government official.
>
> Q. Mr Macmillan said you had had Communist associations. Is that why you were asked to resign?
>
> A. I was asked to resign from the Foreign Office because of an imprudent association with Burgess and as a result of his disappearance.[4]

Kim Philby's coolness, in so publicly denying being a traitor to his country, is still studied as a classic example of how agents in the intelligence sphere should remain calm in adversity, refute all accusations and lie effectively through their teeth when under pressure. Faced with Nicholas Elliott's accusations of treachery in Beirut in January 1963, however, Philby's old confidence and self-assuredness was to become jaded by self-doubt and undermined by the excessive alcohol he consumed to mask his anxiety.[5]

In 1956 there were many changes. The brothers Fidel and Raul Castro arrived in Havana to start a revolution that would lead to the Cuban Missile Crisis of 1962 and France was shaken by the first terrorist attacks in her colony Algeria, the first indications of a traumatic colonial war in which half a million Frenchmen would be called to arms. Khrushchev's strong Congress speech on 'different routes to socialism in different countries' would be taken as a signal to the satellite states of changing times. In spite of his condemnation of Stalin's repression, Khrushchev would feel it necessary to stamp out the waves of unrest and protests that threatened Moscow's tight grip on their Eastern Empire.[6]

In February 1956 at the 20th Congress of the Soviet Communist Party in Moscow, as the delegates were preparing to depart at the end of the sessions, they were called back for an unpublicised 4-hour speech by Nikita Khrushchev that would rock the Communist world and beyond. Beforehand, during the Congress itself, the French Communist guest speaker, Maurice Thorez had given a stirring speech praising Stalin's memory and received a standing ovation.[7] But Khrushchev had a different perspective. The leaders of the fifty-five Communist and Workers' parties, and those of all Eastern European Communist parties, were stunned by the Party Secretary's long, dramatic speech. The historian William Taubman described how they listened in silence, then left the Congress Hall, repeating 'da-a, da-a' (yes) to themselves.[8]

What had shaken them to the core was Khrushchev's damning condemnation of the dictator Joseph Stalin, whom he accused of appalling and cruel abuses of power. Stalin, he said, had been a weak and cowardly leader during the war; he had never visited the troops at the front and was a leader detached and remote from ordinary Russians. Worse, Stalin had terrorised his fellow citizens, ordering hundreds of thousands to be arrested and deported. He had authorised the torture and execution of thousands of 'honest and innocent' Communists, without proper investigation and trial, and had created a climate of fear and desperation throughout the Soviet Union. Stalin's cult of the individual, he said, was alien to the spirit of Marxist-Leninism and he had betrayed Lenin. In criticising Stalin's brutal leadership, Khrushchev was no doubt attempting to appease his own guilt and his own not insignificant part in the Great Terror, especially in the Ukraine. His excuse for never voicing criticism of Stalin at the time, and for not opposing his purges, was that Stalin had 'used them . . . anyone who objected . . . was doomed . . . to immediate destruction'.[9]

Nikita Khrushchev had been tasked with arresting 35,000 'enemies of the people', 5,000 to be shot. He exceeded his quota by arresting 41,305 mostly kulak small farmers and having 8,500 executed. His part in this Great Terror would come back to haunt him.[10]

Geert Mak described Khrushchev as genuinely hoping his speech would restore Communism's reputation and create a more humane and less repressive Soviet Union. In 1955 thousands of political prisoners had been released from both the prisons and the Gulag (Glavnoe upravlenie ispravitel'no-trudovykh lagerei – The Main Directorate of Corrective Labour Camps). Wladek Matwin again: 'Khrushchev revealed that Lenin . . . had tried to put a stop to Stalin . . . Khrushchev condemned the purges, Stalin's waste of lives during the war and the collectivisation of Soviet agriculture, his paranoia and his break with Tito. The Soviet Union never completely recovered from that speech in February 1956.'[11] Over 5½ million people were held in the NVKD's custody at this time. Khrushchev wrote in his memoirs that the figure was 'up to ten million . . . more than an English pirate could have dreamed of'.[12]

William Taubman described how the news of Khrushchev's speech, never publicly released in the Soviet Union, was revealed to the world. The Poles had copied and distributed the official translation of Khrushchev's speech. Israeli intelligence had then passed it on to the CIA. It was then leaked and published in the *New York Times* in June 1956.[13] What was encouraging in Khrushchev's radical speech was that it appeared to have ditched the conventional Marxist-Leninist view that war between Communism and Capitalism was inevitable. His boast was now that Communism had grown so powerful that war was no longer necessary. Socialism would be victorious, through the Communist means of production. In reality, the only products that Communism produced effectively were armaments, rockets and spacecraft. The command economy of the 'workers' paradise' would never produce enough consumer goods in sufficient quantity to satisfy demand, although Khrushchev did try to meet the housing needs of the citizens, including millions of disbanded soldiers.[14] The same month Khrushchev removed his rival Molotov as Foreign Minister and replaced him with Shepilov. (Gorbachev in the 1980s would act in a similar manner by removing Andrei Gromyko and installing his Georgian ally Shevardnadze as Foreign Minister, a crucial manoeuvre in his plan to allow the satellite states to go their own way, the so-called Sinatra doctrine of 'I did it my way'.)

The repercussions of the speech were not long in coming. On 28 June, on 'Black Thursday', Polish workers in Poznan went on strike, calling for 'Bread and Freedom'. The Polish government dealt with the unrest with 2 divisions of Polish soldiers and the security forces, backed up by 300 tanks. Scores of workers were killed and hundreds injured. The Polish Army, however, had never forgotten the heartless way the Red Army had stood back across the Vistula when the Warsaw uprising of 1944 was brutally put down by the Germans. This was illustrated by the ironic joke describing a Polish soldier facing an invasion from both fronts, from Germany and Russia. Which soldier would he kill first, the German or the

Russian?' 'The German,' the Pole replied, 'because business comes before pleasure.'

For Britain a major crisis now occurred that was to spell an abrupt end to its colonial power in Egypt and damage its prestige in the Middle East. The planned Anglo-French operation to seize back the Suez Canal was aborted on the brink of success.

On 26 July 1956 Nasser nationalised the canal, which was owned and operated by the French Suez Canal Company. A crucial motivating factor for him was the proposed financing of the High Dam at Aswan. Britain and the USA had initially agreed to contribute but then changed their minds. Nasser's plan was to use his profits from the Suez Canal to finance the Aswan Dam project. French shareholders would lose their investments. Nasser had been playing off the West against Russia and was 'making Egypt a spearhead for the Arab front against Israel'. Anthony Eden considered Nasser's actions to be 'an act of plunder which threatens the livelihood of many nations' and that 'the lives of the great trading nations of the world' could be 'strangled at any moment by some interruption of the free passage of the Canal'.[15] In December 1955 the British and Americans had offered to finance the Aswan Dam. But Eden, physically ill and with strong medication affecting his judgement and moods, now regarded Nasser as a new Hitler who must be removed. He telephoned Nutting, his Foreign Affairs Minister, declaring; ' I want him destroyed . . . murdered'. When Eden later repeated this to his PUS at the FO, Sir Ivone Kirkpatrick, he replied: 'I don't think we have a Department for that sort of thing, Prime Minister.' Nor did MI6 have a specific department dealing with assassinations. Various schemes were considered by MI6 but dropped. The Prime Minister's order was not carried through.[16] The Soviet Union, in contrast, had a Department 13 of the First Directorate under General Serov for carrying out state assassinations, or 'wet affairs' as they were called. When the order had gone out in 1954 to eliminate the Ukrainian NTS (People's Labour Alliance) émigré leader-in-exile, the chosen assassin, Nikolai Khokhlov, was equipped with a silenced electric gun, disguised as a cigarette packet, which fired lethal bullets, tipped with cyanide. Khokhlov, however, decided to disobey his orders and warned his intended victim that the Central Committee had ordered his elimination, before promptly defecting to the CIA. On Khrushchev's orders, an assassin of Department 13 named Stashinsky, from the East Berlin Karlshorst base, eliminated the two main Ukrainian émigrés in West Germany with a special KGB gun that sprayed cyanide poison gas onto the victims, inducing a heart attack. In 1957 a revenge attempt failed to kill the defector Khokhlov with radioactive thallium.[17]

In Egypt, George Young of MI6 thought that the FO and the government's handling of Middle East Affairs was a 'tale of blunder and disaster . . . we seemed to be blissfully unaware of the extent to which the Arabs had come to resent the physical presence of British troops'. When the British had to withdraw from Suez, Young remarked: 'I became an old man overnight . . . the expedition meant the end of British power and influence in the region . . . it was the last self-conscious fling of the old British style'.[18] Young drew up plans to kill Nasser. Assassination schemes ranged from paying dissident military officers to planting an exploding electric razor, to using poison gas and sending out hit teams. There was official disapproval for these projects and they were quietly dropped. Meanwhile, Nasser had learnt of the plans and the KGB provided him with increased security, including a caged bird that would fall off its perch in the presence of poison gas, in the manner of heroic canaries in the British fighting tunnels of the First World War.[19]

The Prime Minister Eden, despite the policy agreed in the Cabinet, also planned to involve the SIS, working with the Israelis, in Operation OMEGA. The FO and CIA would have little sight of this shelved plan, an extreme covert action to both undermine Nasser's position and topple the Syrian government.[20] In September another plan called Operation PILE-UP was conceived in which the British would deliberately put in requests for excessive shipping traffic through the canal, with the ensuing chaos providing a opportunity for the West to step in. This scheme was abandoned.[21] Plans for a Suez invasion were afoot. The Israelis, threatened by Fedayeen terrorists entering their territory from Egyptian-held Sinai, attended a secret meeting at Sèvres in France with the British Prime Minister, the French Premier and their foreign ministers. (The French saw Nasser as a threat to their presence in Algeria, where he was promoting revolution.)

In Europe, meanwhile, events would soon prove how dangerous Khrushchev's speech was for the hegemony of the Soviet Union over its satellite states and for the future of international Communism. The effects of his speech were long-lasting and significant. Khrushchev's condemnation of Stalin's abuse of power and revelations of his repressive policies threatened the control that the leaders of Eastern European Communist states had over their citizens.[22] In Poland the cracks were beginning to appear. William Taubman described how on 19 October Khrushchev flew unannounced into Warsaw, accompanied by Zhukhov and eleven generals. After his plane was buzzed by Polish jets, he rushed down the steps in a fury, waving his fist angrily, and declaring 'We are ready to intervene.' The unpredictable Khrushchev, although ambitious to be seen as peacemaker, was quick to anger and naturally aggressive. When he ordered Russian troops to move on Polish cities, Gromulka mobilised Polish security forces and told Khrushchev that he would not talk with a loaded gun on the table and that Poland would not 'permit its independence to be taken away'. Gromulka was able to defuse the situation by reassuring Khrushchev and convincing him that Poland would remain a loyal member of the Warsaw Pact. Khrushchev had miscalculated and a compromise was reached.

Just four days later, however, unrest exploded in Budapest with huge student demonstrations. Stalin's statue was toppled, the Hungarian police HQ occupied and 30,000 Soviet troops and tanks entered Budapest and sealed it off. Martial law was imposed but fighting continued with grenades, Molotov cocktails and paving stones. Hundreds of Hungarian civilians and Soviet soldiers were killed. Zhukhov advised withdrawing the troops on 28 October. Soviet tanks and reinforcements meanwhile massed on the Hungarian border. When Hungarian security forces fired on a crowd, angry demonstrators attacked the Communist Party HQ. As the security men left the building they were lynched. Andropov, the future KGB Chairman and Soviet leader, watching from the Soviet Embassy, was appalled. He developed a 'Hungarian complex' that some said he never shook off. Thousands of Hungarian soldiers and several tank commanders joined the resistance, bringing their weapons with them. Radio Free Europe praised these 'freedom fighters'.[23]

The following day, on 29 October, the Israelis invaded Sinai and fought their way rapidly to the Suez Canal. As previously agreed, on 30 October the British and French sent an ultimatum to the Israelis and the Egyptians to withdraw ten miles from either side of the canal to allow the British to occupy Port Said, Ismailia and Suez. The British naval task force had sailed from Malta, 1,000 miles away, two days before the Israeli invasion. From Cyprus a large force of French and British paratroopers and soldiers flew to Egypt. The French and British jets attacked Egyptian airfields for four days. The fleet arrived and captured Port Said.[24] One of Sanderson's close regimental colleagues recalled in 2017:

> In England John was posted into 'B' Company of 1st Btn York and Lancaster regiment, just as we were about to go to Suez in the Autumn 1956. The Company had been selected for arduous training as instructed by the Commander of 3 Division, Major-General Jack Churcher. I was also posted to Bulford at the same stage. In recognition of this training of marching for ten miles fully loaded-up in two hours, and digging in at an anti-nuclear depth, in four hours, the Company had enjoyed increased rations. John thus inherited a particularly fit body of men.[25]

In Hungary on 30 October Nagy announced a coalition government. The Kremlin conceded that the previous Hungarian regime had made 'serious mistakes'. Nagy then miscalculated, declaring Hungary's neutrality and withdrawing from the Warsaw Pact. This was the final straw for Khrushchev. Fearful of unrest spreading from Hungary to other Warsaw Pact countries, and of 'having capitalists on the frontiers of the Soviet Union', Khrushchev, Malenkov and Molotov flew to Poland, Romania and Bulgaria to warn their satellite states of their intention to intervene in Hungary. On 3 November the full force of 15 Soviet divisions and 4,000 tanks moved to surround Budapest. On 4 November they entered the capital, leading to 2 weeks of intense fighting which resulted in 15,000 Soviet and 20,000 Hungarian casualties.[26] Nagy was later tried and executed. An advisor of Khrushchev's remarked: 'He executed Nagy as a lesson to all the other leaders in Socialist countries . . . In his eyes political expediency was superior to morality. Humanity came second to security.'[27]

In Egypt a UN-organised ceasefire had been introduced in Suez at midnight on 6 November. A resolution in the UN, introduced by the Americans, had stopped the invasion before Ismailia and the whole canal could be seized. Khrushchev commented that the Americans had helped their allies 'the way the rope helps the man who is hanged'.[28] To the US threat not to help Britain in her financial crisis was added the Russian threats to launch nuclear rockets on Britain and France, and send 'volunteers' to fight in Egypt.[29]

The CIA discounted the threat of a Soviet attack on Britain or France. Such an action would precipitate outright war. The strongest action by the Soviets that they could envisage would be submarine attacks on British or French ships. The British Ambassador in Moscow dismissed 'the nuclear threat as ugly bluster, as of course it was; it was an early example of what was to be a common Khrushchev technique, posturing for propaganda purposes from a safe position, when it was clear that his bluff would not be called'.[30]

Peter Wright gave a fascinating account of how technological eavesdropping lead directly to policy decisions. By introducing a fault in the Egyptian Embassy telephone in London, MI5 created an opportunity to install a listening device in a telephone receiver next to an Egyptian cipher machine. Every morning when the Egyptian reset the cipher, any sound picked up was sent via a link to GCHQ, where the new setting could now be calculated and the daily cipher broken. Through Operation ENGULF during the Suez crisis, GCHQ were able to obtain a detailed account of Egyptian/Soviet discussions in Moscow. One important topic covered the planned Russian mobilisation of aircraft to confront Britain.

This went straight to the JIC and was a contributing factor in the Britain's decision to withdraw.[31]

As well offending the military pride of the French, Operation MUSKETEER infuriated the Americans: the world's attention was being diverted away from the brutal Soviet invasion of Hungary. Cordial relations between the CIA and SIS were still important, however, during the Suez Crisis.The CIA Watch Committee in Washington was scrutinising NSA intercepts and U2 (Ultra-high altitude CIA spy plane) photographs and could see an attack on Egypt was coming: British ships were sailing through the Mediterranean, military forces were grouping in Cyprus and French jets were flying into Israel. On 28 October 1956 the CIA opposite number of John Bruce Lockhart (John Sanderson's SIS colleague) was pressing him for some indication of the British government's intentions. Lockhart did drop hints, telling him: 'We can't let Suez go, you realise it's the lifeline of our Empire.'[32] The diplomatic relationship between the British and US governments reached an all-time low in this period. However, in spite of the American Ambassador being withdrawn and the State Department issuing an ultimatum, the CIA still continued to provide the British with U2 aerial reconnaissance imagery of Egyptian airfields.[33]

In Paris (A. Beevor and A. Cooper noted) the French Communist Party tried to ignore Kruschchev's Congress speech, such was their devotion to Stalinism. French Communists used to swear they would die with their party membership cards in their pockets (*'mourir la carte dans la poche'*). Many, however, could no longer grit their teeth (*'serrer les dents'*) and ignore the truth. 'Furious French demonstrators attacked the Soviet Embassy . . . Crowds also surrounded the Communist Party headquarters . . . A more serious attack was mounted against the offices of L'Humanité. Groups climbed over the roofs and threw Molotov cocktails . . .The events of 1956 led to a dramatic decline in the Communist Party's influence on intellectual life in Paris.'[34] The Russians were remarkably well-informed about Operation MUSKETEER. The deputy chief of the French section of the NATO HQ Press and Information Department, one Georges Pâques, was a spy working for Soviet Intelligence and had passed over the operational plan for the Anglo-French invasion of Suez.[35]

Meanwhile, Major John Sanderson was aboard the troopship *New Australia* (sailing with *Empire Fowey* and *Asurias*). This left Portsmouth on 2 November (officers travelling 1st Class with commensurate menu) and arrived on the morning of 10 November in the eastern Mediterranean, after an eight-day voyage from the United Kingdom to join units of the Allied fleet 5 miles off the Egyptian coast. The task of ferrying these occupation troops ashore began within 24 hours. Their arrival made it possible to begin the phased withdrawal of the Commando and Paratrooper units that had taken part in the invasion. Air reconnaissance had revealed that the Egyptians were rapidly repairing some of their key airfields in the Canal Zone, and there was still a possibility that hostilities might break out once more if the Russians and Czechs supplied combat aircraft. The danger was highlighted by the fact that the Egyptians at El Cap had reoccupied all their defensive positions and were now sending out reconnaissance patrols right up to the Allied line, where the opposing sides still exchanged occasional bursts of gunfire. On 11 November, the 1st Btn Royal West Kent regiment disembarked and moved up to the tense area, where they relieved 2nd Btn the Parachute Regt.[36]

On 6 November, on the orders of Nasser, the Suez Canal was blocked with forty-seven sunken ships, halting the flow of Middle East oil. Eden was forced to back down and ordered a pull-out from Egypt. British reserves had now fallen by a staggering 15 per cent. The USA refused a temporary loan and sterling was collapsing.[37]

JBS landed in Suez on Armistice Day, 11 November, after the firing was over. His airmail letter of November 1956 read:

> Dear A, Went up to the 'sharp end' today to have a look at the Royal West Kent positions. They are sitting, facing the Egyptians some miles up the canal. It was quite fun climbing up one of those high towers at the canal station and having a peep at the Egyptian positions through my binoculars. They seem to be doing the same as our chaps – i.e. digging, wiring and lying in the sun. We were to have taken over from R.W.K. this week-end, but this has now been changed and Jo Jo's outfit goes there, and we relieve them a week later. In the meantime, we have landed the unenviable task of guarding practically everything in Port Said. My Company has landed the Ammunition Depot, plus the oil installations of Shell. Awful bind! However, I am kept on the go all the time, so life does not seem too dull at present. Don't get the impression I am enjoying it – far from it. Sleeping on a concrete floor does <u>not</u> appeal to me! Thank goodness our vehicles are being unloaded. I get my trailer today but alas only the tent. Had my first beer today for a week. John.

A second letter from *JBS* followed six days later:

> Major J B Sanderson 165827 on Active Service with 1st Bn York and Lancaster Regiment, Suez 17 November 1956.

> Dear A, Have just returned from a conference at the HQ (6pm) and find all my colleagues are on a tour of our posts. Have returned carrying an egg given me by Colonel Mike – he got a few in Cyprus. So tomorrow I shall enjoy a fried egg for the first time since the 'New Australia'. We are still living on the 'Compo' rations though, and will not get fresh food for a long time to come. However, there are various 'packs' which give variety. We also get fresh bread today from the latest 'automotive' bakery War Department WD pattern. Ten men worked all last night, and this machine produced enough bread for 10,000 troops! And jolly good bread it was.
>
> An amusing story about the Egyptians at the 'sharp end'. One or two of our naval gun boats took a party of journalists up the canal on a trip and the Egyptians saw them coming. A few minutes later a harassed UNO officer came over to the Royal West Kent lines and said: 'For God's sake, send those gun boats away, they are causing alarm and despondency amongst the Egyptian Forces who think they are about to be attacked!' Most of them were apparently prepared to 'up sticks' and run for it! John.

JBS later commented: 'Morale was good amongst the troops even if it was not amongst the British politicians. We brokered a small "inter-force" trade exchange with the French forces across the Sweet Water Canal: British supplies of Scotch whisky in exchange for French cigarettes.' His regimental colleague recalled in 2018:

> When in Suez, at a very smart shooting club which had been smashed up by French forces, we had very poor lavatory drainage. John Sanderson insisted that no lavatory paper was to be used. Based no doubt on his Indian experiences, we had to use our hands and a pot of disinfectant was conveniently placed. The whole of the Suez drainage had been destroyed and elsewhere UK forces dug trenches and oil was floated on the top of the spoil. A well-known miscreant in the Company slaughtered a pig and looted a flat. I remonstrated with John that this was not on. He said that this was fair game.[38]

The Royal West Kents, who had embarked on 11 November, were relieved at El Cap on 21 November by the Royal Fusiliers. They in turn were relieved by John Sanderson's 1st Btn the York and Lancaster Regt. The latter was still there when, on 30 November, two companies of Danish UN troops arrived by train from Abu Sueir. Transfer of responsibility to the Danes was completed on 7 December, and the next day the York and Lancaster Regt went to Port Said to embark on HMS *Theseus* on 16 December for the voyage home to the United Kingdom and to Dover Castle, their base.[39]

Peter Wright noted that Eden had reactivated the assassination option after the withdrawal from Egypt but that 'by this time virtually all MI6 assets in Egypt had been rounded up by Nasser. A new operation, using renegade Egyptian officers . . . failed lamentably . . . because their cache of weapons . . . was found to be defective'.[40] British and French forces withdrew by Christmas 1956 and the Israeli Army returned to their starting positions. Egypt had blocked the canal, forcing the shipment of Europe's oil to go around the Cape and across the Atlantic. Low gold and dollar reserves added to Britain's weak position and forced her reluctantly to accept the US position. The Russians then moved in to finance and advise the Egyptians on the Aswan Dam project. Eden resigned in January 1957 and was replaced by Harold Macmillan.[41]

Cradock in his book on the JIC described the Suez affair as 'a story of misuse and neglect of intelligence'. Policymakers disregarded JIC's forecasts and estimates. Strategic errors were compounded by the dissipation of government resources 'through secrecy, duplicity and sheer muddle'. It was extraordinary that the Allied Commander-in-Chief was not informed that the Israeli, British and French plans had been discussed and decided upon in advance. It was only at the last minute that many of the British commanders learned that operation CORDAGE was directed against Egypt and not Israel.[42]

Frustratingly, the Anglo-French operation to seize the canal had been called off on the brink of its success. Nicholas Elliot of M16, who in January 1963 would accost Philby in the Lebanon with his treachery, held 'an abysmal opinion of Eden' and felt that 'having attacked, you should have had the guts, no matter what the United States attitude was, to go ahead with it'.[43] Ironically, twenty-five years later, a future Egyptian President would fall out with his Soviet suppliers, over exactly the same issue of supplies for tanks that frustrated Nasser in his negotiations with the British government. The UN Russian Under Secretary General Arkady Shevchenko, who defected to the Americans in April 1978, revealed that the Soviet Foreign Minister Andrei Gromyko and KGB Major General Ivan Glazkov differed on the issue of military supplies to the Egyptian President Anwar Sadat. The Russian Defence Ministry put pressure on Sadat by withholding the spare parts he needed to service his ageing Soviet tanks and aeroplanes. Eventually Sadat had had enough, closed down all military and naval bases in Egypt and expelled the multitude of Soviet technicians and advisers. This was a blow to the Soviets since Egypt was an important outpost in the Mediterranean, so close to the British bases in Cyprus and was a stepping stone to influence in the Indian Ocean.[44]

The ripples of events in Hungary and Poland threatened to provoke unrest in Russia itself. To pre-empt this, a Commission under Brezhnev declared that 'the dictatorship of the proletariat must be merciless'. Citizens began to be prosecuted under Article 58 of the Stalinist Criminal Code with more than a year in prison. The hardline future First Secretary was preparing the 'Brezhnev Doctrine'. In June 1957 Khrushchev rounded on Molotov, who had joined Malenkov and Shepilov in an attempted politburo coup: 'You wanted to please Stalin, to show how vigilant you were. You sent innocent people to death with taints and a smirk.' Khrushchev later removed his two rivals, exiling them: Molotov as ambassador to Outer Mongolia and Malenkov to Kazakhstan as a manager of a hydroelectric plant.[45] The following four years stabilised Khrushchev's position with the Soviet Union's international reputation greatly enhanced by the launch in October 1957 of Sputnik. The world's first space satellite inspired a 1962 Number 1 bestselling instrumental tune in the USA and Britain called 'Telstar'.

Having dealt with his rivals and crushed any challenges, Khrushchev grew in confidence. His threat and bluster towards Britain and the West, however only increased with his tighter hold on power. William Taubman described, in his acclaimed biography of the Russian leader, how on a visit to Britain Khrushchev bragged petulantly to Anthony Eden's wife over dinner that: 'Soviet missiles could easily reach your island' and advised R.H. Crossman that Britain should: 'join with the Russians because, if not, they would swat us off the face off this earth like a dirty old black beetle'. Although Khrushchev boasted his ICBMs (Intercontinental Ballistic Missiles) could reach anywhere on earth, during the 1960s the Soviets only had a mere four functional ICBMs. They had no bombers that could reach the USA, and half the nuclear weapons the USA thought they had. To reduce costs in the next three years Khrushchev would reduce the Soviet Army by 2.3 million men. Khrushchev was cutting conventional forces, including Navy ships to concentrate on submarine and missile production.[46] A reckless bully by nature, Nikita looked for any signs of weakness in others which he could exploit, as his Presidium colleagues could confirm. Khrushchev had a respectful admiration for Eisenhower, however. In 1957 Khrushchev was 'over the moon' when he was granted his longed for invitation for a tour of the USA. (After its success he would withdraw his ultimatum on Berlin.) In 1960 an incident would happen which would infuriate and then delight Khrushchev.

Dressed in a tight pressure suit and white space helmet, the CIA civilian pilot Gary Powers took off (see map 1, p. 2) in his U2 aircraft No. 360 early on 1 May from a base in the Vale of Peshawar in Pakistan on a 'Green Hornet' spy mission, the twenty-fourth over the Soviet Union and the last U2 flight planned. This mission aimed to fly right across the USSR, ending in Bodø in Norway. It was a Soviet public holiday, the day of the Red Square annual military parade.

The author James Bamford described how Powers passed over Afghanistan and the Hindu Kush, until he crossed the Soviet border at 66,000ft over the Tadjik Republic. The aircraft on this CIA 'Operation GRANDSLAM' was already being tracked by Soviet radar. Khrushchev was woken at 6 a.m. to advise him that a U2 had crossed the Soviet border, heading for Sverdlovsk. The Russian leader ordered that it must be shot down: there had been too many provocative U2 flights since 1956: over Poland, Belarussia, Moscow, Leningrad and the Ukraine. Thirteen MiGs scrambled to shoot Powers down but could not attain the U2's height. It was outside their altitude range. A Soviet ground-to-air rocket, meant for Powers' U2 then hit and destroyed one of the MiG-19s.

Powers was closing fast on his first photographic and radar interception target over the Tyuratam Missile Test Range. (This was the site from where Yuri Gagarin would blast off in his Vostok 1 rocket in April 1961.) As he switched on his Polaroid cameras, however, an S-75 Dvina (SA-2) surface-to-air missile exploded in a fireball behind him, damaging the tail and wings. His aircraft went into a spin from 70,000ft, his cockpit lost pressurisation and his suit inflated. Powers decided to disobey his orders to destroy the aircraft and, at 34,000ft, climbed out of the cockpit. In his haste to get out, Powers had not disconnected his airhoses. Luckily, they separated and after pulling his parachute handle, he floated slowly down towards Russia, before landing on a collective farm near a bemused peasant. In an NSA listening post in Turkey the operators who had been intercepting Soviet radar signals during Powers' flight had suddenly seen the U2 vanish from Soviet radar screens.[47] The shooting down of the Ultra-Secret U2 spy plane and the capture of the pilot Francis Gary Powers created an international incident, satisfied Khrushchev and severely embarrassed Eisenhower.

Two weeks later Khrushchev flew to Paris for the long-awaited four-power conference with de Gaulle, Macmillan and Eisenhower. At the Elysée Palace Khrushchev ranted against 'his friend' Eisenhower's U2 spying in an abusive, irate speech that insulted Ike, annulled his planned visit to Moscow and rejected the possibility of any meaningful negotiations. De Gaulle commented dryly to Khrushchev that the satellite he had launched before leaving Moscow had since overflown French sky eighteen times without his permission, possibly taking pictures. When Khrushchev denied this, de Gaulle remarked that a Soviet satellite's camera had photographed the far side of the moon. The summit was a failure. Khrushchev refused to attend a second session and departed for Moscow in a fit of pique, leaving Eisenhower to declare that Khrushchev was a scoundrel and that it was time 'to cut the tail off the cat'. [48]

In June 1961 Khrushchev would have his first meeting with Eisenhower's successor in Vienna. He would seriously misjudge John F. Kennedy's character and resolve. Kennedy would prove to be a more resilient character than Khrushchev had realised. During the Cuban Crisis Kennedy would rise to the Russian showman's challenge and prove, in the end, to be his nemesis. For Khrushchev, his Cuban misadventure would turn out to be the pride before the fall.

Chapter 22

Military Attaché, Sofia and Berlin Wall, 1961–2

JBS expressed his thoughts on his return to Sofia after twelve years' absence:

> I arrived in Bulgaria for the first time in December 1948, when the show trials were in full swing. They had just hanged the courageous Nikola Petkov, and were about to stage the trial of twenty-five Protestant pastors. I returned to Bulgaria for the second time twelve years later, in 1961. In total, I had spent nearly three years in the country and the opportunity of being able to compare the regime from its infancy in 1948 to the stage it had reached in 1961 was perhaps unique. To have merit, any evaluation of Bulgaria under Communism must be objective. Objectivity, however, is difficult in considering any possible merit in a system which is properly recognised as basically bad. Ideally, the development of the country should be measured apart from the political system. An objective comparison of the economic, educational and social status of Bulgaria from 1948 up to my second tour indicated that measurable progress had been made in these fields. The question which is difficult to answer is, of course, whether comparable or greater progress would have been made under another political system. If you beat people over the head for sixteen hours a day, then there will undoubtedly be material progress. The price the individual has to pay is rigid control of all his actions, dissolution of the family, subservience to a foreign power, and submission to injustice and oppression. In the non-Communist world where progress is not incompatible with freedom, such a price is unthinkable. But the Bulgarian can only compare the Communist system with the dictatorship of

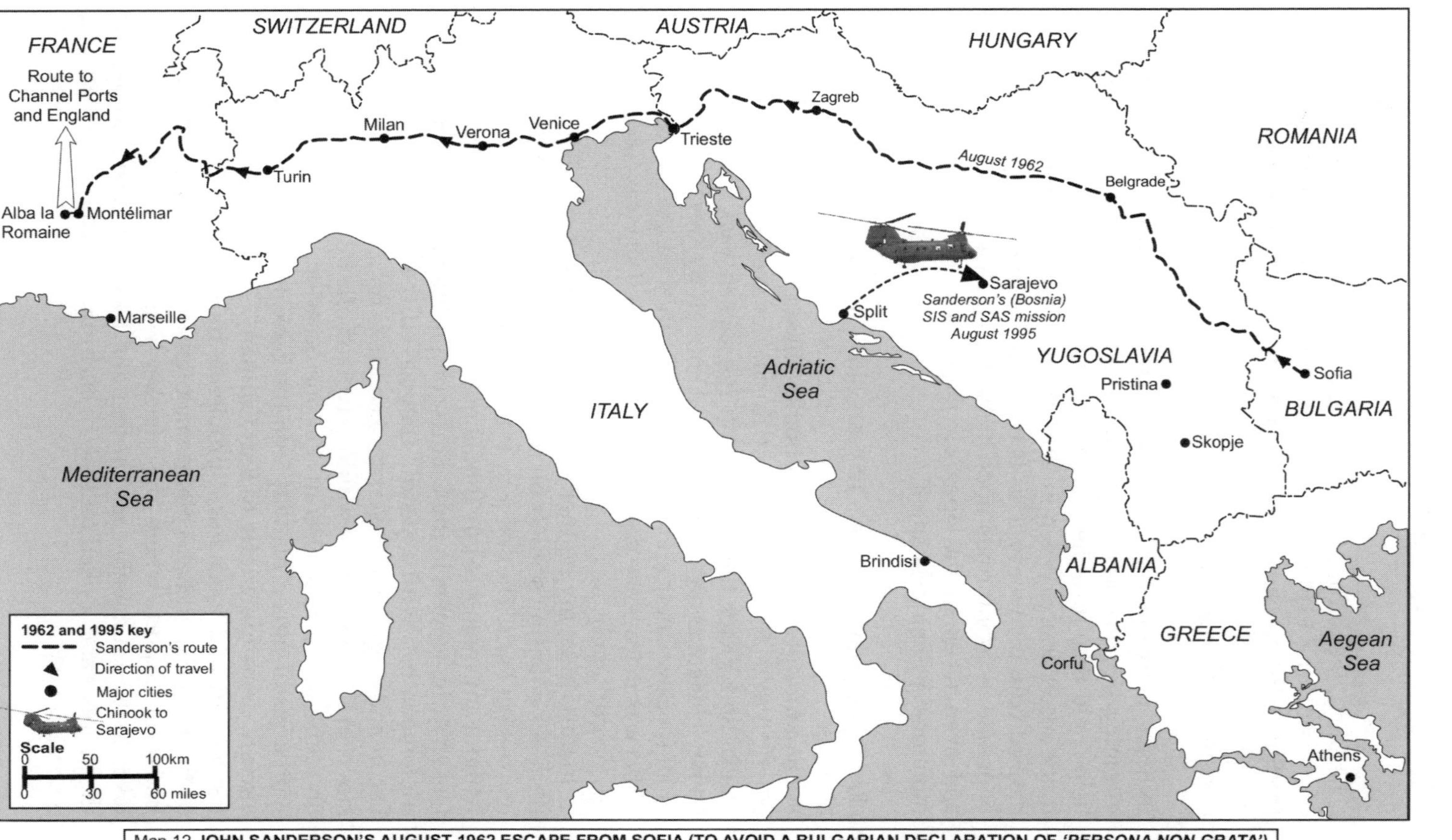

Map 12 **JOHN SANDERSON'S AUGUST 1962 ESCAPE FROM SOFIA (TO AVOID A BULGARIAN DECLARATION OF *'PERSONA NON GRATA'*) including J.B.S'S LAST SIS MISSION: SARAJEVO IN 1995 DURING THE BALKAN WAR**

> Czar Boris, the terror of Imro, and the Turkish occupation. Since oppression and exploitation have been the historical heritage of the Bulgar, he has simply exchanged one master for another.

John's regimental colleague noted in 2018:

> In Sofia, where he had a difficult time, John always left a few incoming personal letters lying around the house. His domestic help could then meet her commitment to reporting information to the secret police. When in Sofia the walls of their house were daubed with the words 'This is the house of the aggressor'. The population was informed upon by those in their apartment block and even when in the open air their conversations could be monitored by being 'beamed'.

John Sanderson's daughter was 12 years old at the time:

> We had four people to help at home: Milka our petite maid, her elderly White Russian husband Kosta, our well-rounded cook Slavka and Victor the driver with his slicked back Teddy boy hairstyle! He was an amiable thug. Although we were very fond of all four, we knew and they knew, that they had to spy on us. Milka was in tears one day when she confessed she was forced to spy on our family.
>
> In the winter, my brother and I used to travel out to Bulgaria from our boarding schools on the Orient Express via the British embassy in Paris. The embassy staff put us aboard the train: once without any money to buy food. Luckily we met up with the two Queen's Messengers in the Guards compartment, protecting the diplomatic bag with a pistol. They saved the day by cooking bacon and eggs for two starving children on a small camping stove. In the summer we would travel to Sofia by plane, usually on a virtually empty aircraft. On one occasion, though, a man with a pistol forced his way into the cockpit and hijacked the aircraft, demanding it fly to East Germany. The pilot pretended the aircraft had mechanical problems, by shutting down one of the engines, and the plane made an emergency landing at Budapest airport, where the hijacker was overpowered and taken away. I remember my brother and I were not alarmed by the incident and looked on it as an exciting opportunity to visit a new country.

> In Sofia our best friends were the children from the American Embassy whose father was head of the CIA. We would often accompany our parents on trips to Varna on the Black Sea and other areas. We were always aware of being followed by the Bulgarian secret police, who we called 'the Georges'. I remember my father crossing the border into Greece and bringing back boxes of oranges which he distributed to children outside our house who had never eaten oranges before. Crossing over to Greece was quite an experience. On the Bulgarian side nothing but a bleak landscape with grim-looking soldiers with guns in wooden lookout posts and then, just a few yards over the border, the contrast of lush, green vegetation and the welcoming smiles of the Greek border guards, offering us refreshments of lemonade and fresh watermelon! The large department store in Sofia was very dismal and the shelves were virtually empty of goods, apart from locally carved wooden boxes and rosewater perfume. The streets of Sofia were spotless: every morning the cobbled streets were washed down. Dogs were not encouraged. I don't remember seeing any dogs, except for our little dachshund who was shot in the end when my father had to leave the country in haste. My father was very fond of Bulgaria and the Bulgarians and I am sure it was his dream to see them part of Europe. He always wanted to return to this beautiful country but sadly never did.

Sofia is located at an altitude of 2,300ft on a curved plain, surrounded by mountains. It has hot summers and very cold winters with the March melted snow turning the streets into a wet slush. Nevsky Cathedral's 50m-high dome, visible throughout Sofia, contains 8kg of gold. Its twelve Moscow-made bells can be heard from 30km away. Sofia has wide avenues, bordered with trees. Mount Vitosha to the south dominates the city.[1]

When Colonel John Sanderson arrived in Sofia on 20 April 1961, twelve years after his first posting to the Legation, British Intelligence was busy debriefing a Russian agent who would prove a very valuable asset in Moscow in the coming Cuban Missile Crisis. At 11 p.m. on the very same day, Colonel Oleg Penkovsky was quietly knocking on the door of Room 360, a specially reserved suite at the Mount Hotel in London.[2] He had slipped away from his Soviet party, who were staying in the same hotel. This was Penkovsky's first meeting with Western Intelligence (two CIA and two MI6 agents), after many unsuccessful attempts to make contact in Moscow. The fruits of his espionage were to prove invaluable for the West, not only for the successful resolution of the Cuban Missile Crisis, in which John Sanderson was to play his part in the Intelligence Division of NATO, but also for a complete reappraisal of NATO tactics and strategy. The young Lieutenant Colonel Penkovsky also dealt a heavy blow to Russian Intelligence, by identifying 600 Soviet intelligence officers, 550 of whom were GRU Soviet military intelligence officers like himself.[3]

By coincidence, whilst a Russian spy was being debriefed in London, a British traitor was being confronted. When George Blake arrived at MI6's Broadway HQ two weeks previously, interrogator Harold Shergold told him: 'There are a few things we'd like to discuss with you about your work in Berlin. Certain problems have arisen.' Blake had been identified through information supplied by a Polish defector, Michal Goleniewski. Blake was soon to confess that he had copied the Berlin station chief Peter Lunn's card index of agents and that he had betrayed 500–600 Allied agents, as well as the entire MI6 OB (Order of Battle).[4] Goleniewski also blew the covers of Gordon Lonsdale and his espionage ring. Lonsdale was an illegal, born a Russian named Konon Trofimovich Molody, who had adopted the identity of a dead Canadian and moved to London in 1955 to take a Chinese course at the School of Oriental and African Studies, hoping to recruit fellow students. Molody ran a large network of Soviet agents, (most of whom were never caught), including the Cohens (Peter and Helen Kroger) and Harry Houghton who, with Ethel Gee, had access to top-secret information on nuclear submarines and anti-sub warfare. Molody also ran an unidentified agent inside Porton Down, the Microbiological Research Establishment. They were all jailed in 1961.[5] Molody was eventually exchanged in April 1964, at the Heerstrasse checkpoint in Berlin, with Greville Wynne, the British accomplice of Colonel Penkovsky, who had served only one year of his eight-year sentence for espionage.[6] Five years previously Penkovsky had served in Turkey as a Military Attaché. In 1961, the First Secretary of the Soviet Embassy in Ankara was a Brigadier General Sudin, in charge of 'illegal residents' (spies) within Turkey, some of whom were Bulgarians. Penkovsky was a friend of 'Sudakov's (Sudin's alias) and would have passed over to his SIS handlers useful intelligence on Bulgarian espionage in Turkey, picked up in conversations with his high-ranking friend.[7]

C/O The Foreign Office London S.W.1 Sofia 12th June 1961.

Dear Family, We have now just returned from sailing down the Danube in a little ferry steamer, from Vidin to Silistra. We thoroughly enjoyed it, although it was disappointing to find the Danube very muddy and brown, and not at all like Strauss'

> 'Blue Danube Waltz'. The river here runs between Romania and Bulgaria with monotonous green trees and swamps, with only the occasional hill on the Bulgarian side. It poured with rain all the time, so perhaps we didn't see the Danube at its best. We disembarked at Silistra, a small town, and drove on to Varna on the Black Sea. We were last there twelve years ago, when there was only one hotel for tourists. Now it has developed into a lovely resort with good clean hotels amidst trees and gardens, soft sandy beaches and clear blue sea (not black!) We were on the shore at 7 a.m. to find it already covered with Bulgarian holiday makers. It seems no hotel serves any form of refreshment, not even morning tea or mineral water. We never leave home without tea-making equipment, a frying pan and eggs and bacon, and usually manage to cook up an English breakfast in the hotel bedroom in rainy days, or by the roadside when the sun shines. From Varna we drove to the Balkan mountains, over the Shipka pass, at least 5,000ft through the clouds, and down across the Valley of the Roses. It is from these plants that the famous Attar of Roses is distilled from the many thousands of rose petals. We stayed one night at Tarnovo, the old capital of Bulgaria – the hotel was perched on a hillside and the nightingales were singing all the evening. John.

James Reeve of the FO's northern department knew both Denis Greenhill and John Sanderson well. In January 1959 Reeve had joined the FCO as desk officer for Hungary, Romania and Bulgaria. He worked in the 'Third Room', as it was called, until 1962. (The Moscow Centre's codename for the Foreign Office was *zaboulok*, 'the back alley'.) Reeve explained in George Rendel's book *The Sword and the Olive* that his department was responsible for Britain's relations with the USSR and the Warsaw Pact satellites. At the height of the Cold War, it was a prestigious department whose head, Tom Brimelow (later ambassador in Moscow and finally head of the FO), was one of the world's leading Kremlinologists. 'The northern department had two assistant heads, Nicholas Henderson, who was responsible for all direct aspects of bilateral relations with the Soviet Union, and Christopher MacAlpine, who supervised our section, which included Byran Cartledge, who became ambassador to Moscow under Mikhail Gorbachev.'[8] The role of desk officers was to give guidance and information to their relevant legations or embassies on their duties vis-à-vis government policies. They also liaised with other Whitehall departments.

Reeve noted that 'in the background were the veiled activities of the intelligence world'. Soviet and Western authorities carefully vetted diplomats' visas and monitored their movements once in post. Diplomatic incidents also arose over the bugging of their conversations. Reeve explained how months of FO negotiations and planning, within Whitehall and between allies, could be frustrated by international incidents. Examples were: the disruption of Khrushchev's Paris conference by Gary Powers' U2 flight; the unauthorised and fatal dive by Commander Crabb under a Russian warship in Portsmouth harbour; the deaths of British passengers in an Israeli aircraft shot down by Bulgaria. Reeve's department also provided advice for British citizens, including businessmen, who travelled to Eastern bloc countries and ran the risk of being compromised by their security services. Ways of entrapping visitors included being entertained by call girls in bugged hotel rooms, equipped with two-way mirrors and hidden video cameras.[9]

JBS described one attempted *operativinaya igri* ('honey pot') on his wife in Paris:

> The Bulgarian authorities had evidently heard of my later posting to NATO in Paris. In 1963 my wife, accompanied by our children, was window shopping on the Champs Elysées when she was approached by a man (whom she later described as being exceptionally handsome!), who attempted, rather clumsily she thought, to strike up a conversation with her in Bulgarian and English. It was a known ploy of the Bulgarian secret service to try to build a relationship and compromise spouses of military men.

Reeve noted: 'There were rarely any exchanges of consequence with London embassies of Eastern bloc countries: some incident or other, such as a Military Attaché shot at, would make nonsense of vague suggestions that bilateral relations could be improved.' Reeve then described the situation of Military Attachés and cameras, no doubt referring to John Sanderson in Sofia, whose SIS defence activities he undoubtedly disproved of:

> A member of one of my client embassies expressed indignation at the lack of fair play in the shadowy activities of defence attachés. We had scolded their attaché in the UK for taking pictures of his children on a picnic that happened to be within telescopic range of an American base. Meanwhile, our attaché in the Balkans was said to be behaving provocatively. My East European colleague

> explained that it was often the practice for his country to provide an unobtrusive escort for Colonel X and his driver in case of mishap. It seemed, however, that the engines of the early Skoda cars used by the minders were not very robust. Our attaché's driver had taken to travelling at a very low speed for the first few miles of any journey, which had a dire effect on the cooling system of the car behind. He would then accelerate off at a high speed.[10]

One incident described by Sanderson's daughter describes the result of such a minor incident on the Bulgarian roads:

> Our family were driving on holiday to Varna. It was dusk when a single sheep ran across the road and was hit by our car. My father got out, pulled the animal's body to the side of the road and walked up to the shepherd in the field to offer him a handful of Leva banknotes as compensation. The old man shook his head and refused the money, saying: 'Don't worry. These sheep don't belong to me. They are owned by the state.' The secret police following our car were less nonchalant, however. That evening in Varna they spent hours in the lobby of the hotel attempting to browbeat our father into signing a long form, admitting his responsibility for destroying Bulgarian state property. He obviously refused and they gave up in the end. There was an amusing incident that evening. My father demonstrated how our hotel room was 'bugged'. He said in a loud voice to my mother: 'They never provide any towels in these hotel rooms.' Five minutes later there was a knock on the door and a maid appeared with a pile of clean towels!

A regimental colleague recalls an incident with the Bulgarian traffic police:

> John was driving along in a residential area of Sofia, when he was overtaken and pulled over by the police and asked to explain why, with a 'NO ENTRY' sign displayed on the road, he had contravened the traffic rule. Local residents came out of their apartments to witness this altercation between a foreigner and the police. Of course, the situation had been stage-managed, with the police placing the traffic sign on the road after his vehicle had passed.[11]

Sir David Omand, a former UK Intelligence and Security Co-ordinator put on record that: 'Intelligence during the Cold War had a very big impact on the shape and size of the British defence programme and on the kinds of equipment we bought and the actual capabilities we built into that equipment, to counter whatever intelligence showed was the capability of the Warsaw Pact forces.' During the Korean War Americans hit exactly this type of equipment failure, when their bazooka and anti-tank rounds were ineffective against the latest well-armoured T-34/85 tanks.[12]

Tony Geraghty described how careful investigation can alter battle tactics. When BRIXMIS soldiers were on tour in the GDR in 1982 they obtained a top-secret manual. This was a lucky find. Amongst rubbish dumped by departing Russian soldiers near the back gate of their barracks was a private logbook full of technical drawings and top-secret detailed information on the specific armour and capabilities of the latest T-64 tank and even the new T-80. This was judged the most important technical intelligence for a decade. The MOD hastened to distribute large quantities of effective new counter-armaments: 1,400 heavy and medium APDFS (armour piercing 'long rod penetrator') anti-tank missiles and 2,500 hand-held anti-tank weapons.[13]

The brief of a Military (Defence) Attaché is to scrutinise a country's military preparedness for a conflict, to establish diplomatic relationships and build trust with his military counterparts from other countries as well as the host nation, and to provide military advice and operational assistance to the MOD, the security services and other government departments. He can also facilitate the entry of British troops into a foreign country. If a covert operation is required, the Attaché can be closely involved in the preparations. Where the opportunity arises, or where he is requested to approach a target individual, a Military Attaché will attempt to recruit opposition intelligence officers as double agents. In Bulgaria this was difficult. Russian and Soviet bloc officers of equivalent rank were well 'looked after' by their respective government and enjoyed an excellent standard of living with preferential treatment at home. Furthermore, defecting would put their family and relatives at home at risk of retribution. *JBS* made one 'pitch' to a Russian officer in Sofia, as told to the author: 'I asked him directly: "Why not come and work for us?" He replied patriotically: "Why should I, John? I have my family in Russia, a good army pension and a dacha in the country. Why should I give all that up for an uncertain future abroad?"'

Western intelligence agencies were rarely successful in recruiting KGB personnel so directly. Most new double agents were 'walk-ins' who offered to spy or defect with information, such as Colonel Penkovsky.

17a

17b

17c

17d

18a

18b

18c

18d

18e

DEMOLITION AND ASSAULT PIONEER COURSE,
ROORKEE – NOV. 1944.

C. A. ACHIESON

SHERMAN.

4 STOOGES.

HAMILTON BRIDGE

MAURICE DOWNHAM.

20a

20b

20c

20d

20e

21a

Hitler's bunker in January 1946. Miss Audrey Jones, Captain John Sanderson's future wife, stands at the position marked 'GARDEN' in the map below. The allied officer in the background points out the spot where Adolf Hitler and Eva Braun's bodies were doused with petrol and burned on 30th April 1945. (Marked 'X' on map below.)This act was witnessed by Erich Mansfield, on police guard in the unfinished concrete tower on right.

21b

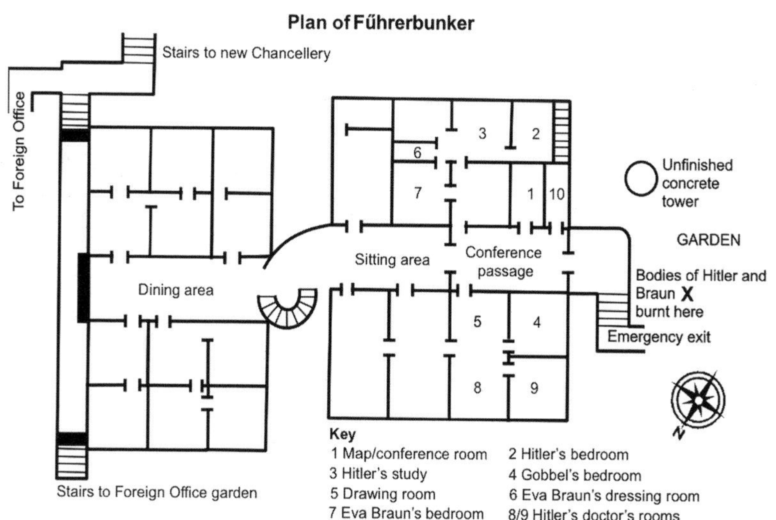

21c

THE OFFICERS
OF THE 1st BN. THE YORK AND LANCASTER REGT.
BERLIN JULY 1947.

22a

22b

22c

22d

23a

23b

23c

23d

23e

24a

You will make us a visit at Marly and have a cup of tea with us.
Yours sincerely
B. Sawochinsky

Château des Ombrages — MARLY-LE-ROI (S.-et-O.) - Tél. 120

24b

24c

24d

24e

24f

Bataillons du Ciel
QUI OSE GAGNE
23e T. №178.390
1/10
LOTERIE NATIONALE
B

LOTERIE NATIONALE

24g

London MIA 1948
and JBS
PHOTO BY:- CRAINE, ROCHE & Co.
72a BLANDFORD ST., BAKER ST., W.1.

25a

BULGARIAN TRIALS REPUDIATED

Confessions "Suspect"

A statement is likely to be made by the Foreign Office to-day on the case of Mr Denis Greenhill, First Secretary of the British Legation in Sofia, whose name was mentioned during the recent trial of Bulgarian pastors. Reports from Sofia have suggested that the Bulgarian Government have decided to declare Mr Greenhill persona non grata.

In view of the British Note to Bulgaria repudiating the "confessions" in so far as they affect alleged activities by the British Legation, the expulsion of a British diplomat might well be followed by reciprocal action against a member of the Bulgarian Legation in London.

Pastor Vasil Ziapkov, the chief accused, who received a life sentence, testified (according to Reuter) that he gave Mr Greenhill information on Black Sea coastal defences. The British Note declared that the whole of the testimony of the so-called "confessions" was suspect.

25b

25c

25d

Министерството на външните работи удостоверява, че Г Полк. Джон Бърден Сандерсън - военен аташе при легацията на Великобритания в София

22. III. 1961 г.

Директор на протокола

Пълномощен министър

25e

Министерството на външните работи удостоверява, че Г-жа Одрей М. Сандерсън, съпруга на полк. Джон Сандерсън, военен аташе при легацията на Великобритания в София

№ 22. III. 1961 г.

Директор на протокола

Пълномощен министър

25f

25g

26a

26b

26c

26d

26e

26f

27a

27b

27c

27d

28a

28b

28c

28d

28e

28f

29a

29b

im Gespräch mit dem Chef der russischen Militärmission, General Sawitzki

29c

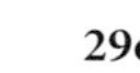

29d

30a

30b

30c

30d

30e

31a

ACHTUNG
Sie verlassen jetzt
West-Berlin

31b

31c

31d

31e

31f

John Burden Sanderson
1921-2001

32a

32b

32c

32d

32e

32f

32g

Stephen Dorril noted that the FO was increasingly bringing MI6 under its control, with traditional ties to the armed forces being downgraded. In 1964 the service intelligence directorates were combined with the JIB (Joint Intelligence Bureau) as the DIS (Defence Intelligence Staff). With Ministry of Defence cutbacks, military officers were no longer to be seconded to MI6. Before his retirement as 'C' in 1966, Dick White would begin to reorganise and to plan the modern SIS. Stations around the world would have to be closed with only seven controllers covering the main areas. This reorganisation would make mounting operations abroad harder.[14]

A previously classified CIA document shows that John faced an uphill task in trying to recruit the Russian colonel who was obviously a family man and patriot. At this time the CIA were learning from the mercurial, unstable but courageous Colonel Oleg Penkovsky but questioned his motives: 'Who are the people that dream of power and glory, and not only frustrated in these dreams but perhaps even ridiculed in their daily lives, become so bitter as to turn their backs on family, friends and nation? . . . A normal, mature, emotionally healthy person, deeply embedded in his own ethnic, national cultural, social and family matrix just doesn't do such things.[15] Colonel Oleg Gordievsky would be one of these exceptions.

As regards diplomatic functions, the round of dinners and cocktail parties that the Western diplomats gave for each other had a dual role: they enabled fruitful discussions and the discreet sharing of information, and provided a relaxing, convivial environment to enjoy the company of other friendly nationalities. For those with a sense of humour, it could provide endless sources of amusement, as *JBS* revealed:

> I was once taken aside at the end of a dinner party by our French host. 'Did you not enjoy the food, John?' she enquired. 'Au contraire,' I replied, 'it was delicious.' The host then pointed out the uneaten chicken legs lying under the chair I had just vacated. The penny dropped: the arm I had noticed moving under the dinner table was that of the Turkish Ambassador, surreptitiously throwing his unwanted chicken legs under my chair, presumably to apportion blame elsewhere.
>
> One event illustrates the crude methods the Bulgarian authorities employed to spy on Western diplomats. At the beginning of a drinks party which we were organising, I noticed a young attractive Bulgarian woman, aged about 20 years old, standing inside the gate of our walled garden.

'I'm very sorry.' she said in Bulgarian, evidently flustered and embarrassed. 'I'm so sorry to tell you this, but I have been ordered to invite myself to your party.'

'Well, you're very welcome to come in', I replied, inviting her inside to join our party. The young lady mingled and, in spite of our warm welcome, evidently felt rather awkward at a cocktail party full of strangers, Of course, nobody would have been discussing secrets at a drinks party. However, no doubt later her controller would have congratulated himself on what a clever affair he had stage-managed.

Following the first Sputnik placed in orbit in October 1957 and Laika the dog's flight in September in a three-stage rocket, the Soviets were manifestly ahead in the space race. Three years later Sputnik V showed they could bring the passenger back alive. On 12 April 1961 Major Yuri Gagarin became the first man to orbit the earth. As his 30m-high Vostok 1 rocket blasted off from Tyuratam missile range he yelled '*Poyekhali*!'('Here we go!'). His flight lasted only 108 minutes. During Gagarin's descent, the hatch of his spacecraft was released at a height of 7km and his ejection seat thrust out of the capsule. A farmer and his daughter watched a man in a helmet and bright orange suit float down by parachute and land nearby. Reassuring them, Gagarin called out: 'Don't be afraid, I am a Soviet like you, who has descended from space and I must find a telephone to call Moscow.'[16]

The next month Commander Alan Shepherd made a 115-mile space flight, followed by Captain Virgil Grissom in July. Major Herman Titov outdid them both on 6 August by flying seventeen orbits in Vostok 11. When Gagarin made a visit to Sofia, John Sanderson was there, with other Western diplomats, to attend his welcome parade. The foreign Military Attachés were also invited to a military training establishment where the exploits of the Soviet Socialist space achievements were exhibited. Yuri Gagarin's photo was proudly displayed (see 27a in the plates). Ten years later the Russians would launch Salyut 1, the first space station. After Soyuz 1 had docked successfully, three cosmonauts spent twenty-four days aboard Salyut. Tragedy struck when the crew separated their orbital module for the return to earth: malfunction caused a loss of atmosphere and they perished in less than a minute. For Russia, the loss was on a par with the USA's grief for President Kennedy.

Khrushchev had been threatening to deal with the issue of a divided Berlin for years. In 1958 he had graphically explained how he would heighten the tension in Europe: 'The leaders of the United States are not such idiots to fight over Berlin . . . Berlin is the testicles of the West, every time I want to make the West scream, I squeeze on Berlin.'[17] The Allies had made clear their resolve to stay in Berlin. John Dulles had told Chancellor Adenauer in 1959 that if the Soviet Union threatened the Allies' rights in Berlin, then it would be a war 'in which we obviously would not forego the use of nuclear weapons'.[18] Adenauer was horrified. In the same year Khrushchev had told Averell Harriman, the US Ambassador in Moscow: 'Your General is talking of tanks and guns defending your Berlin position. They would burn . . . but we don't want to go to war over Berlin.'[19] Although in March Khrushchev had advised Ulbricht it was too dangerous to build a wall, he finally authorised it, but the preparations had to be in secrecy. Khrushchev was driven around East and West Berlin anonymously to inform himself of the layout of the city.[20] President Kennedy had underlined Allied resolve over Berlin in June 1960 when he had told Khrushchev that the national security of the USA was directly linked to that of Berlin. Khrushchev had declared furiously: 'I want peace, but if you want war that is your problem.'[21]

By 1960 the flow of refugees across to the West (Republikflucht was a criminal offence) had increased from 144,000 in 1959 to 200,000. In Berlin the following year, on 12/13 August 1961, barbed wire was unrolled and laid as the first stage of the Berlin Wall. Three days later East German workers removed all the cobblestones in Potsdamer Platz, erected concrete walls, and finally sealed off the 103-mile border around Berlin. On 27 October thirty-three Soviet tanks drove up and positioned themselves at the Brandenburg Gate. Only one crossing point now remained for Western staff, Checkpoint Charlie. When a US diplomat was denied access to East Germany, on General Clay's orders ten US M-48 tanks drew up 50yd from the border, racing their engines. In response ten Russian T-55 tanks roared up to face the M-48s 100yd away. The US gunners loaded live shells. Khrushchev ordered any force to be met with force. The stand-off continued for 16 hours until Kennedy contacted Khrushchev to defuse the situation. One T-55 started its engines and withdrew 5yd. A US tank did likewise. All tanks then withdrew, one by one. A Hot War was averted.[22] By the time the wall was built, one in seven of the East German population, a total of 2½ million refugees, had headed West. Subsequently, a thousand were killed trying to escape. The wall caused disruption to those living in the East near the Berlin Wall. The majority of the 120,000 were obliged to abandon their dwellings to make space for a 'death' strip several hundred metres wide.[23]

Colonel Penkovsky of the GRU had for some time been passing over intelligence on Soviet military preparations in the Soviet Union and the GDR, including the entire Soviet military plan for a possible conflict in

Berlin. As Sanderson explained, Penkovsky was continuously feeding back to his MI6 handlers the Soviet reaction to the firm line the West were taking over Berlin.[24] This was reiterated in Corera's book:

> At the time of the Berlin Wall construction in 1961, Penkovsky had been able to reassure MI6 and the CIA about Khrushchev's intentions and whether he was prepared or not to go to war: 'They are not ready,' Penkovsky had explained, 'Khrushchev's statements about this are all bluff . . . The reasoning is simply this, to strike one sharp blow, let a little blood flow and the Americans and British will be frightened and withdraw. This is what he is banking on.'[25]

In 1961 Colonel Oleg Vladimirovich Penkovsky would use a Minox camera to photograph Soviet plans for the military use of outer space, including senior Soviet commanders' paperwork on 'projects such as global rockets, photo reconnaissance by orbiting satellites and manned space command posts'.[26]

Shortly before the Cuban Missile Crisis and a year into his second tour in Bulgaria as a full Colonel Military, Naval and Air Attaché (at 41 years old, one of the youngest colonels in the British Army), Sanderson received instructions from London to investigate and obtain photographic images of a MiG fighter jet known to be in Bulgaria. He was well-trained in the use of a miniature Minox spy camera, the size of a cigarette lighter that would fit into the palm of his hand. London were interested in developments of the Mikoyan-Gurevich MiG-21F supersonic jet fighter aircraft (NATO codename 'Fishbed' and nicknamed '*balalaika*', or 'pencil', by Polish pilots for the shape of its fuselage). The MiG-21F was introduced in 1959 and served for decades, being produced in Gorky, Moscow and Tbilisi. The K-13 9 missiles, NATO codename ATOLL, carried by the aircraft were introduced in 1960 as 'reverse engineered' copies of a US AIM-19 Sidewinder that the Chinese had delivered to the Russians. Western Intelligence was particularly keen to discover the capability of MiGs and their armaments: successful aerial surveillance above the CCCP (Russian abbreviation for the Soviet Union) depended on their spy-planes' invulnerability to Soviet missiles. The shooting down in 1960 of the Ultra-Secret U-2 spy plane by a surface-to-air missile from a MiG-19-P and the capture of the USAF pilot Francis Gary Powers had created an international incident.[27] As the regimental colleague of Sanderson recollected in 2018:

> In August 1962, in a bold attempt to take photographs of a latest model MiG, John arranged with his American (CIA) opposite number to drive in the middle of the night, with a tail of police or other enemy. John bowled out of the car, in a parachute roll, the US guy driving on, outside a military airbase. When the light came up and aircraft were taking off, he started to photograph the planes. The police arrived. He had to expose his film, celluloid in those days, and he was arrested.'[28]

Sanderson was in a very difficult situation now and he knew that to avoid being declared PNG and to save his country the embarrassment of a highly publicised diplomat exchange he would have to act quickly and leave the country immediately.

This plan was not without risk. In one rather precarious incident in Hungary, Sanderson and the British Military Attaché from Romania were caught up by a car which shadowed them, driven by the secret police which then attempted to run them off the road, luckily without success. As a further example of the Bulgarian Secret Service's callousness, there was the unexpected death, some months after Sanderson's return to Britain, of an effective Western Military Attaché diplomat in Sofia, a family friend, well known to the author. Sanderson was informed later that the Bulgarians had concealed a radioactive substance under this diplomat's bed (evidence of which must have been detected by representatives of the victim's country). John Sanderson explained that the officer's death from cancer, some months afterwards, was believed to be connected to his exposure to the concealed radioactive material. (Account given separately to the author by both John and Audrey Sanderson.)

It was a 'Cold War' but could still be a cruel war. The Bulgarian Secret Service was a ruthless organisation with a long reach, as the assassination of Markov in London later demonstrated. When the Bulgarian Police had arrested Sanderson at the airport perimeter, they were forced to release him since he had 'diplomatic immunity'. He expected to be declared PNG, a stigma that he was very keen to avoid. Sanderson returned to his house in Obirishte Street in Sofia and informed his wife that they would have to leave the country immediately, taking with them only a change of clothes and leaving all their possessions and their dog behind. This news was obviously an unwelcome surprise for Audrey but she stoically agreed. They drove at speed to the Yugoslav border, only 35 miles away, and succeeded in leaving the country, before the border guards could be alerted by the central authorities in Sofia. John must have felt that their safety and security was threatened, even when the Bulgarian border was crossed. They drove in haste across Yugoslavia, still a Communist country, on the good roads to Belgrade. From there, they drove through Italy to Montélimar in the south of France. *JBS* felt their situation was still precarious and that the Bulgarians might still be in pursuit:

> Once on French territory, we drove straight to the Ardèche region of France, where my sister Pat lived near Montélimar. To provide us with the safe cover of four passengers and a child instead of a couple, she agreed to join us, accompanied by her baby daughter and her husband, a former wartime SBS (Special Boat Section) commando, on the drive up to a Channel port and the safety of a ferry bound for England.

In November 2008 John's sister Patricia wrote:

> I remember very clearly my brother and his wife arriving unexpectedly in Alba la Romaine. My husband Vere [Holden-White] and I had moved there in 1958 to be part of an international group of painters-writers-sculptors. The Ardèche had lost more men in the First World War than any other departément. Old stone houses were there to be rebuilt into studios and homes. One day, suddenly, my brother John arrived at my door: 'Come on Pat – bring your daughter – we are off to England – "returning tourists"'. My husband immediately understood and helped pack a few clothes.

Major Vere Holden-White relished the opportunity for adventure. He had been awarded his MC whilst serving with the SBS, his citation signed by Earl Mountbatten. Vere was originally in the Royal Sussex Regt but had left to join the SBS section of No. 2 Commando, whose task was sabotage, reconnaissance of enemy coastlines and landing of agents in hostile territories. In November 1942 he led an SBS team to reconnoitre sites for the Allied North Africa landings near Oran in Algeria and to test a new weapon, a mini-torpedo which could be fired from a canoe, eliminating the dangerous task of fixing limpet mines to ships' hulls. Under fire from shore batteries and machine guns, the canoeists disembarked from naval cutters and paddled into Oran harbour, where they fired their torpedoes at an enemy ship and then a submarine, without effect because of the distance. Landing ashore, they were immediately captured by Vichy sailors but later freed by advancing US troops. In April 1944 he was posted to India where he trained as a parachutist, before carrying out raids against the Japanese on the Arakan coast and patrolling the Burmese rivers, earning himself a mention in dispatches. After the war Vere studied painting at Chelsea School of Art, where he met Patricia Sanderson, a talented painter who had won the Prix de Rome. Patricia's account continues:

> We set off without delay, just as we were, in T shirts and shorts – off we went! On the ship, John went off immediately to see the captain. When he returned, he was smartly dressed in a suit the captain had kindly loaned him. My brother John later said, that his return without incident, was well-received and thanked me for my help. What tension for John, and his wife Audrey also, who was always wonderful and played a great part in helping John.[29]

Once successfully on board, Sanderson contacted the ship's Captain to communicate with London. On docking, he dropped off his sister's family and headed straight up to London to be debriefed at the Foreign Office, following his letter of instruction of 25 November 1960, when departing to Sofia. Instructions from the SIS were very clear: 'Each time you return to this country you will report yourself to the Director of Military Intelligence as well as to the Director of Naval Intelligence, in your capacity as Naval Attaché and to the Assistant Chief of Staff (Intelligence) in your capacity as Air Attaché'. It was a great 'feather in his cap' that Sanderson had managed to return to England without being PNG'd, without publicity and without incident. In spite of his failure to obtain a photo of the Russian MiG, the incident did not damage his career. His annual Confidential Report for 1962 made by Brigadier Green, Deputy Director of MI6, Military Intelligence, the War Office read:

> Lieutenant-Colonel Sanderson continued to give excellent service as Military Attaché, Sofia, up to August 1962, when his recall was demanded by the Bulgarian Government. The reason for this action may have arisen owing to over-confidence (and an error of judgement) on the part of Colonel Sanderson, but it was probably due to bad luck as much as anything. It is certainly no reflection on his initiative and zeal. Overall, he has proved a first rate officer with plenty of energy, drive and common sense. He and his wife were both popular with and esteemed by the diplomatic community. Entirely fit for promotion to the substantive rank of Lieutenant-Colonel. 20th May 1963.

The letter below was sent from the British Legation in Sofia, from Mr Mark M., who lived on the same Sofia street as John:

> My dear John, Disposal of your effects has been difficult . . . they are now with the customs and the house is empty. Old Kosta [the cook] has joined the Legation as boilerman. Cleary [Lieutenant Colonel, US Military Attaché] spoke to me very seriously at Plovdiv where I met him at the U.S. stand. He asked me to tell you that he will be in London in October or November. He would very much like to see you (to talk shop) and, if you are already in Paris, he wondered whether the War Office would let you come back to see him. He spoke of what Henderson (and his predecessors) had done for the Americans when they were here and said that they would like to reciprocate. He was the only one left who had personal experience of that time. Henderson ought to have received a medal from them. So if you can manage it, he would be glad to see you. Perhaps the U.S. Embassy in London will know when he is coming? B. drops in quite frequently to keep us 'au fait' with military affairs but he usually reports orally which increases the risk of error when I pass this on, inexpertly to the F.O. Best wishes to you both, Yours ever, Mark

Letter dated 17 September 1962, Légation de France en Bulgarie:

> L'Attaché Militaire et de L'Air, Colonel P. Murat
>
> Dear John, We cannot express how sorry we are of what happened. Your legation was very discreet but at one M.A. meeting I asked abruptly if the Bulgarian M.A. in London was also withdrawn and he answered very openly that the thing was done, he regretted very much but . . . It is a very pity for you . . . and also for us. We lose our best friends and I lose my best colleague. Recently at one M.A. meeting where there were the two Greeks, the two Americans and Egypt, I could not help myself to get very angry and to tell them that you were the most active M.A. and we have to be thankful for you. One is soon forgotten. Surely the collaboration between the M.A.'s in Sofia will not be the same. I am very tired of our life here. The work is more and more difficult. Since two or three months, a campaign of 'vigilance' is going on in the country. You remember the two motorcars in Chenklevo. Now it is everywhere so: the civilians are working for the milice. Besides the Bulgarians were terribly sensitive in the

> south-west of the country in July and August. Unfortunately I am now the only M.A. who is annoying them.
>
> When we came back from Varna with the family three weeks ago, I discovered that the bar of stabilisations of my car was nearly broken. We nearly had a serious accident. It is a curious thing and I am today in Salonika to repair the car and to get the thing clear. Mes amitiées à tous deux, Sincerely, Paul.

Dennis Greenhill had come across this sabotaging of Western vehicles in Bulgaria 1948, thirteen years previously. Nothing had changed in this regard:

> The vehicles of the treaty enforcement military officers were frequently, dangerously sabotaged by interference with braking systems and filling the sumps with nuts and bolts and other foreign matter. No amount of protest to the authorities made the slightest difference or produced any admission of official guilt. Interference was attributed to 'spontaneous public hostility' to us. With no contact with the Bulgarian 'man in the street' . . . we found it hard to detect any hostility.[30]

Letter dated July 1962 from Lieutenant Colonel Markovich USAF (retired), former Air Attaché in Sofia:

> California, USA 26 July 1962
>
> My Dear John, Your letter was like a refreshing breeze, and I appreciate your thoughts and best wishes for my good health. So the 'Goons' are fast on your tail? I had my heart attack at the right time. Give them my 'love' (Yank style). I have a contact in India, so maybe we can get some real Indian curry, dependent upon the availability and quality. We had a very enjoyable trip from Washington to Calif, and most happy to be in the old home state. I mostly drive the Austin-Healey Sprite as the big Pontiac drinks about two thirds more petrol. I enjoy zipping around town. June sends her love to you both and wishes you all the best for the remainder of your tour, likewise old Marko. My best to all the Western types. Write when you have the opportunity, love to hear about dear old 'beloved' Glorious People Democratic Republic of Bulgaria. Thanks again John for your letter. P.S. What ever happened to the Bulgarian Pilot that landed in Italy? It smells a bit to me.

The aircraft to which Markovich was referring was a Bulgarian MiG 17 which crash-landed in January 1962 in Italy near a Jupiter IRBM (Intermediate-Range Ballistic Missile) base. The MiG was equipped with cameras and was evidently on an espionage mission when the pilot, Sub Lieutenant Solakov, misjudged his height and clipped a tree. After recuperating in hospital, Solakov was detained for a year, then returned to Sofia. Curtis Peebles noted that the Russians had been making probing flights over Western Europe for over ten years with their highest performance fighters, capable of out-accelerating the Western jets if intercepted, with their superior climbing speed. Between 1962 and 1964 there were ninety-five of these penetrations. The Soviets used Eastern bloc pilots (East German, Czech or Bulgarian) to avoid the provocation of Russian pilots being downed. The MiGs flew along their border and then made quick turns into Western airspace, whilst the Soviet ground stations monitored the opposition's radar and electronic data.[31]
Christmas greetings from US friends in Bulgaria:

> Sofia December 1962
> Dear All,
>
> This is the first time in five years that we have spent two consecutive Christmases in the same place. In 1959 we were in Frankfurt, in 1960 Berlin, arriving here in Sofia on Christmas Eve 1961. While our stay behind the Iron Curtain has been interesting to date, we are not so enthralled with this worker's paradise as to want to prolong our residence much beyond one more Christmas. The whole Yule season is officially ignored and barely tolerated here. The only star we will see shining in the heavens of Christmas Eve will be the red star atop the Communist party building.
>
> Tom is the American consul in Sofia. After a year of almost daily exposure to tales of misery, he is of the firm belief that Bulgaria is a poor and hopeless land, inhabited by people whose greatest virtue seems an infinite capacity to endure suffering. In spite of some recent changes, all power remains in the hands of almost the worst elements in the society. These people are firmly dedicated to our destruction, talk of peaceful coexistence to the contrary. To them peaceful coexistence simply means: 'Since we aren't strong enough to kill you now, we'll be peaceful while we wait for a chance.'
>
> In spite of this grim backdrop, our life here has its redeeming features. The enforced isolation from local society makes for

> very close relationships in the western diplomatic colony. In this environment so-called neutrals like Egyptians, Ghanaians and Indonesians consider themselves part of the western group. Our apartment looks from the outside like something the slum clearance project missed. By Bulgarian standards, we're very well off, with a kitchen and a bathroom of our own. We're also aristocrats when it comes to eating, since we can import food or make trips to Greece, Turkey or Yugoslavia, adjoining countries which, although poor themselves, at least have a regular and ample supply of food in the markets. There are almost no fresh fruits and vegetables on the market. A few potatoes, some of them as big as golf balls, are still available.
>
> We can be 90% sure of having a white Christmas in Sofia, albeit a grey one. The first snow blew in on November 25th and temperatures will have a hard time getting above the freezing mark for the next three months. However, the low-grade brown coal here makes for a heavy pall of smog, guaranteeing that the snow does not stay white very long.
>
> Wishing a very Merry Christmas to you from the Blackshear family.[32]

During the Second World War, in Bulgaria, most of the fighting against the Germans had been carried out by the Communists, although they represented only 2 per cent of the population. Initially, after the liberation, the victorious returning partisans had been welcomed by the populace. However, at this stage the Communist Party officials, controlled by the veteran Tsola Dragoytchova, wielded the true power in Bulgaria. The British and US officials in Bulgaria were treated with suspicion and disdain, especially the British. The Allied Armistice Commission did not enjoy the agreed freedom of movement. The Red Army physically prevented the British and US heads of section, two major generals, from visiting the Bulgarian Commander-in-Chief, saying the destination was in a restricted area. The confused Bulgarian people watched the Russians driving Lend-Lease American Jeeps and trucks whilst the Allies, who had provided these vehicles, were treated in an arrogant and offhand manner.[33] An analysis by C. Andrew explained that, because of Bulgaria's traditional Slavic ties to Russia, the Communists had taken over rapidly after the war. After a coup by the Fatherland Front in 1944, CP membership rose through intimidation from 15,000 to 750,000 members. On 1 December 1947 Bulgaria had became 'the Communist People's Militia . . . and an NKVD-supervised secret police, began a reign of terror'.[34] In 1962 *JBS* presented his service colleagues with his view (abridged here) on the history and current situation in Bulgaria:

> The political and social complexion of a nation is a product of its history and the influences that shaped its history. The present status of Bulgaria, as a Communist satellite, affords an interesting example of the hand of history in forming a nation. I feel sure you will prefer to hear an account of life behind the Iron Curtain rather than a detailed history, and will want to know where we in the West stand in relation to the Communist Bloc, and that might be the political outcome in the future. I propose to fill in the background: my theme is a nation conceived in violence and born in bloodshed . . . Bulgaria had her usual bad luck in the First World War. She sided with the Central Powers and came out of the war a genuine loser. She lost to Greece that territory, called 'The White Sea' by Bulgarians, which had given her access to the Aegean. Bulgaria also lost territory, historically claimed as her own, to the new state of Yugoslavia. She lost the Dobrudja to Romania. The inter-war years were marked by internal strife, with right and left vying for political dominance. Although the Communists lacked the organisation and outside support to seize power, when the Boris government crumbled under the impact of the Second World War, they were to inherit a disenchanted nation conditioned to authoritarian rule.
>
> As German fortunes waned, Communist influence in Bulgaria increased. The government, formed in June 1944, belatedly tried to avoid Soviet occupation by officially withdrawing from the war. (The Soviet Union had not seen fit to declare war on the Bulgarian government.) On 9 September 1944 the Red Army invaded the country. The transformation of Bulgaria into a Communist People's Republic and a loyal Soviet satellite followed the now all too familiar pattern: firstly a coalition government with an initial period of tolerance, the seizure of the police and justice ministries, with a subsequent campaign of terror and intimidation by armed forces. A Communist-managed plebiscite abolished the monarchy in September 1946 and in February 1947 a peace treaty was signed. Bulgaria was declared a 'People's Republic' in November 1947 and the stage was set for the subsequent show trials of members of non-Communist groups.

JBS ended with a perceptive prediction:

> What then of the future of Bulgaria? It is unlikely that the Bulgarian people will rise in concert against a system that deprives them of democracy and freedom. You will have gathered that they have no heritage of freedom. There is evidence, however, of disenchantment with Soviet Communism, not only in Bulgaria, but elsewhere in the Soviet bloc. Traditional Bulgarian nationalism is beginning to assert itself, as it has periodically over the centuries. Whilst it would be unrealistic to anticipate any imminent philosophical rejection of Communism, it is not unrealistic to anticipate an eventual rejection of the Soviet domination that imposes it. Bulgaria may one day be 'free', in the sense that, say, Yugoslavia is free, but this freedom will be within the limits imposed by her heritage. To assume otherwise would be to deny the lesson of history.

One individual who looked back later with fond memories of Bulgaria was 'Kim' Philby, now a Moscow resident, and his Polish-Russian wife Rufina. In the summer, his KGB bosses often permitted them to take summer holidays in the Soviet bloc. Philby visited Prague, Sofia and the Black Sea coast, spending the proceeds of the translations of his autobiography. In the late 1970s Philby also made a trip to Cuba by Russian freighter, sailing through the Channel, from where he wistfully commented that the poor visibility prevented him from seeing his old prep school in Eastbourne.[35]

On board this ship Philby was no doubt thinking of his children, abandoned in England when he fled to Russia. His daughter Miranda passed her college diploma and found a job as a secretary to the Bursar of Pembroke College, Oxford. One day her landlady was surprised to receive a big tin of the best caviar from Russia, with a note of thanks from Philby in Moscow.[36] A *Sunday Telegraph* reporter in 1962 described flying from Sofia to Plovdiv where the airport was a grass field occupied by sheep that scattered as he landed. Flying on to Varna, he found 'this much publicised Black Sea holiday resort with gleaming new hotels, erected quickly to lure the tourists, has no restaurants or entertainment. Forced labour camps still exist in Bulgaria, and several have been seen in the mountains. Reports say that 50 people died at one now disbanded camp, through beatings.' *JBS*: 'Two Bulgarians we knew well who worked at the British Legation decided to attempt to cross the border out of Bulgaria. They were shot dead by a border patrol. We used to refer to Bulgaria as "Little Russia" because the conditions were so oppressive.'

Bulgaria saw itself as the little sister of 'Big Brother' Russia. Geert Mak described the terrible conditions of the Bulgarian 'Little Siberia': in the 1950s 100,000 'political prisoners' were detained in dreadful conditions. In Romania, Albania and Czechoslovakia the figures were double that.[37] Nikita Khrushchev often travelled to Bulgaria to a dacha on the Black Sea. It frustrated him that so close over the border in Turkey fifteen American Jupiter missiles at Cigli Airbase were targeted at Russia. He took it personally: 'I see US missiles in Turkey, aimed at my dacha.'[38]

In September 1958 Nigel West described a USAF EC-130 SIGINT Hercules, flying out of the Incirli Airbase in Turkey, being shot down in Armenia with seventeen crew aboard. MiG fighters had deliberately attacked the US aircraft overflying the Soviet border. Eleven crew members had parachuted out. Six bodies were returned. Khrushchev had given the order that any inflying Western planes were to be shot down. In an unprecedented release of SIGINT messages between the five MiG fighter pilots and the ground control (from a tape and transcript of messages intercepted and recorded at a NSA listening post at Trabson in Turkey) Eisenhower appealed for information on the surviving crew. To no avail.[39] The missing men were likely to have been incarcerated in a Russian prison or sent to a gulag in Siberia. On his next holiday to Bulgaria in May 1962, whilst walking on the beach at Varna, Khrushchev proposed: 'Why not throw a hedgehog at Uncle Sam's pants?'[40] He began to consider giving the Americans 'a little of their own medicine' so 'they would learn just what it feels like to have enemy missiles pointing at you'.[41] He would retaliate by sending nuclear missiles to Cuba, pointing at the USA.

Chapter 23

Cuban Missile Crisis, NATO HQ, Paris, 1962

The Hiroshima bomb was the equivalent explosive power of 20,000 tons of TNT (Trinitrotoluene explosive). However, with the new 'nuclear fusion' bomb which compressed isotopes of deuterium, tritium and hydrogen together to form a 'hydrogen' or 'thermonuclear' bomb, the explosion power was frighteningly higher, measurable in megatons, or millions of tons of TNT. A megaton bomb would produce a blast that would blind anyone looking at it within 100 miles, and, having the heat of the sun itself, would melt anything within 3 miles, and burn anyone standing within 20 miles. In 1963 the Soviets had a 58-megaton bomb.[1]

In the autumn of 1962, John Sanderson was relocated to the Intelligence Division of SHAPE HQ in Paris at exactly the moment the Cuban Missile Crisis was taking place. What has not been generally realised is that whilst the Cuban Missile Crisis was heading towards possible meltdown in October 1962, a huge Warsaw Pact Exercise was unfolding in Eastern Europe from 5–10 October. Romanian National Archives on Soviet Marshal 'Sir' Vasili Sokolovski, the Soviet Commander-in-Chief, have revealed the strategic action that the Red Army would have taken if an international military conflict had erupted. (Lord Montgomery had granted Sokolovski an hononorary knighthood at the end of the war in a ceremony at the Brandenburg Gate.[2]) The main course of action defined by the Marshal would have been a strategic offensive, unleashed from the beginning of a conflict:

> The main roles will be played by the troops of the strategic destination missiles, the long-range aircraft and the nuclear submarines equipped with missiles. The offensive, unleashed with nuclear vectors, would be followed by the occupation of western Europe by WTO [Warsaw Treaty Organisation]

> conventional forces. The troop manoeuvres, led by the Polish Colonel-General Spychalski, took place in Poland and partially on East German territory. The 'BALTIC-ODER' exercise involved marines and paratroop units, 32,000 troops, 250 tanks, 300 armoured carriers, 250 aircraft, 5,000 vehicles and 105 vessels. The exercise scenario envisaged Western Forces secretly concentrating their troops under the pretext of military exercises, and carrying out a first strike against the Eastern Forces and attacking in the Wittenburgh–North Berlin direction. The Eastern WTO forces on the seashore front and the Berlin front would respond by carrying out a nuclear strike against the Western forces to stop the latter's offensive. Regrouping their troops, Eastern forces would then start their own offensive in the main direction Breslau–Hamburg. Then the Polish-Soviet-East German troops would attack NATO's main army group on the Berlin Front and their 'Baltic Army Group' on the Baltic seashore front. Close to the Oder River, WTO Reserves would attack the 16th and 1st Airborne Divisions.

An over-enthusiastic Polish general, playing the 'Western' forces in the exercise, suggested setting fire to an area 13,000m^2 with 432 napalm bombs to simulate a 'radioactively contaminated area' but this was refused. Instead, the Commander used six Soviet Mil 'Hook' Mi-6 and thirty-three Mil 'Hound' Mi-4 helicopters (NATO code nicknames) to back up the maritime attack and to carry out a tactical battalion launch in depth to the rear of WTO forces.

> After the firing of fictitious nuclear weapons, 1,200 troops, ten T-54 tanks and eight amphibious tanks disembarked in four waves on the seashore. To counter the 'Western' airborne attack, the WTO engaged a tank division, carrying out live-firing on a Polish fire range from covert positions. The air force bombarded with live ammunition. Next a Soviet mechanised regiment, in a 'Western' role, forced the Oder river West–East in a single wave, supported by the 1st Airborne Division. It took 25 minutes to force the crossing with amphibious tanks, armoured personnel carriers and tanks crossing underwater. Seven Soviet Mil 'hound' Mi-4 and six Mil 'Hook' Mi-6 helicopters, were backed up the Soviet mechanised Division.

Nine years later BRIXMIS would observe NVA troops carrying out night river crossings with tanks fitted with snorkels and mine ploughs, 'hardly a defensive act of war'.[3]

Marshal Andrei Grechko's post-mission critique identified leadership problems, the long distances involved in a Western attack scenario, the use of nuclear weapons on a massive scale creating major difficulties for WTO forces re-grouping post-strike and an inadequate knowledge of foreign languages, especially Russian. (The satellite state military were clearly not understanding all of the Soviet commanders' orders.) Grechko declared that WTO forces must be able fight any aggressor on the aggressor's own territory and stated that this theatre of operations in North-West Europe was extremely important. The Warsaw Pact generals believed that carrying out a strong offensive by destroying the NATO troops on their left flank would enable the destruction of the NATO bloc's main group in Central Europe. The Romanian archive analysis concluded that the military exercises in October 1962, which took place only a few days before the Cuban missile crisis, had no direct connection with the Cuban crisis. NATO military leaders would have monitored these military manoeuvres and analysed them carefully during the last ten days of October when the Cuban Missile Crisis reached its climax.'[4]

This large Warsaw Pact exercise would have been closely followed by BRIXMIS on the ground in Eastern Europe and by the Intelligence Division of SHAPE, where Lieutenant Colonel Sanderson was now based. The gathering storm in Cuba would have certainly increased their workload. In 1968, six years later, the whole NATO nuclear defensive plan for this vitally important Central Europe area would be written by Sanderson for his general in the AFCENT HQ in Holland.

In 1962, Squadron Leader John Aldwinckle was also posted to the Intelligence Division at SHAPE near Paris and the two Johns became firm friends. The Intelligence Division operated as a series of cells, with each cell having limited access to the intelligence obtained by other cells. Aldwinckle, Sanderson and their US boss ran the UKUSA cell, where shared intelligence between NSA and GCHQ was handled. Both officers were there during the Cuban Missile Crisis and continued until 1965. (John Aldwinckle later returned to a similar position at SHAPE in 1970–4, after SHAPE had moved to Mons in Belgium. His last position before retiring at 55 years was managing the Defence Intelligence Centre in the MOD, responsible for daily intelligence briefings to the Cabinet Office.)

In the Kremlin Khrushchev's hold on power depended on the approval of his comrades in the Communist Party and the wider society: the centralised power that Stalin had exercised through fear and intimidation was no longer sufficient: 'Khrushchev had to earn the authority he wielded in domestic and foreign policy. In the international arena, this compulsion led him to rash or adventuristic actions over Berlin, at the UN and in the Cuban Missile Crisis of 1962, which bought the world to the verge of nuclear war.'[5] The historical interpretation of this Cuban crisis has changed over the decades. In 1966 Dr R.C. Mowat wrote, describing a battle of wills that Kennedy won:

> During a week of crisis [22–8 October 1962], when the world was at the threshold of thermonuclear horror, the wills of two men representing two great nations, were in conflict. The steady nerves of the younger man and his colleagues held. Khrushchev was forced to bow to the ultimatum – to stop his ships from trying to pass the American force now quarantining the island, to agree to withdraw the jets and rockets, and to dismantle the bases.[6]

Later, with the knowledge that there was an MI6 mole inside the Kremlin, the dynamics of the crisis became clearer. Thanks to the intelligence handed over by Colonel Oleg Penkovsky and US secret satellite imagery, President Kennedy was able to handle this crisis successfully and face down the Russians: Khrushchev backed down in Cuba and withdrew the missiles. On 26 October the world stepped back from the brink of a cataclysmic conflict between the superpowers, when the Kremlin announced Russia would dismantle its IRBM and MRBM (Medium-Range Ballistic Missile) in Cuba in return for USA guarantees that it would never attack Cuba. The USA in turn removed its Jupiter missiles from Turkey. What has become evident recently is that the situation was rather more complex than it appeared at the time and that Khrushchev's objectives and modus operandi, although highly risky, were not as irrational as first appeared. The Americans had attempted to dislodge Castro in the unsuccessful 'Bay of Pigs' invasion in April. (Kennedy later took full responsibility for the invasion fiasco, in mitigation quoting a Chinese proverb that victory has a hundred fathers but defeat is an orphan.[7]) Khrushchev had a romantic attachment to Cuba, which reminded him of the revolutionary zeal of his youth. As a true Communist, he could not afford to let one of the few examples of a successful Marxist-Leninist fail to carry forward the socialist revolution. The first of Kruschev's aims was to prevent an invasion of Cuba by the USA. This he achieved.

Khrushchev gambled that he could ship and install the nuclear missiles in Cuba, presenting Kennedy with a fait accompli that he would be forced to accept. After all, the Americans had installed Thor and Jupiter missiles on his doorstep in Turkey, as well as in Britain and Italy. There was a strategic element to his gamble also, since the USA had a far greater arsenal of missiles: the Russians felt vulnerable to a first strike.

The Americans, had indeed noted the unidentified cargo aboard the increased shipping heading for Cuba. They did not yet know the reasons for the presence of 6,000 Soviet personnel in Cuba, with their large suspicious crates, but they could not allow this threatening build-up to continue on their doorstep, 90 miles from Florida. Khrushchev failed to achieve his planned surprise. The Americans became fully informed of the threat and they would not acquiesce. Luckily, during the Cuban stand-off and negotiations, as John Sanderson later explained to the author, the West was being supplied with accurate information on the strategy of Nikita Khrushchev and his fellow politburo members in the Kremlin by the brave Penkovsky, who was subsequently uncovered and shot as a traitor. *JBS*: 'Colonel Oleg Penkovsky was invaluable to us during the Cuban Missile Crisis: we knew what the Kremlin was thinking and Kennedy could judge how far he could safely go to call Khrushchev's bluff.' Penkovsky was also passing over intelligence on Soviet military preparations in the Soviet Union and the GDR, including the entire Soviet military plan for a possible conflict in Berlin. As Sanderson explained, Penkovsky was continuously feeding back to his MI6 handlers the Soviet reaction to Kennedy's decisions to call up reserves and increase the US defence budget because of the missiles installed in Cuba.[8]

Because British Intelligence had limited funding for SIGINT, since the end of the Second World War they had relied on the generosity of their US allies in supplying this facility. (The American CIA had continued to give unofficial assistance to SIS during the Suez Crisis in 1956 when they provided U2 aerial surveillance photographs of the Egyptian airfields. The RAF used this imagery when their Canberras bombed Egyptian airfields.) The quid pro quo for this sharing of intelligence was the contribution Britain made from its own intercept stations throughout the Commonwealth and elsewhere, for example at Edirne.[9] 'In the Oval Office on 13 July, Kennedy was personally briefed about Colonel Penkovsky by his CIA Director who explained that Khrushchev was not ready for war.'[10] Over Cuba, chance aerial surveillance had discovered the presence of Russian missiles. Hourly photographic transmits from overflying US planes and detailed secret satellite surveillance images were coming across *JBS*'s desk at SHAPE Intelligence HQ in Paris:

> The American satellite images of the bases that reached our SHAPE HQ in Paris were so clear that we could almost read a newspaper held by a man on the ground and note when he had walked several yards in consecutive photographs. Contrary to what is generally known, NATO headquarters in Paris were

> receiving full up-to-date reports throughout the crisis. Cuba, after all, was still part of the global threat to the West and any defensive response to a Russian threat would have had to have been assessed and coordinated with a European defensive strategy.

These aerial surveillance photographs revealed that the Russians had already installed forty medium-range nuclear-capable missiles, directly and closely threatening the USA.

One crucial document from inside the safe of his friend Chief Marshal Sergei Varentsov, which Penkovsky had photographed with his Minox, was a document entitled 'Methods of Protecting and Defending Strategic Rocket sites', an ultra-secret paper from the HQ of the Soviet Army Missile & Ground Artillery. 'The illustrations, especially those of the camouflage outlines . . . showed distinctly different concealment profiles for Soviet surface-to-surface as compared with surface-to-air weapons . . . for offensive as opposed to defensive missiles'.[11]

A Soviet nuclear battery was drawn up 15 miles from the USA base at Guantanamo Bay awaiting firing orders. Fred Muesagaes, a USAF pilot flying a RF-101 mission, recalled:

> Assigned photographic targets were SAM [Surface-to-Air Missile] sites, airfields, barracks, military installations and of course nuclear missile assembly and deployment sites. Threats were AAA, SAMs and MIG-17s and MIG-21s. Only one MIG-17 was ever airborne but no way could he catch us even if he wanted to. We criss-crossed the island from east of Havana for 1:15 hours. One thing I will never forget is as we approached Guantanamo Bay, I saw dozens of troops running for their AAA emplacements but as we flew by them they were all waving, so I rocked my wings. Not all Cubans were hostile.

Soon these pilots would be 'flying intensive, dangerous and unrelenting missions over Laos and Vietnam'.[12] The photographs that the U2 bought back confirmed without a doubt that the US mainland was now under threat from Soviet nuclear missiles: 'the site layout and camouflage outlines filmed matched exactly those of the Russian medium-range surface-to-surface weapons as reproduced in the purloined report'.[13]

Kennedy debated with his NSC Committee and also consulted the British Ambassador. Of his two options of ordering an air-strike on Cuba or a sea blockade, he decided the safer option was ordering a quarantine blockade area 500 miles around Cuba. Khrushchev had written two messages to Kennedy: the first offered to stop further shipments to Cuba in exchange for a deal not to invade and the second note demanded a Turkish-Cuban missile agreement. Kennedy publicly agreed not to invade Cuba if all the missiles were withdrawn.

On 27 October 1962, dubbed 'Black Saturday' in the White House and the most dangerous day of the Cuban Missile Crisis, three Soviet submarines heading for Cuba approached the US quarantine line. The Soviet submarines had been detected by US listening posts, picking up the 'blast radio transmissions' between the submarines and Soviet High Command. Underwater sonobuoys and SOSUS sound surveillance systems had also tracked the subs' locations through their engine noises. When the USS *Beale* dropped harmless 'signals' practice grenades around the B-59 submarine, it misinterpreted the sounds as exploding depth charges, rather than signals to surface.[14]

The author Gary Slaughter described conditions aboard the *Foxtrot* diesel-powered submarine as being stifflingly unpleasant. Captain Savitsky and his deputy, unable to contact base and believing war had broken out, proposed firing a 15-kiloton nuclear torpedo at a US Navy vessel. The huge aircraft carrier USS *Randolf* was the obvious target in the area. However, second Captain Vasili Arkhipov, whose agreement to fire was necessary, managed to persuade the Captain to calm down and surface the submarine. Nuclear warfare was averted. The sub lay alongside the USS *Cony*. Suddenly a P2V Neptune plane overflew the sub, dropping incendiary devices to activate its photographic cameras. Believing he was under attack, Savitsky turned his sub to bring the torpedo tubes to bear on the USS *Cony*. The ship's signalman was directed to flash an apology to the submarine. Friendly communications were then established. American cigarettes and fresh bread were high-lined to the Soviet submarine, before it turned, submerged and headed for home.[15]

Meanwhile, the President instructed his brother to secretly offer the Russian Ambassador the removal of the American Thor and Jupiter missiles from Turkey within four to five months. Khrushchev accepted Kennedy's offer and the latter specified that if the Soviets revealed the Turkish deal, it would be cancelled. On 26 October the world stepped back from the brink of a thermonuclear conflict between the superpowers, when the Kremlin announced it would dismantle and withdraw all offensive weapons from Cuba. Eventually the US Turkish missiles were removed, the second of Khrushchev's objectives. In this respect Kennedy had sacrificed Turkish security for US security. (Their role was then assumed by Polaris nuclear submarines.) In the end a compromise, potentially damaging for Kennedy's reputation had it been revealed, was secretly reached.[16]

The Cuban Missile Crisis was a high-risk gamble on Khrushchev's part that didn't come off. Although two of Khrushchev's objectives were met, publically it was a humiliating loss of face which tarnished the Soviet Union's international prestige. The failed confrontation was to spell the beginning of the end of Khrushchev's influence and power. The writing had been on the wall anyway for Nikita since his disastrous and eccentric unrestrained behaviour in the UN General Assembly on 1 October 1960. After taking off a shoe, he had used it to bang his desk in a crass attempt to interrupt the Spanish Foreign Minister. He then threatened the minister with his fists as he passed by. The Soviet Foreign Minister Gromyko was furious. The Soviet delegation was horrified.[17] Castro never forgave Khrushchev for backing down. He had been prepared to take the stand-off with Kennedy to its limit. He had always believed Khrushchev's exaggerated boasts about being able to shoot a fly out of space with his missiles. He had not been consulted in the decision to withdraw the missiles. He was furious with Khrushchev, accusing him of being a 'Son of a bitch. Bastard. No cojones.'[18]

At this stage Penkovsky had been under surveillance in Moscow for nine months. George Blake, now in the 'Scrubs' prison, had worked in Berlin for four years alongside Ruari Chisholm, an SIS officer who was now Moscow MI6 station head, under diplomatic cover as a Second Secretary, and he would have passed this on to his KGB bosses. Chisholm was running Penkovsky: his wife Janet would have thus also been under intense KGB surveillance. She, as a member of an SIS officer's family, had been requested, and bravely volunteered, to pick up Minox cassettes from Penkovsky in brush-past encounters, whilst walking her children in Moscow parks. Janet had received a dozen boxes of sweets over two months, some containing secrets that would go directly to the President of the USA.

Ominously, during September and October, nothing was heard from Penkovsky. His arrest was announced on 22 October, six days before Khrushchev agreed to remove his weapons from Cuba and return them to Russia. The KGB 2nd Directorate Chief General Oleg Grbanov had in 1960 ordered a blanket surveillance of the US and British embassies twice a year routinely. Penkovsky, in his overconfidence, had visited the British Embassy without the necessary clearance. The KGB had put a watch on Penkovsky's flat, then sent his neighbours on holiday, installing a pinhole camera. The KGB smeared poisonous chemicals on a chair in Penkovsky's flat. Whilst he was in hospital, they found incriminating espionage evidence. Penkovsky was interrogated, brutally tortured, put on trial and humiliated in court.[19] The spy, who at Moscow airport had passed to his contact Greville Wynne a letter addressed to Queen Elizabeth and President Kennedy which read: 'I ask you to consider me as your soldier. Henceforth the ranks of your armed forces are increased by one man', was finally shot on 16 May 1963.[20] During his trial the Chief Military Prosecutor General Gorny had declared: 'A leading role in this belongs to the Central Intelligence Agency of the US. Like a giant octopus it extends its tentacles into all corners of the earth, supports a tremendous number of spies and secret informants, continually organises plots and murders . . . The British Intelligence Service, an old fox which has been in existence for about 300 years, is no less insidious and astute in its methods. It continues to pursue increasingly deceptive and refined methods but attempts to remain more in the background.'[21]. Although Penkovsky was eventually unmasked, this had not been as a result of a direct betrayal: the fact that he had been run as such a useful penetration agent for two years did much to restore the reputation of MI6 domestically and with the Americans. The wealth of highly classified and top-secret material that Penkovsky supplied to Western Intelligence, much from the GRU secret library, was staggering. This courageous 'Walter Mitty' spy photographed onto Minox cartridges, with consummate skill, everything he could get his hands on over a period of two years, even in areas outside his expertise:

- The 'Alert' stages for preparing Soviet Strategic Rockets together with the times needed to prepare the missiles.
- The drills for setting up the missiles on the launchpads with the pre-firing checks and the actual firing sequences.
- The technical details of missile warheads with graphs of estimated radiation yields. Weaknesses in Soviet Tactical Missile systems needed for a Red Army invasion as well as deficiencies in all Soviet liquid-filled missiles.
- The location sites of many Soviet ICBMs with the ICBM true totals and stocks (revealing that there wasn't a 'missile gap' between Russia and the USA as feared).
- The Red Army's complete OB and signal codes for hundreds of military items. Details of three new battle tanks, one amphibious.
- Top Personnel lists in the army and the Communist Party, including the Kremlin telephone directory.[22]

Most importantly, Pentovsky reported Soviet internal debates on future strategic plans for the 'nuclear age', with a proposed cutback on conventional forces and an increased reliance on missiles. G. Brook Shepherd noted that: 'NATO's decision, made in the early 1960's, to prepare to face chemical warfare as a major weapon in any war with the Soviet Union stems directly . . . from the chilling disclosures Pentovsky had produced . . . Penkovsky's steady and solid flow of information . . . led, quite simply, to a complete rethinking of NATO's strategy and tactics . . . Over a broad front of military planning, the policy of the Western alliance was to be shaped by Penkovsy's revelations for a decade to come.'[23] The revelations would later influence Colonel Sanderson when he came to draft a defence plan for Central Europe with a flexible response of conventional forces and tactical nuclear defences.

The *New York Herald* told its readers that 'Colonel Penkovsky's exposure as a spy blew a huge hole within the entire Soviet information-gathering operation.'[24] He had identified 600 Soviet intelligence officers across the world, 50 of whom were GRU like himself. Soviet Military Attachés in embassies across the world were recalled to Moscow.[25] But the intelligence about the chemical weapons capability of the Soviets was the most highly valued intelligence that Penkovsky handed over. The NATO planners were aware that there was a Soviet chemical warfare programme but its vast scale was unexpected. Documents he supplied revealed the existence of a Seventh Directorate of the Soviet General Staff with responsibility for chemical and bacteriological weapons. There was a network of testing and storage depots throughout Russia. Current exercises were giving priority to chemical weapons over nuclear. Detailed working documents gave such practical data as optimum heights for chemical bursts, as well as the scope of contamination in differing wind conditions, with estimates of casualties. The deadly chemical agent was considered to be a mixture of two gases.[26]

As for Khrushchev, by 1964, after Cuba he had lost the will to rule: he was approaching his 70th birthday. Summoned to appear before a Presidium meeting, he was confronted with fifteen errors he had committed and accused by a committee of his former colleagues. 'Khrushchev tried to defend himself with familiar bluster and vituperation.'[27] He was forced to resign and sent into retirement with a pension. Under Stalin, he would have been shot by a firing squad. Khrushchev had himself handed out this fate to 1,200 security men when he took over as Ukrainian Party boss in 1938. But Russia had changed.[28] Khrushchev had played a significant part in reforming Russia: he had brought the security police under party control, had released millions from the Gulag camps and in so doing so, had succeeded in ending the reign of terror that Stalin had unleashed. The control of society by the security police and the Communist Party, however, was to continue as effectively as under Stalin. A story, supposedly passed around in Russia, illustrates the reticence of ordinary

Russians to express their opinion. Khrushchev had addressed a meeting when one of the audience had bravely asked him: 'Where were you (in the time of Stalin) when these crimes were committed?' 'Who said that?', Khrushchev demanded. There was silence. 'There's your answer then . . . we were all scared'.[29] For Khrushchev:

> Writers, scholars and scientists, officials, managers – all were in the last resort seen as mere cogs in a machine whose function was to impose on a people a grand design elaborated from above . . . Soviet society was almost wholly in thrall to a Stalinist pattern of thought and conduct.[30]

Sir Rodric Braithwaite GCMG (British Ambassador to Moscow, 1988–92) wrote a perceptive analysis of a Soviet system from the 1960s falling into increasing decay: 'the lack of consumer goods, the primitive living conditions, the decrepit factories, the disfunctional agriculture, the lopsided emphasis on heavy industry and defence, the growth rates approaching zero'. Khrushchev understood that the Soviet economy was failing while the capitalist West's economies thrived but his attempts at reform failed. Braithwaite noted that for the next decade and a half the Soviet Union 'floated on a sea of high priced oil'.[31]

In 1971 Khrushchev would look back and assess his political failings: 'My leadership was sometimes more administrative than creative. I was too concerned with restricting or prohibiting . . . today I am opposed to this form of government. I would have opened all the doors and windows if I could.'[32] The Soviet Union would have to wait fourteen years for Mikhail Gorbachev to become General Secretary and begin to do just that.

In 1963 Philby was to confess to Nicholas Elliot in Beirut that 'he had worked for the Soviets since 1946 and had only tipped off Maclean as a friend in 1951'. G. Corera describes how Philby left Beirut in a freighter and eventually arrived before dawn at a small frontier post where one man was waiting for him and said in English, 'Kim, your mission is concluded.'[33] Another version of this story has KGB officers boarding his freighter with a champagne bottle.

John Sanderson was furious when he finally heard the news of Philby's deception and when he realised the implications for all the agents he had recruited over the years and whose trust had been betrayed. It seemed incredible to him that Philby could have deceived the service for so long and got away with it, not to mention the 'knife in the back' for his colleagues. Certainly the Moscow Centre would soon have full details of his own activities, with his cover blown. Philby would be listing the names and details of all his former fellow members in SIS, with information on their backgrounds. In his old age, as he told the author of Philby's betrayal of his country, whilst they strolled beside the Thames, the incredulity was still there in his voice, tinged with a resigned bitterness, even after all the years. Only then, in 1996, did he reveal he had worked for MI6 for decades.

Peter Wright of MI5 described similar reactions:

> Many people in the secret world aged the night they heard Philby had confessed . . . It is one thing to suspect the truth; it is another to hear it from a man's lips. Suddenly there was very little fun in the game anymore; a Rubicon had been crossed . . . To find a man like Philby, a man you might like, or drink with, or admire, had betrayed everything; to think of the agents and operations wasted; youth and innocence passed away, and the dark ages began.[34]

Chapter 24

France Leaves NATO and 'Fairwell'

Paris! Paris outragé! Paris brisé! Paris martyrisé! Mais Paris libéré! Libéré par lui-même, liberé par son peuple avec le concours des armées de la France, avec l'appui et le concours de la France tout entière, de la France qui se bat, de la seule France, de la vraie France, de la France éternelle.

Paris! Paris insulted! Paris broken! Paris martryed! But Paris liberated! Liberated by itself, liberated by its people with the help of the French armies, with the support and help of the whole of France, of the France that fights, of the only France, of the true France, of the eternal France!

Le Général Charles de Gaulle[1]

De Gaulle's liberation speech at the Hôtel de Ville on 25 August 1944 declared to Paris and the world that the city was 'liberated by itself . . . with the help of the French armies'. Ungraciously, no mention was made of all the major sacrifices and casualties that Britain, the US and other Allies had suffered during the liberation of France. General de Gaulle's speech, with its aim of raising French morale after a long and cruel German occupation, omitted to mention the close Allied support given during the liberation of Paris 24–6 August.

The US 4th Infantry Div. had left the honour of entering Paris first to Leclerc's soldiers. On the previous day of 24 August, A. Poirier writes, 'while the Free French and the Spanish Republicans enlisted with Leclerc's 2nd DB started pouring into the boulevards, coming from the south gate of Paris', the US 4th Div. was also on the move into Paris. Through the east gate of Paris and from the Porte d'Italie in the north-east, American, British and Canadian soldiers were driving into Paris. On 26 August, the day following de Gaulle's speech, the US agreed to fly American planes over Paris to deter the Luftwaffe while the General and Leclerc's troops marched down the Champs-Élysées. Later that day enemy sniper fire was still a menace: bullets were flying past the tall, defiant General as he strode determinedly to attend a rapid mass in Notre Dame Cathedral. Afterwards he rang Eisenhower to request American help 'to clean Paris of its few remaining enemies. Two American divisions should do.'[2]

General Charles de Gaulle's animosity towards the Anglo-Saxons had long been harboured. Since his exile in London during the Second World War, de Gaulle had seen himself as representing *l'âme* (the soul) of France, a metaphor for the spirit of French resistance. He frequently referred to himself in the third person. No other Western leader thought in this way, that they 'personified the state'. The General saw himself as continuing the glorious tradition of Louis XIV and Napoleon Bonaparte.

De Gaulle was still bitter that France, as an ally, had not been invited to attend the Great Powers Yalta Conference with Stalin, Churchill and Roosevelt. De Gaulle also never forgave the Americans for withholding military intelligence from him in the closing stages of the war, nor did he forgive Macmillan and the Americans for withholding their nuclear technology from France. The Americans, however, were understandably reluctant to cooperate with a post-war French government whose cabinet included Communists.

The historians A. Beevor and A. Cooper noted that the British Military Attaché in Paris reported back to London the view that de Gaulle's foreign policy was wrong from the start and paradoxical: he was temperamentally anti-Anglo-Saxon. De Gaulle was anti-Communist but he later sought a closer relationship with Russia to aid France in its quest to become the great power which he felt it should be. De Gaulle saw a role for himself as a mediator between the Anglo-Saxons and the Russians.[3]

On becoming head of government in 1958, de Gaulle proposed a tripartite decision-making body to oversee Western military strategy and the sharing of military technology between France, the USA and Britain. Since de Gaulle's election, however, France's military secrets were unwittingly being shared with Moscow: the KGB spy Georges Pâques, employed as an advisor to French ministers in the Elysée Palace, was stealing France's military secrets and passing them over to the Soviet Union. In 1959 Pâques stole the entire organisational plan for the SDECE, whose Director was General Paul Grossin. Pâques was originally recruited in Algeria and would continue to spy for Moscow for twenty years, being in situ when John Sanderson was working in SHAPE HQ near Paris from 1962–3. Pâques was finally 'blown' in 1963.[4] The Russian Lieutenant Colonel Anatoli Golitsyn, a KGB counter-intelligence officer in Finland who defected in December 1961, supplied the information.[5]

C. Andrew and O. Gordievsky revealed that Pâques was part of a Soviet network of spies inside the SDECE called 'The Sapphire Ring'. Pâques, an 'ideological' spy, betrayed to the Russian First Chief Directorate the total NATO defence plan for Western Europe, as well as the Allies' policy over Berlin. Hambleton, a Canadian economist, had also spied for the Moscow Centre, for ten years since 1951. Whilst working in NATO HQ, he would carry secret documents to the car park, where his van was equipped to copy documents rapidly.[6]

De Gaulle refused to envisage the positioning of NATO rockets or nuclear material on French soil until his tripartite demands were met. When in 1959 his proposals were rejected by the allies, France withdrew from the integrated NATO command structure and began the expensive task of developing its own nuclear bomb, 'la force de frappe', together with the means to deliver it. France's post-war prosperity, thanks to the Marshall plan, had put this financially within her reach.

NATO and Russia were now deploying significant numbers of tactical and strategic nuclear weapons across Europe and each side feared a first strike by the other side. The Cuban Missile Crisis only reinforced de Gaulle's view that France had to be a member of the 'nuclear club': it was not a foregone conclusion that the USA would risk a nuclear war to protect Europe.

Britain had been reducing its conventional forces since 1955, basing its defence on a credible nuclear deterrent, backed up since 1957 by a British 'H' bomb (Hydrogen/thermonuclear bomb). The British means to deliver her deterrent, however, were becoming obsolete. The future of warfare obviously lay in rockets launched from the sea or land, not in the air from V-bombers. The failure of the Blue Streak rocket, cancelled in 1960, ended Britain's hopes of becoming an independent military nuclear power. The Americans moved to share their nuclear technology and integrate Britain into the US nuclear strategy, dovetailing their joint operational procedures and targets. As part of the Nassau Agreement, the USA agreed to supply three nuclear submarines to Britain, together with Polaris missiles which Britain would herself arm with nuclear warheads, the systems to be within the NATO command structure.

In 1962 Macmillan was prepared to share the development costs of nuclear technology with France but de Gaulle was too proud to request this. In September of that year the USA had offered to sell nuclear submarines to France, before reconsidering and withdrawing the proposal. De Gaulle wanted no part of a 'multinational' nuclear-armed NATO submarine force: he favoured a 'European deterrent' and began to pull French naval forces out of NATO exercises. De Gaulle saw France as an independent nuclear power outside NATO, without the obligation to rely on the USA for her defence. De Gaulle's EEC partners were stunned when he vetoed Britain's application to join the European Community. Some referred to him thereafter as 'Monsieur Non'.[7]

The Kremlin saw the differences between members of the Western Alliance and the EEC, and Russia's new rapprochement with France, as a way to divide NATO and to favour Russia's long-term objectives in Western Europe. Andrei Gromyko, the Soviet Foreign Minister, embarked on a range of diplomatic treaties, tied to commercial, industrial and technological agreements, as strategies to tie France closer to Russia, with the ultimate aim of inducing France to leave NATO. France and Russia began to share nuclear research and French satellites were launched on Russian rockets. At the same time the KGB embarked on a secret propaganda campaign through French trade associations, newspaper journalists and agents of influence, in an attempt to persuade the French that their membership of NATO, and the basing of US and other troops on French soil, compromised their independence.[8] In March 1966 de Gaulle undertook a state visit to the Soviet Union, where he remarked diplomatically, but realistically: 'How happy we are to have you help us resist American pressure – as we are pleased to have the United States helping us to resist pressure from the Soviet Union.'[9]

The same year, all foreign forces were requested to leave French soil. France remained, however, an active member of the Alliance itself, and French personnel continued to serve at NATO's political HQ in Brussels, as well as in liaison roles in the other military HQ. The French armed forces continued to be part of secret arrangements for cooperating with NATO in wartime, so the Allies could be confident of French forces' support in the event of a crisis or war.[10]

It is interesting to contrast NATO's regretful acceptance of France's decision to distance herself from NATO, with the Soviet Union's heavy-handed reaction, ten years previously, when Imre Nagy, optimistically but, rather unwisely, declared Hungary to be a neutral country outside the Warsaw Pact.

In 1967 the vast infrastructure of US NATO forces in France was shut down, when SHAPE moved to Brussels. The NATO infrastructure had taken nearly two decades to mature, but it was closed and relocated in six months. Negotiations to return land and the thousands of the buildings, airbases, ports, depots, hospitals, schools and housing villages to the French nation took a further two years.[11] With so much unemployment in the area, the Dutch were only too happy to have a new major source of revenue when the AFCENT HQ was installed in the former coal mining area of South Limburg. The base buildings were on the surface, whilst from 1967–9 Lieutenant Colonel Sanderson would work in the NATO Nuclear

(Defensive) Planning Division in the bombproof offices, constructed underground in the old mines.

In 1968, *'les événements'*, an unexpected outbreak of social unrest and protests that harked back to the Hungarian Revolution of 1956, spread across France. In Paris, student demonstrators took to the streets in protest against Capitalism, US 'imperialism', educational failures and perceived social inequalities, whilst 10 million French workers downed their tools in widespread general strike action, occupying schools and factories. These disturbances continued for two weeks, and it appeared there could be civil war. With student revolts, riots and public demonstrations threatening anarchy in the country, de Gaulle flew secretly to South Germany on 19 May to see General Massu in Baden-Baden and ensure the support of the French Army in Germany, in case the situation worsened.[12]

De Gaulle eventually stabilised the political situation by making an emotional appeal to the French nation on television. In August 1944, in a liberated Paris, Charles de Gaulle had marched down the Champs Elysées, striding at the head of joyful Parisians. In 1968 a million demonstrators, carrying banners and de Gaulle's portrait, marched in his support to the Place de la Concorde. Street barricades were finally dismantled and the strikes subsided. In the following month of June, de Gaulle dissolved the National Assembly and fresh elections were held, bringing the Gaullists back into power. In April 1969, however, after a narrow defeat in a constitutional referendum, General de Gaulle resigned his Presidency.

In 1960 de Gaulle had declared *'La France est la lumière du monde. Son génie est d'éclairer l'univers.'* ('France is the light of the world. Its genius is to light up the world.') In terms of culture, he was certainly correct. The historian Jonathan Fenby, however, noted in an article in the *Financial Times* in 2018 that:

> The unpalatable truth was that the ambition for France to 'light up the universe' was beyond the country's capacity, given the decline in its political and economic weight after the traumas of two world wars, or the willingness of citizens to embrace the cause. 'France is worn out, she is made to be supine, not made to fight,' [de Gaulle] told an aide, 'I keep the theatre going as long as I can and then, after me, have no illusion, things will go back to where they were.[13]

François Mitterrand, the future French President, had accused de Gaulle in his 1964 book *Le Coup d'État permanent* of 'operating a permanent coup d'état' with his continual retention of authority and his previous domination of the RPF'.[14]

In late 1969, after three months of French language studies at Tours University, John Sanderson was appointed Liaison Officer with the French Army in Germany, based in Baden-Baden (and living in the house previously occupied by de Gaulle's son Phillipe, a French admiral). There he heard an anecdote that reflected the wit of a French general in the revolutionary days of May 1968: 'Greeting a General named Lecointe and, making a pun on the soldier's name, Charles de Gaulle asked: "Toujours aussi 'con', Lecointe?" ("Still as much a 'con' Lecointe?") To which Lecointe made the tactful reply: "Toujours Gaulliste mon Général!" ("Still a Gaullist, my General!")'

Nigel West noted that the French Secret Service, the DGSE (direction générale de la sécurité extérieure), which is staffed by military personnel, is situated on Boulevard Mortier, in the 20th arrondissement of Paris. It was formerly called Le Service de documentation extérieure et de contre-espionnage (SDECE): the CIA and MI6 sometimes still call it 'the deck'.[15] From 1981–2 the DGSE ran a highly successful Russian agent in Moscow called Vladimir Vetrov, codenamed FAIRWELL. Vetrov was a disillusioned top-ranking KGB officer whose job was examining economic, scientific and industrial intelligence obtained worldwide by Directorate 'T' through espionage. FAIRWELL was one of the most useful Western intelligence spies in the Cold War, providing a list of 250 Soviet Line 'X' officers in embassies across the world who were involved in a vast Soviet global operation to steal the West's technological secrets. Moscow's aim was to save the billions of rubles in Research and Development costs that the Soviet economy could ill afford. France subsequently expelled forty-seven KGB agents and the Americans, informed about FAIRWELL, set up a massive 'sting' operation to feed the Soviets false data, aimed at sabotaging projects based on stolen US technology.

President Mitterrand, whose Elysée Palace had political control of the DGSE, realised the logic of aiding French industry and the national economy, by stealing foreign technology. In 1981 he authorised the setting up of a special Secret Service unit in 'La Piscine' (headed by Pierre Marion, the former head of Air France) to plan operations to acquire scientific information abroad, even from France's allies.[16] J. Adams described the FBI's surprise when they obtained a twenty-three-page French DGSE dossier marked '*Défense Confidentiale*' which revealed French plans for 'acquiring' specific American technology, including the V-22 Osprey tilt-wing aircraft. (This was the revolutionary aircraft concept, originally drawn up by John Sanderson's father in 1942: see his wartime plans, 6c in the plates). France had economic spies within such US companies as IBM and Texas Instruments.[17] In March 2009, under President Sarkozy, France would rejoin NATO's integrated military structure, on the sixtieth anniversary of NATO's formation.

Chapter 25

AFCENT Planning, Holland, 1968–9

The invasion of Czechoslovakia in 1968 demonstrated to the NATO Allies how determined and ruthless the Russians were in keeping down their satellite states. Although the Soviets faced a nuclear-armed, strong and resolute NATO alliance, the latter could not let up their guard in the hope that an invasion from the East would never come. There were signs that the Warsaw Pact had made contingency preparations for an advance westwards. As *JBS* explained to the author in 1970:

> The Soviet tanks were tuned to the same octane fuel used in West German housing central heating systems. They could easily have driven up to the gardens of the private houses or apartment blocks on their advance and refuelled. We knew that Aeroflot planes flying into the UK were military-trained pilots familiarising themselves with the flightpaths in case of a war. The threat was real.

The invasion of Czechoslovakia kicked off on the night of 20/21 August 1968, with Soviet paratroopers seizing Prague airport. It was followed up by the main invasion across 4 frontiers of 400,000 Warsaw Pact forces: 50,000 Poles, 20,000 Hungarians and East Germans, 10,000 Bulgarians and Russians under General Pavlovskii. Tony Gerachty noted that Allied liaison officers had been aware of the build-up of forces, which included a SCUD missile brigade. East German truck drivers were passing notes to BRIXMIS staff several days previously, warning that they were 'going to invade Czechoslovakia'. There were special red bands around the tailplanes of Soviet MiG-21 jets. When the GDR 19 Grenadier Motor Rifle Div. left their barracks with all equipment in July, BRIXMIS watchers said: 'They are off to fight.'[1]

The Russian news agency Tass was reporting: 'the people of Czechoslovakia are showing gratitude for the timely arrival of Soviet troops'. John Sanderson was on holiday in Italy, seated in a restaurant with the author, when he spotted a newspaper headline carrying the news of the Czech invasion. After rushing off at once to telephone his HQ, he immediately cut short the holiday and returned directly to SHAPE where NATO military planners were working full-time to process incoming information and to assess the likely implications of this invasion. There was uncertainty that the thousands of Warsaw Pact troops and Soviet tanks would indeed stop at the Czech/Western border.

The Czechs and Slovaks were told by their government to stay calm and not to actively resist. Alexander Dubček and colleagues were immediately arrested and taken off to Moscow, with Gustáv Husák installed as the Kremlin's stooge. 'Socialism with a human face' would be repressed for two decades by the 'Brezhnev Doctrine'. A 'Russian winter' would freeze out Dubček's 'Prague Spring'.

Moscow always saw Czechoslovakia as the weak link in the Warsaw Pact and had no permanent garrison in the country, with no nuclear weapons stationed there, although they were installed in Hungary, the GDR and Poland.[2] This invasion of Czechoslovakia was an act that Mikhail Gorbachev later refused to repeat in Poland or East Germany. The overt show of aggression was to thoroughly disillusion another sensible Russian, Colonel Oleg Gordievsky, and prove a crucial motivation for his later defection to London. He had first 'dreamed' of living in London after the 20th Party Congress, when Khrushchev had denounced Stalin.[3]

As G. Corera explained:

> The seeds of dissent planted earlier in life and nurtured by the sight of the Wall going up in 1961 had grown into a deep-seated but clandestine conviction that he no longer wanted to work for a 'criminal regime'. Rather than resign, he wanted to subvert from within: 'They've done it! It's unbelievable,' he told his wife over the phone as the tanks made their way through Prague. 'I just don't know what to do.'[4]

Nigel West noted that the Director General John Rennie, who 'had the advantage of a long friendship with Dennis Greenhill, the influential Permanent Under Secretary', was quick to discover how few SIS officers or intelligence sources were operational in Eastern Europe at this crucial moment. The DG (Director General of MI6) would have had little intelligence from his Military Attachés or any advance warning from the Prague M16 station that an invasion by the Warsaw Pact forces was imminent. Fortunately, GCHQ provided hourly updates, 'based on intercepted radio conversations . . . between Prague's taxi drivers, monitored at the NSA–GCHQ base on top of the Teufelsberg in the British sector of Berlin'. This SIGINT intelligence tower picked up signals across East Germany, Poland and Czechoslovakia.[5]

Stephen Dorril described how the new ISC (Intelligence and Security Controller) under Dick White was set up with staff to examine all intelligence information and give its own assessment. It failed during the Russian invasion of Czechoslovakia which caught Whitehall by surprise. JIC and ISC were reporting authoritatively that there would be no invasion.

BRIXMIS in Germany, however, was reporting on the ground that an invasion was being prepared before their eyes. MI6 had no high-level source behind the Iron Curtain, except for these military observers, who knew that GCHQ could not pick up SIGINT on an invasion if the Warsaw Pact's deployment was carried out in radio silence, as was their practice. However, GCHQ became increasingly relied upon by the intelligence community and was well-funded, to MI6's detriment.[6]

Matthew M. Aid wrote that in 1946 a US Army intelligence operator told the Russians that their codes had been broken by Bletchley Park in 1946. (Aid based his book on declassified NSA documents.) This left Britain blind in 1956 at the time of the invasion of Hungary and of Czechoslovakia in 1968. It was not until 1976 that GCHQ finally cracked the Russian cyphers, after almost three decades of failure.

John Sanderson's close friend and colleague in the Intelligence and Planning Division of AFCENT was *Oberstleutnant* Herbert Stobbe of the Bundeswehr (Federal Defence Forces), who had fought in the Wehrmacht during the Second World War. In 1945 Stobbe had surrendered to the Americans but, rather unwisely but faithfully, headed back into East Germany to look for his wife. He was unfortunate to be detained by the Russians and sent to a Siberian prison camp for a decade. There, due to his rank, charm and natural authority, Stobbe became leader of the German contingent. On his eventual release, he returned to find his wife 'alive and well' and they were happily reunited. Reintegrated back into the German Army, Colonel Stobbe continued his career where it had left off, only this time on the US and British side.

Herbert Stobbe told the author a story about John and the Chief of NATO forces, General Jürgen Bennecke, who had served in the wartime Jäger Div. as an *oberstleutnant* (awarded the prestigious German Gold Cross):

SITUATION: 1969 HQ, AFCENT, Emma Mine Brunssum, Netherlands

John Sanderson and I, two stories underground, no daylight, rewriting a strategic paper. An MP calls John to see the new Commander-in-Chief, General Bennecke who is due to give his first briefing at SHAPE and wants to do it in English, although he is still struggling a bit with his English. As he has a brilliant memory, Bennecke intends to memorise the speech overnight. In one passage, Bennecke wants to reassure that we do not need to be too frightened of the Russian soldier.

John adds the words: 'The Russians are not ten feet tall.'

The audience cannot believe that Bennecke is that fluent in English and try to trick him by the question: 'What do you mean by ten feet tall?'

But John had foreseen this question and had previously added several replies to the most likely questions. So Bennecke, having learned the answers too by heart, shot back with a joke. Nobody doubted that Bennecke had improved his English overnight.

Audrey and John were invited to dine at the Commander in Chief's house and there must have been a lot of laughter that evening.[7]

It is interesting to note that the descriptive words which John Sanderson wrote for General Bennecke were also used by Sir Roger Hollis (Director of M15 from 1956–65) referring to the Russians. During a meeting with Peter Wright about the Gordon Lonsdale spy affair Hollis said: 'They're not 10 feet tall, you know, Peter!' – '10 feet tall' was obviously a catchphrase used in intelligence briefings or perhaps picked up in a conversation with Hollis, to note that the strength of the Russian bear was often exaggerated.[8]

Wright was convinced that Hollis was the 'Fifth' Russian agent in the British intelligence services. Wright accurately retranslated the two words of *'otdel upravalenie'* in a list of important Soviet agents inside British establishments, supplied by Konstantin Volkov, who had attempted to defect from Turkey. This gave the sentence 'I know that one of the agents is fulfilling the duties of head of a section of the British Counterintelligence Directorate', i.e. Roger Hollis from 1941–5 in MI5, not MI6.[9]

The suspicions that Hollis was the agent were unfounded; he suffered them stoically.

JBS described the intelligence of the observant 'eyes in the sky':

> In the Brunnsum headquarters, with the technological sophistication and accuracy of the satellite surveillance of the Soviet Union, NATO was able to keep very close tabs on the opposition. Proof of this was the 'smart' observation of the movements of a Russian Division. AFCENT Intelligence simply tracked the caravan used by the Commanding General to pinpoint the location of his Division.

G. Corera, in an interview with John Scarlett, Chief of SIS from 2004–9, noted that eavesdropping by GCHQ, working closely with the US NSA, yielded significant intelligence from the monitoring of foreign phone calls. According to Scarlett: 'There are quite a lot of people out there who are planning seriously to try and kill us, and it is our job, as the Secret Intelligence Service, to protect the country and protect its citizens . . . cooperating with dozens of services in key areas of the world – of course, starting with the United States.'[10]

Percy Cradock quoted a 1955 JIC paper which concluded that the highest proportion of targets the Soviet planners would aim to hit would be located in and around the major UK cities and that these cities would be easy to locate. A JIC paper in August 1957 dealt with the effects of hydrogen bombing on the UK generally:

> To render the UK useless as a base for any form of military operations, the simplest and most effective method of attack would be by surface bursts effected in suitable meteorological conditions. These, besides causing local damage, would cause very considerable areas of the country to be affected by fallout. We are advised that something like ten 'H' bombs, each of a yield of about ten megatons, would effectively disrupt the life of the country and make normal activity completely impossible.[11]

The hazardous effects of actual radioactive substances, released by a nuclear explosion, were well known now: the catastrophic nuclear accident at Chernobyl in April 1986 in the Ukraine, carried radioactive particles across a wide swathe of Europe, whilst the Fukushima Daiichi nuclear disaster in 2011 also released radioactivity into the atmosphere.

According to Margaret Thatcher, detente in the early 1970s was based on the ABM (Anti-Ballistic Missile) Treaty, signed in 1972 in the period of the 'Balance of Terror' or MAD (Mutually Assured Destruction). This treaty banned the superpowers from deploying a strategic missile-defence system, the theory being that if both sides were vulnerable to attack, neither would start a nuclear war. The Russians, however secretly circumvented this treaty by building an early warning station at Krasnoyarsk and NATO, for its part, moved away from MAD with its 'flexible response'. This was removed in the Gorbachev era. Faced with the greater number of Warsaw Pact divisions, NATO had been planning and adopting a 'flexible nuclear response' since the end of the 1960s.[12]

The NATO approach was a graduated conventional and nuclear response, rather than an all-out strategic retaliation. John Sanderson in SHAPE HQ had been responsible for rewriting the plan for the defence of Central Europe with a tactical 'flexible defensive response' adopted between 1968 and 1971. This set a flexible threshold for the firing of tactical nuclear weapons, combined with conventional force defences, to hit invading Soviet forces.

Tactical nuclear weapons would target reinforcements coming up behind the advancing Warsaw Pact forces, in their satellite 'buffer' states. The theory was that the risk of an escalation beyond the nuclear threshold was a deterrent to aggression. There would be a planned 'gradual escalation of nuclear defence' to deter Soviet aggression, and the Russians would know that the West 'meant business'.

> Lt-Colonel John Sanderson, 1967–9, Assessment Report by Colonel A. Walker MBE, MC (HQ, AFCENT Reviewing Officer)
>
> During this period Lt-Colonel Sanderson has been directly responsible for coordinating a major revision and complete rewrite of the basic plan for the defence of the Central Region. In carrying out this project, he has shown a high degree of competence as a staff officer and an exceptional ability in organising, directing and reconciling the activities of the large number of agencies concerned.

This review took place at a crucial time of the Cold War. John Sanderson was afterwards offered an important post in the USA as the British Liaison Intelligence Officer with American Intelligence (CIA and FBI) in Washington (similar to that post occupied by Kim Philby). He turned the post down: he didn't want his daughter to settle in America and stay on the other side of the 'Big Pond' when the time came for the family to return to the UK.

Chapter 26

Liaison Officer, French Army, Germany, 1969–71

A French general, having worked with Colonel Sanderson in NATO and noted his good relationships with the French Army in the past, notably in Bulgaria with Colonel Murat and in SHAPE in Paris, had requested the MOD to appoint Sanderson as the British Liaison Officer with the French Forces in Germany. When this was agreed, Sanderson and his wife were sent to Tours University on a six-month intensive French Language course, before being posted in 1969 as British Liaison Officer with the French Army in Baden-Baden, in the French sector of West Germany. This arrangement dated back to the Army Liaison Agreement of 14 November 1944 ('Control machinery in Germany') between America, Britain and the Soviet Union. In March 1945 France had been invited to join. 'Article 2: Each commander-in-chief in his zone of occupation will have attached to him military, naval and air representatives of the two other commanders-in-chief for liaison duties.[1]

Whilst Sanderson was working closely with the French Army in Baden-Baden, the Russians knew virtually everything about French policy towards Russia. Andrew and Mitrakhin explained that the Soviet Sixteenth Directorate (SIGINT) could read vast amounts of French diplomatic communications.[2] A French cipher clerk (JOUR) in the Quai d'Orsay in Paris ('Le Ministre des Affaires étrangères' codenamed ELITA) had provided information on the cipher machines in the French Embassy in Moscow and in NATO HQ. JOUR had been a Soviet agent for over thirty years, having handed over to the KGB during the 1962 Cuban Missile Crisis the exact copies of all traffic communications between Paris (where Sanderson was in SHAPE HQ) and the French embassies in Washington and Moscow.[3]

In 1971 John Sanderson's family, including the author, took a trip to Berlin on the French military train that left from South Germany, stopped at Helmstadt on the border of East Germany, where John Sanderson joined the night train and continued along the rail corridor to West Berlin. In the morning, the train stopped for 20 minutes in East Germany. The author opened the curtains of his sleeper compartment to see an unsmiling and well-armed German border guard facing him through a high fence, not 2m away. Behind him, 100 metres away, East German guards with eager Alsatian dogs on leashes were walking rapidly up and down the platform of a station. On arrival in Berlin the family stayed in the officers' club of the French Army base. The next day the author took a day-long 'tourist' trip by bus, which zigzagged through the well-guarded and fortified crossing point of Checkpoint Charlie into East Berlin. A drive through the Eastern sector ended at a 'showcase' GDR hotel where the obligatory West German marks were spent.

'Die Grenze ist geschlossen' ('The border is closed'). General Marcus Wolf, the inspiration for John Le Carré's fictional character Karla, was the GDR's HVA (GDR foreign intelligence service) spy chief, heading up the highly successful East German intelligence service. HVA had their secret agent Gunter Guillaume, one of 7,000 in the GDR, installed as the Liaison Officer for the Chancellor of the Federal Republic Willy Brandt, giving the spy complete access to all Brandt's confidential papers.[4] Wolf mentioned the French Berlin base in his memoirs, an extract of which appeared in *Le Monde*. He described how the HVA targeted as a priority the French officers' Napoleon Quarter of West Berlin. A French Legionnaire veteran named Bruno Kranick, who often camped in the GDR, was identified and recruited as a paid agent of HVA counter intelligence. Kranick, who worked in the political office of the French HQ, was a mercurial individual and difficult to handle. Nevertheless, he handed over vital strategic intelligence on the Western Powers' reaction to the construction of the Berlin Wall on 13 August 1961. With the additional information the HVA received from sources inside the West German, American and British headquarters, they concluded that the Allies would neither oppose the wall's construction nor retaliate. After the *abgrenzung* ('fencing off') of West Berlin, the HVA communicated daily with Kranick through infrared radio messages beamed across to his apartment, situated close to the wall.[5]

Tony Geraghty noted that 197,000 East Germans had defected to the West in 1960, before the wall went up. Their prisons held 10,000 political prisoners, including those accused of spying for the CIA, MI6, the French

DGSE or the West German BND (West German foreign intelligence agency). By 1983 the GDR Stasi would be 85,000-strong. Their computer files would hold the names of 5 million East German citizens and their shelves would stretch for 18km.[6]

In 1970 Willy Brandt, the former Mayor of West Berlin who had been elected Chancellor in October 1969, in a policy of rapprochement and easing of tension between East and West (his *Neue Ostpolitik*), cosigned with Kosygin and Gromyko the Moscow Treaty, a non-aggression pact. In December Brandt spontaneously knelt in penance and homage (*kniefall von Warschau*) at the Warsaw ghetto memorial.[7]

In London in 1971 Oleg Lyalin, a KGB agent posing as an official of a trade delegation, defected to Britain. He offered information in exchange for a new life with his Russian secretary, Irina Teplyakova. Lyalin revealed that the Thirteenth Department ('wet affairs') had been replaced in 1968–9 by a Department V which was controlled by Directorate 'S' of Yuri Andropov, later to be General Secretary of the politburo. Lyalin was the Department V officer in the *rezidentura* in London. Nigel West noted that this new department was also tasked with running sabotage operations and using fifth-column agents to create mayhem in time of war, i.e. disguising agents as Whitehall messengers to drop poison gas capsules in government underground corridors.[8] Lyalin had been recruited by John Sanderson's SIS colleague (from Bulgarian days when organising stay-behind networks) Major Tony Brooks. Lyalin had been spotted during routine surveillance, having an illicit affair with his secretary and agreed to work for MI5. In August 1971 his defection was spurred by his arrest in London for drink-driving. He claimed asylum a year later.[9] At least thirty or forty Soviet Intelligence officers in this country were actually running secret agents in government or industry. Following Lyalin's revelations, 105 Soviet intelligence officers were expelled from Britain under Operation FOOT: 90 were Soviet diplomats known to be KGB or GRU officers and another 15 were not re-admitted to Britain. The operation was handled by John Sanderson's friend (from Sofia in 1949), Sir Denis Greenhill, the PUS, who was later offered the post of 'C' but turned it down, whilst accepting Chair of the JIC. Greenhill had been preparing to act against the Soviets in Britain, since a meeting he had held at the FCO in March 1971, attended by 'C', the Chairman of the JIC, the Cabinet Secretary, the MI5 DG (Director General) and the PUSs of the Home Office, the MOD and the DTI (Department of Trade and Industry). The MI5 DG had recommended the removal of a hundred Soviets due to evidence of Soviet penetration of the FCO, the MOD, the army, navy and air force, the Labour Party,

Transport House and the Board of Trade. This action severely disrupted the KGB's Third Department and the careers of a significant number of KGB and GRU individuals.[10]

In 1973 in Russia there were half a million KGB agents: this figure would increase to 700,000 in 1986. In the twenty years after Khrushchev's fall, the CPSU (Communist Party of the Soviet Union) continued to stifle change in government and reinforce its hold over society.[11]

Ryszard Kapuściński described how the writer Yurii Boriev saw an analogy between the Soviet Union and a train. Lenin sets off at the controls of a locomotive speeding towards a bright new future but he is soon forced to stop when the tracks run out. He urges the workers to labour extra hours to lay more rails. The train sets off again, now with Stalin in charge. When the train inevitably grinds to a halt, Stalin orders half of the conductors and passengers to be shot and tells the rest to get out and lay more track. Now Khrushchev sets off in the driving seat. When the train stops again, he directs the passengers to move the rails from the rear of the train and to re-lay them in front of the engine. Then Brezhnev takes over control of the train. When the track runs out, he gives orders for the blinds to be lowered and the stationary carriages rocked so the passengers think the train is still in motion.[12]

Leonid Brezhnev, a vain and non-intellectual leader, did nothing radical to reform the Communist system during his eighteen years in power, but rather consolidated the political elite's power, whilst putting off the change necessary for Soviet society. The Party and the other privileged in society, the *nomenklatura*, continued to have access to special food, housing and other privileges. The 'Brezhnev doctrine' justified military and domestic intervention in satellite countries that threatened the cohesion of the Soviet bloc. Brezhnev continued the high Soviet military expenditure on the one hand, whilst offering detente to the West with the other.[13] Brezhnev realised that it would be impossible, in a climate of confrontation, to acquire the technology necessary to modernise Soviet industry. His thinking on detente was that if he lulled the West into a false sense of security, he would have more opportunity to achieve Soviet ambitions in the third world.

In 1967 a series of treaties were signed, forbidding nuclear tests in space, and in 1971, the banning of the placing of nuclear weapons on the ocean floor. In the SALT (Strategic Arms Limitation) 1 Treaty of 1972 the number of strategic nuclear launchers were frozen (the Soviets had 1,618 against the US total of 1,054, although the US had multiple-head rockets). A system of verification was set up with reconnaissance from satellites. Each side was also permitted two ABM locations, one near their capital city, the other near an ICBM site, to act as a deterrent against a first strike. In 1974 Gerald Ford signed an agreement with Brezhnev to limit to 2,400 the number of launchers and 1,320 for multi-head rockets. From 1974, however, this detente gave way to an arms build-up and a more confrontational policy towards NATO. The year 1975 was seen as the high point of detente when the Helsinki accords were signed. The post-1945 changes in European boundaries were accepted, as well as the Soviet buffer states. There was an agreement of notification of all military exercises involving more than 25,000 men. There were also important clauses on human rights and freedom of expression, which the West did not hesitate to follow up to the Soviets' discomfort.[14]

The development of Cruise missiles and the Soviet 'Backfire' Tupolev Tu-26 bomber, however, delayed ratification of SALT II, which was finally signed in Vienna in 1979, with a SALT III planned in 1985. This was not an effective limiting treaty and appeared to give the Soviets the opportunity to catch up with the USA in missile numbers and eliminate the West's technological advantage.[15] Western intelligence was in a 'blind' situation in 1982, due to the traitor Geoffrey Prime betraying the Cosmic Secret that Britain and the USA had cracked the Soviet high-grade military codes. The Russians subsequently changed all their cipher codes, making it impossible for their traffic to be read at a crucial period of the Cold War.[16] 'It meant the West was left blind to Moscow's intentions during the 1980–1 Solidarity crisis in Poland.'[17]

The election of Cardinal Karol Wojtyła, the Archbishop of Kraków as Pope John Paul II in October 1978 was the significant event in Poland's quest for freedom. The Mitrokhin Archive reveal how strong was the support for Wojtyła and how powerful were his beliefs. The KGB understood how challenging were his views but they dared not arrest him. Andrew and Mitrokhin wrote that 'the contrast between the discredited Communist regime and the immense moral authority of the first Polish Pope was plain for all to see'.[18] A report of the SB (Polish Internal Security Service), the counterpart of the KGB, was sent to the Moscow Centre by the Warsaw *rezident*:

> Wojtyła holds extreme anti-communist views . . . his accusations are that: the people are deprived of its sovereignty . . . collectivisation has led to the destruction of the individual and of his personality . . . the basic human rights of Polish citizens

> are restricted, there is an unacceptable exploitation of workers, whom the Catholic Church must protect against the workers' government, Catholics are treated as second class citizens, that an extensive campaign is being conducted to convert society to atheism and to impose an alien ideology and that the Catholic Church is being denied its proper cultural role . . . 90% of the population is Catholic.

The Hungarian Revolution of 1956 and the Prague Spring of 1968 had failed but the Catholic Church, Polish solidarity and the union of the same name, Solidarność, founded in September 1980 in the Lenin shipyard in Gdańsk under Lech Wałęsa, had gained too strong a support amongst the population. In June 1979 a million Poles had welcomed the Pope home, a demonstration of John Paul II's popular grassroots support.[19]

With eighteen Russian and Warsaw Pact divisions exercising on Poland's border, the risk for NATO that a crackdown in Poland could be a precursor to a further movement westwards of the Warsaw Pact could not be excluded. Brezhnev had decided: 'OK, we don't march into Poland now, but if the situation gets any worse we will come.'[20]

Eight months exactly after John Paul II was shot in St Peter's Square, Rome, martial law was declared by General Jaruzelski on 13 December 1981, with 10,000 Poles arrested on day one. When the Pope, who had narrowly escaped death in the assassination attempt, made a long-awaited return to Poland in April 1983, he was met by adoring crowds everywhere. The following month martial law was suspended. In October Wałęsa was awarded the Nobel Peace Prize.[21] The superpowers, meanwhile, had continued their arms race: the Soviets deployed 'Blackjack' bombers and were developing new ICBMs, whilst the Americans constructed a new multi-missile submarine platform and the new ICBM 'Peacemaker'. The INF (Intermediate-Range Nuclear Force) treaty talks on SS-20 and Cruise missiles in Europe started in Geneva in 1981. The START (Strategic Arms Reduction Treaty) talks began in 1982 but were suspended in 1983 when President Reagan announced research on the 'Star Wars' SDI (Strategic Defence Initiative). The INF would finally be signed in 1987 by Reagan and Gorbachev.[22]

With Brezhnev's death in November 1982, and under the successive General Secretaries, with a more educated Soviet urban elite aspiring towards a more prosperous and independent life, the pressure for change within Russia grew. Gorbachev, glasnost and perestroika were on their way. Within seven years of Gorbachev becoming General Secretary in March 1985, the Soviet Union would fall apart. The START treaty would eventually be signed just before the Soviet Union dissolved and would finally come into force in December 1994, three years after its collapse.

Chapter 27

Kim Philby in Berlin, 1981

Philby was invited in 1981 by Marcus Wolf, the East German spymaster, to lecture in a theatre at the HQ of the Stasi in East Berlin. Addressing the audience as 'Dear Comrades', Philby spoke for an hour with self-assurance and pride about his life and career as a spy, from his recruitment at Cambridge to his departure to Moscow aboard a freighter in January 1963. The 1981 recording of this lecture was located in 2016 by the BBC and broadcast by the BBC Defence Correspondent Gordon Corera.[1]

On the tape Comrade General Wolf introduced Philby, in German, as having spent '30 years in the enemy camp'. Philby, who was born in the Punjab, India on 1 January 1912, started his talk in English, discussing his Indian childhood in India:

> It is perfectly true that I was born into the ruling class of the British Empire. When I was born, my father was District Commissioner in India, and as such, he was a young man ruling several million Indians. So why am I, his son, talking to you like this, both our organisations dedicated to smashing every vestige of imperialism off the face of the earth?

The Soviets wanted him to be a long-term penetration agent. 'It was essentially a long range project. No immediate results were expected or could have been expected. It was made perfectly clear to me that the best target in the eyes of the Centre in Moscow would be the British Secret Service.' The Soviets knew Cambridge students would have successful careers in the British Home Civil Service and they spread their net widely. 'Looking back to my recruitment I find the strangest thing about it, is the fact that I was recruited at all.' He was a young man with no work at the time and without access to any secrets. All he had in the eyes of the astute KGB were 'impeccable bougeois origins and a bourgeois education'.

Philby said he was approached to join SIS when a journalist: 'I was sitting in my office in the Times with very little to do, when suddenly the telephone rang and a voice asked me if I'd be interested in special work for the British Government.'

Recruited into SIS, Philby started working on German, Spanish and Portuguese espionage. He found it easy, with lax SIS security, to obtain documents, from a friend in the archives department, on a wider range of subjects than his immediate geographical responsibility. (Stalin was said to be very proud of these vast numbers of MI6 documents in his files.)

> I would get to the point where two or three times a week I'd meet him after office hours for drinks. He became a close friend, and in my confidence, so I can ask for papers which have nothing to do with German espionage on Spain or Portugal but which he would nevertheless send me as a friend whom he trusted.
>
> Every evening I left the office with a big briefcase full of reports which I had written myself, full of files taken out of the actual documents, out of the actual archives.
>
> I was to hand them to my Soviet contact in the evening. The next morning I would get the file back, the contents having been photographed, and take them back early in the morning and put the files back in their place. That I did regularly, year in, year out.
>
> You have probably all heard stories that the SIS is an organisation of mythical efficiency, a very, very dangerous thing indeed. Well, in a time of war, it honestly was not. If there had been proper discipline in the handling of papers in SIS that would have been quite impossible. But there was, in fact, no discipline.

Philby was then appointed number two in the new MI6 section devoted to counter espionage against Russia. His KGB handler's next instructions were for him to take over the top job in his section by removing his boss, Felix Cowgill.

> I said: 'Well are you proposing to shoot him or something?'
>
> He said: 'No, but all the same, you are going to be head of that new department.'
>
> So I said: 'Well my instructions from the Centre are that I must get rid of my own boss and take his place, yes?
>
> And he said: 'Yes'.

His handler suggested Philby managed it through bureaucratic intrigue. 'So I set about the business of removing my own chief. You oughtn't to listen to this,' he tells the audience of secret service officers to much laughter. He succeeded, by getting his colleagues to plot against their head.

> It was a very dirty story. But, after all, our work does imply getting dirty hands from time to time but we do it for a cause that is not dirty in any way. I have to admit that was the most blatant intrigue against a man I rather liked and I admired but the instructions stood and nothing I could do would alter them.

When he was posted to Washington DC as MI6's liaison with the CIA and FBI, Philby was to betray the Albanian émigré operation to overthrow the Communist regime. Philby claims that by compromising the Albanian operation – he was a member of the four-man High Command team organising it and had full access to the plans – he had helped prevent a third world war, since it thwarted an MI6 operation inside Bulgaria which, he said, could have led to a world war. (This Washington liaison position was later offered to John Sanderson. He turned down this influential position which could have put him in the running for becoming 'C'.) Philby explained his role in Washington: 'I was a member of the High Command and I had all this information . . .'.

Philby passed on the details of SIS infiltration operations in the Baltic, Poland, East Germany and the Balkans to Moscow, including those planned by *JBS*, who told the author in 1995, with bitterness in his voice – even after all those years – that 'Philby betrayed all my agents.'

Philby knew that Bulgaria had being targeted by SIS, but told the Stasi recruits that after Albania: 'If they had been successful the next target would have been Bulgaria. And if they had started that sort of operation in Bulgaria, the Soviet Union would have undoubtedly been immediately involved in World War Three.' Philby deluded himself that his betrayal and the death of so many men in Albania had averted another world war. It is unlikely that the Soviet Union would have gone to war with the West over Bulgaria.

The defection of Guy Burgess together with Maclean, a diplomat but not in SIS, was a disaster for Philby: 'It absolutely destroyed my position in SIS. I might I think, possibly have been chief of the whole outfit, I don't know, but anyway one of the first three, say.' There had been an outside chance after his Washington post as Liaison Officer that he could have been shortlisted for the post of 'C', as may have Sanderson if he had accepted the Washington post. As regards the investigation that followed

Burgess' defection: 'I felt slightly relieved to find that the old class instinct has asserted itself and that the investigation that had begun some months before had concentrated almost entirely on the locally recruited servants of the embassy.'

Philby had been dismissed in July 1951 by MI6. Then in November 1951 he was cross-examined by Sir Helenus 'Buster' Milmo QC. Nobody who attended the hours of questioning believed that Philby was innocent. Numerous lies had been found in his two written statements after Burgess and Maclean's defections. But Philbys survived by remaining silent and not confessing. Philby was never really trusted again but was posted to Beirut under cover as a newspaper journalist.[2]

New evidence surfaced in 1963, however. Philby's friend Nicholas Elliott flew to Beirut and confronted Philby: 'You took me in for years. Now I'll get the truth out of you even if I have to drag it out. I once looked up to you. My God how I despise you now. I hope you've got enough decency to understand why.' Philby, taken aback for once, admitted working for the Soviets but only up to 1946. Duplicitous to the end, the typewritten account that he handed over the next day was aimed to clear Anthony Blunt and to incriminate two innocent SIS colleagues, Tim and Tony Milne, whose careers were finished as a result.[3] Philby's version, told to the Stasi in Berlin, differed substantially from Elliott's actual words.

> He said to me, 'Now Kim we are old friends. I have defended you always in the past. Now evidence has come to hand that proves conclusively that you were working for the Soviet Union up to 1949. Now what have you got to say about that?'
>
> And I said: 'Well I haven't anything to say in particular'.
>
> And he said: 'Look here, well, I've seen the evidence myself and I am convinced, I am convinced that it must be true.'
>
> And so I had to stall him.

Another MI6 officer, Peter Lunn, John Aldwinckle's chief in Berlin, was then left to watch over him.

> Four days after my friend Elliott's departure for London, reports reached Beirut of a heavy snowfall in the mountains north of Lebanon and ideal conditions for skiing. And he decided, four days after my other friend had gone back to London, to take a four day holiday skiing in the mountains – and he was the only man in Beirut who knew anything about my case. Four days after he left, I got the signal for departure. I left my flat, went to

> the rendezvous – and away. And I heard afterwards that half an hour after I left my flat Peter Lunn rang up, asking for an urgent meeting the following morning. But the following morning I was gone, way beyond the borders of Lebanon.

It seems that the return of Philby for trial in London was not something the FO would welcome. It's very possible that they left Philby with the opportunity to flee to Moscow.

The enthusiastic Stasi audience then asked him questions. How did he get away with it for so long? Philby's explanation:

> There were many people in SIS who were involved in my recruitment into SIS, my promotion in SIS, who had worked with me in SIS, and given me a lot of information in SIS, those people would be very, very anxious personally to see me made innocent, including the chief of the whole organisation, who had made me head of his counter-espionage. Furthermore, because I had been born into the British governing class, because I knew a lot of people of an influential standing, I knew that they would never get too tough with me. They'd never try to beat me up or knock me around, because if they had been proved wrong afterwards, I could have made a tremendous scandal.

Philby offered a final piece of advice:

> They interrogated me to break my nerve and force me to confess. And all I had to do really was keep my nerve. So my advice to you is to tell all your agents that they are never to confess. If they're confronted with a photograph of themselves, whether with a Soviet contact or a German contact, it's a fake. If they confront you with a report in your own handwriting, it's a forgery – just deny everything. Only admit what is harmless. Admit anything you safely can. But deny that essential link with any foreign intelligence service and you're alright.

This advice to 'Never Confess!' was an outright lie and Philby was deceiving himself and the East German audience. In London in 1955 Philby had indeed repeatedly denied being a Soviet agent. In January 1963, however, when his friend Nicholas Elliott of SIS had confronted Philby in Beirut with his treachery, Philby had made a partial admission to working for Soviet Intelligence. H. Trevor-Roper, an SIS colleague of Philby from 1941, wrote scornfully of his egocentricity. His perceptive analysis of Philby's character was a damning indictment of a man he knew well: Philby's 'critical spirit, his intellectual purity, his moral conscience' died when he decided to unquestioningly serve his communist masters. Trevor-Roper went on to say that 'Philby touched nothing that he did not destroy . . . Institutions, persons, friendships, marriage, all crumbled around him.'[4]

During his spying years in Britain Kim Philby had always assumed he had the status of a KGB officer. When he reached Moscow he learned he was only viewed as a KGB 'agent'. True to form, he deceived the readers of his biography that he was an intelligence 'officer' and 'disinformed' visiting Western journalists that he held the rank of a colonel in the KGB.[5]

Philby died in Moscow in 1988 just before the collapse of the Communist ideal which he had spent his life serving. His ex-colleague John Sanderson, however, had the great satisfaction of watching the fall of the Berlin Wall on television news, seated next to his son, the author.

Chapter 28

Operation RYAN and Exercise Able Archer, 1983

Operation RYAN – Ракетное Ядерное Нападение – nuclear missile attack

> A thermonuclear war cannot be considered as a continuation of politics by other means (re: Clausewitz), it would be a means of universal suicide . . . The experience of past wars shows that the first use of a new technical or tactical method of attack is usually highly effective even if a simple antidote can soon be developed. But in a thermonuclear war the first blow may be the decisive one and render null and void years of work and billions spent on creation of an anti-missile system.
>
> Andrei Sakharov, June 1968[1]

The nuclear physicist Sakharov wrote these words exactly fifty years ago. Originally seen as the 'father of the Soviet hydrogen bomb', he was awarded the Nobel Peace Prize in 1975 for his work as a human rights activist. The dissident Sakharov had condemned the Soviet invasion of Afghanistan in 1979 and was exiled to Gorky in 1980, where he remained isolated from his social circle and persecuted by the KGB, on Yuri Andropov's instructions. The deterrent effect of retaliation with an atomic bomb, had kept the peace in Europe since 1945. The dangers and risk of war, however, had multiplied, as the superpowers' arms budgets rocketed and new missiles threatened a war that, in John Sanderson's perceptive words in 1948 in Paris, 'would not last very long', that could actually be over very quickly. The Cold War between the West and Russia was now entering its final phase. Within seven years, the Soviets' Eastern European empire would break up and, within a decade, the Soviet Union would be gone. It was twenty-three years since Nikita Khrushchev banged his shoe on the table in the UN, then two years later shipped missiles to Cuba, threatening the USA in its backyard and risking a global war. The world had watched and held its breath then. In 1983, as the Cold War entered its most dangerous months, the real threat of war went largely unnoticed by the general public, concerned as they have been by the build-up of menacing missiles in Europe. Soviet fears that the USA might think a 'first strike' nuclear conflict 'winnable' began over twenty years before, in October 1961, when the US Deputy Secretary of Defense Gilpatric had declared: 'We have a second-strike capability which is at least as extensive as what the Soviets can deliver by striking first. Therefore we are confident that the Soviets will not provoke a major nuclear conflict.'[2] The Americans were indicating to Moscow that a 'first strike' by Soviet ICBM rockets would not neutralise US offensive capabilities but would be met by retaliatory strikes on Russian targets. However, from their end of the telescope, the Russians thought the USA believed that it could survive a retaliatory strike by Russia, after a first strike by themselves, and still win a war.

In March 1983 Reagan announced on national television his intention to deploy SDI, a space-based missile-defence system, as a 'defence shield' to protect the US public. The announcement had a profound effect in Moscow. If SDI worked, the implications were cataclysmic, making the strategies of deterrent and MAD redundant. The USA could launch a nuclear first strike without fear of a Soviet retaliatory response.[3] The Russians' fear of the US 'Star Wars' programme, however, was that they could not hope, technologically or financially, to match this missile shield which would (theoretically) make the USA invulnerable to Soviet missiles and still able to strike the USSR with impunity.

Soviet conventional forces in Europe were expanding to a worrying level. Brigadier John Learmont, Chief of the BRIXMIS Mission, had reported in 1983: 'During the past twenty months I have witnessed the biggest re-equipment programme undertaken by GSFG [Group of Soviet Forces in Germany] since World War II. The improvement is both qualitative and quantative. The threat posed is totally different from that presented in late 1982.'[4]

Forces of the Warsaw Pact, May 1980, Twenty-Fifth Anniversary of Formation

	Russia	Bulgaria	Czechoslovakia	Hungary	GDR	Poland	Romania
Infantry	3.66 million	150,000	185,000	105,000	160,000	320,000	181,000
Divisions	173	8	10	6	6	15	10
Tanks	50,000	1,800	3,400	1,250	2,500	3,400	1,500
Combat Planes	4,350	170	460	150	335	680	330
Naval Ships	1,280	50	–	–	150	112	86

(including non-nuclear submarines)

Source: Claude Delmas, *Le Pact de Varsovie* (Presse Universitaire de France, 1981), p. 47.

Taylor Downing noted that the Americans were doubling their defence budget and budget deficit, with orders for new BI-B bombers, Tomahawk cruise and Pershing II missiles, new M-1 Abraham Battle tanks, fighter-bombers and Stealth aircraft. On the sea, new ships were sailing and, under the waves, new Trident submarines, on a 'crusade of freedom' to challenge what Reagan saw as 'the Evil Empire'.[5] Another US ploy to apply pressure on the Soviets was their use of PSYOPS navy and air force probes near the Russian borders which greatly unnerved the Russians, as General Jack Chain, US SAC Commander, recalled: 'Sometimes we would send bombers over the North Pole and their radars would click on.' And Dr W. Schneider, Under Secretary of State: 'It really got to them. They didn't know what it all meant. A squadron would fly straight at the Soviet airspace, and other radars would light up and units would go on alert. Then at the last minute the squadron would peel off.'[6]

The author S. Vistica noted that in March 1981 Reagan authorised the navy to exercise near maritime approaches to the USSR in places where no US warships had gone before. In August/September an Armada of eighty-three NATO ships led by the carrier Eisenhower sailed through the Greenland-Iceland-UK Gap undetected, using concealed and deception measures, turning the Allied force into a quasi-stealth fleet, even eluding a Soviet low-orbit, active-radar satellite launched to locate it. As the warships came within Soviet long-range reconnaissance planes' operating areas the Soviets could identify but not track them. The navy fighters made unprecedented simulated attacks on the Soviet planes as they refuelled in-flight.[7]

The author S. Hersh described sabre-rattling by the US Navy, which in 1983 dispatched aircraft carrier battle groups on exercises off the north and east coasts of the Soviet Union. The potential military and industrial targets located inland were subject to simulated surprise attacks. In the fjords of Norway the admirals positioned submarine escorts and further aircraft carriers. Under the Arctic ice cap, US submarines practised attacks on Soviet SSBMs (nuclear-powered ballistic missile submarines). American warships patrolled the Bering and Baltic seas. Off the Crimean peninsula, where the Russian Baltic fleet was based, American intelligence SIGINT ships were anchored, listening and recording.[8]

Thatcher later wrote: 'All these exercises were a demonstration that the US and her allies could match and surpass menacing Russian exercises. However, there is no doubt they left the Soviets increasingly worried and frightened.'[9] In the autumn of 1983 the USA deployed Cruise missiles (for sea, air or ground launching with a flying time from West Germany to Moscow of 4–6 minutes) and Trident II and Pershing II missiles (capable of destroying Soviet underground missile silos and 'command and control bunkers') to counter the USSR's SS-20 threat. From the Soviet perspective, their SS-20s with a range of 2,500 miles did not threaten the US mainland. As *Time Magazine* noted, IRBM + NATO = ICBM: US rockets within Europe were the equivalent of strategic missiles threatening Moscow.[10] In 1983 this was precisely the threat of a first-strike Western attack that the paranoid General Secretary Yuri Andropov and his Old Guard in the Presidium were mistakenly worried about, with Pershing II and Cruise missiles threatening, within 6 minutes of flying time, to vaporise the Soviet leadership before they could reach their nuclear bunkers. Vladimir Kryuchkov, head of the First Chief Directorate, was convinced that the West intended to decimate the Soviet Union. Andropov informed his KGB residences abroad: 'Not since the end of the Second World War has the international situation been as explosive as it is now.' Anatoli Dobrynin, the long serving ambassador in Washington, saw Andropov's attitude as 'a paranoid interpretation' of President Reagan's policy.[11]

The Kremlin had committed two major strategic errors leading up to this situation. Firstly, by invading Afghanistan in 1974, they had started a war that turned out to be their 'Vietnam', with thousands of young conscripts repatriated in body bags, billions of rubles in treasure expended with nothing to show for it and world opinion turning against them and ending detente. The second error was the stationing of upgraded missiles (with technology, known to NATO as stolen from the West by Soviet agents), the mobile SS-20s in Eastern Europe, which threatened the West and escalated the Cold War.[12] In 1981 President Reagan had proposed 'the zero-zero' withdrawal of SS-20s, as a condition for the USA not deploying new IRBMs in Europe but Moscow had said: '*Niet*.'[13] Gordon Brook-Shepherd explained that the KGB was ordered to investigate whether a political decision had been reached by the West to carry out a nuclear strike on Russia, while the GRU were to monitor military evidence for a possible attack. The *residentzia* were told 'Don't Miss it!' – '*Niet Prozerot*!' In London the MI6 double agent Oleg Gordievsky was well-placed to warn British Intelligence of Operation RYAN when General Kryuchov had told Gordievsky's department that: 'Belligerent imperialist circles are preparing new weapons systems which could render a sudden attack feasible.'[14]

In January 1983 a Top Secret assignment was sent from Moscow to the London *Rezident*:

> 17.02.1983 TOP SECRET COPY No 1 LONDON
> COMRADE YERMAKOV (A.V. GUK.)
> PERMANENT OPERATIONAL
>
> **Assignment to Uncover NATO Preparations for a Nuclear Missile Attack on USSR**
>
> In view of the growing urgency . . . discovering promptly any preparations by the adversary for a nuclear missile attack [RYAN] on the USSR, we are sending you a permanent . . . assignment [POA] and briefing. The objective . . . is to . . . uncover any plans in preparation by the main adversary [the United States] for RYAN and to organise a continual watch for indications of a decision . . . to use nuclear weapons against the USSR or immediate preparations being made for a nuclear missile attack.[15]

Nigel West described how Colonel Oleg Gordievsky, who had positioned himself in charge of the Russian desk in Moscow, had alerted London to this 'largest Soviet peacetime operation in history, run jointly by the KGB and the GRU'. This was passed on to Number 10 to Margaret Thatcher. Gordievsky, codenamed FELIKS then OVATION, was the most valuable MI6 double agent since Colonel Oleg Penkovsky two decades previously. The Soviet invasion of Czechoslovakia in 1968 had deeply affected him, as the Hungarian invasion in 1956 had disillusioned Penkovsky.[16]

The author T. Downing noted that Gordievsky was a university entrant into the Soviet Foreign Ministry before his first posting to Berlin, just after the wall went up. In 1963 he had moved to the KGB where he underwent three years of training. Gordievsky hated the Soviet Union and saw it as one big concentration camp. Gordievsky's first KGB posting had been to Copenhagen in 1972. A second posting to Denmark was as a Press Attaché, the same Secret Service cover that SIS officer John Sanderson used in Sofia in 1949. In Copenhagen Gordievsky made contact with MI6 where his first case officer was an MI6 Russian speaker, John Scarlett, later to become 'C'. Gordievsky revealed that there was a Soviet spy named Gunvor Haavik inside the Norwegian Foreign Ministry. (It was through Norwegian waters that the Soviet naval fleets and submarines passed, heading from Murmansk to the Atlantic.) When Haavik was arrested, the Moscow Centre tried to find the source of the leak, drawing up a list of seven possible suspects to try to identify the Western mole. Although on the list, nothing was proved against Gordievsky. He later named a Norwegian Arne Treholt as a spy selling NATO top-secret documents to the KGB.[17]

Gordievsky was run as an agent inside the KGB Third Department for twelve years, from 1972 until 1985. In December 1982 Gordievsky had identified Michael Bettaney as a Soviet mole working inside MI5's counter espionage department. Bettaney was sentenced to twenty-three years in prison. Gordievsky also had a valuable information source outside the Third Directorate, in the person of his brother, who had trained as an illegal in the FRG. Gordievsky's comprehensive intelligence was a gold mine to MI6. He revealed the posting details of all his colleagues in the KGB. Between 1978 and 1983, 316 espionage agents were withdrawn from 43 countries. In 1983 alone 111 Soviets were PNG'd from 16 countries.[18]

Operation RYAN's aim was to identify warning signs that an attack from the West was imminent. Yuri Andropov, who had initiated RYAN in 1981, thought that the NATO exercise was a 'ruse of war', a deception (*maskarova*), to cover up an actual attack on the USSR. A KGB memo was sent to Soviet embassies in all NATO countries and major cities around the world declaring that 'the threat of the outbreak of nuclear war has reached dangerous proportions'.[19]

Nigel West wrote that in May 1981 the KGB had drawn up a list of 292 indicators in the areas of economy, the political, military and intelligence services and civil defence. Significant observations might add to the evidence being collated by fifty KGB officers in Moscow of a planned Western surprise nuclear attack.[20]

Exercise Able Archer, 2–11 November 1983

> 'The world did not quite reach the edge of the nuclear abyss during Operation RYAN. During ABLE ARCHER 83 it had, without realising it, come frighteningly close . . . closer than at any time since the Cuban missile crisis.'[21]

G. Brook-Shepherd explained that:

> [Able Archer] was a top secret exercise, staged to enable the western alliance to practise its own nuclear release procedures in . . . an all-out war. As a matter of routine, Warsaw Pact intelligence began to monitor the exercise . . . and Western intelligence began to monitor the monitors . . . It soon became clear to both British and American listening centres that something had gone badly wrong . . . a sharp increase was registered in both the volume and the urgency of the Eastern bloc traffic. The incredible seemed to be happening . . . that the Warsaw Pact suspected it might really be facing nuclear attack at any moment.

The Russians were assuming that the West was using an exercise as a cover for a real invasion. On 8–9 November the Kremlin had panicked, 'having noted what appeared to be significant changes in the Able Archer message formats'.[22]

Gordon Corera commented: 'Part of the Soviet land-based missile force went on to its own heightened alert. The world was not on the brink of war but there was a danger that, as in the First World War, mobilisations and preparations could be embarked upon from which no one could back down.'[23]

Andrew and Gordievsky described a Moscow Centre memo of February 1983:

> of the highest importance [is] to keep a watch on the functioning of communications networks and systems since through them information is passed about the adversaries' intentions and, above all, about his plans to use nuclear weapons . . . changes in the method of operating communications systems and the level of manning may in themselves indicate the state of preparation for RYAN.[24]

During Able Archer 83, NATO forces simulated going through all the alert stages from DEFCON 5 to DEFCON 1 (NATO's five alert stages (5–1) up to imminent war; Operational Readiness No. 1 is declared when there are obvious indications that war is inevitable and may start at any moment). This progression led KGB agents to mistakenly report the alert moves from 5 to 1 as actual. Part of the scenario which NATO war gamers were playing in Mons SHAPE HQ was a Warsaw Pact nuclear attack on Colonel Sanderson's former AFCENT HQ in Limburg, Holland.[25]

Andrew and Gordievsky described Soviet Intelligence as reporting that NATO was indeed using unique procedures, not seen previously, as well as new more sophisticated message formats that could possibly indicate an imminent nuclear attack.[26]

Given this level of perceived threat, the Soviet forces were put on nuclear strike alert. The historian J. Hughes-Wilson noted that, with panic taking hold in the Kremlin, a flash signal went out to all KGB *rezidentura* abroad announcing an 'intelligence of war status'. In East Berlin Marcus Wolf, like Gordievsky in London, thought RYAN was a ludicrous overreaction. In Washington Dobrynin commented later: 'Both sides went a little crazy.' Gordievsky reported that on 8/9 November the Kremlin issued a FLASH Top-Secret 'warning of war' signal, putting the Warsaw Pact on a war footing. Ammunition was prepared for aircraft, tanks were driven to battle readiness and troops moved to their dispersal stations. MI6 files, from British agents operating inside the Kremlin and the Soviet High Command at the time, reveal that Moscow thought that NATO was preparing for war.[27]

Downing, in 1983, noted that Moscow Centre had received, through Marcus Wolf's HVA, a 'Cosmic Top Secret' report from his spy TOPAZ (Rainer Rupp), who was head of the NATO Current Intelligence group. This annual document laid out all the exact locations and details of NATO military forces and equipment, with details of the known Warsaw Pact assets. This reliable HVA spy was able to reassure Moscow that no NATO first-strike attack was in fact planned. Downing noted that a nuclear war was nearly started by accident in an isolated incident in September 1983 when a Lieutenant Colonel Petrov in a Soviet 'early warning' missile attack station, which was monitoring US Minuteman ICBMs in the USA, received repeated satellite signals detecting the flares of US missile launches. Not seeing evidence of missiles from the satellite's photographic detectors, the sensible Petrov reported these to Moscow as 'false alarms' and, luckily for humanity, not as a massive US 'first-strike' attack on the Soviet Union. The 'OKO' (EYE) satellites were later found to have misinterpreted the sun's reflection on high clouds as missiles engine flares.[28]

The Russian alert only stood down, however, when the exercise Able Archer terminated on 11 November. President Reagan was advised of Soviet perceptions of a likely NATO 'first strike' and took note, reducing his 'Evil Empire' rhetoric.

Exercise LIONHEART, September 1984

When Yuri Andropov died in February 1984 and Konstantin Chernenko took over as General Secretary, East–West tensions eased off slightly. Margaret Thatcher and Vice-President Bush attended Andropov's funeral in Moscow and earned Russian respect for their respectful attendance.

Moscow Centre, however, still continued to send flash messages out and demanded reports on the West's preparation for nuclear war. In April NATO issued, in error, a telegram erroneously reporting that NATO communications systems were almost set on a 'war footing'. Andrew and Gordievsky noted that the death of the hardline Marshal Ustinov and removal of his deputy weakened the belief in the credibility of RYAN amongst the leadership.[29]

In September 1984, NATO forces held their annual exercise, this year called LIONHEART, the largest British reinforcement exercise since the Second World War. This was the last year (1983–4) that John Sanderson was in military service as the Administrative Officer of a TA Reserve regiment: he would have been involved in the mobilisation of this TA unit for these Continental exercises in 1983 and 1984. Sanderson had been in continuous service since 1938, forty-six years in total.

Exercise LIONHEART comprised Exercise FULLFLOW, involving all troops in the rear Combat Zone, and Exercise SPEARPOINT, involving the 1st British Corps ('Blue' force) with 97,000 men and 750 main Challenger battle tanks under the command of Lieutenant General Ferndale. The 3rd and 4th Armoured Divs with 2nd Infantry Div. were deployed in the Corps rear whilst the 6th Airborne Bde was held in reserve. The 'Orange' force 'enemy' of 12,000 men was represented by the 1st German Panzergrenadier Bde, the 1st US Tiger Bde and the 4th Netherland Armoured Bde. Supporting in the rear were the 5th Airborne Bde (UK), the Life Guards, the 10th Gurkha Rifles and elements of the Parachute regiments. The RAF and Allied forces, consisting of 13,000 airmen with Harriers and new Tornados were also in action as part of the 2nd Allied Tactical Air Force for both 'Orange' and 'Blue' sides.[30]

Spetsnaz (Soviet Special Forces) 'Spetsialnoye Nashacheniye' Defector

The invasion of Czechoslovakia in 1968 had had a profound effect, as it had for Oleg Gordievsky, on Red Army intelligence officer Lieutenant Vladimir Rezun. Rezun realised that the Soviet Army, of which he was part, was not rolling in as a liberator, as it had in 1944. Rather it came as oppressor of a sympathetic and relatively prosperous and free country under Dubček. When Rezun had defected in 1978, he brought with him detailed knowledge of the ruthless Spetsialnoye Nashacheniye, or Special Purpose Forces, who were trained to find and eliminate, at the very start of a conflict, NATO military commanders and their enemy's leaders. Rezun described the structure of 'Aquarium', the Russian GRU Military Intelligence HQ based on Moscow's Khodinka airfield, with full details of the GRU members in foreign embassies and their agents.[31]

G.Brook-Shepherd described the Spetsnaz ethos:

> These special sabotage and terrorist units had been integrated into every layer of the Soviet military, naval and intelligence network. Each of the 41 Soviet armies [had] a Spetsnaz company of 115 men, commanded by a major, as part of its regular strength . . . They were drafted in because they were considered tough and ruthless enough to meet the requirements of turning out a terrorist in uniform, driven by single-minded savagery . . . All the beatings . . . insults and humiliations he has suffered are steps on the path to a brilliant, suicidal feat of heroism . . . only someone who has been driven barefoot into the mud and snow . . . and has proved every day with his fists his right to existence – only this kind of man is capable of showing one day that he is the best.[32]

The scenario account below, by a SHAPE historian, was used by the Joint Chiefs of Staff in Washington DC and the MOD in London. Released by NATO, it details the hypothetical lead-up to the Able Archer 83 exercise and explains why the soldiers in the 1984 exercise were wearing gas and chemical suits:

> The exercise scenario began with Orange (the hypothetical opponent) opening hostilities in all regions on 4 November and Blue (NATO) declaring a general alert. Orange initiated the use of chemical weapons on 6th November. These events had taken place before the start of the exercise and were simply part of the written scenario. There had thus been three days of fighting and a deteriorating situation before the start of the exercise. The purpose of the exercise was to test procedures for transitioning from conventional to nuclear operations. As a result of the Orange advance and its persistent use of chemical weapons, SACEUR [Supreme Allied Commander Europe] requested political guidance on the use of nuclear weapons early on Day 1 of the exercise on 7th November 1983.[33]

Below is an account compiled from an interview the author carried out with a 5th Airborne Bde paratrooper who took part in Exercise LIONHEART in September 1984, in an assault force playing Orange (Spetsnaz) forces. Spetsnaz special forces would have met their match in combat if they came across these tough Para Airborne soldiers. Told with a touch of 'gallows' humour and irreverence, so typical of the British Airborne soldier, this story illustrates just how close NATO and Warsaw troops always were to actual armed conflict. It is worth noting that the paratroopers were issued with encumbering chemical and biological gear on this exercise. In the Able Archer 83 exercise, Orange forces persistently simulated using chemical weapons.

> Exercise Lionheart 1984 involved the mobilisation of every regular soldier and reservist throughout NATO countries to test NATO's defences and counter attack capabilities in the event of a Soviet land invasion of Western Europe through West Germany. After Exercise Archer the previous year, the Soviets and their allies were understandably paranoid about all of this US-inspired sabre-rattling. Our job during these exercises was playing the Reds or, rather, 'Orange Forces' (calling us 'Red Forces' was considered a bit too much).
>
> As paratroopers, we naturally assumed the role of the Red Army's Spetsnaz special forces, their equivalent of the British SAS or American Delta Force units. The Delta Force units were pretty good, as long as the pilots, who were delivering them to the objective, didn't get either lost or distracted and drop us over-hastily in the wrong position.
>
> One day my company was tasked with seizing a bridge over the river Weser, in one of those boring little northern German market towns where nothing much ever happens, except for market day. And the occasional airborne invasion by Orange Forces, testing Blue Forces' reaction times, in the face of a bit of good old Hitlerian Blitzkrieg. As far as the Ivans were concerned, Blitzkrieg had worked well for their Nazi soulmates in 1940 and 1941 so why change the format? Assault gliders, however, being a thing of the past on both sides of the Iron Curtain by 1984, we duly staggered out to the waiting Chinooks in full NBC gear, gas masks and all. Some genius of a staff officer somewhere had decreed that since the Soviets were likely to use chemical and biological weapons before attacking, their point units would be wearing Nuclear Biological Chemical protective coveralls and masks. For those of you who have never tried to put on a helmet and parachute over an NBC hood and gas mask, I will leave it to your imagination. Still, at least this time, we weren't required to parachute onto the objective.
>
> Our joy at this was, however, somewhat tempered by finding that the Chinooks belonged to our alleged allies, the Americans,

because one never knew where one was going to end up when one boarded an American flying machine. Well, this time, they really excelled themselves.

After an hour or so of vomit-inducing low-level flying to simulate wartime conditions, the Loadmasters signalled 'Action Stations' and we stood up. (You could tell who'd cheated, lifting his gas mask a bit to breathe, by the steamed-up glass.) So now we had several blind men to lead along on the Arnhem-style battle march into town, to take and hold this bridge for advancing Orange Forces armoured units. Down went the tailgate and out we went. I suppose someone was yelling 'Go!' but unlike films, you can't hear anything, hence hand signals and lemming-like mass-action. As we dropped into all-round defence in the grass and cowpats, we saw the other Chinook disgorging our mates some thirty feet from the ground. Most of them were hospital cases, as a result. Oh yes, the pilot had dropped the tailgate as he came in to ground level. Maybe American soldiers are slow to de-bus but British paras tend to head for the light like trapped rats, biting, mauling and mutilating anyone who gets in the way, including loadmasters . . .

Despite losing half the lads, we stumbled and staggered into town, the partially sighted leading the blind, as gasmasks steamed up. There were no Blue Forces in sight so we took the bridge and, using some borrowed civilian cars, set up barricades at each end. There was a railway bridge a little way downstream, so we sent some guys to block that too, with a car. The fact that it wasn't on our maps of the objective, hadn't quite sunk in yet. Before long, there were tailbacks of natives beeping and honking. Some of them were intelligent enough to get out of their cars and trucks and ask us what we were doing. We replied in a Russian language, gleaned from Sven Hassel novels. Dressed as we were, so close to the border, we could have been Russian. The female natives were smart enough to run for it, just in case.

Eventually, Der Polizei turned up. They weren't too polite – so we shot them. But as we only had blanks, we then had to take them prisoner. More cops turned up. They were disarmed and tied up. Still no Blue Forces. A while later, the Burgermeister turned up with the police commander. They spoke very good English but it didn't do them much good. We took them prisoner too. And so the day wore on. At one point, our OC gave the order to remove gas masks. Off they came and on went the red berets.

We even sang to the locals and our captives in German, to cheer them up: the WW2 German paratrooper anthem Rote Scheint Der Sonne, which they liked, and the Horst Wessel Lied, which they pretended not to like so much. Someone told us we could be arrested for singing it. But how? We'd captured the town's police force. The mayor kept telling us we were in the wrong town. Well, we'd figured that out by then. The Yanks had dropped us in the wrong place.

But the British Paratrooper never retreats, unless ordered to do so by Very Senior Airborne Officers. We tended not to pay attention to non-Airborne officers, except Generals. We were careful of Generals. And so, the bridge remained ours. It was market day in the town and we did allow a few farmers to herd their livestock across the river. Eventually a Very Senior Airborne Officer turned up and told us that we could stand down and follow him off the bridge. We were commended for doing a 'jolly good job'. As we stripped off the NBC kit and rolled it up for the sweaty tab back to the trucks, waiting over a mile away at the end of the tailback, some of us asked why Blue Forces hadn't reacted. The Very Senior Airborne Officer smiled and said that we were in the wrong place but that this was not our fault.

In conclusion, all the Red Army would have had to have done, prior to unleashing Blitzkriegsky, would have been to send some schoolboys to acquire our military plans and then target all obstacle crossings not mentioned therein. The staff officers at NATO HQ would presumably have sat there, stunned by the fact that the enemy wasn't in the right places and that, therefore, they could not order a counterattack. The Ivans would have been on the North Sea coast by teatime, never mind Christmas . . . However, the Russians, for all their faults, have never traditionally been an invasive nation, except for Siberia, Mongolia, northern Asia, Poland, Finland, the Baltic States, Hungary, Czechoslovakia and Afghanistan, to name a few exceptions to this much-vaunted rule. They have long-feared invasions from the West.

On one other occasion, at night this time, one of our sections was wandering around near the border in Spetsnaz reconnaissance mode. The previous day, the Ivans and their East German allies had been treated to the sight of over seven hundred main battle tanks heading for the border in attack formation and stopping just short. So they were probably feeling rather paranoid, especially with hundreds of thousands of NATO troops mobilised for war along the Iron Curtain and with Britain and the USA in the hands of the Plutonium Blond (The Iron Lady) and President 'Raygun' Reagan. Anyway, having nothing else to do on a country lane at three in the morning in the rain, our section stopped a Land Rover. The driver and his passenger, Royal Air Force NCOs, claimed not to be part of the exercise. Well, they would have said that, wouldn't they, to paraphrase Mandy Rice-Davies. They were stripped naked and tied to a telegraph pole by the side of the road and away went our lads on a joyride. The trailer contained ration packs, booze destined for an officers' mess and small torch batteries, to which they helped themselves a few clicks down the road, before dumping the trailer, which was only part of the ensemble ever found, with the Land Rover disappearing into a river somewhere.

A few days later, the SIB (Special Investigations Branch) of the British Army's Royal Military Police turned up at the battalion location and, in effect, arrested everyone. The toms and Junior NCOs were locked up in the garrison tennis courts. The two RAF NCOs were swiftly identified, as we were all ordered to remove our berets and file past the victims of the Spetsnaz ambush, who seemed none the worse for their experience.

Rumour Control indicated that the ambushed 'blue jobs' had been on their way in the Land Rover to deliver new code sheets and radio frequencies to three nuclear-equipped forward strike squadrons. These squadrons were not part of Lionheart and the Reds, already somewhat paranoid, were watching them like hawks, alert for any unusual changes in their daily routine.

The patrol commander, being easily identifiable by dint of his physique – unusually large for a parachutist – and his colour, was given a swift leg-up over the fence at the back and taken away by one of our officers. Nobody was arrested in the end as the RAF men had no real chance of associating the fresh-faced innocents filing past them, with the blacked-up savages who'd importuned them so rudely a few nights before.

Many years later, a cassette containing a documentary about the Iron Curtain was circulated amongst former members of our battalion. In it, a Russian ex-major spoke about 'Operation Lionheart' and the mock-attacks that had scared Moscow rigid. He had been in charge of an observation post, tasked with

> monitoring radio traffic between three forward strike squadrons of the Royal Air Force.
>
> It must be pointed out that they were not listening in and that, even if they had they been listening in, British military radio communications were conducted in Batco, or battle code (except in the case of Contact Reports, when it was presumed that the enemy would know locations anyway and so encoding the messages was futile.) What the Russian Major and his staff was looking for, as they stared at the screen were the blips indicating the regular change, not just of the Batco the net frequency which is also changed once or more a day, to keep ahead of enemy codebreakers. The Major and his German underlings were, apparently, particularly interested in these squadrons since they were nuclear-equipped. When the expected net frequency change, (signalled by radio check procedures between HQ and its sub-units), did not occur, this irregularity had our vodka-fuelled foe in a cold sweat. Empowered to launch a preemptive strike, but unable to raise his HQ, and even less so the Kremlin, the Major spent an uncomfortable few minutes, before making the correct decision and not starting World War Three, by firing missiles at three RAF bases in northern Germany.
>
> The eight dirty-faced boys, detailed to act as Spetsnaz infiltrators, had always felt that the arrival of an army of hard-eyed SIB men that September day in 1984 was a bit of an overreaction, in relation to the injured pride of a couple of 'blue jobs', and the disappearance of a Land Rover. When they learned how they might have caused mushroom clouds over Germany, however, it was their turn to sit there in a cold sweat.[34]

NATO's first Secretary General Lord Ismay made clear the Western Force commanders' apprehension: 'The supply lines of the Western zones were highly vulnerable to any advance against them from the East. There would be scenes of appalling and indescribable confusion . . . if we were ever attacked by the Russians.'[35]

On the other side of the Iron Curtain, amongst the WTO military commanders, the conclusion was no doubt the same, though 'the powers that be' would be reticent to voice this frank and dangerous view. J. Adams noted that when Gordievsky finally defected in September 1985, SIS distributed a fifty-page briefing, 'Soviet Perceptions of Nuclear Warfare', which covered Gordievsky's information on Operation RYAN. President Reagan was shocked when he read through the whole report and this knowledge led to his language being less belligerent. The running of Gordievsky as an MI6 agent greatly raised its prestige in Washington and the CIA.[36]

In April 1985 Gordievsky disclosed that the Aeroflot charter manager and four embassy diplomats were intelligence officers; thirty-one Soviets were later PNG'd.[37] In the same month, Gordievsky's luck finally ran out when an event occurred that nearly cost his life. On 16 April Aldrich Ames, a senior officer in the CIA counter intelligence Soviet Division with fifteen years' service, walked into the Soviet Embassy in Washington and offered to spy for money and reveal all CIA operations in Eastern Europe and the Soviet Union. After initially passing on the names of two US spies in the embassy, within three months Ames had betrayed twenty Western agents, including the KGB General Dmitri Polyakov, an American double agent for twenty years.

T. Downing described Ames as the CIA's worst counter-intelligence and operational failure of the last half of the Cold War. The CIA, however, could not accept that there was a mole in their organisation and blamed a compromised SIGINT code. Gordievsky was one of the 20 GRU and KGB agents 'blown' by Ames and was recalled to Moscow for an urgent meeting with Chebrikov, the Chairman of the KGB, and Kryuchkov, head of the First Chief Directorate. Gordievsky was driven off for a meeting with a General and a Colonel of counter intelligence. In spite of being disorientated by a doped glass of brandy and ordered to confess (*Prinznaysya*!), Gordievsky kept his nerve and revealed nothing, helped by his own presence of mind and a pep pill MI6 had provided.

Released under KGB observation, Gordievsky activated an MI6 plan to spirit him out of Russia. Without warning his family, he threw off surveillance by repeatedly changing routes and transport, using the standard espionage ploy of 'dry cleaning'. He took a train, then a bus to the Finnish border, where he met up with British Embassy staff in a wood. Hidden in the boot of their Ford Sierra, he was smuggled over the Vygo border into Finland, where his handler Joan awaited him. As far as is known, Gordievsky was the sole MI6 agent to ever escape from the USSR. He was too valuable a source for the risks not to be taken.[38]

When Gordievsky arrived back in Britain, the MI6 controller of the Western hemisphere Alastair Rellie held a welcoming party in the garden of his Chelsea home. Rellie and Gordievsky became good friends and the two used to go off on short trips to France, the Russian disguised with a false moustache and beard. Both were later to be awarded the CMG for 'exceptional service'. Rellie had joined SIS in 1963, the year Philby defected. In 1970 he replaced Daphne Park in Africa and was later adept at running

Eastern bloc agents. During the Falklands conflict Rellie organised the MI6 war room and was involved in the successful operation to deny the Argentinians further French Exocet missiles to use on the British naval task force. Shortlisted for the post of 'C', Rellie was appointed director of counter intelligence and security 1990–2. His curiosity in retirement led him to visit Albania and North Korea as a 'tourist', another SIS officer who never quite retired. Rellie died in April 2018, aged 83 years.[39]

In 1987, Gordievsky briefed the Prime Minister on her planned visit to the Soviet Union. Her television interview in Moscow was very well received. Thatcher, in her usual forthright manner, took the opportunity to pass on to the Soviet audience information that they had not previously had revealed to them.[40]

In 1994 on his arrest, the CIA traitor Aldrich Ames confessed to having betrayed Gordievsky as a British double agent.[41]

Chapter 29

Gorbachev and the End of the Cold War

> I've always thought that the most powerful weapon in the world was the bomb and that's why I gave it to my people, but I've come to the conclusion that the most powerful weapon in the world is not the bomb but it's the truth.
>
> Andrei Sakharov

Sakharov made the first speech at the first session of the Congress of People's Deputies on 25 June 1989.[1] The Cold War was really a metaphor for a stand-off between the Soviet Union on one side and the USA, Canada and Western Europe on the other. Many factors have been suggested by G. Minsk for the end of Communism in Europe: Reagan's Star Wars, Brandt's *Ostpolitik*, John Paul II, Solidarity, the opening of the Hungarian border, the pressure of the refugees from the GDR on the FRG's embassy, and finally Gorbachev's perestroika.[2]

The historian Serhii Plokhy identified three separate, but interconnected, stages in the end of the Cold War. The first was when the countries of Eastern and Central Europe became independent and rejected Communist doctrine in 1989–90, the second was a period when the Soviet state itself ceased to have a Communist political system and the last stage was the break-up of the USSR itself.[3] It is simply not true, as is sometimes claimed triumphantly, that it was the USA's aim to cause the break-up the Soviet Union, and that they succeeded in doing so. This misconception still holds sway widely in both the USA and Russia. It has been refuted by Jack Matlock, the capable and experienced US Ambassador to Moscow (1987–91).[4] Matlock noted that during the Reagan administration, a top-secret US NSDD 75 (National Security Decision Directive) contained 'no suggestion of a desire to destroy the Soviet Union or to establish US military superiority, or to force the Soviet union to jeopardise its own security. Instead US goals were 'to promote, within the narrow limits available to us, the process of change in the Soviet Union towards a more pluralistic political and economic system'.[5] The Bush administration believed that if one of the superpowers made moves to dismantle another this would inevitably result in a strong counter-reaction and cause a serious political conflict. Only in November 1991 did the Bush administration recognise Ukraine's independence, after their December referendum. There was grave concern in Washington about the security of the Soviet Union's nuclear weapons and the nightmare of nuclear weapons going astray and ending up in the wrong hands. (The US offered $550 million to dismantle them.[6]) The break-up of the Warsaw Pact, as the Eastern European and Baltic States regained their sovereignty, had greater effect on the disintegration of the Soviet Union than US foreign policy.[7]

Professor Brown, who was convinced in the early 1980s that Gorbachev would become General Secretary, and advised Margaret Thatcher of this, noted that Gorbachev's main aim in the beginning was to revitalise and improve the existing Communist system not to dismantle it.[8] William Taubman wrote that Mikhail Gorbachev had been greatly influenced by Khrushchev. Gorbachev's contemporaries thought of themselves as 'the children of the 20th Party Congress'. Gorbachev drew encouragement from Khrushchev's memoirs: his glasnost policies aimed to continue the reforms that Khrushchev had initiated and that Brezhnev had stultified.[9]

Since the 'Prague Spring', 'reform' was a word excluded from the accepted Communist lexicon. Instead Gorbachev used the synonym 'perestroika' which could mean different things to different people, and, importantly, changed its meaning over time. Professor Brown noted that in 1985 it meant changing the system through 'social and economic reform', whilst in 1987 it meant 'radical political reform' and by 1987 it stood for 'politically transformative change'.[10] Gorbachev was the main stimulus for this radical shift in Soviet politics but he had a delicate balancing act to perform. Professor Brown's notes and observations from a speech Gorbachev gave in London record that Gorbachev's views evolved, during the seven years that he was President, as a result of his open mindedness: 'Until 1988 I had the same illusion as previous reformers . . . that the system could be improved. In 1988 I realised we needed systematic reform. The system had to be replaced.'[11] Gorbachev used the term 'The socialist idea', but his interpretation evolved and it became not the authoritarian Soviet socialism, but rather a Western type of 'social democracy'. Gorbachev's beliefs, and the actions he took to carry them through, were the crucial factors in ending the Cold War, not US military power and the challenges of the SDI, as some historians wrongly believe. Reagan had great faith in personal relationships, as did Thatcher. Reagan liked Gorbachev and thought him someone with whom he could negotiate sincerely. He engaged with Gorbachev and took the advice of his Secretary of State George Schultz, rather than his defence chiefs and the CIA.[12]

With a succession of sick old leaders, Brezhnev, Andropov and then Chernenko, in 1985 the politburo welcomed the youthful, energetic Gorbachev, who was a very skillful communicator and persuasive politician. He had carefully positioned himself as second secretary and had deliberately hidden his radical views from the politburo. On the very evening of Chernenko's death, Gorabachev struck whilst the iron was hot by calling an immediate politburo meeting. The next day he was voted in as General Secretary of the Central Committee. At Chernenko's funeral, he spoke to each of the Eastern European leaders in turn to explain the new thinking. Gorbachev was a persuasive humanitarian, with a social conscience that had much in common with the Moral Rearmament Movement of Oxford post-war, including the historian Dr R.C. Mowat. Professor Brown noted that in October 1985 Gorbachev read out 'several heart-rending letters' from mothers of Soviet soldiers killed in action in Afghanistan.[13] (The situation of the severely injured on their return to Russia was dreadful – stumps, dirty bandages and a lack of wheelchairs and housing.[14]) His politburo colleagues thought he would regenerate the old system and in time their support for him diminished, as their interests and powers faded. They could have challenged and dismissed Gorbachev but he continued to gain their approval for major policy changes over the next five years, until he became President of the Soviet Union and no longer needed his decisions to be collectively agreed.[15] Ronald Reagan had first declared the Soviet Union to be an 'Evil Empire' in early 1985 (he later rejected the term in Red Square, Moscow) at the time of his SDI proposals. The British FCO regarded SDI as a distraction from serious arms control negotiations and an impediment to better relations with Russia. When Thatcher visited Reagan she stated: 'Even if an SDI system proved 95% successful, a significant success rate, over 60 million people would still die from those weapons that got through . . . SDI is only a research programme. Our objective is both to maintain a military balance and to enhance, not weaken deterrence.'[16] Thatcher described how she and Reagan met 'to discuss the strategy we should now pursue towards the Soviet Union . . . over the years ahead. I began by saying that we had to make the most accurate assessment of the Soviet system and the Soviet leadership . . . We all had to live on the same planet'. Thatcher's policy, far from attempting to destabilise the Soviet Union, was one of 'constructive engagement'.[17]

Stalin, the instigator of the Cold War, had created a politburo organisation where all power resided in the General Secretary. This now worked in Gorbachev's favour. None challenged him except for Yeltsin, who in 1987 was First Secretary of the Moscow Party Committee and thus independent. Gorbachev could dismiss and appoint those he thought held similar views as himself and would support his policies. His main focus of activity was in the foreign policy area. His replacing of the hardline Andrew Gromyko as Foreign Minister by his inexperienced protegé Eduard Shevardnadze was a clever move: Gorbachev wanted to control foreign affairs. Gromyko had agreed to move on when offered the prestigious post of Head of State. Gorbachev then brought in the experienced Anatoli Dobrynin (ex-Russian Ambassador in Washington), installing Alexsandr Yakovlev (the ex-Russian Ambassador in Canada) in the Politburo and also appointing Cherniaev as his main policy advisor. The long-serving Foreign Minister Gromyko looked on the Soviet occupation of the satellite bloc as the prize bought with Red Army blood in 1945. The Old Guard felt a certain prestige and pride in controlling Eastern Europe. It was hard for them to accept letting go of this. Dobrynin summed it up: 'Gromyko's chief priority was . . . the upholding of our gains of the hard war that defeated Nazi Germany. A disciple of Stalin's, he did not attach much importance to moral aspects of foreign policy such as human rights.'[18]

Morality and change were at the heart of Gorbachev's reforms. A major contribution to the end of the Cold War, and something not generally realised, were the ideas developed in research institutes before perestroika, where Gorbachev's *Novoye Myshlenniye* (New Political Thinking) had taken seed. Georges Mink described how, since 1986, two small groups of experts (political and scientific) had been meeting discreetly, often in secret, in academic institutes. Each expert advised Gorbachev and Yakovlev. They focussed on the politics of one particular country in Eastern Europe, managing its changes and, where necessary, pushing them forwards. They came up with the key words that characterised Gorbachev's changes: perestroika (restructuring), glasnost (transparency) as well as 'Europe, our common home'. They advised on how to anticipate resistance to change and how to action the new strategic objectives. They concentrated in particular on two countries with a history of resistance to Stalinisation: Hungary and Poland. Step by step, for two years they managed the inevitable end of the Soviet Empire, striving to build a new political structure.[19] The KGB, realising radical structural changes to the system were inevitable, had supported Gorbachev in the winter of 1984, seeing him as Chernenko's successor, and gave him detailed policy briefings. In return, Gorbachev supported the KGB which had a powerful foreign intelligence section and a large manpower domestically: countless informers, 200,000 border guards and 400,000 officers.[20]

In October 1986 at the Reykjavik Summit, General Secretary Gorbachev decided to offer deep cuts in nuclear weapons. (He had been deeply affected by the Chernobyl nuclear disaster on 26 April 1986.) This initiative was taken up by the USA the following year, when the superpowers agreed to the removal of all intermediate-range missiles from Europe, without an abandonment of SDI. Thatcher pointed out: 'the American President had effectively just won the Cold War – without firing a shot'. Thatcher's view, however, that the end of the Cold War was due to Reagan's presidency alone, was simply not true.[21] But President Ronald Reagan was a force for change. In June 1987 he stood at the Brandenburg Gate in Berlin and declared: 'If you seek peace, if you seek prosperity for the Soviet Union and Eastern Europe, if you seek liberalisation, come here to this gate. Mr Gorbachev, open this gate . . . tear down this wall!'.[22]

Gorbachev, meanwhile, was planning large cuts in Soviet conventional forces and he next moved to manage the *siloviki*, the power of the army, the military-industrial complex and the KGB. Gorbachev appointed a politburo ally Zaikov to a commission managing the *bolshaia piaterka* ('the big five'): the Ministers of Foreign Affairs and Defence, the Chairman of the KGB, the Head of Intelligence and the Head of the military-industrial complex. A *malaia piaterka* ('the small five') dealt with arms control and security policy. In May 1987 19-year-old West German student Matthias Rust took off from Helsinki in a small Cessna aircraft and, skillfully flying at tree height to avoid radar, managed to reach Moscow and land safely on a bridge near in Red Square. Gorbachev was furious and, before sacking him, asked the Deputy Minister of Defence sarcastically if it was the road traffic police that had detained Rust – '*Uznali ot GAI*?' Gorbachev had once again turned the situation to his advantage politically by sacking the Minister of Defence, the Chief of Air Defence and a hundred conservative senior military officers.[23]

In June 1988 Gorbachev called a special conference. His prior report to the politburo had replaced the words *blagodarya nashey sile* ('thanks to our military strength') with the more apposite 'thanks to our new thinking'. Gorbachev then announced to the 5,000 conference delegates the reforms that would spell the end of the Communist system: a new parliament would replace the Supreme Soviet. One-third of the seats could be nominated by the Communist Party whilst the rest would be elected.

A president would run the Soviet Union and an elected parliament. Elections to the new parliament would take place in the spring.[24]

Unrest was soon to appear in the Baltic States as they understood there would be no 'Brezhnevian' repression. Angus Roxburgh, a newspaper correspondent in Moscow, noted that on 20 August 1988 in Tallinn (changed from the Russian spelling of 'Talin') Estonia's Popular Front published their programme and the radio station read out the 'secret protocols' of the 1933 Molotov-Ribbentrop Pact (where Hitler and Stalin had divided Eastern Europe into spheres of influence). Gorbachev installed his old friend Vaino Välijas as party leader in Estonia. Within a week the blue, black and white tricolour national flag was legalised, after a forty-eight-year ban. The Popular Front, the local Communist Party and the city council of Tallinn were singing from the same hymn book of change, understanding the need for self-government and independence.

In Lithuania, in a huge demonstration in September 1988, the Free Lithuania League taunted riot police with chants of 'Occupiers!'. The Communist Party restored the independence era flag and the national anthem. Half a million Lithuanians gathered in Cathedral Square to sing hymns and wave red, green and yellow flags. Vilnius Cathedral was returned to the Catholic Church after forty-eight years as an art museum.[25] On 7 December 1988, exactly forty years after Captain John Sanderson sat in the Security Council Meetings in the UN in Paris watching Stalin's henchmen, Gorbachev addressed the assembly of the UN urging 'freedom of choice' for all, and signalling that the Soviet satellites were free to 'choose their own paths'. He unilaterally announced cuts of 500,000 men from the Soviet military, with 10,000 tanks, 8,500 artillery guns and 800 combat aircraft leaving Eastern Europe as well as similar large forces withdrawals from Manchuria and the Chinese border.[26] The growing liberalisation in the Soviet Union raised expectations in Eastern Europe. In 1989 the Communist states in Poland, Hungary, East Germany, Czechoslovakia, Romania and Bulgaria would each fall in turn. As Gorbachev explained (in an interview with *Le Monde* in 2008): '1989 was the beginning of the political spring, when we created the parliament and the new government. The European union in the West and Eastern Europe were reformed by perestroika . . . Europe had to breathe with two lungs'.[27] Gorbachev flew to East Berlin to tell Honneker that change must not be resisted. Gannadi Gerasimov, the Soviet spokesman, explained to the East German leader: 'We have the Frank Sinatra doctrine now.' The Soviet bloc would be permitted to 'go its own way'. On 7 October 1989, on the fortieth anniversary of the GDR in Berlin, thousands of East Berliners marched through the streets, defiantly resisting the violence of the Volkspolizei whilst ironically shouting the Communist slogan '*Wir sind das folk*!' ('We are the people').[28] Gorbachev described this day:

> 'The Polish Prime Minister lent towards me and said: "Do you understand German?" I replied: "Enough to understand what the demonstrators are saying?" He replied: "Then you understand it's the end."' So that was how it was. Meanwhile, Honneker was behaving as if he understood nothing: he was singing, joining in all the artificial enthusiasm.

Gorbachev explained that the opening of the Berlin Wall on 9 November 1989 had ushered in the Velvet Revolution in Eastern Europe which held the promise of a 'common European home' (a process that would be fraught with new dangers). Gorbachev considered unwise the US and Western European view that recent events proved the superiority of the West's systems and values over Communism and that they signalled the defeat of Russia in the Cold War. Gorbachev described President Mitterrand's attitude as: 'We like Germany so much that we would like there to be two Germanies.'

Colonel John Sanderson had, since the 1970s, made clear his strong views that a divided Germany was a necessity for the maintenance of peace in Europe. He was convinced that both NATO and the Russians shared the same post-war *realpolitik*: by keeping Germany divided, they averted the dangers of a resurgent, united Germany in the heart of Europe.

Gorbachev described Margaret Thatcher as 'aggressively hostile to the reunification of Germany' and believed 'she had to face reality' and accept that 'the process of reunification was underway'. Gorbachev believed that 'the Germans were free to choose for themselves their own types of mutual arrangements', recognising that the 1990 New Year East German mass demonstrations were the signal that Russia had to change direction in its politics and consider the Germans' desire for unification.

Gorbachev described meeting President Bush and declaring they were no longer enemies and that the Cold War was over. Gorbachev regretted that after 1989: 'What was negative was . . . what followed. Even when preparing Borscht, the national dish, a cook can make mistakes with the seasoning.'[29]

It was not just the seasoning, however, that caused the failure of Gorbachev's attempts to institute effective institutional changes. It was the recipe itself and his timing, which in cooking is vital. The

Soviet economy needed radical, rapid reforming. In 1991 he delayed instituting the necessary structural economic changes, and really did not understand the methods of doing so. Gorbachev was a Communist who believed the Communist system needed reforming not abolishing, in contrast to Yeltsin who wanted it destroyed. Gorbachev's main weakness was that he had little understanding of how to reform the Soviet Union's creaking and inefficient market economy. When in July 1991 Gorbachev met John Major in London, the British Prime Minister realised this failure:

> Gorbachev expounded a very Victorian image of private ownership. His understanding of privatisation was negligible: he seemed to believe it was no more than a benevolent state selling a company to a profiteering private owner who would worsen the service and increase the price. He had no concept of the free market, and the merits of competition were alien to him . . . Gorbachev had changed the face of Russia, yet he was unable to grasp even the basic essentials of the free market into which he had released his country.'[30]

Gorbachev was elected President of the Soviet Union on 15 March 1990, with 95 per cent of the vote. Yeltsin was elected Mayor of Moscow with 5 million votes. The new executive presidency had an authority separate from the CPSU. The politburo was now merely the highest body of a party divested of its 'leading role' in controlling the state. It could only watch as power flowed to President Gorbachev and the leaders of Soviet republics, above all to Boris Yeltsin's Russian republic. Within the CPSU, members no longer felt inhibited in expressing their own opinions. In 1989 they were proposing divergent policies in their quest for seats in the new parliament.[31]

The rejection of Communism in the Eastern European satellite states, together with the liberalisation and green shoots of democracy appearing in the Soviet political system, was welcomed as a green light by the three Baltic republics, the Georgians and the western Ukrainians to seek their own independence, a move that previously would have guaranteed a heavy-handed response from Moscow. The rapprochement and dialogue between the two former ideologically opposed opponents in the Cold War gave impetus within the Soviet Union to nationalists seeking separation. The changes in Eastern Europe, especially Poland with the victory of Solidarity in the 1989 election, had huge repercussions. The Baltic States would never have imagined in 1985 that six years later they would cease to be Communist and part of the Soviet Union.[32]

There were Soviet forces ready to resist these moves for freedom and independence and urging the involvement of Gorbachev, under threat of ousting, to install martial law. Yakovlev, Gorbachev's aid, explained that Gorbachev was blameless. The harsh repressions in the Baltic States and Georgia that resulted in several deaths were organised by the putschists who would place Gorbachev under house arrest on 18 August 1991. Except for the disturbances in Baku, Gorbachev had intervened to end occurrences of violence by the authorities the next day. Gorbachev was against the use of force in resolving conflicts. Yakovlev wrote in 2003 that the last Soviet leader went into history 'without blood on his hands'.[33]

Thus the seismic changes that shook Eastern and Central Europe in 1989 originated in Moscow, not in Western capitals. Stalin and subsequent leaders had imposed a tyrannical hold on the satellite states of Eastern Europe by force for decades but the courageous policies of Mikhail Gorbachev allowed Eastern Europe countries to regain their freedom, respecting their dignity and their 'right to choose' their own political and economic systems. By keeping Soviet troops in their barracks, he had signalled that the old days of repression were over. This, in turn, set a precedent for the republics in the Soviet Union itself, encouraging their political hopes for self-determination and independence. In 1989 the Communist states fell in Poland, Hungary, East Germany, Czechoslovakia, Romania and Bulgaria. From July 1990 Ukraine, Armenia, Turkmenistan, Tadzhikistan, Kazakhstan and Kirghizia declared sovereignty.[34]

For the Communist leaders of Central Europe, however, Gorbachev was a traitor and a gravedigger burying Communism.[35] It is ironical that the metaphor of a 'domino effect' that the West applied to the spread of Communism in South-East Asia in the 1960s is most apt as a description of the changes that occurred in reverse in Eastern Europe decades later. In Sofia in 1989, the day before a visit by President Mitterrand, the Bulgarian Communist Party leader and Head of State Todor Zhivkov gave an interview to S. Kauffman of *Le Monde*. A wily 78-year-old peasant, he joked about his future and talked of his prospective retirement aged 95 years. He had been in power since 1954. The concept of a multi-party system didn't concern him for there would never be any other party than his in power in Sofia. He admitted that a growing opposition was agitating and that he had been obliged to arrest twenty-five individuals, 'causing trouble' prior to the French President's visit. 'However,' he remarked, 'the situation will be controlled, don't you worry about that.' It was Zhivkov who should have worried. The conversation was his last as Head of State. Before the year was out, the long reign of the leader who boasted 'I set my watch by Moscow time' was over. Mitterrand's breakfast meetings with University academics and dissidents, including the future democratic Bulgarian leader Zhelu Zhelev (1990–7), were fruitful.

The fall of Zhivkov took place a day after the fall of the Berlin Wall on 10 November 1989 in a palace coup organised by a fellow politburo member, Mladenov, a politician who appeared open to political pluralism. Only eight months later, however, he resigned after film evidence showed him proposing to use tanks against demonstrators. In early 1990 the Communist Party's leading role was removed from the constitution. In October 1991 the UDF (Union of Democratic Forces) defeated the BSP (Bulgarian Socialist Party), led by Zhelev.[36]

In 1990–1 Gorbachev made a tactical retreat, which disillusioned his radical reformer friends and further alienated the military and the KGB, as well as the hardline communists. Gorbachev wanted to replace the Soviet system but certainly not the Soviet State. He made a number of unwise staff changes that helped the hardliners: he replaced the liberal minister of the interior with Boris Pugo and appointed Gennadi Yanaev as Vice-President, both of whom would take part in the August 1991 coup attempt against him. Then in March 1991, he held a referendum on keeping the USSR as a renewed federation of equal sovereign republics. (The Baltic States and three of the Soviet republics refused to hold the referendum.) Over 70 per cent (of the 80 per cent taking part) voted 'yes'.[37]

In April 1991 Gorbachev launched the Nogo-Ogarevo process to negotiate a new Union Treaty. The negotiations excluded the politburo and the Communist Party. Yeltsin was demanding that more federal powers be ceded to the republics and his resounding victory in the June 1991 made his position even stronger. Gorbachev, believing that he had laid the foundations for the new treaty and had dealt with the hardliners, left in early August for his presidential holiday home in the Crimea, planning to return to Moscow to sign the Union Treaty on 20 August. It was, however, a serious error to leave Moscow at such a crucial time. Gorbachev's position was not fully secure and he had ruffled many feathers.[38]

The former British Ambassador to Moscow Sir Rodric Braithwaite described Gorbachev as destabilising a failing system in his reform attempts. It was not 'that Mr Gorbachev failed to manage the genie of nationalism. By 1989 the genie was right out of the bottle.' Sir Rodric wrote that, instead of sending in the tanks, Gorbachev had attempted to create a voluntary federation of Soviet republics. This was a 'solution that most western leaders preferred to the nightmare of "Yugoslavia with nukes" – the bloody disintegration of a nuclear superpower.'[39]

The attempted coup by Communist hardliners in August and Yeltsin's political manoeuvres put paid to these plans.

Chapter 30

Coup by South African Intelligence

An Intelligence Coup: Hands-on Inspection of a Russian T-72 Battle Tank With its Manual

In an interview with the author, Scott Charman a South African ex-soldier entrepreneur, explained how between 1989 and 1992 he had carried out one of the most masterly deals of the Cold War Communist era by brokering agreements to bring out of a WTO country some of the latest Russian military hardware, sophisticated equipment that Western Military Intelligence experts were all too keen to examine.

As an experienced young soldier in the SADF (South African Defence Force) during the South African Border War, Scott led patrols in armoured vehicles into Angola and South West Africa (renamed Namibia on independence) to fight a bush war with PLAN (People's Liberation Army of Namibia), an armed wing of SWAPO (South West African People's Organisation). In 1975 Scott took part with the Capetown Highlanders of 71 Brigade in Operation SAVANA, in the north of Namibia, where he came under fire from Russian Katyusha rockets. The South Africans called the Soviet rockets 'Redeye' because you could see them coming towards you and had time to dig in rapidly. Luckily, the sandy soil of Namibia absorbed the explosion: you could be 10m away from the impact and survive unharmed. In the Second World War Katyusha rockets were nicknamed 'Stalin's organ': the multiple rocket launcher resembled an organ and the rocket had a distinctive howl which unnerved the German soldiers.[1]

The 'winds of change' blowing through Africa after de-colonisation, which had led to tens of African states gaining independence, became a gale in Angola which had ceased to be a colony of Portugal in 1974, after a coup in Lisbon.[2] The military struggle in Angola involved some of the heaviest fighting in Africa since the end of the Second World War. The SADF armed UNITA (National Union for Total Independence of Angola) forces against the Marxist MPLA (People's Movement for the Liberation of Angola) rebels, who were backed by Soviet advisors with billions of rubles of Russian defence equipment including tanks and missiles, as well as 12,000 Czech rifles from Cuba. Thousands of Cuban forces, sent over by Fidel Castro to wage a revolutionary war in Angola, intensified the conflict.

The South African government, meanwhile, was struggling with the African National Party and portrayed their military bush campaigns as a necessary and vital military containment of Communist expansionism. The historian Jeremy Isaacs noted that the South African Army, joined by mercenaries, fought their way to within 100 miles of Luanda, the capital, where independence was being prepared, but they were defeated at Ebo. In Angola, Charman was advancing in an armoured car when he came under fire from Russian tanks and, thinking it an uneven contest, withdrew rapidly. By the time the fighting finally ended, and the MPLA had installed the People's Republic of Angola, hundreds of thousands had died.

After Namibia gained its independence in March 1990, the UN brokered fishing rights for international trawlers to fish off the Namibian coast. The basic Namibian ports could not, however, handle the complicated engine repairs European ships needed: Scott, now in Maritime security and ship chartering, used his entrepreneurial skills and extensive personal connections to ease various ships' entry into South African ports for repairs, via UK flag agency representation. Through helping Eastern ships to maintain their fishing fleet, far from their Baltic ports, Scott was able to make useful connections with important individuals in Poland, whose country had a desperate need for foreign currency, at this crucial time of social unrest. In 1989 a secret deal was allegedly arranged by Scott Charman for the purchase by South Africa of the latest self-loading, V12 diesel engined, three-man T-72 main Russian battle tanks in use by the WTO army, together with their comprehensive user manuals. Two brand-new T-72 tanks, with their very long 125mm smoothbore barrels, were discreetly shipped out of Szczecin, suitably wrapped and shielded from satellite 'eyes' in specially lined containers installed on the deck of a Polish refrigeration ship, chartered by Scott. Once in South Africa, the military hardware was made available for inspection by grateful Western military experts. By offering this technical aid to the Western Intelligence Services, the beleaguered apartheid government hoped for a quid pro quo support from their respective governments.

Further similar shipments in 1990 and 1992 included Soviet RT231 (Infra RED) air-to-air missiles for the MiG-23 fighter jet and their RT231R

Radar Seeker systems, Shilka ZSU trucks, with ground-to-air radar-guided 23 mm anti-aircraft cannon, mounted on the T72 chassis, as well as three types of high-altitude Russian radars: the SA8, SA13 (infra-RED) and the large SA6 surface-to-air guidance system. Acquiring the technical knowledge of these radar systems was extremely useful to US/UK forces, later enabling Tornado GR1 jets during the First Gulf 'Desert Storm' War to jam the Russian radar systems of Saddam Hussein's air defences. Photographs show the equipment being shipped and examined by the Western experts. In one image Scott Charman tests the heat-seeking capabilities of a Russian SA13 Missile by rotating a lighted cigarette in front of the guidance system.

In the 1990s, in the window of glasnost existing in Yeltsin's time, Scott Charman visited Moscow as part of an international Defence Cooperation delegation to meet representatives of Rosvooruzhenie, the Russian state arms sales organisation. (The Bush administration in 2006 would impose sanctions on its successor Rosoboronexport for supplying weapons to Iran, in breach of US sanctions.[3]) During the meeting, the Russian general in charge of Rosvooruzhenie boomed down from the head of a table around which were seated twenty-two people: 'Mr Charman, we know all about you!'

Chapter 31

Yeltsin and the End of Communism

On 18 August 1991, Gorbachev's Black Sea dacha in the Crimea was surrounded and he and his family were put under house arrest. The KGB Head of the Ninth Department Plekhanov stormed in, leading a group that included Gorbachev's Chief-of-Staff Boldin and General Varennikov, who had commanded the Soviet forces in Vilnius in January when demonstrators had been killed. When the General aggressively demanded Gorbachev's resignation as President, he received his answer in unequivocally strong language from the Soviet leader.

The plotters informed Gorbachev that he would be under arrest very soon and that Yeltsin had already been arrested. This was untrue: the indecisive KGB Chairman Kryuchkov had cancelled this order. This was the first of several mistakes the disorganised leaders of the putsch were to make. Furthermore, the Commander-in-Chief of the army had not backed the putsch and there was not full support amongst senior army officers, or all of the KGB, for a change of government.[1]

Gorbachev refused to hand over power, even temporarily, to a self-appointed State Emergency Committee. The next morning, however, the Soviet Vice President Gennadi Yanaev, with trembling hands, announced at a badly organised press conference that the putsch organisers represented such a body. Yeltsin refused to cooperate when the KGB Chairman telephoned him at his dacha. A further error of judgement by the plotters permitted Yeltsin to travel to the Russian Parliament, the Moscow White House.[2] (The same day the three Baltic republics reaffirmed their independence. In September they would join the UN.[3])

On 19 August 1991 in London, when PM John Major heard the news that Gorbachev was being held hostage in the Crimea, he had a call put through to Moscow to Yeltsin, trapped in the Russian Parliament and 'highly excited'. When Major told Yeltsin that the British were 'watching events with extreme anxiety, he burst out with an impassioned plea for support'. Yeltsin said that Gorbachev was isolated and, although there was a curfew in place, thousands of demonstrators were protesting against the coup. Yeltsin interrupted Major to say that tanks were heading to capture the White House, shouting that he had possibly only a few minutes left. He asked Major and the West to demand Gorbachev's release.[4]

Yeltsin then left the building to confront the tanks. Courageously clambering onto a tank and rallying resistance, he turned the tide against the coup attempt. The tank commander ordered his men to encircle the parliament and turn their vehicles around so their guns faced away from the White House, deterring any attack. The coup lasted a further two days but Boris Yeltsin's dramatic gesture had saved the day.[5]

Following his political instinct, with the White House surrounded by troops and tanks, Boris Yeltsin had marched out and defiantly called for Gorbachev to be released. The televised images of his courageous act were broadcast to Russia and around the world.

Yeltsin called for 'the unity of the Soviet Union and the unity of Russia' and warned that the illegal and immoral action of the self-appointed State Committee would 'return us to the epoch of the Cold War and the isolation of the Soviet Union from the world community'.[6] Whilst self-defence units of be-medalled Afghan veterans rallied around the Parliament and large crowds of Muscovites and other citizens denounced their attempted coup, demonstrators were toppling the statue of Felix Dzershinsky which stood in front of the Lubyanka Square KGB HQ.[7]

On 21 August the tanks withdrew from the streets of Moscow. The attempted coup was over. Gorbachev's misfortune in the Crimea had given a strong political advantage to Yeltsin. For Boris all talk of a new Union Treaty was over, although Gorbachev on his return still wanted to push it through. On 23 August, Yeltsin suspended the Communist Party in front of tens of millions of television viewers. The *Daily Telegraph* of 24 August reported the public humiliation of Soviet President Gorbachev by the Russian President Boris Yeltsin and his deputies. 'A hesitant and flustered Soviet leader . . . was shouted down as he defended the Communist Party and urged the Russian parliament to show restraint'. Yeltsin interrupted an address by Gorbachev, handing him the minutes of a cabinet meeting from the first day of the coup which revealed that almost all Gorbachev's ministers had betrayed him. When Yeltsin made a show of signing a decree suspending the activities of the Communist Party, Gorbachev pleaded with him, repeating: 'Boris Nikolayevich'. The newspaper reported that 'Yeltsin cast a cursory glance at his long-term adversary, smiled and sighed. Deputies rose in unison, clapping and cheering.'[8] Thus Communist Party activities were banned in the Russian republic and their 'leading role' was over. On 1 December 90 per cent of Ukraine voted for independence.[9]

Gorbachev's attempts to win support for a new and voluntary federation, or confederation, were frustrated. True to his conciliatory style, he would have made major concessions to keep Ukraine in a new reconstituted Union, but Yeltsin would only envisage a confederation dominated by the Russian republic.[10] With Ukraine's expressed desire for independence in their referendum the Soviet Union, in Professor Archie Brown's words, was 'doomed to extinction', even before the meeting in Belarus on 8 December that 'unilaterally pronounced its last rites'.[11]

In December 1989, after a meeting with President George H. W. Bush aboard the *Maxim Gorky* in Malta, Gorbachev had said: 'We want you in Europe. You need to be in Europe. We don't consider you an enemy any more. Things have changed.'[12] Bush had replied: 'We buried the Cold War at the bottom of the Mediterranean Sea.'[13]

On 17 September to 'drive the ultimate nail in the coffin of the Soviet Union' (in Professor Brown's words), the leaders of the three Slavic republics of Russia, Ukraine and Belorussia met in a hunting lodge on the Polish border to sign a joint declaration that the 'Soviet Union has ceased to exist'. The agreement was ratified soon afterwards by the other republics.[14]

On 25 December the red flag of the Soviet Union, with its gold star, hammer and sickle, was lowered from the Kremlin, to be replaced by a new white, blue and red flag. Mikhail Gorbachev left office the same day. The Russian Federation would be granted the USSR's permanent seat on the UN Security Council.

In 1962, at the end of his tour in Bulgaria, *JBS* ended his FO analysis by describing Bulgaria's probable future:

> There is evidence, however, of disenchantment with Soviet Communism, not only in Bulgaria, but elsewhere in the Soviet Bloc. Traditional Bulgarian nationalism is beginning to assert itself, as it has periodically over the centuries. While it would be unrealistic to anticipate any imminent philosophical rejection of Communism, it is not unrealistic to anticipate an eventual rejection of the Soviet domination that imposes it. Bulgaria may one day be 'free', in the sense that, say, Yugoslavia is free, but this freedom will be within the limits imposed by her heritage. To assume otherwise would be to deny the lesson of history.

Braithwaite's prognosis on Russia ended with the similar conclusion to Sanderson: 'Five months after that flag come fluttering down, I wrote it would take Russia decades, perhaps generations, to overcome its economic, imperial and other difficulties. But it was not, I told London, mindless optimism to think Russia might eventually develop its own, no doubt imperfect, democracy. But it still seems a tenable proposition.'[15] But it was almost impossible to square the circle of radical change in a former Marxist-Leninist society, where the granting of new freedoms left central control less effective. There were too many vested interests and the system had been too repressive for too long. Gorbachev had feared the confusion that an abrupt changeover to a free market would cause. Yeltsin would find that his market reforms brought destabilising, rapid changes to Soviet society and the economy, with few winners and many impoverished losers. It was enormously difficult to try to change the Soviet economy to a market economy in such a short timescale.

Angus Roxburgh described the steps Yeltsin took to move Russia from a command economy to a market economy. In January 1992 he ended state control of prices so that the free market dictated prices, including food, previously kept low. Inflation took off, wiping out the values of state pensions of the old who still had to survive on 300 rubles a month, which was totally insufficient. Poverty would increase and life expectancy plummet.[16] Yeltsin privatised the entire economy, selling off the major state assets, having distributed a nominal value 'coupon' to each citizen, most of which ended up in the hands of a few rich businessmen. Those managing state assets manoeuvred to acquire them as personal businesses. The Russian Mafia organised protection rackets for the smaller companies. The economic wealth of the country in banks, the media, industry and natural resources ended up in the hands of oligarchs, mainly ex-Communists or KGB, previously seen as the 'Shield and the Sword' of the Communist Party.[17]

In 1993 the Russian Parliament opposed these rapid changes in society, that they saw as unfair and disruptive. With the legitimacy of a referendum supporting him, Yeltsin then dissolved the Parliament. To force the deputies to vacate the building, he cut off the power, water and communications. The army were ordered in to shell the White House and they set it on fire, causing the occupants to evacuate. Spetsnaz forces tackled protestors in the TV studios. Three months later a new Duma was elected.[18]

In 2002 Margaret Thatcher noted: 'Although the scale and violence of Russian crime has snowballed since the end of the USSR, its psychological and systematic roots were planted under Communism'.[19] Corruption under Brezhnev was notorious. From the mid-1980s crime became fully institutionalised, not least through the activities of the KGB. In 2002 Russia was thought to have 3,000 to 4,000 criminal gangs operating.

The Russian Ministry of Internal Affairs said organised crime controlled 40 per cent of the turnover of goods and services. Half of banks were controlled by criminal syndicates. From the mid-1980s crime became fully institutionalised, not least through the KGB which 'sold cheaply acquired Soviet commodities abroad at world prices, putting the proceeds into disguised foreign accounts and front companies . . . lines of business came to include money laundering, arms and drugs trafficking etc.'.[20]

Mikhail Gorbachev, a law graduate, realised that a fair society needed: 'the rule of law, contested elections, freedom of the press, freedom of assembly, and the accountability of rulers to the people as a whole'.[21] Sadly, there is little evidence of these principles in today's Russia.

Chapter 32

TA Reserve, Last SIS Mission to Sarajevo, 1995

JBS's final military appointment:

> Following my retirement from the regular army and my appointment as an administrative officer in a TA base, a prospective employee arrived in 1980 for an interview in my barracks. Having welcomed him to a seat in my office, I noticed that the man was staring at me with a rather stunned expression on his face. When I enquired what was the matter, he replied: 'I was a prisoner in a Japanese POW camp in Thailand in 1945 when you dropped in by parachute to liberate us. I will never forget your smiling face.'

In 1984, on his last day in the army at the age of 63 years, Lieutenant Colonel John Sanderson left Her Majesty's Service forty-seven years after he joined up as a boy soldier. He opened his office safe, took out the Luger pistol that had accompanied him on his postings since Berlin days, and instructed his warrant officer to return it to the armoury.

On his final drive home from the barracks, he spotted some travellers at the side of the road sitting on an upturned bathtub next to their caravan. Slowing down his car, and winding down his window, he handed them his half-full box of the finest Havana cigars with the words: 'You'd better smoke these, they're too dangerous for me!' John Sanderson would have needed the pistol: eleven years later there was time for one last dangerous mission in the Balkans.

Special Air Service in Bosnia: Bosnia Operations

On 6 April 1994 at Gorazade a seven-man SAS (Special Air Service) team directed air strikes against Serb positions, which were relayed to F-16 fighters, which pounded the Serb positions. Unfortunately, during their retreat from Gorazade, one SAS soldier was killed.

In August of 1995 the SAS was in action again, when its men, who had infiltrated Serb lines that ringed Sarajevo, reported the exact location of Serb armour, artillery and anti-aircraft units.[1]

1995 Mission to Sarajevo

The prosecuting counsel of the Hague war crimes trial declared that one must go back to the Second World War to find a parallel in European history with the siege of Sarajevo. 'Not since then had a professional army conducted a campaign of unrelenting violence against the inhabitants of a European city so as to reduce them to a state of mediaeval deprivation in which they were in constant fear of death.' The counsel said that there was nowhere a citizen of Sarajevo could be safe from deliberate attack: homes, schools and hospitals were all targeted.[2]

Sir Christopher Meyer described the bloody civil war that erupted in 1991 when Yugoslavia split into Croatia, Serbia and Bosnia (where the horrors of concentration camps, ethnic cleansing and mass rape occurred). The Balkan conflict caused the death of 110,000 Bosnians and left 2 million homeless. Thatcher warned in 1992 that Serbia would not listen until forced to do so. 'Waiting until the conflict burns itself out will not only be dishonourable but also very costly: refugees, terrorism, Balkan wars drawing in other countries, and worse.'[3]

Sarajevo had once been a cosmopolitan city inhabited by Croatians, Muslims and Serbs living peacefully together. In the first two years of the civil war, however, Bosnian Serb artillery killed 10,000 of its 350,000 inhabitants, who sheltered in the shelled buildings of the besieged city, deprived of electricity, fuel, food and water. Of those killed by sniper fire, mortars or shells, 3,000 were children: 6 whilst tobogganing in the snow.[4] The siege had become a stalemate: the Bosnian Army could not break out and the Serbs, whose artillery was sited strategically around the city, lacked the shells to force Sarajevo into submission.[5]

The UN Security Council, in an attempt to end the slaughter, declared 'that the capital city of the Republic of Bosnia-Herzegovina, Sarajevo . . . should be free from armed attacks and other hostile acts'. The Security Council Resolution 824 of May 1993 discussed setting up 'safe havens' as a protection form ethnic cleansing. Sadly, this resolution for UN protection was shown to be ineffectual in Srebinica.[6]

Sir Christopher Meyer outlined the history of the hostilities in Sarajevo. The Serb siege had started in 1992 and would last four years. The Serbs shelled the population from the hills around and within the city, as well as from the suburbs. The toll from one ruthless attack alone, on a football game, was fifteen dead and eighty injured. After the Markale marketplace massacre in 1994, which killed 68 civilians and injured 200, the UN threatened to strike the Serb artillery from the air if they were not withdrawn as instructed. They were pulled back, but only temporarily. Finally, following the terrible massacre in mid-July 1995 by the Bosnian Serbs of 8,000 male Muslims at Srebrinica, which the Dutch UN peacekeeping force was powerless to prevent, the five powers of the USA, Britain, France, Germany and Russia finally agreed to dispatch a strong Anglo-French rapid reaction force to protect Sarajevo.[7]

The London Conference decided to withdraw all UN forces from Serb-held territory. The UNIPROFOR (UN Protection Force) mission was suspended. Gorazde and all UN weapon-collecting sites were abandoned. This permitted NATO to launch strategic air strikes against Serb HQ, air defence systems and logistic bases.[8] Stephen Dorril described how the British Secret Service ran very few federal intelligence sources within the former Yugoslavia. (Macedonia was also an area of concern; sources had pointed to MI6 using airdrops in an operation to set up arms dumps on the border of Macedonia, as part of a stay-behind network.) As a result of this intelligence deficiency, the JIC established a CIG (Current Intelligence Group) on the Balkans. Within eighteen months, MI6's Controllerate had formed several ethnic, military and political sources at a high level. Dorril noted that: 'the service lacked appropriate linguists and had to start more or less from scratch'. One solution was to recall past Balkan interpreters with FCO and military expertise in the Balkans. In SIS retirement was a flexible concept. John Sanderson was contacted and asked if he was prepared to undertake an intelligence mission in the Balkans for HMG (Her Majesty's Government). Volunteering without hesitation, he began to brush up on his linguistic skills (noted by the author, though his father offered no explanation).

Dorril explained that the Americans at this time were not sharing all their area intelligence with the British. General Sir Michael Rose, the Commander-in-Chief of the UN Protection Force and a former head of the SAS, realised in 1995 that his Sarajevo HQ was being 'bugged' by the Americans and that all his communications were being intercepted. Apparently, this was because Washington judged that bombing the Serbs in NATO air strikes was now the only way to make them sit down again and negotiate seriously. The US administration considered the British to be too supportive of the Bosnian Serbs. When the Americans monitored the communications of SAS scouts deep in Bosnian territory, they discovered that the SAS were deliberately failing to identify Serb artillery positions.

This perceived lack of trust caused friction and led to a 'behind the scenes' confrontation between the CIA and MI6.[9] Evidently as a result of this furore, fences had to be mended and decisions taken at a higher political level to restore the special relationship through appropriate military action.

In August 1995 a British Chinook helicopter flew in low over the city of Sarajevo, where eighty years earlier the assassination of Archduke Franz Ferdinand had triggered the outbreak of the First World War. Inside the chopper, looking with interest at the city below, was a distinguished-looking, silver-haired gentleman of 74 years, accompanied by his 'increment' escort, a fully equipped unit of SAS soldiers. (These were most probably members of the 22 SAS Sabre Sqn which works with SIS.[10]) The passenger was a retired British lieutenant colonel, a respected ex-diplomat and member of MI6, an interpreter in Balkan languages and an FCO expert on Macedonia and Bulgaria. His family believed he was holidaying on a Greek island in the peaceful Aegean. However, he had taken a different route back from Athens.

The Serb artillery was still laying siege to Sarajevo, causing terrible casualties to the civilian population, including a second market massacre at 11 a.m. on 28 August in which thirty-seven civilians were killed. Bosnia's capital had been under siege for forty months. People were still being killed by the sniping and shelling from the mountains, as they went about their daily lives in a struggle to survive. Colonel Sanderson had been sent to liaise with local contacts and play a small part in bringing peace to the bloody stranglehold on the beseiged city.

Sarajevo airport was in UN hands, although the flight in was hazardous for the UN C-130 aircraft. There were signs warning of snipers: '*PAZITE, SNAJPER*'.[11] General Sir Michael Rose described a hazardous helicopter flight into the Kosevo stadium in Sarajevo, which he had made:

> Right under the noses of the Serb guns . . . our route took us along the battle line for five miles, from where we were within range of small arms fire from both sides . . . We had an excellent view of Sarajevo as we roared down the main street of the city, level with the tops of the tower blocks and the Serb trenches on the hills behind . . . the stadium subsequently became a UN-designated helicopter-landing zone.[12]

After his Chinook landed, in *JBS*'s words: 'I met up with a waiting contact. We had a discussion and examined a map. I then returned to brief the SAS officer who thanked me, got back into the helicopter and took off with his men to undertake their assigned task.' NATO forward air controllers received their directed target identification. The mission was successful. In December that year, the Dayton Peace Agreement was signed. General Sir Michael Rose, the Commander of UNPROFOR who for exactly a year from January 1993 had displayed such wisdom, diplomacy and patience in Sarajevo in an almost impossible mission to keep the Bosnian and Serbs combatants apart and restrained, described the NATO military actions against the Bosnian Serbs in August and September 1995. Rose noted that the 2-week air offensive involved 3,500 aircraft sorties and 100 cruise missiles striking 400 separate Bosnian targets. The onslaught from the air was only part of an intense strategic campaign to end the Bosnian War, in which John Sanderson's SAS colleagues played their part. The UN Rapid Reaction Force targeted the Bosnian Serb heavy weapons in the hills around Sarajevo with artillery and mortar fire. The most crucial factor was 'the emergence of a political settlement that all sides would accept'.[13]

As the Foreign Secretary Douglas Hurd had noted, Britain had no interest specifically in the former Yugoslavia: 'Not important strategically. Our interest was simply to make it more decent place. To stop people killing each other.'[14] The diplomat Christopher Meyer, however, explained why an international intervention was necessary and what would have been the strategic implications of a continuing war: 'Left to their violence, the southern Slavs could have destabilised the whole of southern Europe, wrecking NATO, humiliating the UN, dragged in Greece and Turkey, and creating a serious antagonism with Russia, just as we were all celebrating the end of the Cold War.'[15]

John Sanderson certainly played a small part in bringing peace to Bosnia and the Balkans, a region he had first known in 1949, almost half a century before. As a result of his last secret action, unrecognised officially, he probably saved many lives.

Chapter 33

The Two Johns and *Kriegsglück*

Per Ardua ad Astra – 'Through Hardship to the Stars'

RAF motto

Wing Commander John Aldwinckle lived until just after his 90th birthday, passing away on 24 October 2012. A week later the British press gave full-page coverage to the traitor George Blake celebrating his 90th birthday in his Russian dacha near Moscow.

Utrinque Paratus – 'Ready for Anything'

Parachute Regiment motto

Lieutenant Colonel John Sanderson died aged 80 years on 21 December 2001, ironically the 'official' birthday of Joseph Stalin. Just six years earlier, Sanderson had been 'on government service' in the Balkans, serving his Queen and the cause of European peace one final time. A hundred days before he died, the twin towers in Manhattan were struck, setting in motion a 'Global War on Terror' and a subsequent violent clash between Militant Islam and the West. A new Cold War in Europe has confounded those who hoped that the demise of the Soviet Union would bring a reconciliation between old adversaries.

After the many adventures of his extraordinarily eventful life, John Sanderson was very fortunate to pass away peacefully in his bed. Because his father had survived the First World War, he had always been convinced that he too would come through the Second World War alive. He was very fortunate to have done so: both father and son had been wounded by shellfire in battle. They certainly had 'Lady Luck' on their side, with the odds were stacked against their survival. The German soldiers' *kriegsglück*.

At the time Sanderson died, Britain was again rushing off to intervene in a far-off Middle East countries, where 'The Great Game' had been played for centuries and on whose borders he had been stationed in 1942. The day before he died, when asked by his family how he was, the old soldier replied with a smile: 'I've been lying here, working out how I would set up a forward base for our troops.'

In the evening of his life, Field Marshal Bernard Montgomery penned in his memoirs a fitting and perceptive tribute to his old comrades in arms. Half a century before, in September 1910, as a young subaltern in the Royal Warwickshire Regt Montgomery had acted as best man for his distant relative, St John Philby, on the occasion of his marriage to Miss Dora Johnston in Murree Cathedral in the Rawalpindi district of the Punjab. Montgomery would never have imagined that the fruit of this marriage, Kim, would, like his father, betray Great Britain.[1]

> Montgomery: The British soldier is 'second to none' in the communities of fighting men . . . How often he has stood firm before tyranny and oppression. In the midst of the noise and confusion of the battlefield, the simple homely figure of the British soldier stands out calm and resolute – dominating all around him with his quiet courage, his humour and his cheerfulness, his unflinching acceptance of the situation. May the ideals for which he has struggled never vanish for the world.
>
> I shall take away many impressions into the evening of life. But the one which I shall always treasure above all is the picture of the British soldier – staunch and tenacious in adversity, kind and gentle in victory – the man to whom the nation has again and again, in the hour of adversity, owed its safety and its honour.[2]

In 2018 one of Sanderson's closest friends, a York and Lancaster regimental colleague, recollected:

> At Dover Castle in 1957, Captain John Sanderson was organising the presentation of new colours to the 1st Battalion the York and Lancaster Regiment by the Earl of Scarbrough. He discovered that there was no 'Regimental Collect' and so he wrote one himself. John's text is read on every November 11th Remembrance Day Service at the regimental memorial in Weston Park in Sheffield:

> Almighty God who canst save by many or by few and dost bid us to endure to the end that we might be saved, strengthen we pray thee, the York and Lancaster Regiment, that, as our perseverance has not been found wanting in battle, so may we be blessed in enduring all temptations, and at length, receive the crown of life, through Christ our Lord. Amen.

For over twenty-eight years a high wall divided Berlin, Germany and Europe. It has now been down longer than it stood, a symbol of a fractured Europe. When on 26 June 1963 President John F. Kennedy visited Berlin and the wall, he spoke to Berlin and to the world:

> There are many people in the world who really don't understand . . . what is the great issue between the free world and the Communist world. Let them come to Berlin. There are some who say that Communism is the wave of the future. Let them come to Berlin . . . Lasst sie nach Berlin kommen . . . Freedom is indivisible, and when one man is enslaved, all are not free. When all are free, and we look forward to that day, when this city will be joined as one, and this country, and this great continent of Europe is a peaceful and hopeful globe.[3]

In Bulgaria, Stalin's Peak has been renamed 'Musala' meaning 'Near God'.

Appendix I

Locations of Operations Flown by John Aldwinckle with 148 Squadron, August–November 1944

Key	Date	Operation	Place	Comment
WAR	13/14 Aug		Warsaw	Dropped supplies
KF	15/16 Aug	KINGFISHER	North Italy	No detail available on precise location
L	17/18 Aug	LIFTON	North Italy	No detail available on precise location
504	18/19 Aug	504 (z)	South-west Lodz	Dropped supplies
AL	21/22 Aug	ALDSWORTH	Ceva, North-west Italy	Between Cuneo and Genoa. Off map
R	22/23 Aug	ROOSTER	Thrace, near Turkish border. D/P at 41.07N and 26.08E	Dropped 3 agents ('Joes'), 15 containers, 15 packages
Tl	25/26 Aug	TIDALWAVE	At 46°26′N and 14°26′E at Kranjska Gora, south-west of Klagenfurt.	Now Kranj, Slovenia
AB	28/29 Aug	ABRAM	West Italy	Mondovi (few miles west of Ceva) Off map

Key	Date	Operation	Place	Comment
PA	5/6 Sep	PIDDOCK/ ASSURANCE	North Italy (2 targets)	No further details
TW	7/8 Sep	TWILFIT	Yugoslavia	No further details
AU	9/10 Sep	AUST	Bulgaria	No further details
C	9/10 Sep	CREEK	North Italy	No further details
TOC	12/13 Sep	CICERO/ VINDICTIVE	Castelnovo ne' Monti North Italy	Between Regio Emilia and La Spezia No further details
K	16/17 Sep	KITE	Zennare, North Italy	Zennare, south-west of Venice. 15 containers and 5 packages dropped
KF WA		WATERFALL	North Italy	Agents refused to jump
WA AP	26/27 Sep	APPLE / PECULIAR	Italy	No further details
TU	7/8 Oct	TUNGSTEN/ PLATINUM	Czechoslovakia	Unable to find target in solid cloud and had to abandon drop
TO	11 Oct	TOWNBUCKET	Araxos, Greece	15 containers and 40 packages
B	12 Oct	BREAD	Megara	West of Athens
D	17 Oct	DARIEN	Krvaskopolje, North Yugoslavia	Likely in the area of Dragatus, Slovenia 15 containers, 21 packages dropped
WAL	21 Oct	WALTZ	North-west Italy	Unable to complete mission due to heavy cloud obscuring drop area. Off map
L	23 Oct	LOCHMARAN	Pajanja, Albania	South of Tirana. 41°18′N and 19°7′E. Now Pajan. Dropped 15 containers and 28 packages

Key	Date	Operation	Place	Comment
TIN	25 Oct	TINKER	Albania	Did not complete operation as incorrect reception signals at target area
G	29 Oct	GUNMAN	Berat, Albania	Dropped 15 containers and 16 packages
PR	31 Oct	PRIMUS	Shëngjergj, Albania	Dropped 15 containers and 55 packages
E	1 Nov	ELLIS	Shëngjergj, Albania	No details but assume containers dropped
I	4 Nov	ICARUS	Yugoslavia	Strong cross winds at base meant John's Halifax was the only aircraft to get airborne. Completed drop of arms to partisans
S	9 Nov	SUNFLOWER	North Yugoslavia	No further details
EA	26 Nov	ELLIS/ANGEL	Albania	No further details
Additional flights made by 148 Squadron before John Aldwinckle's posting				
KA	11/12 Jun		Karlova, Bulgaria	North of Plovdiv. Agent drop

Notes

Introduction: by Myles Sanderson

1. Nigel West, *Spycraft Secrets. An Espionage A–Z* (History Press, 2016), pp. 184–5.
2. William Taubman, *Khrushchev. The Man. His Era* (Simon & Schuster, 2017), p. 279.
3. website ww2talk.com/airgraphs. KYT 20/1/2007.
4. Harold Adrian Russell Philby, *Kim Philby: My Silent War* (Arrow, 2003), p. 16.
5. Taylor Downing, *1983. The World at the Brink* (Little, Brown, 2018), p. 111.
6. Website en.wikipedia.org/wiki/Francis_Gary_Powers.

Chapter 1: Indian Childhood

1. Website sis.gov.uk/our-history ~Beginnings.

Chapter 2: Return to Britain, 1929

1. Alan Axelrod, *The Real History of the Cold War: A New Look at the Past* (Sterling, 2009), p. 12.
2. John Lewis Gaddis, *We Now Know. Rethinking Cold War History* (Oxford University Press, 1997), p. 6.
3. 'Humble Pie', *Time* magazine, 25 October 1926.
4. Gaddis, *We Now Know*, pp. 8–9. Jerrold L. Schecter and Vyacheslav Luchkov (trans and eds), *Khrushchev Remembers: The Glasnost Tapes* (Little, Brown, 1990), p. 37.
5. Website red_flag_of_the _paris_commune.
6. Geert Mak, *In Europe. Travels Through the Twentieth Century* (Vintage, 2008), pp. 452–3.
7. Denis Greenhill, *More by* Accident (Wilton 65, 1992), p. 50.
8. Rudyard Kipling and Zohreh T. Sullivan, *Kim Authoritative Text, Backgrounds, Criticism* (W.W. Norton, 2002), p. 225.
9. Christopher Andrew and Vasili Mitrokhin, *The Mitrokhin Archive* (Penguin, 1999), p. 76.
10. West, *Spycraft Secrets*, p. 116—17.

Chapter 3: Army Enlistment, Cliffs of Dover and War, 1938–42

1. William Shakespeare, *Richard II*, Act 2, Scene 1.
2. Axelrod, *The Real History of the Cold War*, pp. 22–3.
3. Mak, *In Europe*, p. 452.
4. Christopher M. Andrew and Oleg Gordievsky, *KGB: The Inside Story of its Foreign Operations from Lenin to Gorbachev* (Hodder & Stoughton, 1990), p. 203.
5. David Stafford, *Flight from Reality: Rudolf Hess and His Mission to Scotland, 1941* (Pimlico, 2002), pp. 5–15.
6. B.H. Liddell Hart, *The Sword and the Pen 'Mein Kampf'*, trans. J. Murray (Littlehampton Book Services, 1978), pp. 249–50.
7. David Stafford, *Churchill & Secret Service* (Abacus, 1997), p. 14.
8. John Erikson, 'Rudolf Hess: A Post-Soviet Postscript', in David Stafford, *Flight from Reality: Rudolf Hess and His Mission to Scotland, 1941* (Pimlico, 2002), pp. 39–42.
9. Stafford, *Flight from Reality*, pp. 3, 23.
10. Winston Churchill, *The Second World War*, 6 vols (Cassell, 1951), Vol. II, p. 282.
11. Arthur, *Forgotten Voices*, pp. 97–8.
12. Polish letters, insignia and photographs (Sanderson Archives).
13. Website un.org/en/sections/history-united-nations-charter/1941-atlantic-charter.
14. Richard Sim, Interview with Major John Sim's son, March 2108.
15. Tim Leadbeater, *Britain and India 1845–1947* (Hodder Murray, 2008), p. 99.

Chapter 4: Hut 6 at Bletchley Park and ULTRA

1. Interview with Helene Aldwinckle, Bletchley Park Oral History Project, 2003.
2. F.W. Winterbotham, *The Ultra Secret* (Weidenfeld & Nicolson, 1974).
3. John Jackson (ed.), *Solving Enigma's Secrets: The Official History of Bletchley Park's Hut 6* (BookTower Publishing, 2014). The original Bletchley Park three-volume history, TNA, HW 43/72.

Chapter 5: Voyage Back to India, Khyber Pass and Sikhs

1. Leadbeater, *Britain and India*, pp. 102–3.
2. 'Quit India Movement', *Congress Sandesh* magazine, Vol. 18, No. 12, August 2016.
3. Churchill, Winston.Speech. Mansion House.11th November 1942 website theguardian.com/theguardian/2009/nov/11/churchill-blood-sweat-tears.

4. Hugh Trevor-Roper, *The Secret World* (I.B. Taurus, 2014), p. 146 in a review of F.H. Hinsley and A. Stripp, *Codebreakers: The Inside Story of Bletchey Park* (Oxford University Press, 1993).

Chapter 6: The Arakan Battle, December 1942–May 1943

1. Julian Thompson, *Forgotten Voices of Burma* (Ebury, 2009), p. 101.
2. Frank McLynn, *The Burma Campaign 1942–45* (Vintage, 2011), p. 41, quoting Adrian Fort, *Archibald Wavell: The Life and Times of an Imperial Servant* (Jonathan Cape, 2009) p. 55.
3. Thompson, *Forgotten Voices*, p. 47.
4. William Slim, *Defeat into Victory* (Pan Books, 1999), p. 125.
5. John Grehan, and Martin Mace, *The Fall of Burma, 1941–1943* (Pen & Sword Military, 2015), pp. 112–13.
6. Michael Hickey, *The Unforgettable Army: Slim's XIVth Army in Burma* (Spellmount, 2003), p. 73.
7. Thompson, Julian, *The Imperial War Museum Book of the War in Burma, 1942–1945: a Vital Contribution to Victory in the Far East* (Pan Books in Association with the Imperial War Museum), 2003, p. 43.
8. Jon Latimer *Burma: the Forgotten War* (Murray, 2004), pp. 140, 150.
9. Thompson, *War in Burma*, p. 43.
10. Latimer, *Burma*, p. 141.
11. Ibid., p. 74.
12. Slim, *Defeat into Victory*, p. 152 and Latimer, *Burma*, p. 142.
13. Latimer, *Burma*, p. 146.
14. Thompson, *Forgotten Voices*, p. 254.
15. Latimer, *Burma*, p. 254.
16. Slim, *Defeat into Victory*, p. 154.
17. Birdwood, *The Sikh Regiment*, pp. 260–1.
18. Robert Lyman, *Slim, Master of War* (Constable, 2005), p. 97.
19. McLynn, *The Burma Campaign*, p. 98.
20. Birdwood, *The Sikh Regiment*, p. 261.
21. Slim, *Defeat into Victory*, p. 156.
22. Latimer, *Burma*, p. 147.
23. Hickey, *The Unforgettable Army*, p. 78.
24. War Diary of 6/11th Sikh Regiment Indian Army 1942–1943, TNA.
25. Hickey, *The Unforgettable Army*.
26. Birdwood, *The Sikh Regiment*, p. 262.
27. Thompson, *Forgotten Voices*, p. 59.
28. Slim, *Defeat into Victory*, p. 160.
29. Latimer, *Burma*, p. 143.
30. McLynn, *The Burma Campaign*, p. 89.

31. Birdwood, *The Sikh Regiment*, pp. 263–4.
32. Hickey, *The Unforgettable Army*, pp. 81, 107.
33. Thompson, *Forgotten Voices*, p. 50.
34. Latimer, *Burma*, p. 150.
35. John Hughes-Wilson, *A Brief History of the Cold War: The Hidden Truth about How Close We Came to Nuclear Conflict* (Robinson, 2006), p. 56.
36. Arthur, *Forgotten Voices*, pp. 396–7.
37. Churchill, *The Second World War*, Vol. V, p. 497.
38. Ibid., Vol. V, p. 498.
39. McLynn, *The Burma Campaign*, p. 301.
40. Thompson, *War in Burma*, p. 151.
41. Rajeshwor Yumnam, Battle of Sangshak documentary script, courtesy of Maurice Bell's family.

Chapter 7: The Battle of Sangshak, March 1944

1. Kohima Memorial words. Poem by John Maxwell Edmonds (1875–1958).
2. Wikipedia: 'Battle of Sangshak'.
3. Yumnam, account of the Battle of Sangshak.
4. Hickey, *The Unforgettable Army*, pp. 157–8.
5. Obituary Brigadier M.R.J. 'Tim' Hope-Thomson, the *Daily Telegraph* and 152nd Indian Parachute Btn (50th Indian Parachute Bde) war diary account (handwritten) by OC Lieutenant Colonel Paul Hopkinson (typed up from Paradata website).
6. Yumnam, account of the Battle of Sangshak.
7. Louis Alan, *Burma: The Longest War 1941–45* (J.M. Dent & Sons, 1984), p. 216.
8. Hopkinson, war diary.
9. Yumnam, account of the Battle of Sangshak.
10. Arthur, *Forgotten Voices*, pp. 157–8.
11. J.P. Cross, *Jungle Warfare: Experiences and Encounters* (Guild Pub., 1989).
12. Hopkinson, war diary.
13. Ibid.
14. Arthur, *Forgotten Voices*, pp. 380–1.
15. Hopkinson, war diary.
16. Hickey, *The Unforgettable Army*, p. 159.
17. Hopkinson, war diary.
18. Author interview, Major Maurice Bell, 50th (Indian) Parachute Bde, Signals Section.
19. Ibid.
20. Hopkinson, war diary.

21. Alan, *Burma*, p. 216.
22. Hickey, *The Unforgettable Army*, p. 159 and imphalcampaign.blogspot.co.uk, Basil Seaton account by Rajeshwor Yumnam.
23. Author interview, Major Maurice Bell.
24. War diary of 152nd Indian Parachute Btn (50th Indian Parachute Bde), TNA.
25. Churchill, *The Second World War*, Vol. VI, pp. 500–1.
26. Thompson, *War in Burma*, p. 151.
27. Author interview, Major Maurice Bell.
28. Laurence Binyon, 'Ode of Remembrance. For the Fallen', *The Times*, 1914.

Chapter 8: D-Day, 1944

1. Binyon, 'Ode of Remembrance'.
2. Arthur, *Forgotten Voices*, pp. 299, 301.
3. Interview, Andrew Cooper (son of pilot Ted Cooper), February 2018.
4. Stephen E. Ambrose, *Pegasus Bridge* (Simon and Schuster, 1985), pp. 40, 52. Major Howard, en.wikipedia.org/wiki/John_Howard.
5. Peter Harclerode, *'Go To It!' An Illustrated History of the 6th Airborne Division* (Caxton, 2000). Personal narrative of John Sim, courtesy of Sim family.
6. Major John Sim, 'Joining the 12th Yorkshire Parachute Battalion', section: 'We land in Normandy, 6th June 1944', pp. 7–10. A personal narrative written by John Sim as a contribution to Cornelius Ryan's *The Longest Day*. Courtesy of the Sim Family Archives.
7. Tony Sim, funeral ovation for Major John Sim MC and obituary for Major John Sim MC, *The Times*, 23 January 2107 (John Sim died on Christmas Eve, 2106, aged 96 years.)
8. John Christopher, *The Race for Hitler's X-Planes* (History Press, 2013), pp. 108–9, 179 and Wikipedia.
9. Mak, *In Europe*, p. 388.

Chapter 9: SOE – RAF Operations from Italy, 1944

1. Major Peter Greenhalgh DFC TD, Royal Artillery, Wartime Personal Papers, Imperial War Museum Archives; also archives from Army Museum of Flying.
2. John Grehan, *RAF and the SOE: Special Duties Operations in Europe During WW2. An Official History* (Frontline Books, 2016), p. 126.
3. Major General C.J. Venter, Director General, South African Air Force, 8 September 1944, quoted in Oliver Clutton-Brock, *Trusty to the End, The History of 148 (Special Duties) Squadron 1918–1945* (Mention the War Publishing, 2017), p. 558.

4. Norman Davies, *Rising '44: The Battle for Warsaw* (Macmillan, 2003), p. 307.
5. Sir John Slessor, Marshall of the RAF, *Autobiography, The Central Blue* (Cassell & Co. Ltd, 1956), p. 612.
6. Davies, *Rising '44*, p. 165.
7. Clutton-Brock, *Trusty to the End*, p. 556 and TNA, File HS4/184.
8. Laurence Rees, *Behind Closed Doors. Stalin, the Nazis and the West* (BBC Books, 2008), pp. 285–6 and BBC interview.
9. TNA, 148 Squadron Operations Record Book, August 1944, AIR/27/996.
10. Neil W. Orpen, *Airlift to Warsaw* (Foulsham & Company Ltd, 1984), p. 68.
11. Ibid., p. 79.
12. Ibid., p. 65.
13. Davies, *Rising '44*, p. 307.
14. Grehan, *RAF and the SOE*, p. 126.
15. Davies, *Rising '44*, p. 307.
16. Ibid., p. 309, personal recollection written in 2002 by Mr Alan McIntosh, Downer, Australia.
17. Ibid., p. 310.
18. Ibid., pp. 312–13, quote from M.J.R., *Destiny Can Wait, Polish Airforce in WW2* (1949).
19. Davies, *Rising '44*, p. 226.
20. Personal logbook of John Aldwinckle and 148 Sqn Operations Record Book.
21. Rees, *Behind Closed Doors*, p. 286.
22. Ibid., pp. 295, 299.
23. Davies, *Rising '44*.
24. TNA, HS 7/11, quoted in Clutton-Brock, *Trusty to the End*, p. 553.
25. Clutton-Brock, *Trusty to the End*, pp. 560–1.
26. Andrew and Gordievsky, *KGB*, p. 283.
27. Taubman, *Khrushchev*, p. 328.
28. Helene Aldwinckle, Bletchley Park Oral History Project, 2013. https://bletchleypark.org.uk/roll-of-honour/8921.
29. Trevor-Roper, *The Secret World*, p. 143.
30. Andrew, and Mitrokhin, *The Mitrokhin Archive*, p. 717.
31. Nigel West, *SIGINT Secrets: The Signals Intelligence War, 1900 to Today* (Weidenfeld & Nicolson, 1988), pp. 132, 255.
32. Winterbotham, *The Ultra Secret*.
33. Trevor-Roper, *The Secret World*, p. 143.
34. Gordon Welchman, *The Hut 6 Story* (McGraw-Hill Book Co. Inc., 1982, repr. 1997, 1998, 2000 and 2001).
35. West, *SIGINT Secrets*, p. 256.

Chapter 10: Elephant Point and POW Liberation, 1945

1. Otto Preston Chaney, *Khukhov* (Malcolm Mackintosh, 1974), p. 307.
2. Alan Axelrod, *The Real History of the Cold War*, pp. 32–4.
3. Chaney, *Khukhov*, p. 308.
4. Tony Geraghty, *Brixmis: The Untold Exploits of Britain's Most Daring Cold War Spy Mission* (HarperCollins, 1997), pp. 8, 9, 12, 20.
5. Churchill, *The Second World War*, Vol. VI, pp. 536–8.
6. John B. Sanderson interview, ITV programme *Kilroy*, May 1985.
7. Axelrod, *The Real History of the Cold War*, pp. 43, 97–8.
8. Churchill, *The Second World War*, Vol. VI, pp. 538–9.
9. Ibid., pp. 498–9.

Chapter 11: The Atomic and Plutonium Bombs

1. Axelrod, *The Real History of the Cold War*, p. 52.
2. Gaddis, *We Now Know*, p. 85.
3. Simon Sebag Montefiore, *Stalin: The Court of the Red Tsar* (Weidenfeld & Nicolson, 2004), p. 454.
4. J. Pimlott, *La Guerre Froide* (Aladdin, 1987), p. 22.
5. Axelrod, *The Real History of the Cold War*, pp. 97–8.
6. Mak, *In Europe*, pp. 560–1.
7. D. Middleton, *The struggle for Germany* (Cape, 1959), p. 13 and R.C. Mowat, *Ruin and Resurgence 1939–1965* (Blandford Press, 1966), pp. 196–7.
8. E. Davidson, *The Death of Germany* (Cape, 1959), p. 288.
9. Churchill, *The Second World War*, Vol. VI, pp. 545–6.
10. Audrey M. Jones, original Sanderson Family Archives document.
11. Churchill, *The Second World War*, Vol. VI, p. 546.
12. Ibid., Vol. VI, p. 546.
13. Ibid., Vol. VI, pp. 551–3.
14. Ibid., Vol. VI, pp. 548, 550–1.
15. Lawrence Rees, *Behind Closed Doors*, pp. 373–4 and FRUS, The Conference of Berlin, 1945, Vol. 2, pp. 359–62.
16. Churchill, *The Second World War*, Vol. VI, p. 551.
17. Axelrod, *The Real History of the Cold War*, p. 56.
18. Montefiore, *Stalin*, p. 533.
19. Axelrod, *The Real History of the Cold War*, p. 49.
20. Churchill, *The Second World War*, Vol. VI, pp. 556–8.
21. Neil Kagan and Stephen G. Hyslop, 'World War II. The Spies and Secret Missions that Won the War', *National Geographic Magazine*, 2017, pp. 104, 107–8.
22. John. B. Sanderson, ITV programme *Kilroy*, May 1985.
23. Axelrod, *The Real History of the Cold War*, pp. 49, 64.

24. Ibid., p. 49.
25. Craig Brown, article on Ronald Searle, *Sunday Times*, June 2010.
26. Greenhill, *More by Accident*, p. 46.
27. Keith Jeffery, *MI6: The History of the Secret Intelligence Service, 1909–1949* (Bloomsbury, 2010), pp. 762–7.
28. Knightley, *Philby*, p. 262.
29. Philby, *Philby*, p. 16.
30. Jeffery, *MI6*, p. 768.

Chapter 12: The Iron Curtain, Berlin and Hess

1. Norman Cousins, *The Improbable Triumvirate* (W.W. Norton, 1972), pp. 52–3.
2. Gaddis, *We Now Know*, p. 14.
3. West, *Spycraft Secrets*, p. 191.
4. Jeffery, *MI6*, p. 656.
5. Ibid., pp. 657–8.
6. Ibid., pp. 658–9.
7. Ibid., p. 678.
8. Ibid., pp. 659–60.
9. Roger Hermiston, *The Greatest Traitor: The Secret Lives of Agent George Blake* (Aurum, 2013), p. 64.
10. Axelrod, *The Real History of the Cold War*, p. 88.
11. Ibid., pp. 94–6.
12. Winston Churchill, *His Complete Speeches 1897–1963*, Vol. VII.
13. Gaddis, *We Now Know*, p. 20.
14. Axelrod, *The Real History of the Cold War*, p. 99.
15. Ibid., p. 96.
16. Gaddis, *We Now Know*, pp. 40–1.
17. Montefiore, *Stalin*, p. 511.
18. Hughes-Wilson, *A Brief History of the Cold War*, p. 26.
19. Stephen Dorril, *MI6: Fifty Years of Special Operations* (Fourth Estate, 2000), pp. 99–100.
20. Ibid., p. 104.
21. Ibid., pp. 105–6.
22. Ibid., p. 101.
23. Andrew and Gordievsky, *KGB*, pp. 230, 302–3.
24. Dorril, *Fifty Years of Special Operations*, pp. 106–9, 114–15.
25. David Stafford, *Flight from Reality*, p. 323.
26. Albert Speer, *Inside the Third Reich, Memoirs*, trans. R. and C. Winston (Macmillan Company,1970), pp. 523–4.
27. Dorril, *Fifty Years of Special Operations*, p. 109.

28. Isaacs and Downing, *Cold War*, pp. 40–1, 44, 47.
29. Philip H.J. Davies, *MI6 and the Machinery of Spying* (Frank Cass, 2005), p. 196.
30. Nigel West, *At Her Majesty's Secret Service: The Chiefs of Britain's Intelligence Agency, MI6* (Greenhill, 2006), p. 75.
31. Tim Leadbeater, *Britain and India 1845–1947* (Hodder Murray, 2008), p. 132.

Chapter 13: Intelligence Corps Depot, MI4, London

1. Antony Beevor and Artemis Cooper, *Paris After the Liberation, 1944–1949* (Viking, 2007), p. 245.
2. Gaddis, *We Now Know*, pp. 41–2.
3. John Keep, *Last of the Empires: A History of the USSR, 1945–1991* (Oxford University Press, 1995), pp. 45–6, 54.
4. Pimlott, *La Guerre Froide*, p. 6.
5. Isaacs and Downing, *Cold War*, p. 47.
6. Axelrod, *The Real History of the Cold War*, p. 114.
7. Ibid., p. 12.
8. 'Humble Pie', *Time* magazine, 25 October 1926.
9. Gaddis, *We Now Know*, pp. 8–9.
10. Keep, *Last of the Empires*, p. 10.
11. Ibid., pp. 11–13, 18. Keep referred to Aleksandr I. Solzhenitsyn, *One Day in the Life of Ivan Denisovich* (New American Library, 1962).
12. Jeffery, *MI6*.
13. Major General J.F.C. Fuller (military analyst for *Newsweek*), article in *IMAGES*, French magazine, 9 November 1947 (trans. by author).

Chapter 14: Start of the Cold War, Berlin Airlift, 1948

1. Andrew and Mitrokhin, *The Mitrokhin Archive*, p. 449.
2. Axelrod, *The Real History of the Cold War*, pp. 57, 123, 129–30, 134–5.
3. Isaacs, and Downing, *Cold War*, p. 57.
4. Axelrod, *The Real History of the Cold War*, p. 222.
5. Dorril, *Inside the Covert World of Her Majesty's Secret Intelligence Service*, pp. 355–7.
6. Ibid., pp. 361–3.
7. Ibid., pp. 363–4, 388.
8. Philby, *Kim Philby*, p. 156.
9. Dorril, *Inside the Covert World of Her Majesty's Secret Intelligence Service*, p. 368.
10. Ibid., pp. 368–9.
11. Isaacs and Downing, *Cold War*, pp. 65–6.
12. Ibid., pp. 67–9.
13. Axelrod, *The Real History of the Cold War*, pp. 225–9.

14. Isaacs, and Downing, *Cold War*, pp. 73–80.
15. Lord Greenhill, British Diplomatic Oral History Programme, 14 February 1996.
16. Agnès Poirier, *Left Bank. Art Passion and Rebirth of Paris*, 1940–1950 (Bloomsburg, 2018), p. 272.

Chapter 15: Paris Mission and UNO, 1948

1. West, *Spycraft Secrets*, p. 81.
2. Andrew and Gordievsky, *KGB*, p. 384.
3. Andrew and Mitrokhin, *The Mitrokhin Archive*, pp. 1, 199, 602 and J. Schecter and P. Derabin, *Recollections of the KGB Defector Peter Derabin. The Spy Who Saved the World* (Scribners, 1992), p. 273.
4. Andrew and Mitrokhin, *The Mitrokhin Archive*, p. 201.
5. Jeffery, *MI6*, pp. 718–19.
6. Andrew and Mitrokhin, *The Mitrokhin Archive*, p. 118.
7. Jeffery, *MI6*, pp. 719–20.
8. Mak, *In Europe*, p. 590.
9. Gaddis, *We Now Know*, p. 41.
10. Isaacs and Downing, *Cold War*.
11. US Foreign Relations Diplomatic Papers, 'Conference Document No. 12. Information from the Soviet delegation', Vol. 1, 1943.
12. Philby, *Kim Philby*, p. 130.
13. Ibid., p. 139.
14. Dorril, *Inside the Covert World of Her Majesty's Secret Intelligence Service*, p. 39, referring to Nicholas W. Bethel, *Spies and other secrets* (Viking, 1994), p. 299 and Thomas Powers, *The Man who Kept the Secrets: Richard Helms and the CIA* (Washington Press, 1979), p. 54.
15. Beevor and Cooper, *Paris After the Liberation*, pp. 326–7.
16. French website Wikipedia: Le RFP 'Le Rassemblement du peuple français'.
17. Paul V. Gorka, *Budapest Betrayed: A Prisoner's Story of the Betrayal of the Hungarian Resistance Movement to the Russians* (Oak Tree Books, 1986), pp. 119–21.
18. Dorril, *Inside the Covert World of Her Majesty's Secret Intelligence Service*, pp. 175–7.
19. Ben Macintyre, *A Spy Among Friends: Kim Philby and the Great Betrayal* (Bloomsbury, 2014), pp. 89–90.
20. Beevor and Cooper, *Paris After the Liberation*, p. 296.
21. Ibid., pp. 116, 119.
22. T. Morgan, *Valley of Death: The Tragedy at Dien Bien Phu that Led America into the Vietnam War* (Random House, 2010), p. 97.

23. Jeffery, *MI6*, p. 678–9.
24. Beevor and Cooper, *Paris After the Liberation*, p. 130.
25. Ibid., p. 295.
26. Jeffery, *MI6*, p. 678.
27. Ibid., p. 680.
28. Ibid., pp. 681–2.
29. Keep, *Last of the Empires*, p. 81.
30. Andrew and Mitrokhin, *The Mitrokhin Archive*, pp. 152–3.
31. James Reeve, *Cocktails, Crises and Cockroaches: A Diplomatic Trail* (Radcliffe Press, 1999), p. 69.
32. Beevor and Cooper, *Paris After the Liberation*, p. 357.
33. Andrew and Mitrokhin, *The Mitrokhin Archive*, p. 213.
34. Beevor and Cooper, *Paris After the Liberation*, p. 329.
35. Hughes-Wilson, *A Brief History of the Cold War*, p. 80 and Roger Hermiston, *The Greatest Traitor: The Secret Lives of Agent George Blake* (Aurum, 2013), p. 151.
36. Dorril, *Inside the Covert World of Her Majesty's Secret Intelligence Service*, pp. 366–7.
37. Sydney Stanley, né Kohsyzcky, a fraudster had been able to get preferential treatment in return for money bribes. Belcher resigned after an inquiry.
38. Beevor and Cooper, *Paris After the Liberation*, pp. 369–70.
39. Bob Conquest, 'Back to Bulgaria', *National Review*, January 1994.
40. Jeffery, *MI6*, p. 671.
41. Ibid., p. 672.
42. Ibid., p. 673.
43. Ibid., p. 674.
44. Obituary of Anthony Brooks, SOE agent, *Daily Telegraph*, 15 May 2007.
45. West, *At Her Majesty's Secret Service*, pp. 74–5.
46. Jeffery, *MI6*, pp. 675–6.

Chapter 16: Behind the Iron Curtain, Bulgaria, 1949

1. Evan Galbraith, 'Hot Spots in the Cold War', *National Review Periodical*, 24 January 1994.
2. Dorril, *Inside the Covert World of Her Majesty's Secret Intelligence Service*, p. 376.
3. Greenhill, *More by Accident*, pp. 55–6.
4. Ibid., p. 54.
5. Ibid., p. 60.
6. Lord Greenhill, British Diplomatic Oral History Programme, 14 February 1996.
7. Ibid., p. 64.

8. Ibid., p. 45.
9. J.B. Sanderson, typed trial report (Sanderson Archives).
10. Greenhill, *More by Accident*, pp. 65–6.
11. Ibid., p. 66.
12. Lord Greenhill, British Diplomatic Oral History Programme, 14 February 1996.
13. 'Bulgarian Murder Squad Exposed', *Daily Telegraph*, 31 July 2010.
14. Andrew and Gordievsky, *KGB*, p. 542
15. West, *Spycraft Secrets*, p. 46.
16. Conquest, 'Back to Bulgaria'.
17. Christopher and Mitrokhin, *The Mitrokhin Archive*, pp. 2–3, 191.
18. Tom Boyer, obituary of John Cairncross, the *Independent*, 9 October 1955.
19. Gaddis, *We Now Know*, pp. 50, 117, 123–4.
20. Montefiore, *Stalin*, p. 51 and Kapka Kassabova, *Street Without a Name* (Portobello Books, 2008), p. 151.
21. *Canberra Times*, 8 October 1949.
22. Knightley, *Philby*, p. 156.
23. *The Times* report from Vienna, 29 December 1949.
24. Gordon Corera, *The Art of Betrayal: Life and Death in MI6 from the Cold War to the Present* (Phoenix, 2012), p. 154.
25. 'Death of U.S. Attaché – Foul Play', *Canberra Times*, 27 February 1950 and Pierre Miquel, *La IVe République 1944–1959* (Larousse, 1993) ; trans. by the author.
26. Keep, *Last of the Empires*, pp. 26, 41, 77.
27. Colonel M.D. Egan, 'US GO HOME', thesis, 2013.
28. Alan Whicker, *Within Whicker's World* (Elm Tree Books, 1982), pp. 111–12.

Chapter 17: Clandestine War Behind the Iron Curtain

1. William Blake,'The Sick Rose', *Songs of experience*.
2. Website numbers-stations.com/cia/OBOPUS%20BFIEND, Report, p. 1.
3. Dorril, *Inside the Covert World of Her Majesty's Secret Intelligence Service*, pp. 382–3.
4. Website numbers-stations.com/cia/OBOPUS%20BFIEND, Report, pp. 4, 10–11, 13.
5. Dorril, *Inside the Covert World of Her Majesty's Secret Intelligence Service*, pp. 377–8.
6. Ibid., pp. 384–5.
7. Ibid., pp. 386, 368.
8. Ibid., p. 389.
9. Galbraith, 'Hot Spots in the Cold War'.

10. Percy Cradock, *Know Your Enemy: How the Joint Intelligence Committee Saw the World* (Murray, 2002), p. 54 quoting TNA, CAB 81/134 JIC (46) 85 of 14 February 1947.
11. David Stafford, *Churchill & Secret Service*, pp. 386, 388–9.
12. Cradock, *Know Your Enemy*, p. 110.
13. Askold Krushelynycky, 'Ukrainian Partisans', *Daily Telegraph*, 18 July 2002.
14. Dorril, *Inside the Covert World of Her Majesty's Secret Intelligence Service*, pp. 235–7.
15. Knightley, *Philby*, p. 162.
16. Tony Northdrop, 'Cold War Warrior Made it Hot for Hoxha', *Australian Newspaper*, 6 September 2000.
17. Dorril, *Inside the Covert World of Her Majesty's Secret Intelligence Service*, p. 391.
18. Ibid., pp. 395, 400–2.
19. Isaacs and Downing, *Cold War*, p. 127.
20. Dorril, *Inside the Covert World of Her Majesty's Secret Intelligence Service*, p. 396.
21. Andrew and Gordievsky, *KGB*, p. 532.

Chapter 18: Edirne Intelligence Centre, Turkey

1. Hughes-Wilson, *A Brief History of the Cold War*, pp. 99–100.
2. Dorril, *Inside the Covert World of Her Majesty's Secret Intelligence Service*, p. 206.
3. Dorril, *Fifty Years of Special Operations*, p. 207.
4. Ibid.
5. West, *At Her Majesty's Secret Service*, pp. 61, 67.
6. Dorril, *Inside the Covert World of Her Majesty's Secret Intelligence Service*, p. 363.
7. Knightley, *Philby*, p. 142.
8. Philby, *Kim Philby*, p. 132.
9. Davies, *MI6 and the Machinery of Spying*, pp. 208, 209 and Anthony Cavendish, *Inside Intelligence* (Sterling, 1987), pp. 2–3.
10. Peter Wright, *Spycatcher* (Dell, 1987), pp. 57–8.
11. Keep, *Last of the Empires*, p. 186.
12. Corera, *The Art of Betrayal*, pp. 72–3.
13. Knightley, *Philby*, p. 272.
14. Philby, *Kim Philby*, pp. 9–10.
15. Knightley, *Philby*, p. 191.
16. Philby, *Kim Philby*, pp. 130–2.
17. Knightley, *Philby*, p. 144.

18. Philby, *Kim Philby*, pp. 133–4.
19. Dorril, *Inside the Covert World of Her Majesty's Secret Intelligence Service*, pp. 212–13.
20. Nigel West, *The Faber Book of Espionage* (Faber and Faber, 1993), p. 463.
21. C.M. Woodhouse, *Something Ventured* (HarperCollins, 1982).
22. G. Brook-Shepherd, *The Storm Birds* (Weidenfeld & Nicolson, 1989), pp. 62–3.
23. Knightley, *Philby*, pp. 151–2, 69–70 and West, *At Her Majesty's Secret Service*, pp. 60, 85.
24. West, *The Faber Book of Espionage*, pp. 463–6.
25. Philby, *Kim Philby*, p. 141.
26. Ibid., pp. 163–7, 19, 143–4.
27. Andrew and Gordievsky, *KGB*, pp. 316–17; C. Andrew's interview with Yuri Nosenko, 15 November 1987.
28. Ibid., p. 21.
29. Radio France report, 'French Highway Swallowed KGB Treasure', 14 March 1993.
30. West, *Spycraft Secrets*, p. 217.
31. Jonathan Leake, 'Soviet spy maps of UK better than our own', *Sunday Times*, 22 October 2107, reviewing Alexander Kent and John Davies, *The Red Atlas* (University of Chicago Press, 2107).
32. See photograph of *JBS* with bear and Turkish peasant.
33. Dorril, *Inside the Covert World of Her Majesty's Secret Intelligence Service*, pp. 601–2.
34. Ibid., p. 550.
35. Knightley, *Philby*, p. 184.
36. Cradock, *Know Your Enemy*, p. 220.
37. Brook-Shepherd, *The Storm Birds*, pp. 179, 181.

Chapter 19: Cyprus–Egypt Intelligence SIS Course, 1953

1. Keep, *Last of the Empires*, p. 41.
2. Tom Parfitt, 'The Power and the Glory', *The Times*, 8 May 2018.
3. Mak, *In Europe*, pp. 442, 601.
4. Ibid., 599–601.
5. Archie Brown, *The Rise and Fall of Communism* (Vintage, 2010), pp. 233–4, Andrew and Mitrokhin, *The Mitrokhin Archive*, pp. 2–3, 191, 713–15 and Montefiore, *Stalin*, pp. 578–9.
6. Taubman, *Khrushchev*, pp. 361–4.
7. BBC News report from Tel Aviv, BBC webpage, 22 April 2108.
8. Gaddis, *We Now Know*, pp. 224–5.
9. dur.ac.uk/library/projects/woodsudan.

10. Wikipedia: General Charles Gordon.
11. Dorril, *Inside the Covert World of Her Majesty's Secret Intelligence Service*, p. 601.
12. Stephen Grey, *The New Spymasters* (Penguin Books Ltd, 2016), pp. 85–6.
13. West, *At Her Majesty's Secret Service*, pp. 114–16.

Chapter 20: Gold Tunnel, Berlin, 1953–6

1. Richard Aldwinckle, author interview (my father's career in the RAF and SIS), January 2018.
2. Geraghty, *Brixmis*, pp. 62–3.
3. Charles Bremner, 'Cold War Secret Army Files Vanish', *The Times*, 10 January 2018.
4. David Stafford, *Spies Beneath Berlin* (John Murray, 2002).
5. West, *At Her Majesty's Secret Service*, pp. 73–6.
6. George Blake, *No Other Choice* (Jonathan Cape, 1990), pp. 168–9.
7. Gaddis, *We Now Know*, pp. 388–9, 394.
8. Stafford, *Spies Beneath Berlin*, p. 115.
9. Hermiston, *The Greatest Traitor*, pp. 180–1.
10. West, *At Her Majesty's Secret Service*, p. 70.
11. Stafford, *Spies Beneath Berlin*, p. 96.
12. Wright, *Spycatcher*, p. 59.
13. G. O'Toole, *Encylopaedia of US Intelligence and Espionage* (Fact on File, 1988), pp. 66–7.
14. David E. Murphy, Sergei A. Kondrashev and George Bailey, *Battleground Berlin* (Yale University Press, 1997), pp. 208–31.
15. Hermiston, *The Greatest Traitor*, p. 196.
16. Roger Boyes, *The Times*, 7 November 2012.
17. Aldwinkle, author interview.
18. West, *Spycraft Secrets*, p. 78.
19. Aldwinkle, author interview.
20. David Charter, 'Berlin Wall Tunnel Tells of Last Hope', *The Times*, 13 January 2018.

Chapter 21: Suez Invasion, 1956

1. Dorril, *Inside the Covert World of Her Majesty's Secret Intelligence Service*, pp. 604–5.
2. Hughes-Wilson, *A Brief History of the Cold War*, p. 135.
3. West, *At Her Majesty's Secret Service*.
4. Gordon Corera, Security Correspondent, BBC News recording, 4 April 2016.
5. Corera, *The Art of Betrayal*, p. 93.

6. Mak, *In Europe*, p. 606.
7. Brown, *The Rise and Fall of Communism*, p. 241.
8. Taubman, *Khrushchev*, pp. 273, 279–80.
9. Montefiore, *Stalin*, p. 532.
10. Mak, *In Europe*, p. 452.
11. Ibid., p. 601.
12. Keep, *Last of the Empires*, p. 77.
13. Taubman, *Khrushchev*, p. 284.
14. Mak, *In Europe*, p. 606 and Isaacs and Downing, *Cold War*, p. 134.
15. Mowat, *Ruin and Resurgence*, pp. 265–6.
16. Dorril, *Inside the Covert World of Her Majesty's Secret Intelligence Service*, pp. 607, 613.
17. Andrew and Gordievsky, *KGB*, pp. 385.
18. Dorril, *Inside the Covert World of Her Majesty's Secret Intelligence Service*, pp. 600, 607, 647–8.
19. Corera, *The Art of Betrayal*, pp. 79–80.
20. Ibid., p. 117.
21. Ibid., p. 120.
22. Brown, *The Rise and Fall of Communism*, p. 25.
23. Taubman, *Khrushchev*, pp. 295–6 and Isaacs and Downing, *Cold War*, pp. 132–5.
24. Mowat, *Ruin and Resurgence*, pp. 267–70.
25. Interview with York and Lancaster colleague of John Sanderson, 2017.
26. Taubman, *Khrushchev*, p. 296–9.
27. Gaddis, *We Now Know*.
28. Taubman, *Khrushchev*, p. 360.
29. Mowat, *Ruin and Resurgence*, p. 196.
30. Cradock, *Know Your Enemy*, pp. 127–8.
31. Wright, *Spycatcher*, pp. 106–7.
32. Dorril, *Inside the Covert World of Her Majesty's Secret Intelligence Service*, pp. 641–2.
33. West, *At Her Majesty's Secret Service*, p. 90 and West, *Spycraft Secrets*, p. 23.
34. Beevor and Cooper, *Paris After the Liberation*, p. 379.
35. Brook-Shepherd, *The Storm Birds*, pp. 198, 202–3.
36. Robert Jackson, *Suez, The Forgotten Invasion* (Airlife Pub., 1996), p. 117.
37. Dorril, *Inside the Covert World of Her Majesty's Secret Intelligence Service*, p. 646.
38. Interview with York and Lancaster colleague of John Sanderson, 2017.
39. Jackson, *Suez*, p. 118.
40. Wright, *Spycraft*, p. 202.
41. Mowat, *Ruin and Resurgence*, pp. 265–70.
42. Cradock, *Know Your Enemy*, pp. 132–3.

43. Dorril, *Inside the Covert World of Her Majesty's Secret Intelligence Service*, p. 647.
44. Brook-Shepherd, *The Storm Birds*, pp. 260, 264.
45. Taubman, *Khrushchev*, pp. 323, 368–70.
46. Ibid., pp. 356–7.
47. James Bamford, *Body of Secrets How America's NSA & Britain's GCHQ Eavesdrop on the World* (Century, 2001), pp. 43–52 and Taubman, *Khrushchev*, pp. 442–5.
48. Taubman, *Khrushchev*, pp. 460–5, 468 and Harold Macmillan, *Harold Pointing the Way* (Macmillan, 1969), p. 210. TNA, prem 11/2992, pp. 41–6.

Chapter 22 : Military Attaché, Sofia and Berlin Wall 1961–2

1. George William Rendel, *The Sword and the Olive: Recollections of Diplomacy, 1913–1954* (Murray, 1957), pp. 137–8.
2. Corera, *The Art of Betrayal*, p. 142.
3. Brook-Shepherd, *The Storm Birds*, pp. 168, 180, 196.
4. Corera, *The Art of Betrayal*, pp. 48, 142–3.
5. Andrew and Gordievsky, *KGB*, pp. 364, 366–7.
6. West, *At Her Majesty's Secret Service*.
7. Oleg Vladimirovich Pen'kovskiĭ, *The Penkovsky Papers; A Translation of an Article Introducing the Diary of Oleg V. Penkovsky and Portions of the Diary* (Caracas, 1966), pp. 29–30 and Dorril, *Inside the Covert World of Her Majesty's Secret Intelligence Service*, p. 705.
8. Reeve, *Cocktails, Crises and Cockroaches*, pp. 122–3.
9. Ibid., pp. 125–6.
10. Ibid., p. 128.
11. Author interview, York and Lancaster colleague of John Sanderson, 2018.
12. Hughes-Wilson, *A Brief History of the Cold War*, p. 92.
13. Geraghty, *Brixmis*, pp. 209–10.
14. Dorril, *Inside the Covert World of Her Majesty's Secret Intelligence Service*, pp. 723–4.
15. CIA, 'More on the Recruitment of Soviets', *Studies in Intelligence*, Vol. 9, winter 1965.
16. Website esa.int/About_Us/Welcome_to_ESA/ESA_history/50_years_of_humans_in_space/The_flight_of_Vostok_1.
17. Gaddis, *We Now Know*, p. 140, quoting (as told to Richard Rusk) Dean Rusk, *As I saw it* (Norton, 1990), p. 227.
18. Gaddis, *We Now Know*, p. 141, quoting Memorandum, Dulles-Adenauer conversation of 8 February 1959. FRUS, 1958–60, viii, 346.
19. Gaddis, *We Now Know*, p. 242.
20. Taubman, *Khrushchev*, p. 505.
21. Isaacs and Downing, *Cold War*, p. 173.

22. Ibid., p. 182.
23. Mak, *In Europe*, p. 709.
24. Pen'kovskiĭ, *The Penkovsky Papers*, pp. 29–30.
25. Corera, *The Art of Betrayal*, p. 158.
26. Brook-Shepherd, *The Storm Birds*, p. 169.
27. Bamford, *Body of Secrets*, p. 153.
28. Author interview with former regimental colleague of JBS.
29. Patricia Holden-White, letter to author, November 2008.
30. Greenhill, *More by Accident*, p. 62.
31. Peebles, *Guardians*, pp. 221–3. Original source: *New York Times*, 21 and 23 January 1962 and 4 January 1963.
32. Sanderson Family Archives, letter from the Blackshear family.
33. Robert Kee, *1945: The World We Fought For* (Penguin Books, 1995), pp. 93–5.
34. Andrew and Gordievsky, *KGB*, p. 291.
35. Knightley, *Philby*, pp. 238–9.
36. Author interview with the former landlady of Philby's daughter, 2017 and Anthony Cave Brown, *Treason in the Blood: H. St John Philby, Kim Philby, and the Spy Case of the Century* (Houghton Mifflin, 1994), p. 543.
37. Mak, *In Europe*, p. 597.
38. Gaddis, *We Now Know*, p. 264.
39. West, *The SIGINT Secrets*, p. 270.
40. Isaacs and Downing, *Cold War*, p. 183.
41. Gaddis, *We Now Know*, p. 264.

Chapter 23: Cuban Missile Crisis, NATO HQ, Paris, 1962

1. André Fontaine, *La Guerre Froide, 1917–1991* (La Martinière, 2006), pp. 36–7.
2. Geraghty, *Brixmis*, p. 18.
3. Ibid., p. 164.
4. Source: Romanian Central Historical National Archives (ANIC), Central Committee of the Romanian Communist Part, Chancellery Collection – file 56/1960, 19; 46/1961. 11-21, 28/1962, 111. Parallel History Project on Cooperative Security ETH (Swiss Federal Insititute of Technology, 2000–8). Marshall V. Sokolovskii (ed.), *Strategia Militara* (Bucharest Military Publishing House, 1972), p. 353–4. (Courtesy of Major Petre Opris, Ph.D., 'Warsaw Pact Military Exercises During the Cuban Missile Crisis of October 1962: The Romanian Point of View (Bucharest University)).
5. Keep, *Last of the Empires*, pp. 54–5.
6. Mowat, *Ruin and Resurgence*, p. 327.
7. Klaus P. Fischer, *America in White, Black and Gray* (Continuum Publishing Group, 2016), p. 86.
8. Pen'kovskiĭ, *The Penkovsky Papers*, pp. 29–30.

9. West, *At Her Majesty's Secret Service*, pp. 58–90.
10. Corera, *The Art of Betrayal*, pp. 157–8.
11. Brook-Shepherd, *The Storm Birds*, pp. 163–4.
12. Doug Gordon, *Tactical Reconnaissance in the Cold War: 1945 to Korea, Cuba, Vietnam and the Iron Curtain* (Pen & Sword Aviation, 2006), p. 180.
13. Brook-Shepherd, *The Storm Birds*, p. 165.
14. Website archive2.gwu.edu Post 24/10/12, No. 399 Briefing Book.
15. Website taskandpurpose.com and Gary Slaughter, *Sea Stories. Memoirs of a Naval Officer (1956–67)* (Fletcher House, 2016).
16. Cradock, *Know Your Enemy*, pp. 179–88.
17. Brook-Shepherd, *The Storm Birds*, pp. 258–8.
18. Gaddis, *We Now Know*, p. 238 and Taubman, *Khrushchev*, p. 579.
19. 'Penkovsky's Progress', *Times Literary Supplement*, 16 December 1965.
20. Corera, *The Art of Betrayal*, p. 140.
21. Pen'kovskiĭ, *The Penkovsky Papers*, pp. 276–7.
22. Brook-Shepherd, *The Storm Birds*, pp. 164–9.
23. Ibid., p. 167–8.
24. Pen'kovskiĭ, *The Penkovsky Papers*, p. 18.
25. Brook-Shepherd, *The Storm Birds*, pp. 195.
26. Ibid., pp. 168.
27. Keep, *Last of the Empires*, p. 62.
28. Ibid., p. 46.
29. Ibid., pp. 48–9.
30. Ibid., p. 63.
31. Sir Rodric Braithwaite, British Ambassador to Moscow, 'The Myths of Russia Old and New', *Financial Times*, November 2011.
32. Keep, *Last of the Empires*, p. 63.
33. Corera, *The Art of Betrayal*, p. 89.
34. Wright, *Spycatcher*, p. 220.

Chapter 24: France Leaves NATO and 'Fairwell'

1. Website reseau-canope.fr/cnrd/ressource/texte/3948.
2. Poirier, *Left Bank*, pp. 70, 71, 76, 78.
3. Beevor and Cooper, *Paris After the Liberation*, p. 217.
4. Andrew and Gordievsky, *KGB*, pp. 335, 369.
5. Brook-Shepherd, *The Storm Birds*, pp. 198, 202–3.
6. Andrew and Gordievsky, *KGB*, pp. 368–9.
7. Mowat, *Ruin and Resurgence*, pp. 341–5, 350–1.
8. Beevor and Cooper, *Paris After the Liberation*, p. 382.
9. Robert G. Kaufman, *Henry M. Jackson. A Life in Politics* (University of Washington Press, 2000), p. 180.

10. Webpage: shape.nato.int/page214871012 shape.
11. Egan, 'US GO HOME'.
12. Mak, *In Europe*, p. 653.
13. Jonathan Fenby, 'France Cannot be Without Grandeur', *Financial Times*, 16/17 June 2018.
14. Wikipedia, 'Le Coup d'État permanent', Mitterrand.
15. West, *Spycraft Secrets*, p. 164.
16. Wikipedia, 'The Fairwell Affair'.
17. James Adams, *The New Spies: Exploring the Frontiers of Espionage* (Hutchinson, 1994), pp. 121–6.

Chapter 25: AFCENT Planning, Holland, 1968–9

1. Geraghty, *Brixmis*, pp. 158–61.
2. Isaacs and Downing, *Cold War*, pp. 264, 267.
3. Colonel Oleg Gordievsky, interview, *Guardian*, 11 March 2103.
4. Corera, *The Art of Betrayal*, p. 251.
5. West, *At Her Majesty's Secret Service*, pp. 127–32.
6. Dorril, *Inside the Covert World of Her Majesty's Secret Intelligence Service*, p. 727.
7. Colonel Herbert Stobbe, German Army, personal account given to author, 2001.
8. Wright, *Spycatcher*, p. 181.
9. Ibid., pp. 352–3.
10. Gordon Corera, interview, 'Take our best weapon, 007 – a moral compass', *Sunday Times News Review*, 27 July 2009.
11. Cradock, *Know Your Enemy*, p. 59. JIC (57) 7 of 16 February 1955 and TNA, 158/2, JIC (57) 12 of 12.
12. Margaret Thatcher, *Statecraft: Strategies for a Changing World* (HarperCollins, 2002), p. 53.

Chapter 26: Liaison Officer, French Army, Germany, 1969–7

1. Geraghty, *Brixmis*, p. 5.
2. Alexander Furshenko and Timothy Naftali, 'Soviet Intelligence and the Cuban Missile Crisis', *Intelligence and National Security*, Vol. 13 (1998), pp. 70–1.
3. Andrew and Mitrokhin, *The Mitrokhin Archive*, pp. 601, 609.
4. Geraghty, *Brixmis*, pp. 163–4.
5. Marcus Wolf, 'Memoirs of a Spy', extracts, *Le Monde*, Hors-Serie, September 2009, p. 81 (author translation).
6. Geraghty, *Brixmis*, pp. 107, 236.
7. Website: en.wikipedia.org/wiki/Willy_Brandt.

8. West, *Spycraft Secrets*, p. 41.
9. Article, *New York Times*, 25 February 1995.
10. West, *At Her Majesty's Secret Service*, pp. 137–9.
11. Keep, *Last of the Empires*, p. 183.
12. Ryszard Kapuściński, *ImperiumGranta* (Random House, 1994), pp. 307–8, describing Yurii Boriev.
13. Keep, *Last of the Empires*, pp. 197–8.
14. Fontaine, *La Guerre Froide*, pp. 26–7.
15. Ibid., pp. 28–9.
16. Michel M. Aid, *The Secret Sentry: The Untold History of the National Security Agency* (Bllomsbury Press, 2009), pp. 31–2.
17. Michael Smith, article, *Sunday Times*, 24 May 2009.
18. Andrew and Gordievsky, *KGB*, pp. 662, 729.
19. Ibid., pp. 662–3.
20. Ibid., p. 676 and Carl Berstein and Marco Politi, *His Holiness: John Paul II and the Hidden History of Our Times* (Doubleday, 1990), p. 243.
21. Andrew and Mitrokhin, *The Mitrokhin Archive*, pp. 691, 702–3.
22. Fontaine, *La Guerre Froide*, pp. 34–5.

Chapter 27: Kim Philby in Berlin, 1981

1. H.A.R. Philby, *The Philby Tape*, BBC Radio 4, 5 April 2016, discussed by Gordon Corera.
2. Nigel West, *A Matter of Trust, MI5, 1945–72* (Coronet, 1982), pp. 64–5.
3. Knightley, *Philby*, p. 214.
4. Trevor-Roper, *The Secret World*, pp. 72, 83.
5. Andrew and Mitrokhin, *The Mitrokhin Archive*, p. 81.

Chapter 28: Operation RYAN and Exercise Able Archer, 1983

1. Andrei Sakharov, 'Essay, Reflections on Peaceful Coexistence', website sakharov-archive.ru/English/.
2. Cradock, *Know Your Enemy*, pp. 61–6 and Documents on Disarmament (US Govt Printing, 1961), pp. 544–5.
3. Downing, *The World at the Brink*, pp. 100–2, 104–5.
4. Geraghty, *Brixmis*, p. 10.
5. Downing, *The World at the Brink*, pp. 52–4, Peter Schweizer, *Victory: The Reagan Administration's Secret Strategy that Hastened the Collapse of the Soviet Union* (NY Monthly Press, 1994), p. 8.
6. S. Hersh, *The Target is Destroyed* (Random House, 1986), p. 17.
7. Simon Vistica, *Fall from Glory* (G.L. & Schuster, 1996), pp. 105–35.
8. Hersh, *The Target is Destroyed*, p. 18.

9. Thatcher, *Statecraft*, pp. 10–11.
10. Gaddis, *We Now Know*, p. 264.
11. Andrew and Mitrokhin, *The Mitrokhin Archive*, pp. 278–9, quoting Anatoli Dobrynin, *In Confidence: Moscow's Ambassador to America's Six Cold War Presidents* (Times Books, 1995), p. 523.
12. Downing, *The World at the Brink*, pp. 75–7.
13. Ibid., p. 94.
14. Brook-Shepherd, *The Storm Birds*, pp. 320–1.
15. Andrew and Gordievsky, *KGB*, p. 605.
16. West, *At Her Majesty's Secret Service*, pp. 118–19.
17. Downing, *The World at the Brink*, pp. 120–7.
18. West, *At Her Majesty's Secret Service*, pp. 152, 156.
19. Corera, *The Art of Betrayal*, pp. 67–8.
20. West, *Spycraft Secrets*.
21. Andrew and Gordievsky, *KGB*, p. 605.
22. Brook-Shepherd, *The Storm Birds*, pp. 329–30.
23. Corera, *The Art of Betrayal*, pp. 269, 488.
24. Christopher M. Andrew and Oleg Gordievsky, *Comrade Kryuchkov's Instructions. Foreign Operations, 1975–1985* (Stanford University Press, 1994), p. 79.
25. Downing, *The World at the Brink*, p. 230.
26. Andrew and Gordievsky, *KGB*, pp. 599–600.
27. Hughes-Wilson, *A Brief History of the Cold War*, pp. 298–9, 293.
28. Downing, *The World at the Brink*, pp. 131–5, 194–201, 250–1.
29. Andrew and Gordievsky, *KGB*, pp. 505–7.
30. Commemorative UK Stamp Cover Information Sheet, 17 September 1984.
31. Victor Spetznaz Suvorov, *The Story of the Soviet SAS* (Hamish Hamilton, 1987).
32. Brook-Shepherd, *The Storm Birds*, pp. 278–9, 277, 273, 284, 286, 290.
33. Dr Gregory Pedlow, Source Exercise Scenario, Able Archer NATO Exercise, 1983, National Security Archive of the original (16 June 2013), Wikipedia.
34. Author interview, an ex-lance corporal of the Parachute Regt, 2013. He was a former 5th Airborne Paratrooper on Exercise LIONHEART, 1984 in West Germany.
35. General Lionel Hastings, Lord Ismay, *NATO The First Five Years, 1949–54* (Bosch Dat, 1954), p. 30.
36. Adams, *The New Spies*, p. 35.
37. West, *At Her Majesty's Secret Service*, pp. 159, 161.
38. Downing, *The World at the Brink*, pp. 278–82.
39. Alastair Rellie, obituary, *The Times*, 26 April 2018.
40. Percy Cradock, *In Pursuit of British Interests* (John Murray, 1997), p. 100.
41. West, *At Her Majesty's Secret Service*, pp. 119, 159.

Chapter 29: Gorbachev and the End of the Cold War

1. Angus Roxburgh, *Moscow Calling: Memoirs of a Foreign Correspondent* (Birlinn, 2017), p. 192.
2. Georges Mink, 'Scenarios pour une fin d'empire', *Le Monde*, Hors-Serie, September 2009, pp. 50–1.
3. Serhii Plokhy, *The Last Empire: The Final Days of the Soviet Union* (Basic Books, 2014), p. 396.
4. Ibid., p. 263.
5. Archie Brown, 'Perestroika and the End of the Cold War', *Cold War History*, Vol. 7, No. 1, February 2007, p. 8 and J.F. Matlock Jr, *Reagan and Gorbachev: How the Cold War Ended* (Random House, 2004), pp. 52–4.
6. Roxburgh, *Moscow Calling*, p. 414.
7. Brown, 'Perestroika and the End of the Cold War', p. 165.
8. Archie Brown, 'The Change to Engagement in Britain's Cold War Policy. The Origins of Thatcher-Gorbachev Relationship', *Journal of Cold War Studies*, Vol. 10, No. 3, Summer 2008, p. 14; a two-day seminar held at Chequers, September 1983.
9. Taubman, *Khrushchev*, p. 648.
10. Archie Brown, 'The Gorbachev Factor Revisited', *Problems of Post-Communism*, Vol. 58, Nos 4–5, July/August/September 2011, p. 57.
11. Archie Brown, Notes takes taken during Gorbachev's speech at Central Hall, London, 29 October 1996.
12. Brown, 'The Gorbachev Factor Revisited', p. 57 and Roxburgh, *Moscow Calling*, p. 143.
13. Brown, ' Perestroika', p. 4.
14. Ibid., p. 9.
15. Brown, 'The Change to Engagement in Britain's Cold War Policy', pp. 16–17.
16. Ibid., p. 17.
17. Brown, 'The Gorbachev Factor Revisited', p. 60.
18. Brown, 'Perestroika', pp. 7, 12 and Dobrynin, *In Confidence*, p. 574.
19. Mink, 'Scenarios pour une fin d'empire', p. 52.
20. Andrew and Gordievsky, *KGB*, p. 512.
21. Thatcher, *Statecraft*, p. 10.
22. Roxburgh, *Moscow Calling*, p. 198.
23. Brown, 'The Gorbachev Factor Revisited', p. 61 (Zasedanie Polibiuro Tsk KPSS 30 Maia 1987 goda NSA, 'Volgogonov Collection', R1646, p. 485).
24. Roxburgh, *Moscow Calling*, p. 159.
25. Ibid., pp. 169–72.
26. Isaacs and Downing, *Cold War*, p. 372.

27. Daniel Vernet, Interview with Mikhail Gorbachev, *Le Monde*, Hors Série, November 2008, trans. by author.
28. Roxburgh, *Moscow Calling*, p. 198.
29. Vernet, Interview with Mikhail Gorbachev.
30. John Major, *John Major: The Autobiography* (HarperCollins, 1999), pp. 499–500.
31. Archie Brown, 'Review Essay. The End of the Soviet Union', *Journal of Cold War Studies*, Vol. 17, No. 4, Fall 2015, p. 158.
32. Ibid., p. 159.
33. Aleksandr Yakovlev, *Sumerki* (Materik, 2003), pp. 519–20.
34. Isaacs and Downing, *Cold War*, p. 403.
35. Mink, 'Scenarios pour une fin d'empire', p. 52.
36. Sylvie Kauffman, '1989. The People Awake', *Le Monde*, Hors-Serie, September 2009, trans. by the author, p. 18.
37. Archie Brown, *The Rise and Fall of Communism* (Bodley House, 2009), p. 541.
38. Ibid., pp. 563–6.
39. Braithwaite, 'The Myths of Russia Old and New'.

Chapter 30: Coup by South African Intelligence

1. Wikipedia.org/wiki/South_African_Border_War.
2. Isaacs and Downing, *Cold War*, pp. 304–7.
3. Wikipedia, 'Rosoboronexport'.

Chapter 31: Yeltsin and the End of Communism

1. Brown, *The Rise and Fall of Communism*, p. 569.
2. Brown, p. 570.
3. Isaacs and Downing, *Cold War*, p. 406.
4. Major, *John Major*, p. 500.
5. Daniel Sandford, 'Moscow coup 1991: with Boris Yeltsin on the tank', BBC News, 20 August 2011.
6. Timothy J. Colton, *Yeltsin* (Basic Books, 2008), pp. 199–200.
7. Roxburgh, *Moscow Calling*, pp. 202–3.
8. *Daily Telegraph* article, 24 August 1991.
9. Brown, *The Rise and Fall of Communism*, pp. 571–2.
10. Plokhy, *The Last Empire*, pp. 401–2.
11. Brown, 'Review Essay. The End of the Soviet Union', p. 161.
12. Isaacs and Downing, *Cold War*, p. 395.
13. Brown, *The Rise and Fall of Communism*, p. 569.
14. Ibid., p. 572 and Mak, *In Europe*, p. 749.
15. Braithwaite, 'The Myths of Russia Old and New'.
16. Roxburgh, *Moscow Calling*, pp. 216, 223, 246.

17. Mak, *In Europe*, pp. 750–1.
18. Roxburgh, *Moscow Calling*, pp. 251–3.
19. Thatcher, *Statecraft*, pp. 77–8.
20. F.W. Ermarth, 'Seeing Russia Plain: The Russian Crisis and American Intelligence', *National Interest*, No. 55, 1999, spring, p. 10.
21. Brown, 'The Gorbachev Factor Revisited', p. 63.

Chapter 32: TA Reserve, Last SIS Mission to Sarajevo, 1995

1. Website, eliteukforces.info/special-air-service/history/bosnia.
2. Sir Christopher Meyer, *Getting Our Way* (Weidenfeld & Nicolson, 2009), pp. 244–5.
3. Ibid., pp. 234–5.
4. General Sir Michael Rose, *Fighting for Peace. Lessons from Bosnia* (Warner, 1998), pp. 1, 224, 350–1.
5. Mak, *In Europe*, p. 794.
6. Rose, *Fighting for Peace*, p. 61.
7. Meyer, *Getting Our Way*, pp. 243, 250–1.
8. Rose, *Fighting for Peace*, p. 68.
9. Dorril, *Inside the Covert World of Her Majesty's Secret Intelligence Service*, p. 790.
10. West, *At Her Majesty's Secret Service*, p. 113.
11. Meyer, *Getting Our Way*, p. 244.
12. Rose, *Fighting for Peace*, p. 123.
13. Ibid., p. 348.
14. Meyer, *Getting Our Way*, p. 246.
15. Ibid., p. 258.

Chapter 33: The Two Johns and *Kriegsglück*

1. Cave Brown, *Treason in the Blood*, p. 13.
2. Website, news.bbc.co.uk, 26 June 2008.
3. Website, americanrhetoric.com/speeches.

Bibliography and Sources

Other Sources

J.B. Sanderson Sources

Family letters from Bulgaria, Turkey, Egypt, Sudan etc., Sanderson Family Archives. Letter to author from Patricia Holden-White, November 2008

Letter from the Blackshear family, Sanderson Family Archives

Letters sent by *JBS* from Paris to his wife, 1948–9, Sanderson Archives

Polish letters, insignia and photographs in Sanderson Archives

Sanderson, John B., ITV programme *Kilroy*, May 1985

Interviews

Author interview, Richard Aldwinckle (My father's career in the RAF and SIS), January 2018

Author interview, Major Maurice Bell, 50th (Indian) Parachute Bde, Signals Section, 2015

Author interview, Scott Charman (alias for a former South African Intelligence officer), 2017

Author interview, Andrew Cooper (son of pilot Ted Cooper), February 2018

Author interview, an ex-lance corporal of the Parachute Regt, 2013

Author interview, former landlady of Philby's daughter, 2017

Author interview, Richard Sim, son of Major John Sim, March 2018

Author interview, Colonel Herbert Stobbe, German Army, personal account given to author, 2001

Author interview, York and Lancaster colleague of John Sanderson, 2017 and 2018

Author interview, son of Luftwaffe pilot KIA 1943, re Berlin airlift, Gerhard, May 2018

Bletchley Park Oral History Project, interview with Helene Aldwinckle, 2013

Family history passed verbally to author by his father John B. Sanderson
Gordievsky, Colonel Oleg, *Guardian*, 11 March 2103
Greenhill, Lord, British Diplomatic Oral History Programme, 14 February 1996

Obituaries

Brooks, Anthony (SOE agent). *Daily Telegraph*, 15 May 2007
Cairncross, John, *Independent*, by Tom Boyer, 9 October 1955
Hope-Thomson, Brigadier M.R.J. 'Tim', *Daily Telegraph*, 29 May 1990
Northdrop, Tony, 'Cold War Warrior Made it Hot for Hoxha', *Australian Newspaper*, 6 September 2000
Sim, Major John, MC, *The Times*, 23 January 2107, and funeral ovation

Miscellaneous

Aldwinckle, John. Personal logbook and 148 Sqn Operations Record Book
Bell, Major Maurice. Account of Battle of Sangshak, published in the Brigade Association Newsletter (courtesy of the Bell family)
Binyon, Laurence. 'Ode of Remembrance. For the Fallen', *The Times*, 1914
Brown, Archie. Notes takes taken during Gorbachev's speech at Central Hall, London, 29 October 1996
Corera, Gordon, Security Correspondent. BBC News recording, 4 April 2016
Davies, Norman. Personal recollection written in 2002 by Mr Alan McIintosh, Downer, Australia
Egan, Colonel M.D. 'US GO HOME', thesis
Congress India Movement, Vol. 18, No. 12 August 2016.
'Humble Pie', *Time* magazine, 25 October 1926
Kohima Memorial words. Poem by John Maxwell Edmonds (1875–1958)
O'Toole, G. *Encylopaedia of US Intelligence and Espionage*, Fact on File, 1988, pp. 66–7
Philby, H.A.R., *The Philby Tape*, BBC Radio 4, 5 April 2016, discussed by Gordon Corera
Sandford, Daniel. 'Moscow coup 1991: with Boris Yeltsin on the tank', BBC News, 20 August 2011
Sim, Major John. 'Joining the 12th Yorkshire Parachute Battalion', section: 'We land in Normandy, 6th June 1944', pp. 7–10, a personal narrative written by John Sim as a contribution to Cornelius Ryan's *The Longest Day*. Courtesy of the Sim Family Archives
Radio France. Report, 'French Highway Swallowed KGB Treasure', 14 March 1993
US Foreign Relations Diplomatic Papers. 'Conference Document No. 12. Information from the Soviet delegation', Vol. 1, 1943

Venter, Major General C.J., Director General, South African Air Force. 8 September 1944, quoted in Oliver Clutton-Brock, *Trusty to the End, The History of 148 (Special Duties) Squadron 1918–1945*, Mention the War Publishing, 2017, p. 558
Yumnam, Rajeshwor. Battle of Sangshak documentary script

Articles

Braithwaite, Sir Rodric (British Ambassador to Moscow). 'The Myths of Russia Old and New', *Financial Times*, November 2011
Bremner, Charles. 'Cold War Secret Army Files Vanish', *The Times*, 10 January 2018
Brown, Archie. 'The Change to Engagement in Britain's Cold War Policy. The Origins of Thatcher-Gorbachev Relationship', *Journal of Cold War Studies*, Vol. 10, No. 3, Summer 2008, pp. 14; a two-day seminar held at Chequers, September 1983
Brown, Archie. 'The Gorbachev Factor Revisited', *Problems of Post-Communism*, Vol. 58, Nos 4–5, July/August/September 2011
Brown, Archie. 'Perestroika and the End of the Cold War', *Cold War History*, Vol. 7, No. 1, February 2007
Brown, Archie. 'Review Essay. The End of the Soviet Union', *Journal of Cold War Studies*, Vol. 17, No. 4, Fall 2015
Brown, Craig. Article on Ronald Searle, *Sunday Times*, June 2010
'Bulgarian Murder Squad Exposed', *Daily Telegraph*, 31 July 2010
Charter, David. 'Berlin Wall Tunnel Tells of Lost Hope, *The Times*, 13 January 2018
CIA. 'More on the Recruitment of Soviets', *Studies in Intelligence*, Vol. 9, winter 1965
Congress India Movement, Vol. 18, No. 12 August 2016
Conquest, Bob. 'Back to Bulgaria', *National Review*, January 1994
Corera, Gordon. Interview, 'Take our best weapon, 007 – a moral compass', *Sunday Times News Review*, 27 July 2009
Ermarth, F.W. 'Seeing Russia Plain: The Russian Crisis and American Intelligence', *National Interest*, No. 55, 1999, Spring
Fenby, Jonathan. 'France Cannot be Without Grandeur', *Financial Times*, 16/17 June 2018
Fuller, Major General J.F.C. (military analyst for *Newsweek)* article in *IMAGES*, French magazine, 9 November 1947 (trans. by author)
Furshenko, Alexander and Timothy Naftali. 'Soviet Intelligence and the Cuban Missile Crisis', *Intelligence and National Security*, Vol. 13 (1998)

Galbraith, Evan. 'Hot Spots in the Cold War', *National Review Periodical*, 24 January 1994

Kagan, Neil and Stephen G. Hyslop, 'World War II. The Spies and Secret Missions that Won the War', *National Geographic Magazine*, 2017

Kauffman, Sylvie. '1989. The People Awake', *Le Monde*, Hors-Serie, September 2009, trans. by the author

Krushelynycky, Askold. 'Ukrainian Partisans', *Daily Telegraph*, 18 July 2002

Leake, Jonathan. Soviet spy maps of UK better than our own, *Sunday Times*, 22 October 2017, reviewing Alexander Kent and John Davies, *The Red Atlas* (University of Chicago Press, 2107)

Longmans, M.E. Green & Co. *Annual Register of 1943, Review of Events at Home and Abroad*

Mink, Georges. 'Scenarios pour une fin d'empire', *Le Monde*, Hors-Serie, September 2009, pp. 50–1

Parfitt, Tom. 'The Power and the Glory, *The Times*, 8 May 2108

'Penkovsky's Progress', *Times Literary Supplement*, 16 December 1965

Slaughter, Gary. 'A Soviet Nuclear Torpedo, An American Destroyer, and the Cuban Missile Crisis', taskandpurpose.com/cuban-missile-crisis-nuclear-torpedo/4/9/2016, about Gary Slaughter, *Sea Stories. A Memoir of a Naval Officer (1956–1967)*, Fletcher House, 2016

Smith, Michael. Article, *Sunday Times*, 24 May 2009

Vernet, Daniel. Interview with Mikhail Gorbachev, *Le Monde*, Hors Série, November 2008, trans. by author

Wolf, Marcus. 'Memoirs of a Spy', extracts, *Le Monde*, Hors-Serie, September 2009

'Yeltsin and the Coup Attempt', *Daily Telegraph*, 24 August 1991

Websites

en.wikipedia.org/wiki/Francis_Gary_Powers
sis.gov.uk/our-history, Beginnings
un.org/en/sections/history-united-nations-charter/1941-atlantic-charter
Wikipedia, Battle of Sangshak
en.wikipedia.org/wiki/John_Howard
bbc.co.uk/programmes, BBC News report from Tel Aviv, 22 April 2108
dur.ac.uk/library/projects/woodsudan
Wikipedia: General Charles Gordon
archive2.gwu.edu Post, 24 October 2012, No. 399, Briefing Book
taskand purpose.com
shape.nato.int/page214871012
Wikipedia, 'The Fairwell Affair'

en.wikipedia.org/wiki/Willy_Brandt
sakharov-archive.ru/English/, Andrei Sakharov, 'Essay, Reflections on Peaceful Co-existence'Wikipedia, Dr Gregory Pedlow, source Exercise Scenario, Able Archer NATO Exercise, 1983, National Security Archive of the original (16 June 2013)
Wikipedia: 'Rosoboronexport'
eliteukforces.info/special-air-service/history/bosnia
americanrhetoric.com/speeches (Kennedy speech)
Wikipedia, Le RFP, 'Le Rassemblement du peuple français'
Wikipedia, 'Le Coup d' État permanent', Mitterrand
esa.int/About_Us/Welcome_to_ESA/ESA_history/50_years_of_humans_in_space/The_flight_of_Vostok_1
numbers-stations.com/cia/OBOPUS%20BFIEND
red_flag_of_the _paris_commune
bletchleypark.org.uk/roll-of-honour/8921
php.isn.ethz.ch/lory1.ethz.ch/collections/
taskandpurpose.com/cuban-missile-crisis-nuclear-torpedo/

Archives

FRUS

The Conference of Berlin, 1945, Vol. 2, pp. 359–62

Imperial War Museum

Greenhalgh, Major Peter, DFC TD, Royal Artillery, Wartime Personal Papers (also archives from Army Museum of Flying)

Romanian Central Historical National Archives (ANIC)

Central Committee of the Romanian Communist Part, Chancellery Collection – file 56/1960, 19; 46/1961. 11-21, 28/1962, 111. Parallel History Project on Cooperative Security ETH/ PHP, Swiss Federal Insititute of Technology, 2000–8. Marshal V. Sokolovskii (ed.), *Strategia Militara*, Bucharest Military Publishing House, 1972, pp. 353–4. (Courtesy of Major Petre Opris, Ph.D., 'Warsaw Pact Military Exercises During the Cuban Missile Crisis of October 1962: The Romanian Point of View (Bucharest University))

TNA

148 Sqn Operations Record Book, August 1944, AIR/27/996
Bletchley Park three-volume history, HW 43/72SOE, 'History of Special Operations (Air) in the Mediterranean Theatre', HS 7/11

War Diary of 6/11th Sikh Regt Indian Army, 1942–3
War Diary of 152nd Indian Para Btn (50th Indian Para Bde)

Books

Adams, James. *The New Spies: Exploring the Frontiers of Espionage*, Hutchinson, 1994
Aid, Matthew M. *The Secret Sentry: The Untold History of the National Security Agency*, Bloomsbury Press, 2009
Ambrose, Stephen E. *Pegasus Bridge*, Simon and Schuster, 1985
Andrew, Christopher M. and Oleg Gordievsky. *KGB: The Inside Story of its Foreign Operations from Lenin to Gorbachev*, Hodder & Stoughton, 1990
Andrew, Christopher and Vasili Mitrokhin. *The Mitrokhin Archive*, Penguin, 1999
Arthur, Max. *Forgotten Voices of the Second World War*, Ebury, 2005
Axelrod, Alan. *The Real History of the Cold War: A New Look at the Past*, Sterling, 2009
Bamford, James. *Body of Secrets. How America's NSA & Britain's GCHQ Eavesdrop on the World*, Century, 2001
Beevor, Antony and Artemis Cooper. *Paris After the Liberation, 1944–1949*, Viking, 2007
Berstein, Carl and Politi, Marco. *His Holiness: John Paul II and the Hidden History of Our Times*, Doubleday, 1990
Bethel, Nicholas W. *Spies and Other Secrets, Viking*, 1994
Birdwood, Colonel F.T. *The Sikh Regiment in the Second World War*, Naval & Military Press, 2014
Blake, George. *No Other Choice*, Jonathan Cape, 1990
Brook-Shepherd, G. *The Storm Birds*, Weidenfeld & Nicolson, 1989
Brown, Anthony Cave. *Treason in the Blood: H. St John Philby, Kim Philby, and the Spy Case of the Century*, Houghton Mifflin, 1994
Brown, Archie. *The Rise and Fall of Communism*, Bodley Head, 2009
Cavendish, Anthony. *Inside Intelligence*, Sterling, 1987
Chaney, Otto Preston. *Khukhov*, Malcolm Mackintosh, 1974
Christopher, John. *The Race for Hitler's X-Planes*, History Press, 2013
Chuchill, Winston. *Winston Churchill: His Complete Speeches, 1897–1963*, ed. Robert Rhodes James, 8 vols, Chelsea House Publications, 1974
Churchill, Winston. *The Second World War*, 6 vols, Cassell, 1951
Clutton-Brock, Oliver, *Trusty to the End, The History of 148 (Special Duties) Squadron 1918–1945*, Mention the War Publishing, 2017
Colton, Timothy J. *Yeltsin*, Basic Books, 2008

Corera, Gordon. *The Art of Betrayal: Life and Death in MI6 from the Cold War to the Present*, Phoenix, 2012
Cousins, Norman. *The Improbable Triumvirate*, W.W. Norton, 1972
Cradock, Percy. *In Pursuit of British Interests*, John Murray, 1997
Cradock, Percy. *Know Your Enemy: How the Joint Intelligence Committee Saw the World*, Murray, 2002
Crankshaw, Edward. *Khrushchev Remembers*, Little Brown, 1970
Cross, J.P. *Jungle Warfare: Experiences and Encounters*, Guild Pub., 1989
Davidson, E. *The Death of Germany*, Cape, 1959
Davies, Norman. *Rising '44: The Battle for Warsaw*, Macmillan, 2003
Daves, Philip H.J. *MI6 and the Machinery of Spying*, Frank Cass, 2005
Delmas Claude. *Le Pact de Varsovie*, Presse Universitaire de France, 1981
Dobbs, Michael. *One Minute to Midnight: Kennedy, Khrushchev, and Castro on the Brink of Nuclear War*, Hutchinson, 2008
Dobrynin, Anatoli. *In Confidence: Moscow's Ambassador to America's Six Cold War Presidents*, Times Books, 1995
Dobson, Christopher and Ronald Payne. *The Dictionary of Espionage*, Grafton, 1986
Dorril, Stephen. *M16: Fifty Years of Special Operations*, Fourth Estate, 2000
Dorril, Stephen. *M16: Inside the Covert World of Her Majesty's Secret Intelligence Service*, Free Press, 2000
Downing, Taylor. *1983. The World at the Brink*, Little, Brown, 2018
Gordon, Doug. *Tactical Reconnaissance in the Cold War*, Pen & Sword, 2006
Edwards, Leslie. *Kohima: The Furthest Battle: The Story of the Japanese Invasion of India in 1944 and the 'British-Indian Thermopylae'*, History Press, 2009
Fischer, Klaus P. *America in White, Black and Gray*, Continuum Publishing Group, 2016
Fontaine, André. *La Guerre Froide, 1917–1991*, La Martinière, 2006
Foot, M.R.D. *SOE: An Outline History of the Special Operations Executive 1940–46*, British Broadcasting Corporation, 1985
Fort, Adrian. *Archibald Wavell: The Life and Times of an Imperial Servant*, Jonathan Cape, 2009
Gaddis, John Lewis. *We Now Know. Rethinking Cold War History*, Oxford University Press, 1997
Geraghty, Tony. *Brixmis: The Untold Exploits of Britain's Most Daring Cold War Spy Mission*, HarperCollins, 1997
Gordon, Doug. *Tactical Reconnaissance in the Cold War: 1945 to Korea, Cuba, Vietnam and the Iron Curtain*, Pen & Sword Aviation, 2006
Greenhill, Denis. *More by Accident*, Wilton 65, 1992
Grehan, John. *RAF and the SOE: Special Duties Operations in Europe During WW2. An Official History*, Frontline Books, 2016

Grehan, John and Martin Mace. *The Fall of Burma, 1941–1943*, Pen & Sword Military, 2015

Grey, Stephen. *The New Spymasters*, Penguin Books Ltd, 2016

Hamilton-Paterson, James. *Empire of the Clouds*, Faber and Faber, 2010

Harclerode, Peter. *'Go To It!' An Illustrated History of the 6th Airborne Division*, Caxton, 2000

Hart, Adrian Liddell. *The Sword and the Pen: Selections from the World's Greatest Military Writings*, Cassell, 1976

Hermiston, Roger. *The Greatest Traitor: The Secret Lives of Agent George Blake*, Aurum, 2013

Hersh, S. *The Target is Destroyed*, Random House, 1986

Hickey, Michael. *The Unforgettable Army: Slim's XIVth Army in Burma*, Spellmount, 2003

Hinsley, F.H. and A. Stripp. *Codebreakers: The Inside Story of Bletchey Park*, Oxford University Press, 1993

Hughes-Wilson, John. *A Brief History of the Cold War: The Hidden Truth About How Close We Came to Nuclear Conflict*, Robinson, 2006

Isaacs, Jeremy and Taylor Downing. *Cold War: For 45 Years the World Held its Breath*, Bantam, 1998

Ismay, Lord, General Lionel Hastings. *NATO The First Five Years, 1949–54*, Bosch Dat, 1954

Jackson, John (ed.). *Solving Enigma's Secrets: The Official History of Bletchley Park's Hut 6*, BookTower Publishing, 2014

Jackson, Robert. *Churchill's Moat: The Channel War 1939–1945*, Airlife Pub., 1995

Jackson, Robert. *Suez, The Forgotten Invasion*, Airlife Pub., 1996

James, Lawrence. *Raj: The Making and Unmaking of British India*, Abacus, 1997

Jeannesson, Stanislas. *La Guerre Froide*, La Découverte, 2002

Jeffery, Keith. *MI6: The History of the Secret Intelligence Service, 1909–1949*, Bloomsbury, 2010

Jeffreys-Jones, Rhodri. *In Spies We Trust: The Story of Western Intelligence*, Oxford University Press, 2015

Kapuściński, Ryszard. *Imperium Granta*, Random House, 1994

Kassabova, Kapka. *Street Without a Name*, Portobello Books, 2008

Kaufman, Robert G. *Henry M. Jackson. A Life in Politics*, University of Washington Press, 2000

Kee, Robert. *1945: The World We Fought For*, Penguin Books, 1995

Keep, John L.H. *Last of the Empires: A History of the USSR, 1945–1991*, Oxford University Press, 1995

Kent, Alexander and John Davies. *The Red Atlas*, University of Chicago Press, 2107

Kipling, Rudyard and Zohreh T. Sullivan. *Kim. Authoritative Text, Backgrounds, Criticism*, W.W. Norton, 2002

Knightley, Phillip. *Philby: The Life and Views of the K.G.B. Masterspy*, Andre Deutsch, 1988

Latimer, Jon. *Burma: The Forgotten War*, Murray, 2004

Leadbeater, Tim. *Britain and India 1845–1947*, Hodder Murray, 2008

Liddell Hart, B.H. *The Sword and the Pen 'Mein Kampf'*, trans. J. Murray, Littlehampton Book Services, 1978

Macintyre, Ben. *A Spy Among Friends: Kim Philby and the Great Betrayal*, Bloomsbury, 2014

McLynn, Frank. *The Burma Campaign: Disaster into Triumph 1942–45*, Vintage Books, 2011

Macmillan, Harold. *Harold Pointing the Way*, Macmillan, 1969

Major, John. *John Major: The Autobiography*, HarperCollins, 1999

Mak, Geert. *In Europe. Travels Through the Twentieth Century*, Vintage, 2008

Matlock, J.F., Jr, *Reagan and Gorbachev: How the Cold War Ended*, Random House, 2004

Meyer, Sir Christopher. *Getting Our Way*, Weidenfeld & Nicolson, 2009

Middleton, D. *The Struggle for Germany*, Cape, 1959

Miquel, Pierre. *La IVe République 1944–1959*, Larousse, 1993

Montefiore, Simon Sebag. *Stalin: The Court of the Red Tsar*, Weidenfeld & Nicolson, 2004

Montgomery of Alamein, Viscount Bernard Law. *The Memoirs of Field-Marshal the Vt Montgomery of Alamein*, Collins, 1958

Morgan, Ted. *Valley of Death: The Tragedy at Dien Bien Phu that Led America into the Vietnam War*, Random House, 2010

Mowat, R.C. *Ruin and Resurgence 1939–1965*, Blandford Press, 1966

Murphy, David E., Sergei A. Kondrashev and George Bailey. *Battleground Berlin*, Yale University Press, 1997

Orpen, Neil W. *Airlift to Warsaw*, Foulsham & Company Ltd, 1984

Parker, Philip. *The Cold War Spy Pocket Manual*, Pool of London Press, 2015

Peebles, Curtis. *Guardians: Strategic Reconnaissance Satellites*, Ian Allan, 1987

Pen'kovskiĭ, Oleg Vladimirovich. *The Penkovsky Papers; A Translation by P. Deriabin of an Article Introducing the Diary of Oleg V. Penkovsky & Portions of the Diary*, Collins, 1965

Philby, Harold Adrian Russell. *Kim Philby: My Silent War*, Arrow Books, 2003

Pimlott, J. *La Guerre Froide*, Aladdin, 1987

Plokhy, Serhii. *The Last Empire: The Final Days of the Soviet Union*, Basic Books, 2014

Poirier, Agnès. *Left Bank. Art Passion and the Rebirth of Paris, 1940–1950*, Bloomsbury, 2018

Powers, Thomas. *The Man who Kept the Secrets: Richard Helms and the CIA*, Washington Press, 1979

Rapport, Leonard, and Arthur Northwood Jnr. *Rendezvous With Destiny. A History of the 101st Airborne Division*, 101st Airborne Division Association, 1948

Rees, Lawrence. *Behind Closed Doors. Stalin, the Nazis and the West*, BBC Books, 2008

Reeve, James. *Cocktails, Crises and Cockroaches: A Diplomatic Trail*, Radcliffe Press, 1999

Rendel, George William. *The Sword and the Olive: Recollections of Diplomacy, 1913–1954*, Murray, 1957

Rose, General Sir Michael. *Fighting for Peace. Lessons from Bosnia*, Warner, 1998

Roxburgh, Angus. *Moscow Calling: Memoirs of a Foreign Correspondent*, Birlinn Ltd, 2017

Rusk, Dean. *As I saw it*, Norton, 1990

Schecter, J. and P. Derabin. *Recollections of the KGB Defector Peter Derabin. The Spy Who Saved the World*, Scribners, 1992

Schweizer, Peter. *Victory: The Reagan Administration's Secret Strategy that Hastened the Collapse of the Soviet Union*, NY Monthly Press, 1994

Scott, Paul. *Jewel in the Crown*, Readers Union Heinemann, 1967

Seaman, Harry. *The Battle at Sangshak, Burma, March 1944*, L. Cooper, 1989

Shulsky, Abram N. and Gary J. Schmitt. *Silent Warfare*, Potomac Books, 2002

Slaughter, Gary. *Sea Stories. A Memoir of a Naval Officer 1956–67*, Fletcher House, 2016

Slessor, Sir John, Marshal of the RAF. *Autobiography, The Central Blue*, Cassell & Co. Ltd, 1956

Slim, William. *Defeat into Victory*, Pan Books, 1999

Smith, Stephen D. *Underground London: Travels beneath the City Streets*, Abacus, 2004

Sokolovskii, Marshal V., *Strategia Militara*, Bucharest Military Publishing House, 1972

Soldatov, Andreĭ and I. Borogan. *The New Nobility: The Restoration of Russia's Security State and the Enduring Legacy of the KGB*, PublicAffairs, 2010

Solzhenitsyn, Aleksandr I. *One Day in the Life of Ivan Denisovich*, New American Library, 1962

Speer, Albert. *Inside the Third Reich, Memoirs*, trans. R. and C. Winston, Macmillan Company, 1970, pp. 523–4

Stafford, David. *Churchill & Secret Service*, Abacus, 1997

Stafford, David. *Flight from Reality: Rudolf Hess and His Mission to Scotland, 1941*, Pimlico, 2002

Stafford, David. *Spies Beneath Berlin*, John Murray, 2002

Suvorov, Victor Spetznaz. *The Story of the Soviet SAS*, Hamish Hamilton, 1987

Taubman, William. *Khrushchev. The Man. His Era*, Simon & Schuster, 2017

Thatcher, Margaret. *Statecraft: Strategies for a Changing World*, HarperCollins, 2002

Thompson, Julian. *Forgotten Voices of Burma*, Ebury, 2009

Thompson, Julian. *The Imperial War Museum Book of the War in Burma, 1942–1945: A Vital Contribution to Victory in the Far East*, Pan Books in Association with the Imperial War Museum, 2003

Trevor-Roper, Hugh. *The Secret World*, I.B. Taurus, 2014

Vistica, Simon. *Fall from Glory*, G.L. & Schuster, 1996

West, Nigel. *The Faber Book of Espionage*, Faber and Faber, 1993

West, Nigel. *At Her Majesty's Secret Service: The Chiefs of Britain's Intelligence Agency, MI6*, Greenhill, 2006

West, Nigel. *A Matter of Trust, MI5, 1945–72*, Coronet, 1982

West, Nigel. *The SIGINT Secrets: The Signals Intelligence War, 1900 to Today*, Weidenfeld & Nicolson, 1988

West, Nigel. *Spycraft Secrets. An Espionage A–Z*, History Press, 2016

Whicker, Alan. *Within Whicker's World*, Elm Tree Books, 1982

Winterbotham, F.W. *The Ultra Secret*, Weidenfeld & Nicolson, 1974

Woodhouse, C.M. *Something Ventured*, HarperCollins, 1982

Wright, Peter. *Spycatcher*, Dell, 1987

Yakovlev, Aleksandr. *Sumerki*, Materik, 2003

Index